D1065766

written and illustrated
by Ross Campbell

additional greytones
Bo Bradshaw

super special thanks to
Michelle Silva

published by SLG Publishing
Dan Vado: President & Publisher
Jennifer de Guzman: Editor-In-Chief

www.slgcomic.com
www.shadoweyes.net

SLG Publishing
P.O. Box 26427
San Jose, CA 95159

First Printing:
ISBN: 978-1593622084

printed in Indonesia.

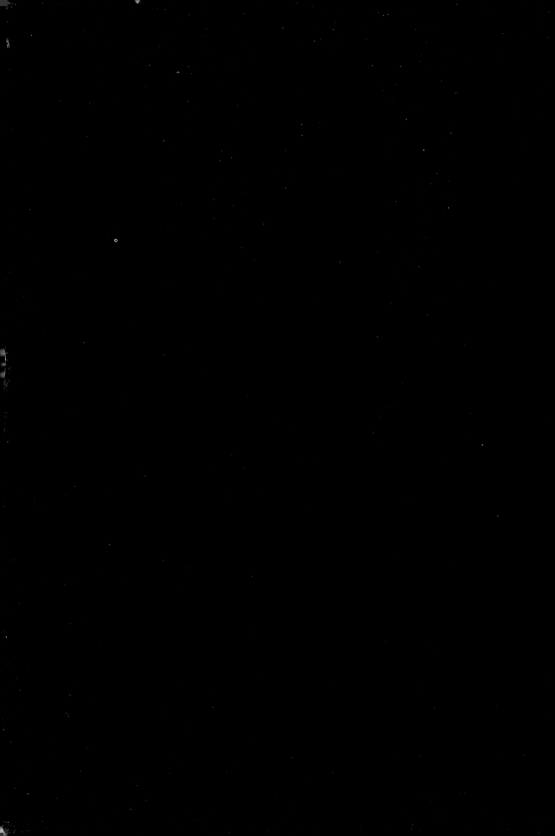

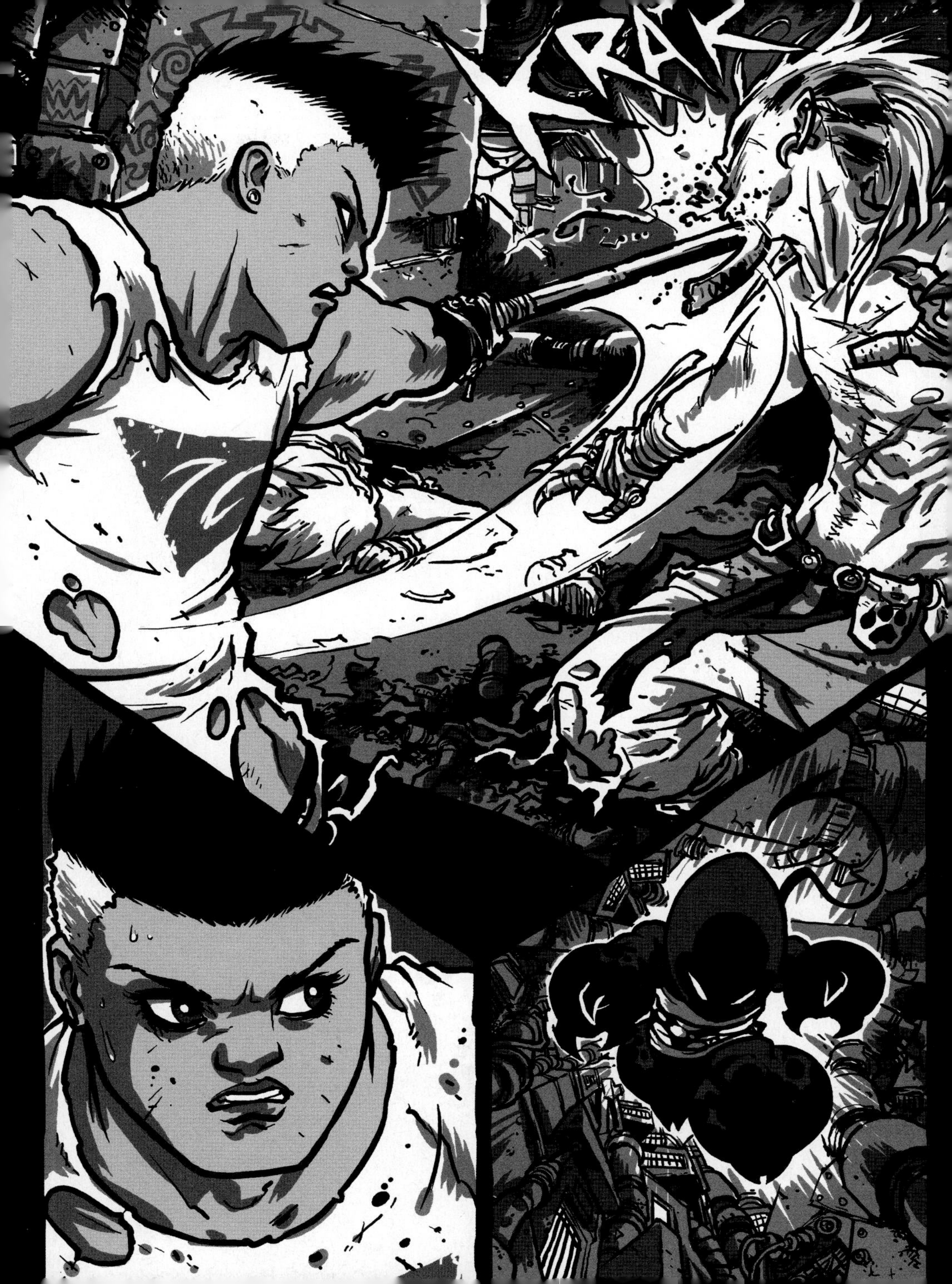
KRAK

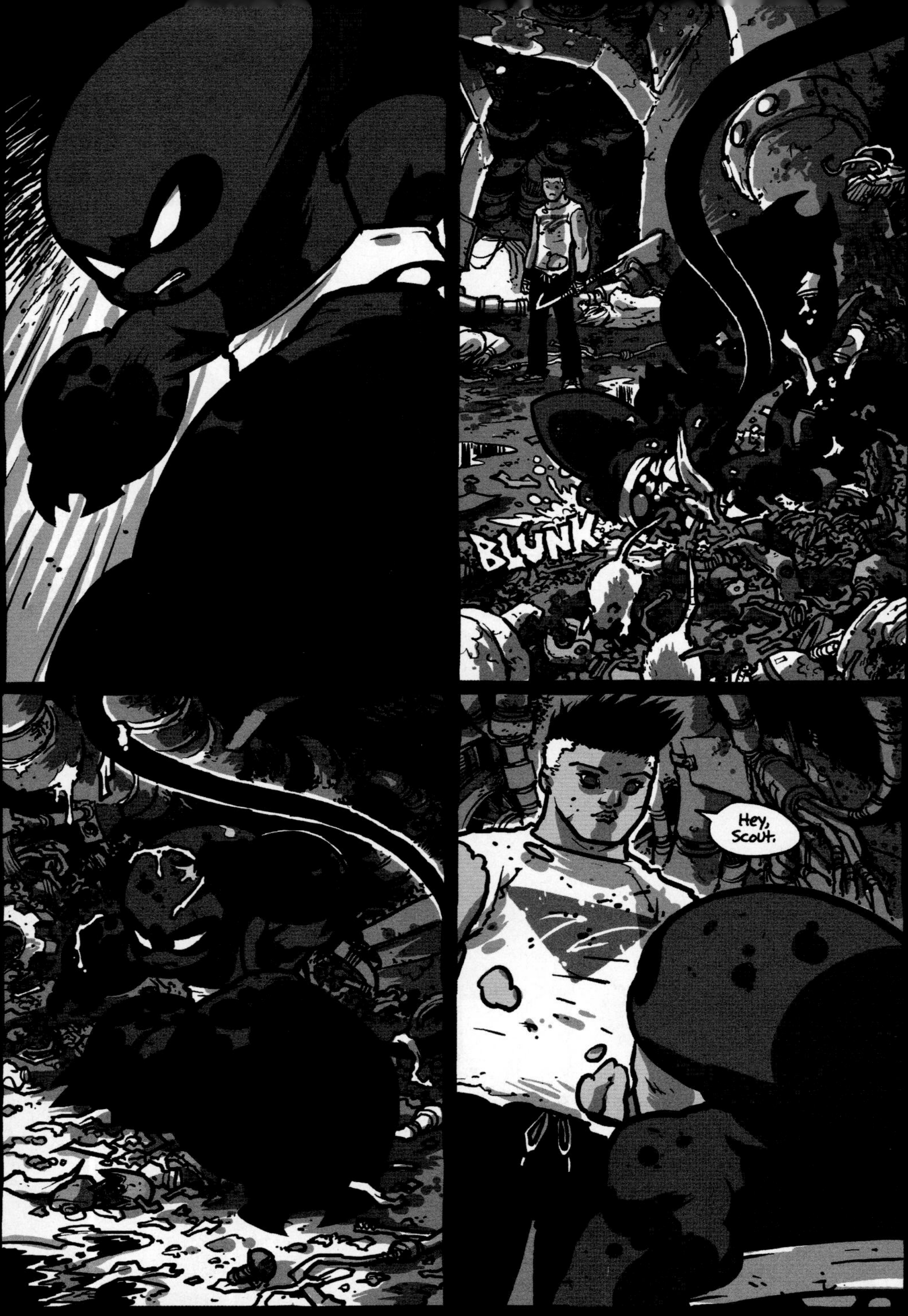
BLUNK
Hey, Scout.

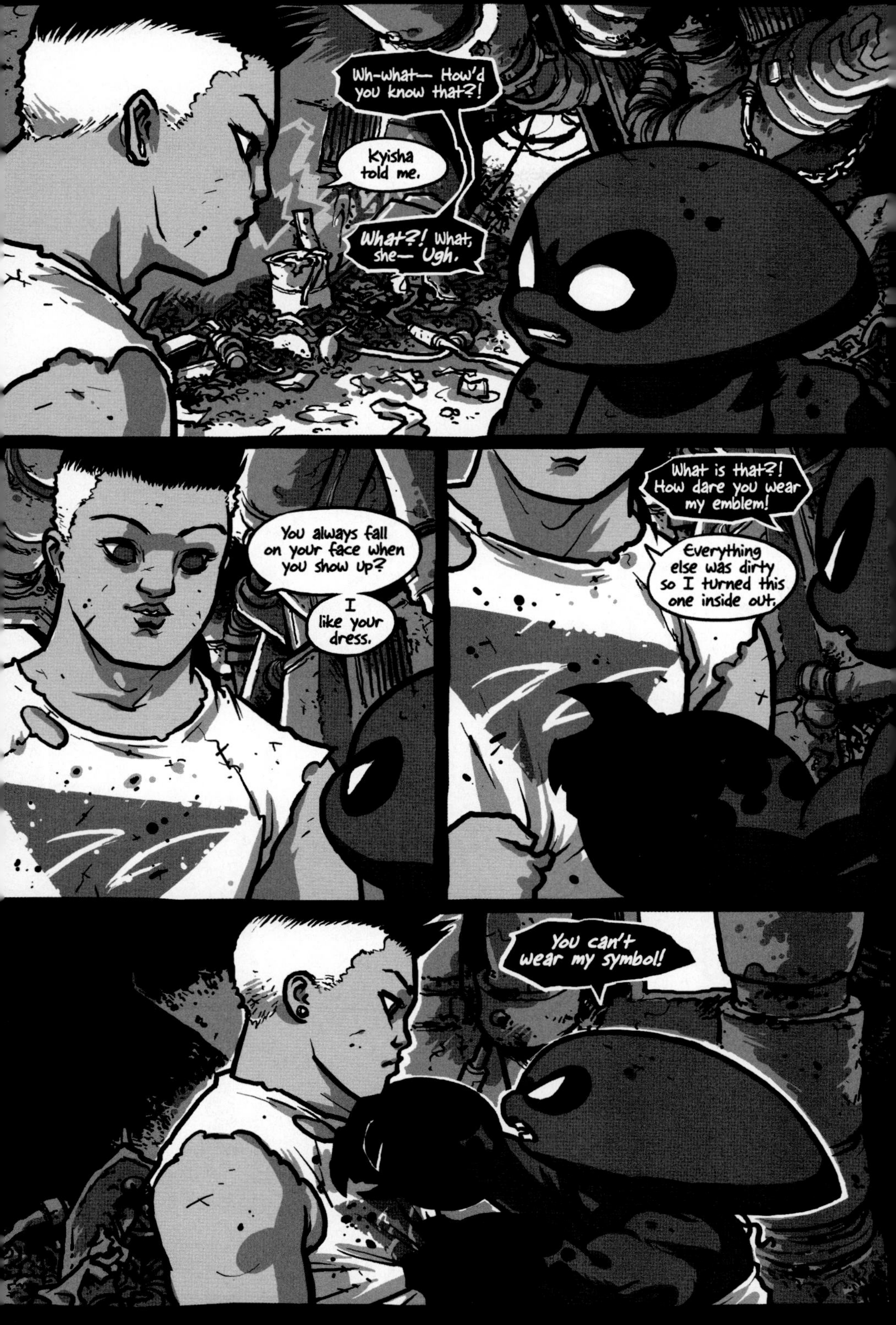
Wh-what— How'd you know that?!
Kyisha told me.
What?! What, she— Ugh.
You always fall on your face when you show up?
I like your dress.
What is that?! How dare you wear my emblem!
Everything else was dirty so I turned this one inside out.
You can't wear my symbol!

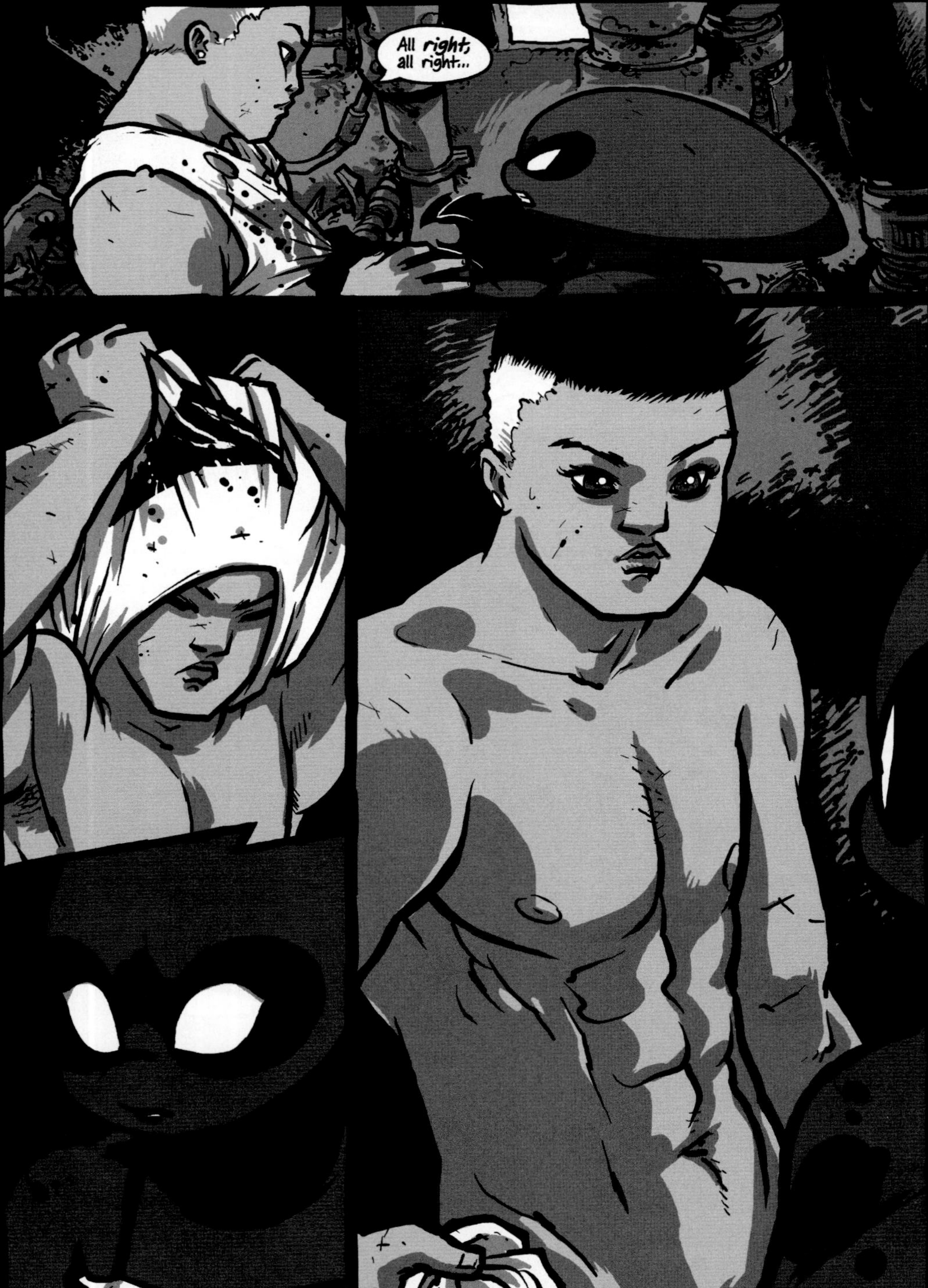
All right, all right...

SHADOWEYES IN LOVE

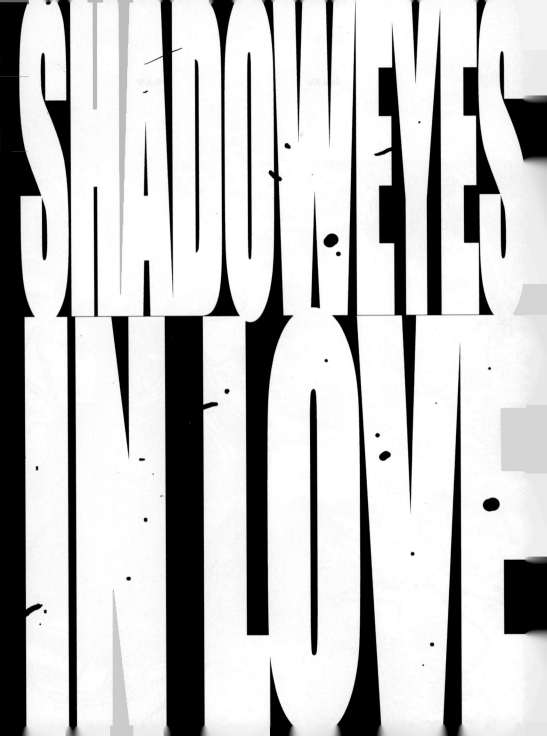

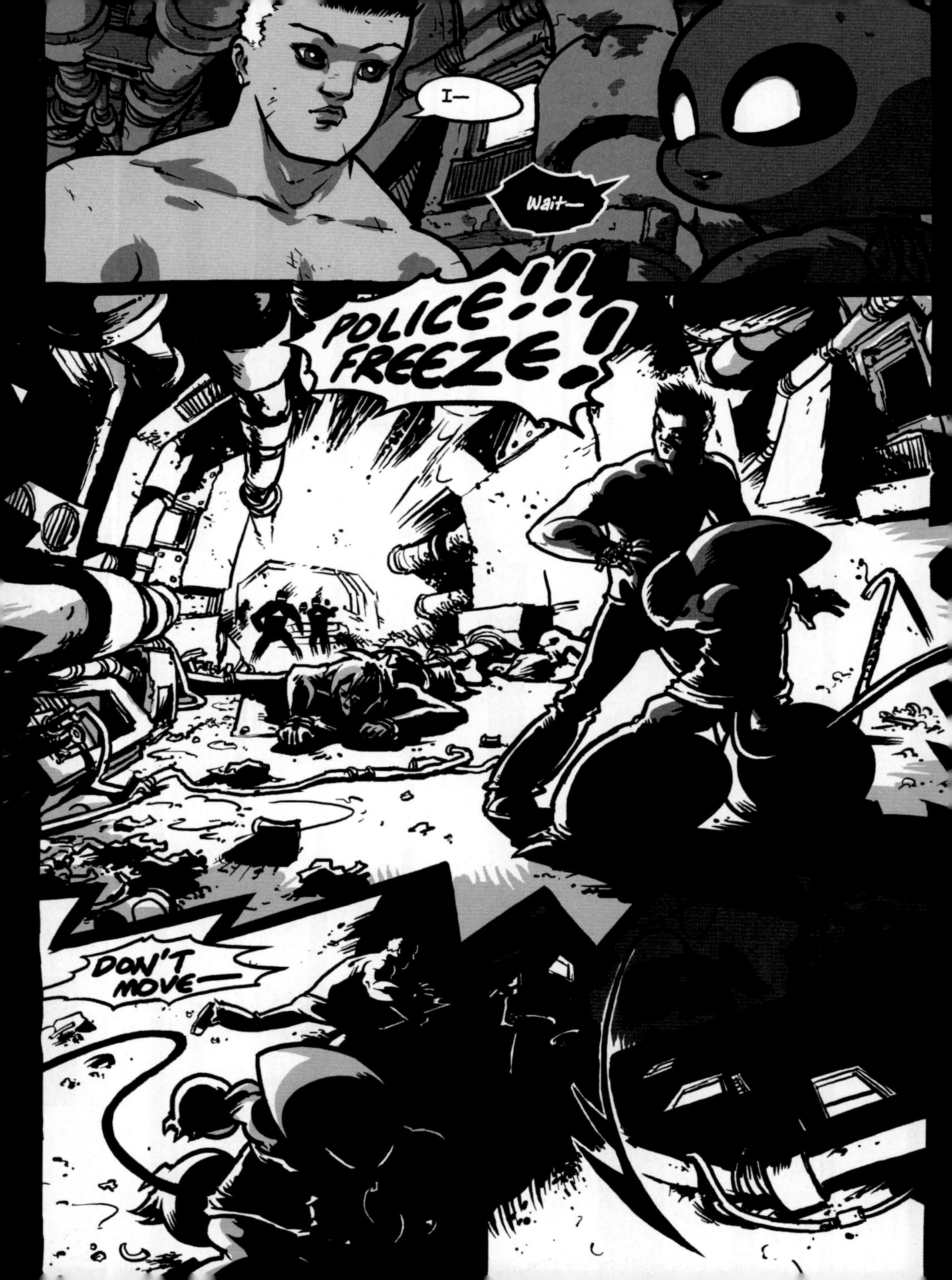
I—
Wait—
POLICE!!! FREEZE!!
DON'T MOVE—

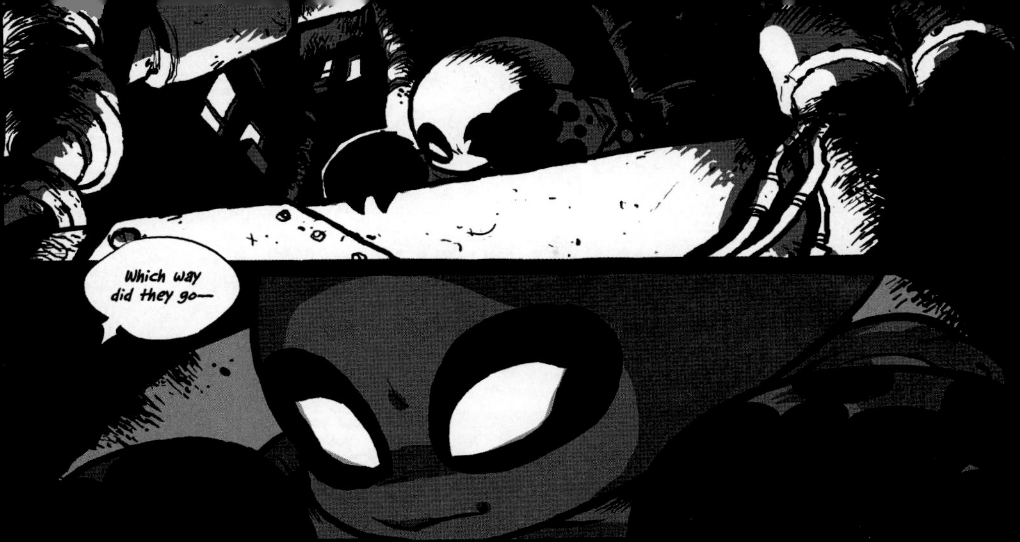
Which way did they go—

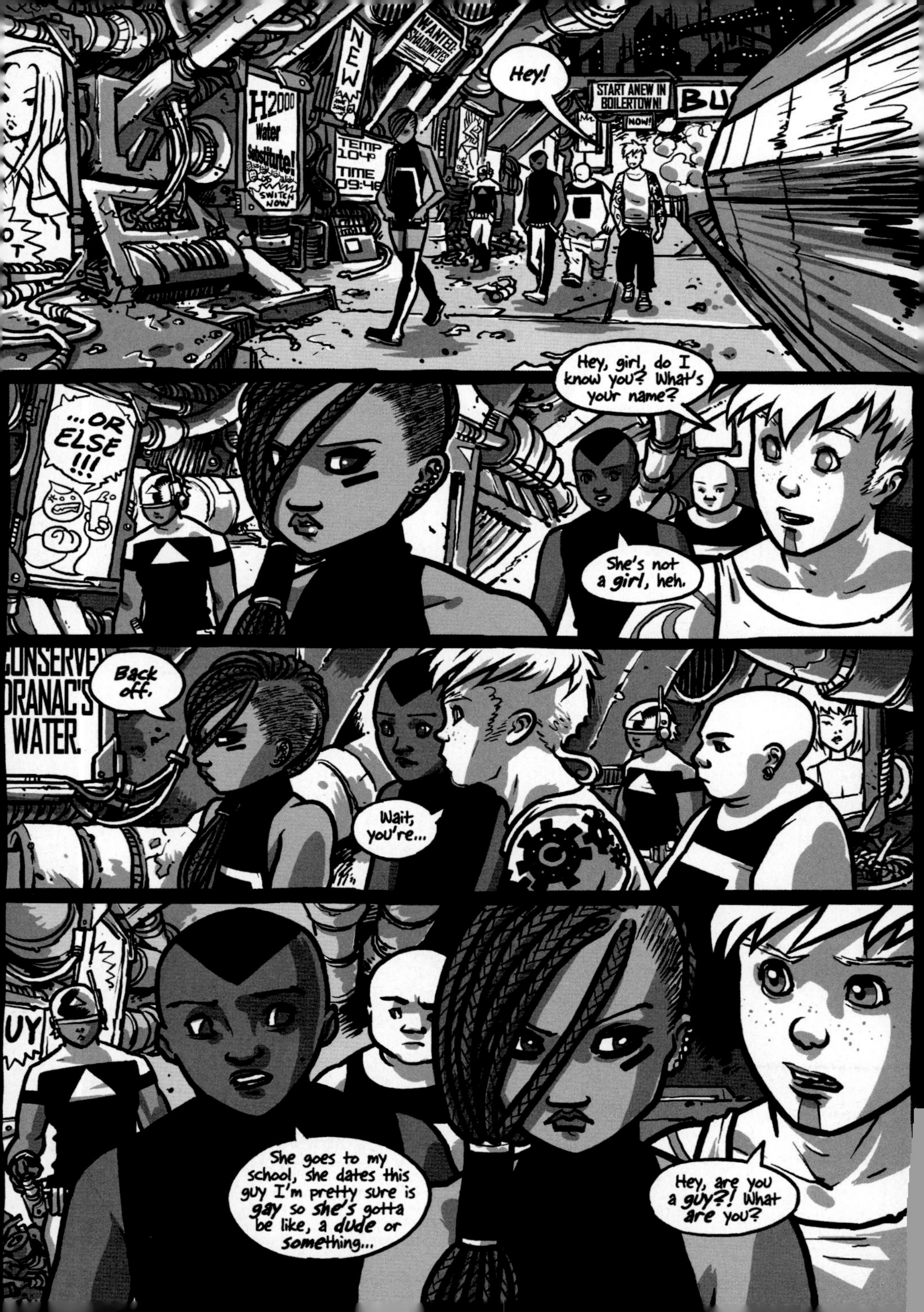
WANTED: SHADOWEYES
NEW
H2000 Water Substitute!
SWITCH NOW
TEMP
TIME
START ANEW IN BOILERTOWN!
NOW!
Hey!
...OR ELSE !!!
Hey, girl, do I know you? What's your name?
She's not a girl, heh.
CONSERVE DRANAC'S WATER.
Back off.
Wait, you're...
She goes to my school, she dates this guy I'm pretty sure is gay so she's gotta be like, a dude or something...
Hey, are you a guy?! What are you?

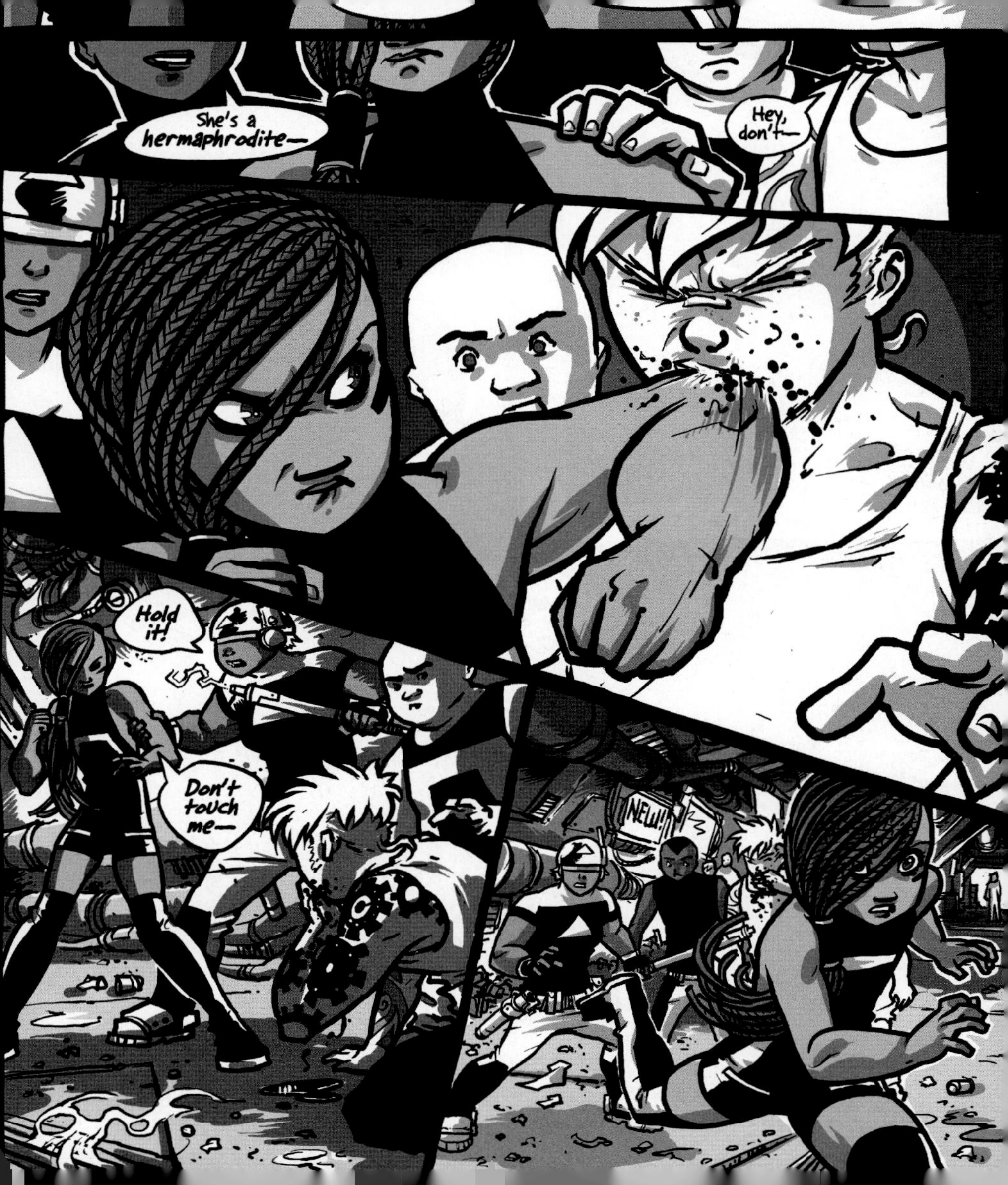
She's a hermaphrodite—
Hey, don't—
Hold it!
Don't touch me—
NEW!

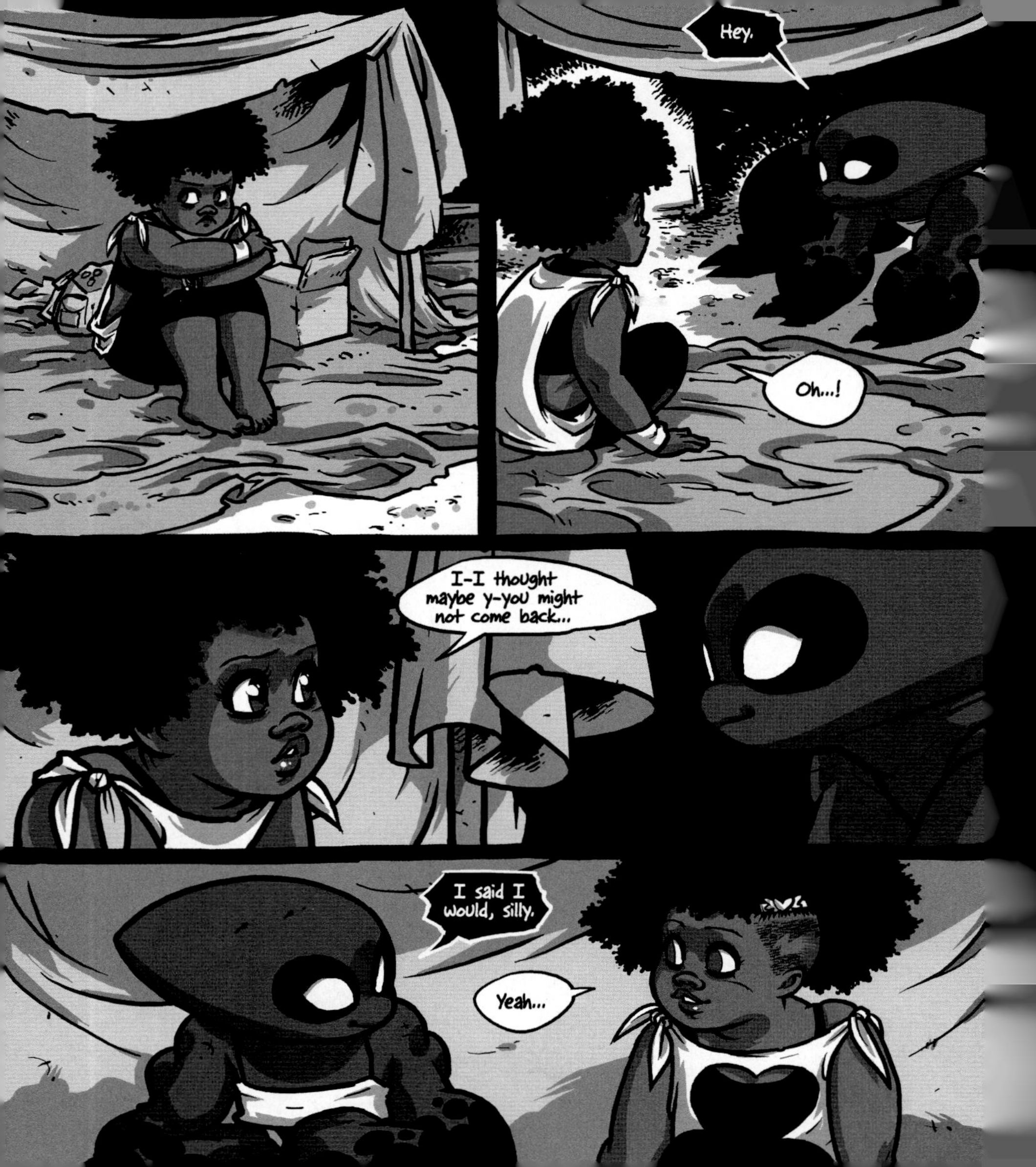
Hey.
Oh...!
I-I thought maybe y-you might not come back...
I said I would, silly.
Yeah...

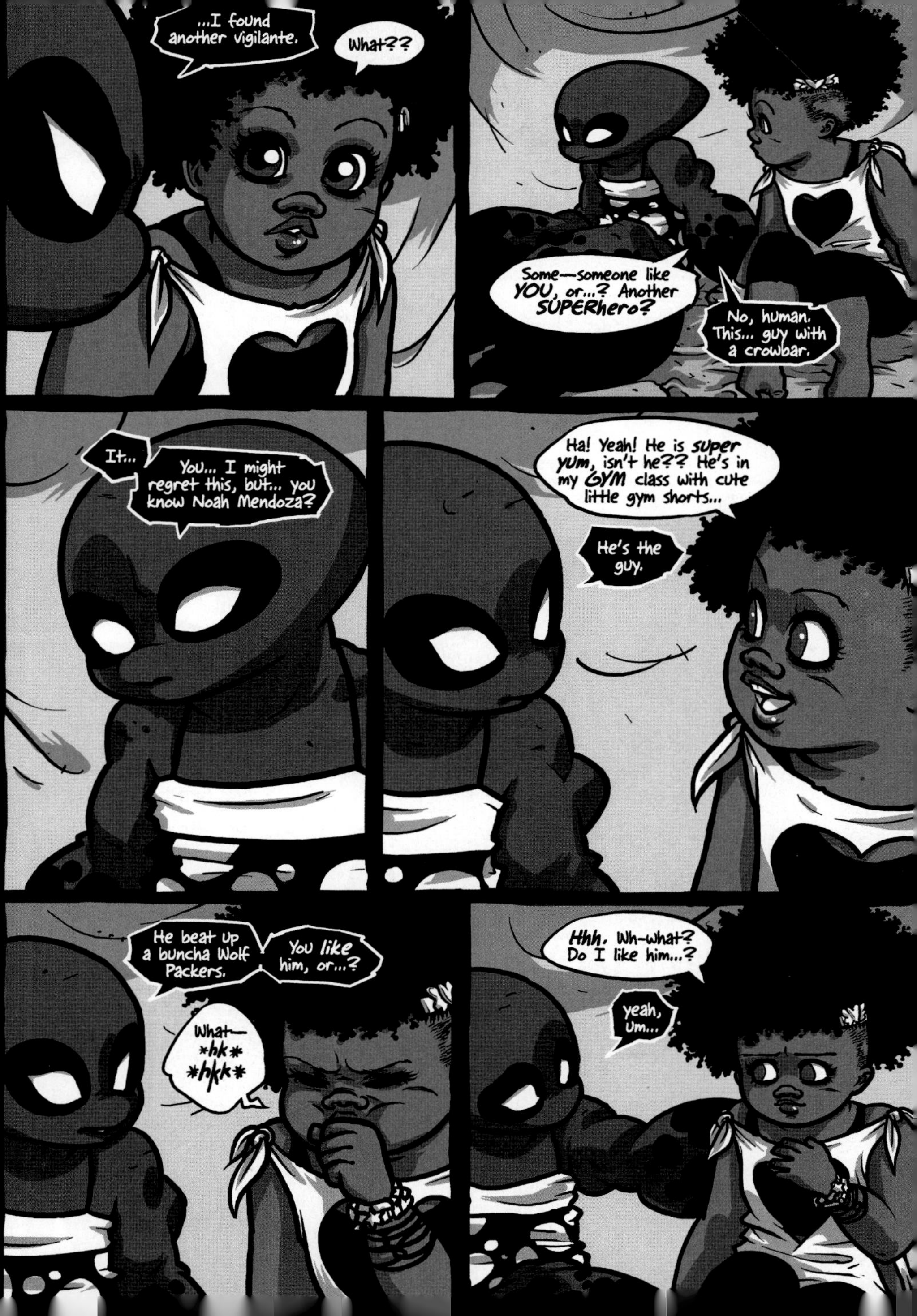
...I found another vigilante.
What??
Some—someone like YOU, or...? Another SUPERhero?
No, human. This... guy with a crowbar.
It...
You... I might regret this, but... you know Noah Mendoza?
Ha! Yeah! He is super yum, isn't he?? He's in my GYM class with cute little gym shorts...
He's the guy.
He beat up a buncha Wolf Packers.
You like him, or...?
What— *hk* *hkk*
Hhh. Wh-what? Do I like him...?
yeah, um...

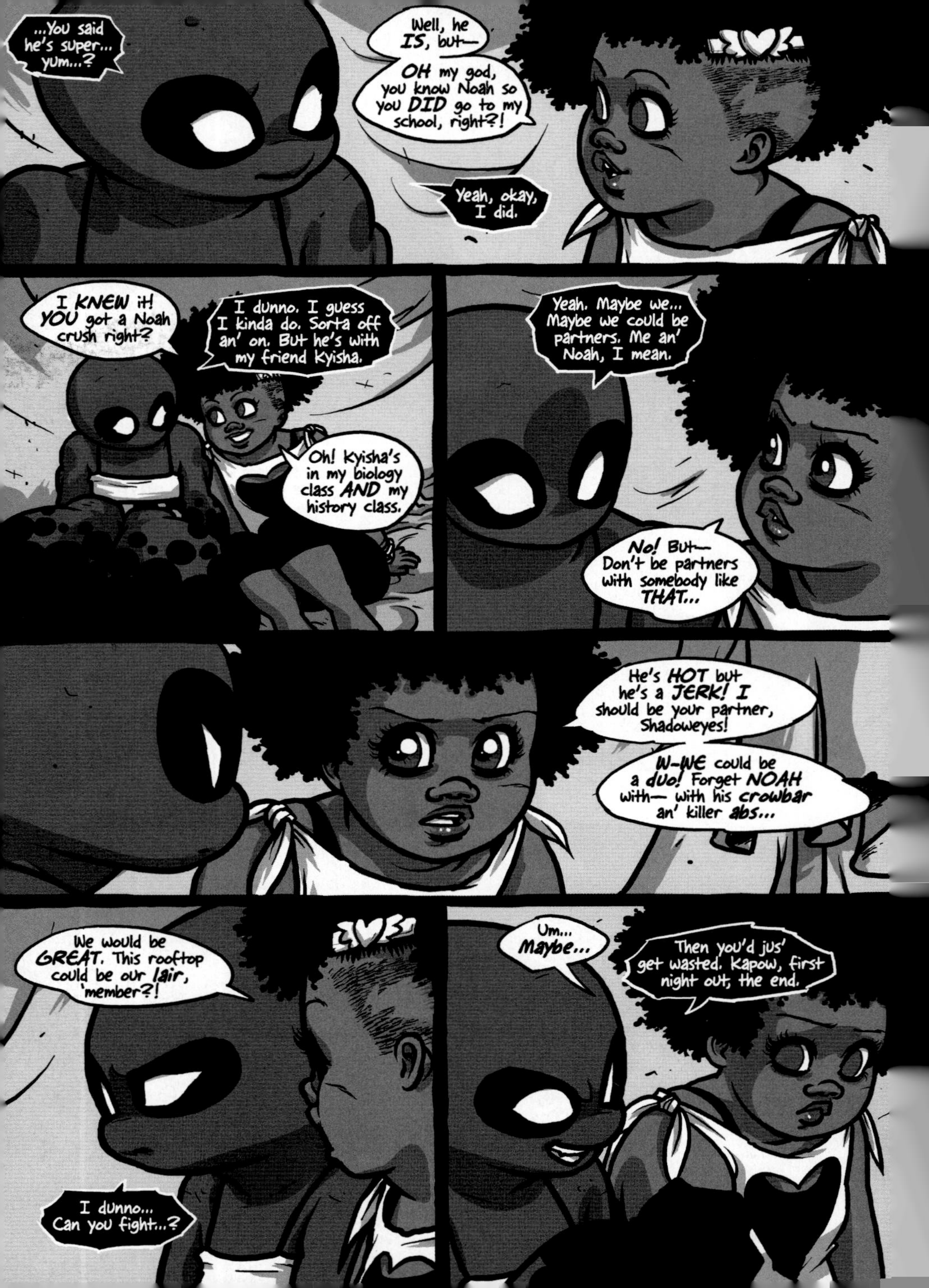
...You said he's super... yum...?
Well, he IS, but—
OH my god, you know Noah so you DID go to my school, right?!
Yeah, okay, I did.
I KNEW it! YOU got a Noah crush right?
I dunno. I guess I kinda do. Sorta off an' on. But he's with my friend Kyisha.
Oh! Kyisha's in my biology class AND my history class.
Yeah. Maybe we... Maybe we could be partners. Me an' Noah, I mean.
No! But— Don't be partners with somebody like THAT...
He's HOT but he's a JERK! I should be your partner, Shadoweyes!
W-WE could be a duo! Forget NOAH with— with his crowbar an' killer abs...
We would be GREAT. This rooftop could be our lair, 'member?!
I dunno... Can you fight...?
Um... Maybe...
Then you'd jus' get wasted. Kapow, first night out, the end.

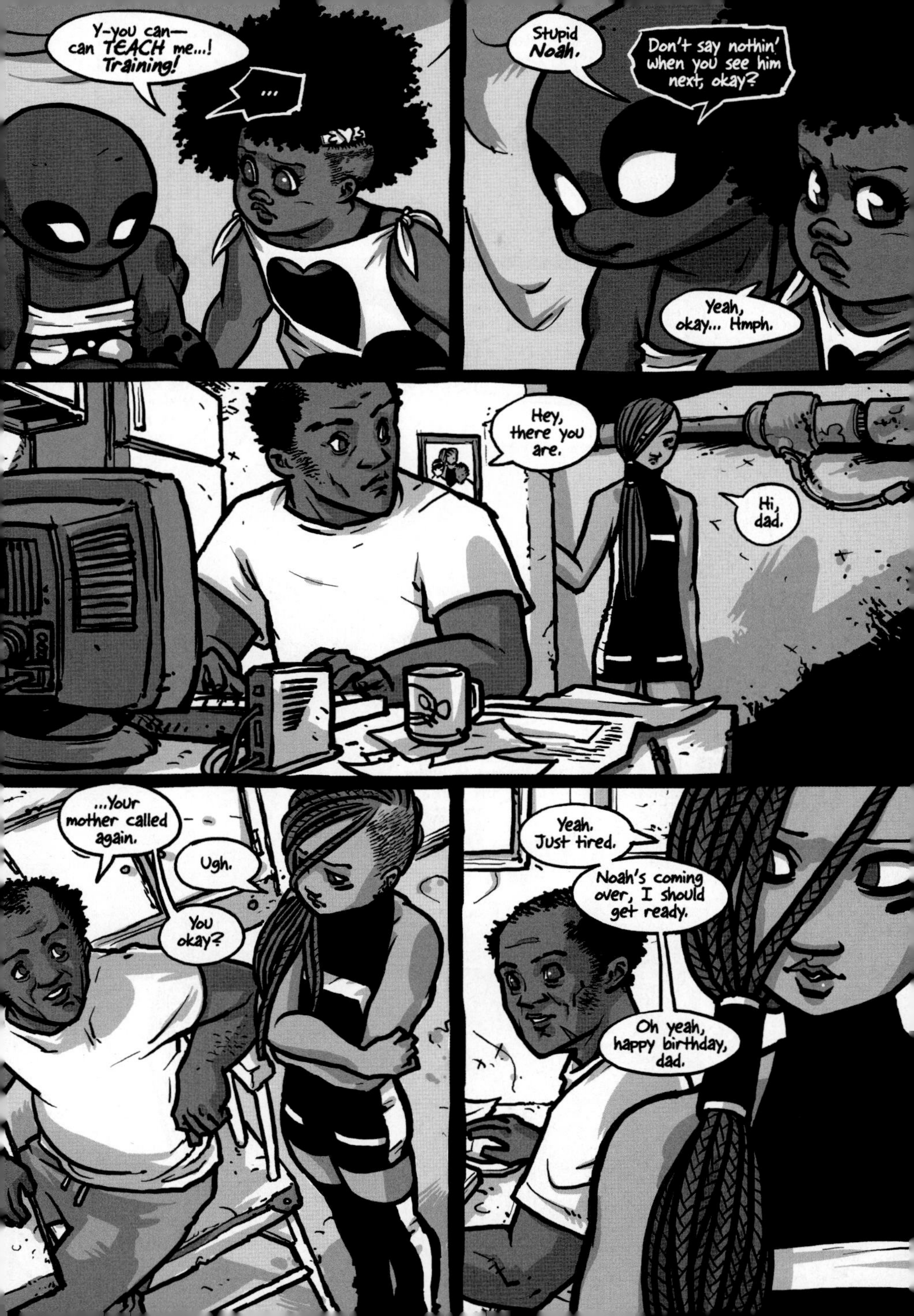
Y-you can—can TEACH me...! Training!
...
Stupid Noah.
Don't say nothin' when you see him next, okay?
Yeah, okay... Hmph.
Hey, there you are.
Hi, dad.
...Your mother called again.
Ugh.
You okay?
Yeah. Just tired.
Noah's coming over, I should get ready.
Oh yeah, happy birthday, dad.

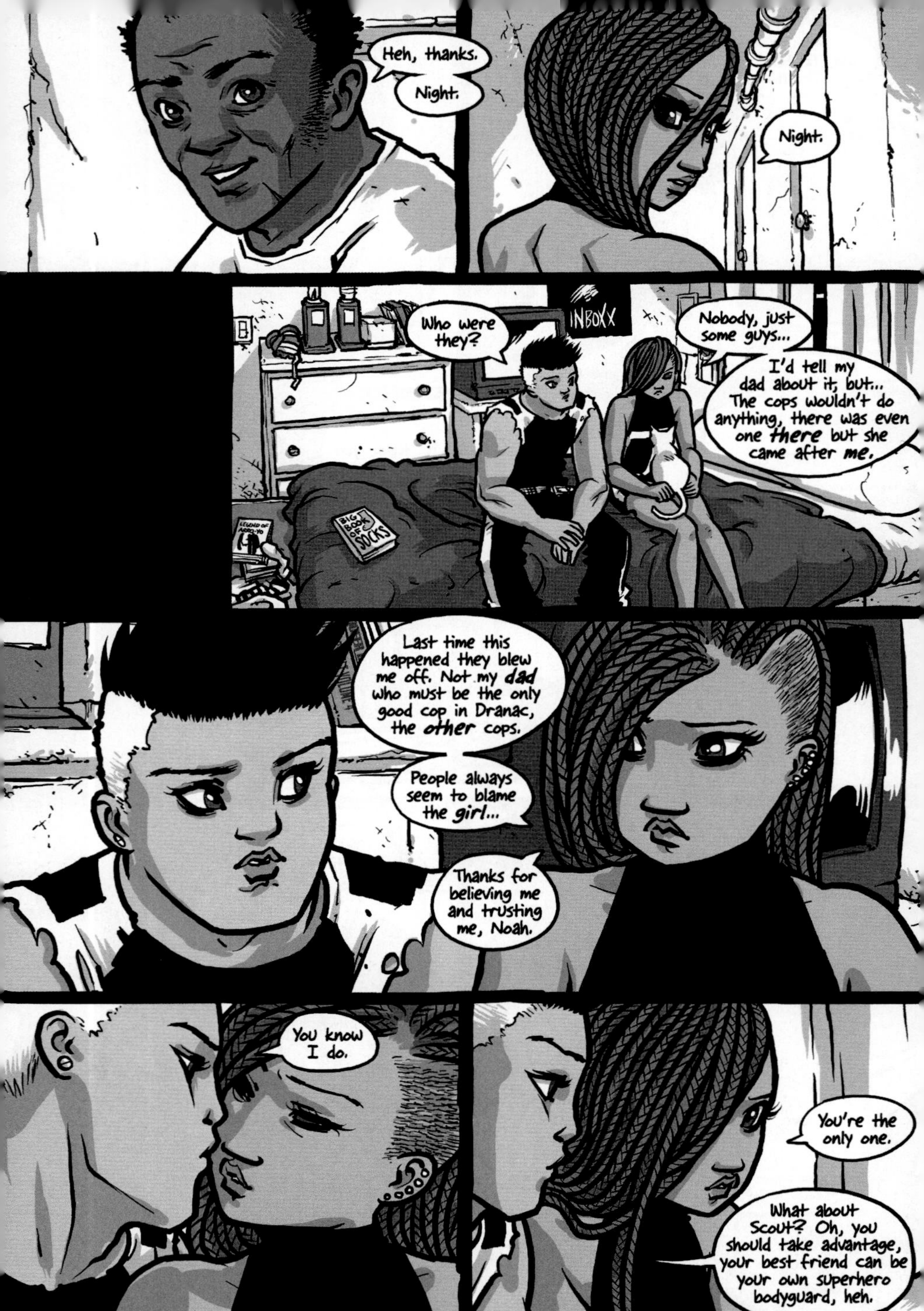
Heh, thanks.
Night.
Night.
INBOXX
Who were they?
Nobody, just some guys...
I'd tell my dad about it, but... The cops wouldn't do anything, there was even one there but she came after me.
LEGEND OF ARRO-YO
BIG BOOK OF SOCKS
Last time this happened they blew me off. Not my dad who must be the only good cop in Dranac, the other cops.
People always seem to blame the girl...
Thanks for believing me and trusting me, Noah.
You know I do.
You're the only one.
What about Scout? Oh, you should take advantage, your best friend can be your own superhero bodyguard, heh.

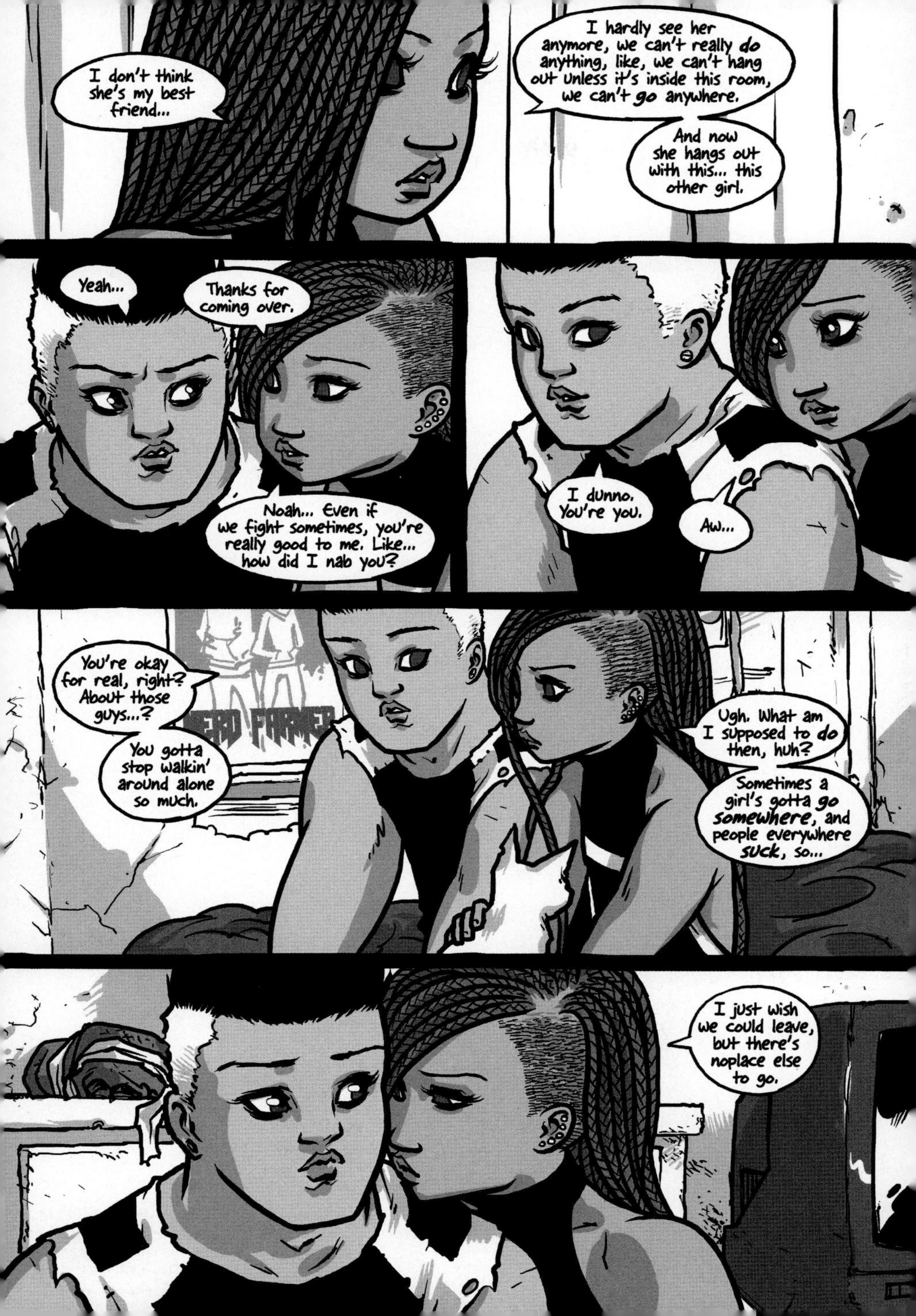
I don't think she's my best friend...
I hardly see her anymore, we can't really *do* anything, like, we can't hang out unless it's inside this room, we can't *go* anywhere.
And now she hangs out with this... this other girl.
Yeah...
Thanks for coming over.
Noah... Even if we fight sometimes, you're really good to me. Like... how did I nab you?
I dunno. You're you.
Aw...
You're okay for real, right? About those guys...?
You gotta stop walkin' around alone so much.
Ugh. What am I supposed to *do* then, huh?
Sometimes a girl's gotta *go somewhere*, and people everywhere *suck*, so...
I just wish we could leave, but there's noplace else to go.

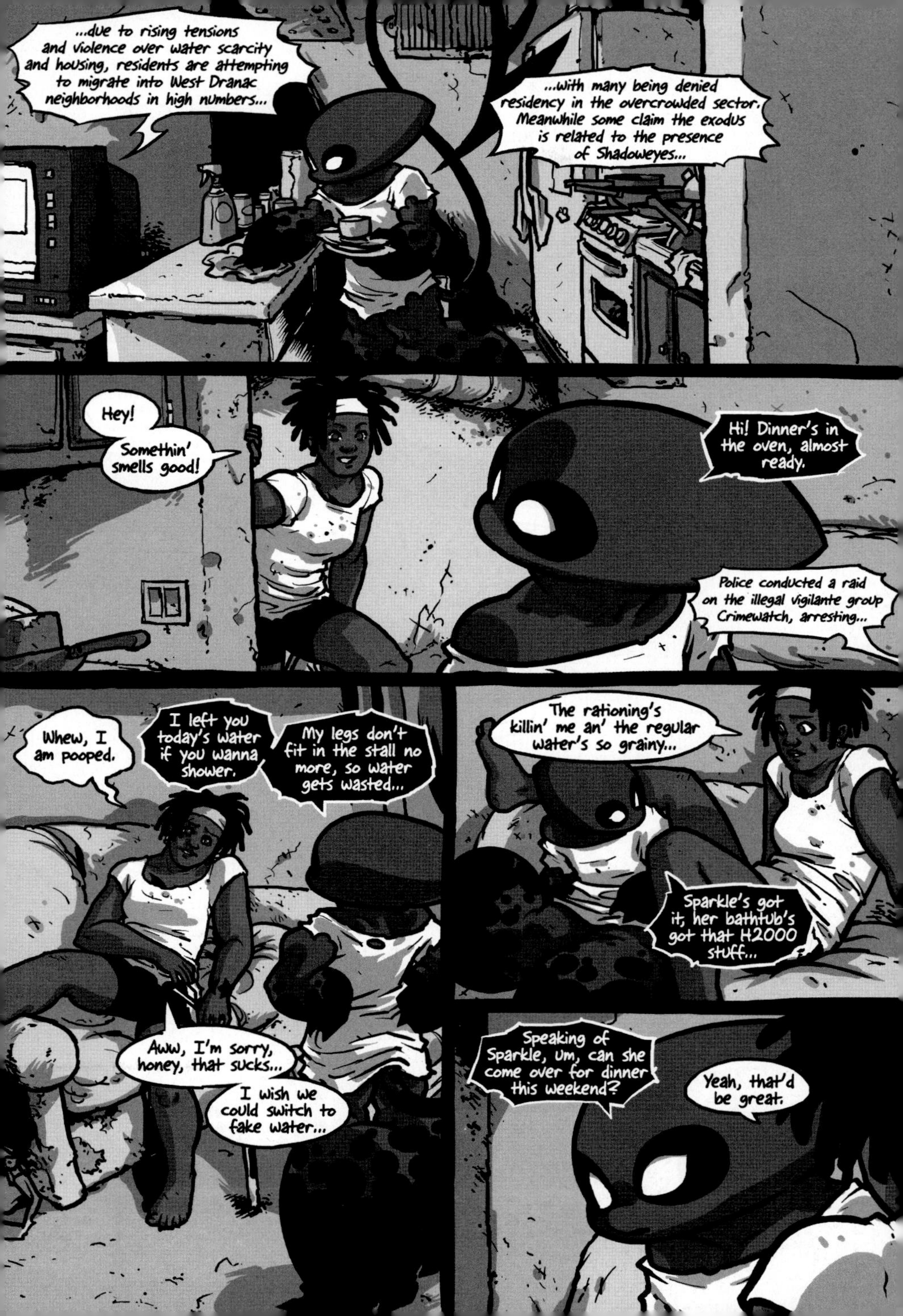
...due to rising tensions and violence over water scarcity and housing, residents are attempting to migrate into West Dranac neighborhoods in high numbers...
...with many being denied residency in the overcrowded sector. Meanwhile some claim the exodus is related to the presence of Shadoweyes...
Hey!
Somethin' smells good!
Hi! Dinner's in the oven, almost ready.
Police conducted a raid on the illegal vigilante group Crimewatch, arresting...
Whew, I am pooped.
I left you today's water if you wanna shower.
My legs don't fit in the stall no more, so water gets wasted...
Aww, I'm sorry, honey, that sucks...
I wish we could switch to fake water...
The rationing's killin' me an' the regular water's so grainy...
Sparkle's got it, her bathtub's got that H2000 stuff...
Speaking of Sparkle, um, can she come over for dinner this weekend?
Yeah, that'd be great.

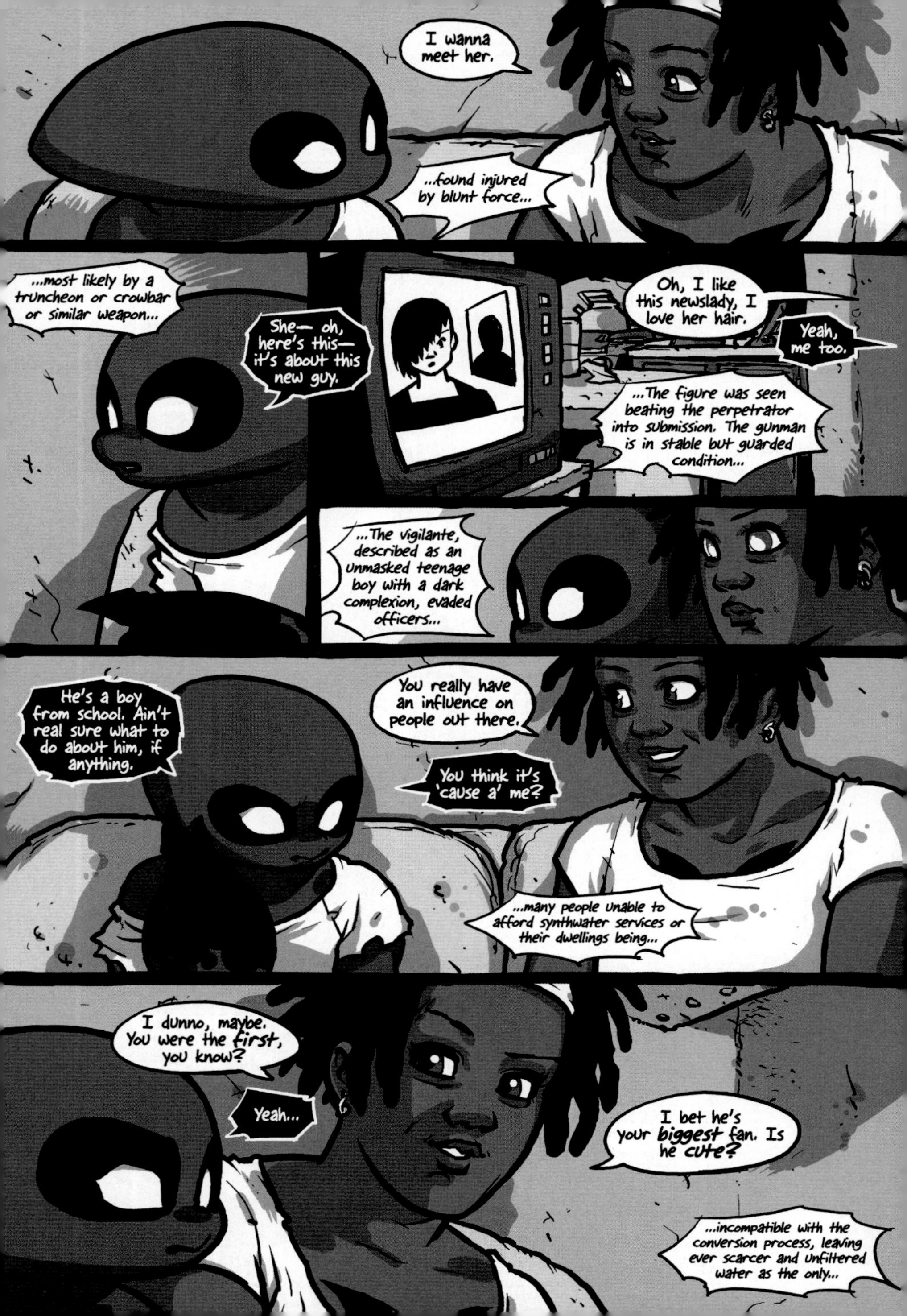

I wanna meet her.
...found injured by blunt force...
...most likely by a truncheon or crowbar or similar weapon...
She— oh, here's this— it's about this new guy.
Oh, I like this newslady, I love her hair.
Yeah, me too.
...The figure was seen beating the perpetrator into submission. The gunman is in stable but guarded condition...
...The vigilante, described as an unmasked teenage boy with a dark complexion, evaded officers...
He's a boy from school. Ain't real sure what to do about him, if anything.
You really have an influence on people out there.
You think it's 'cause a' me?
...many people unable to afford synthwater services or their dwellings being...
I dunno, maybe. You were the *first*, you know?
Yeah...
I bet he's your ***biggest*** fan. Is he ***cute?***
...incompatible with the conversion process, leaving ever scarcer and unfiltered water as the only...

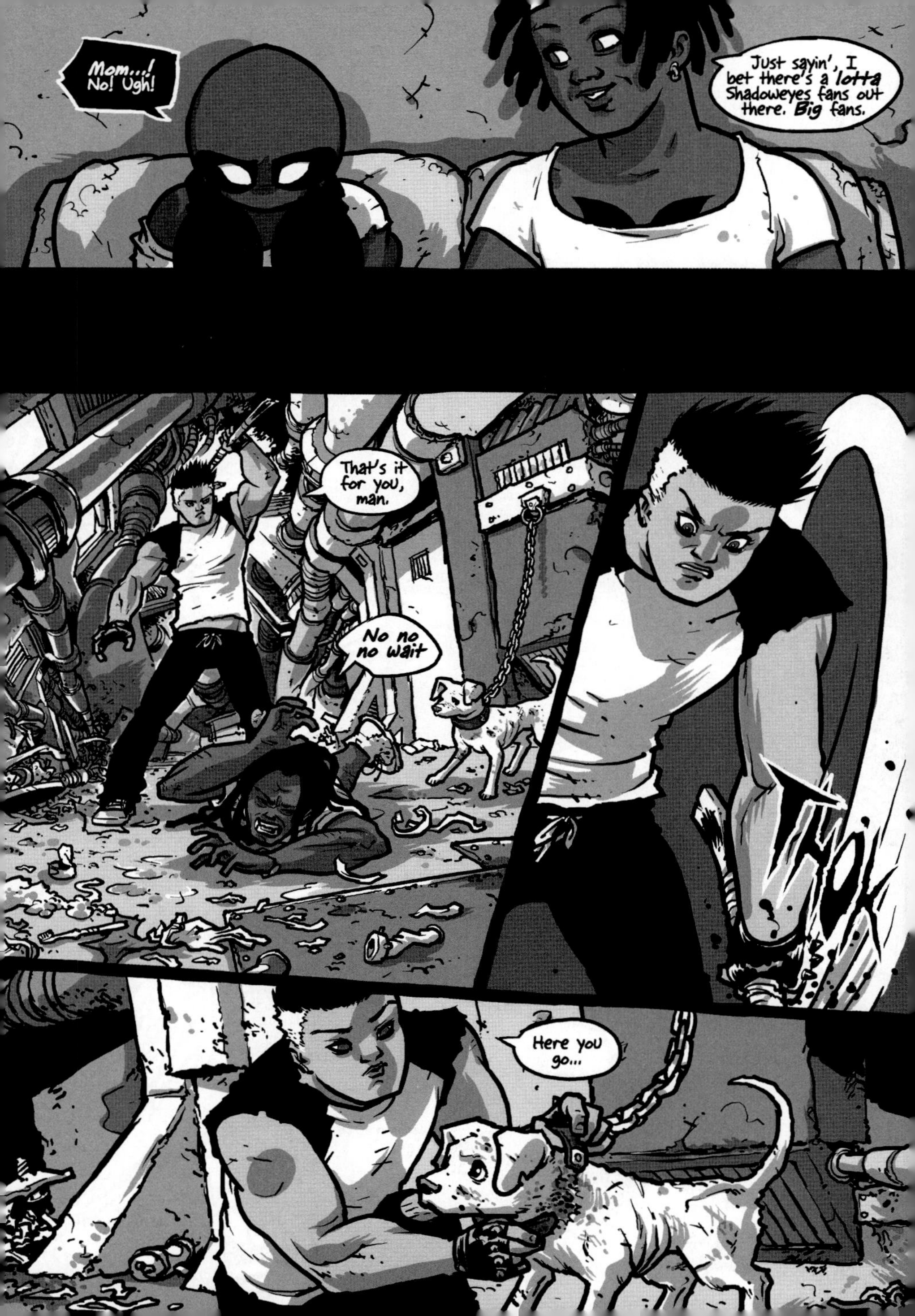
Mom...! No! Ugh!
Just sayin', I bet there's a *lotta* Shadoweyes fans out there. *Big* fans.
That's it for you, man.
No no no wait
THOK
Here you go...

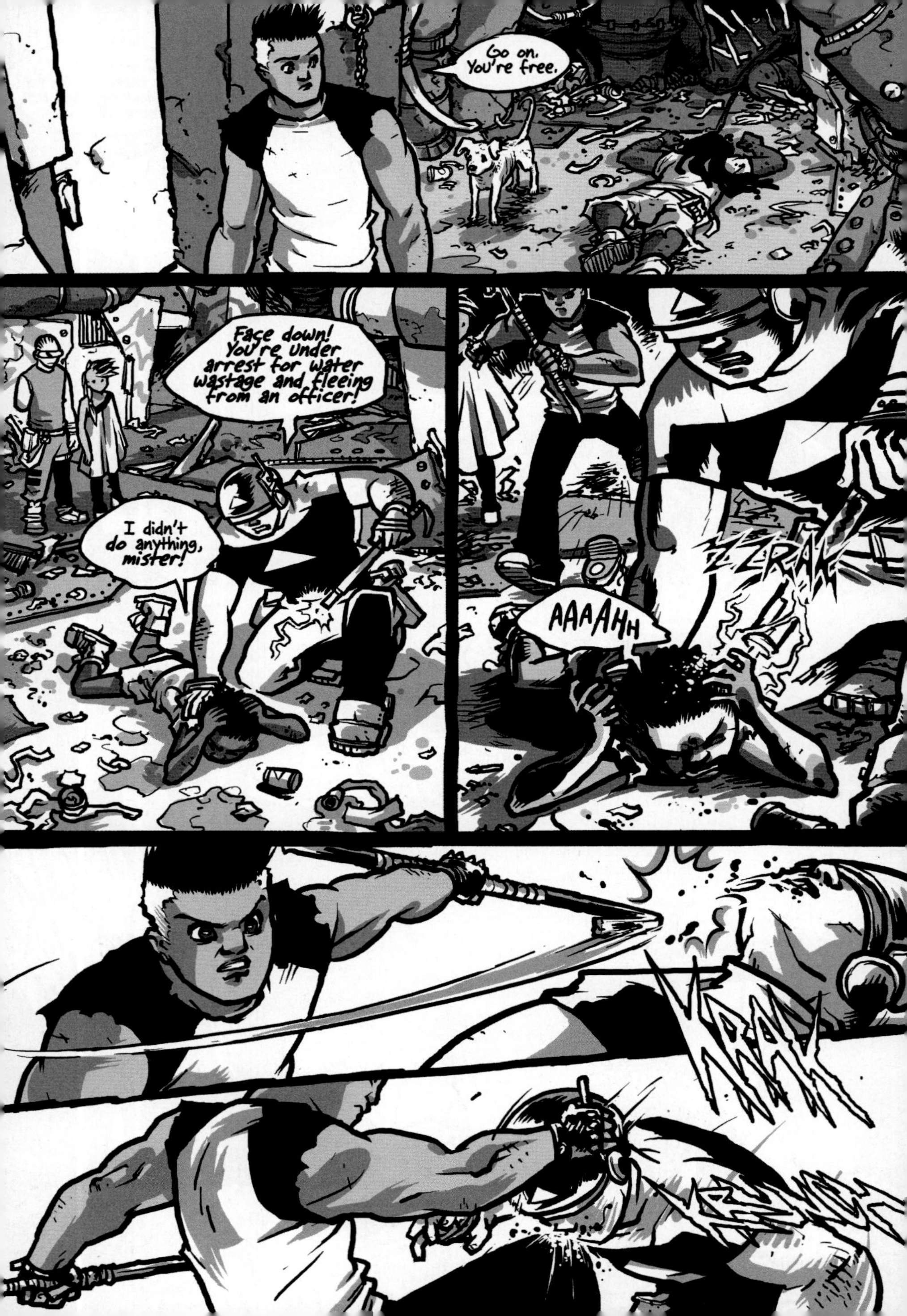
Go on. You're free.
Face down! You're under arrest for water wastage and fleeing from an officer!
I didn't do anything, mister!
ZZZRAK
AAAAHH

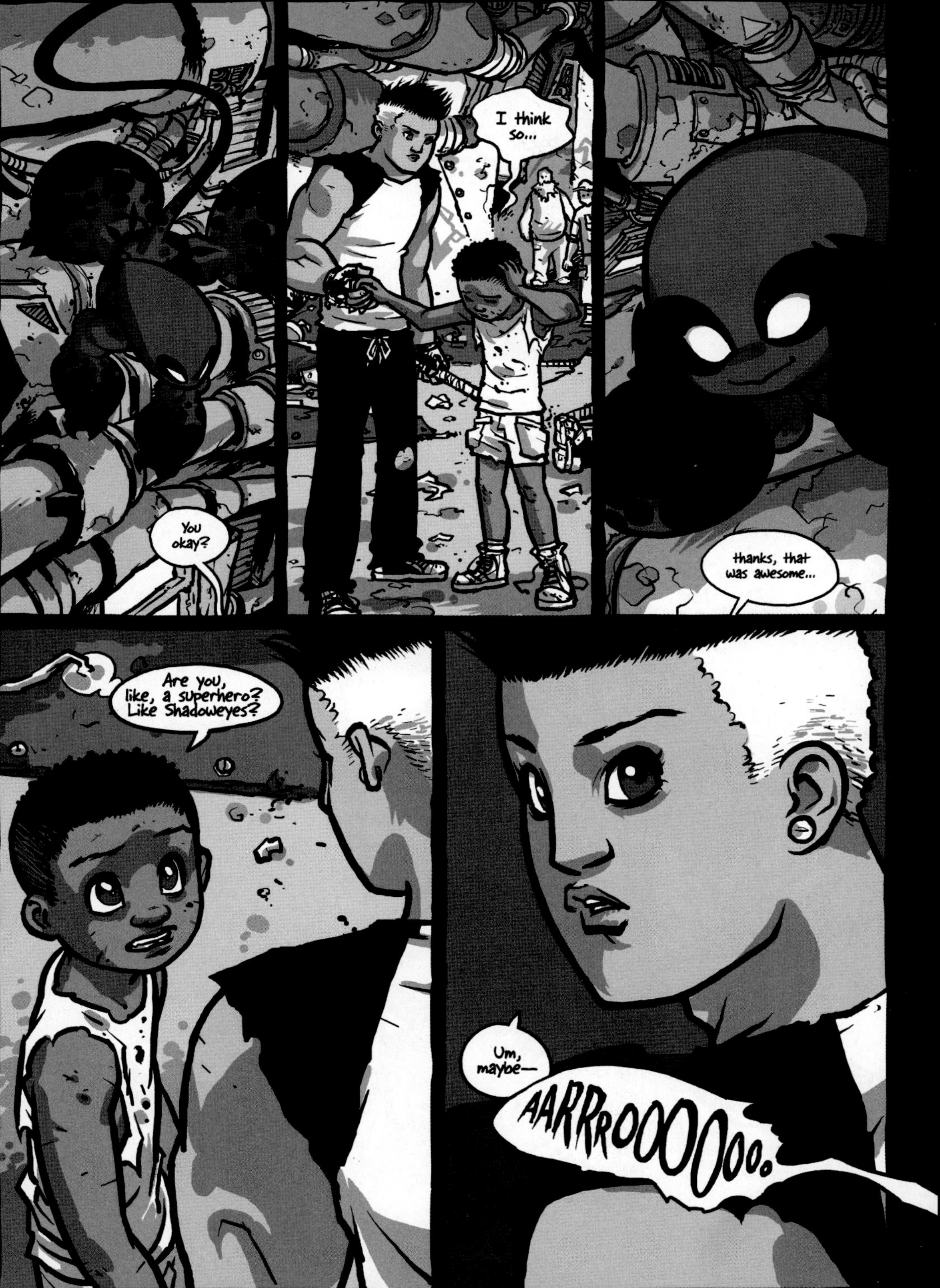
You okay?
I think so...
thanks, that was awesome...
Are you, like, a superhero? Like Shadoweyes?
Um, maybe—
AARRROOOOOoo.

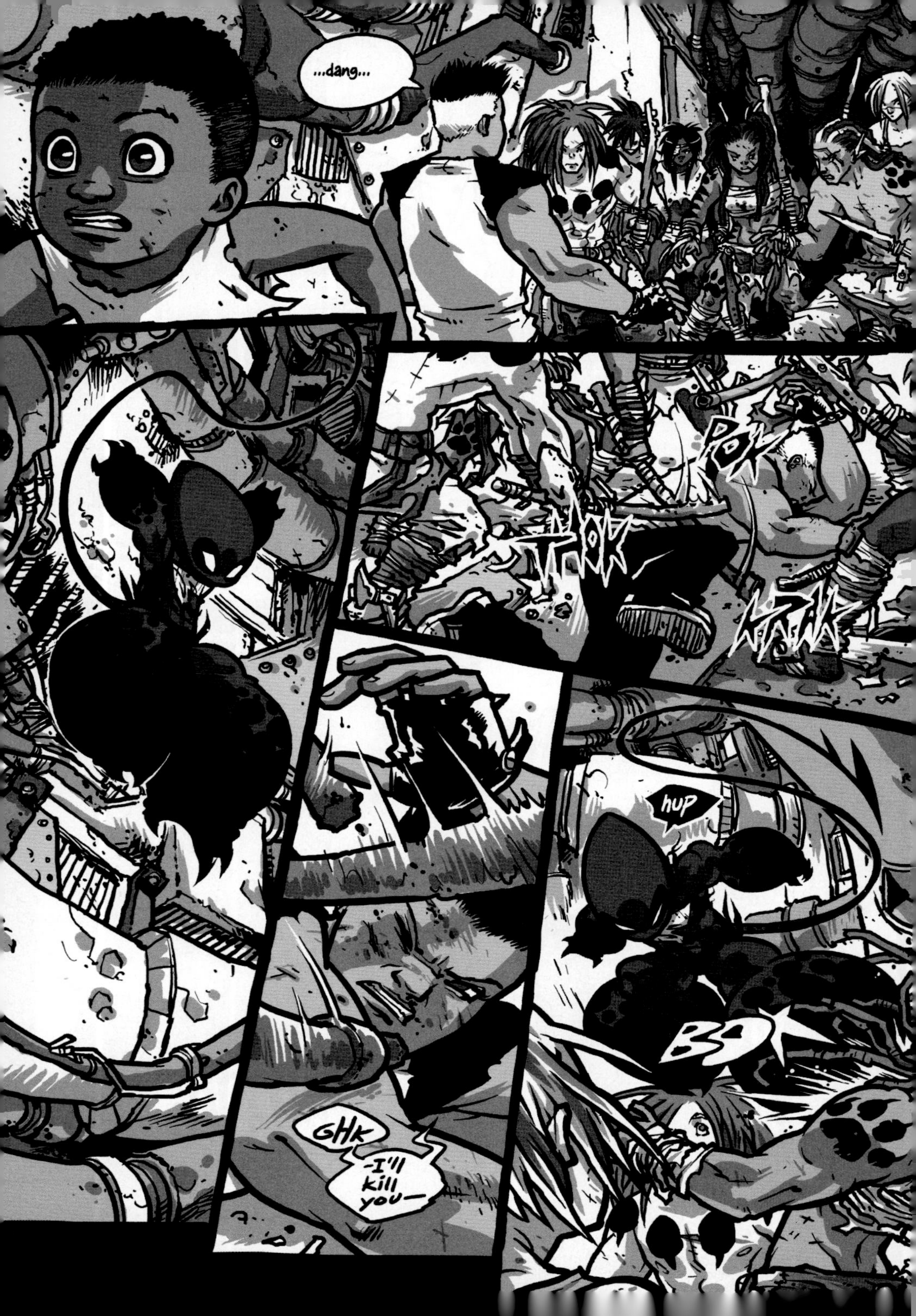
...dang...
POK
THOK
KRAK
hup
GHK
-I'll kill you—

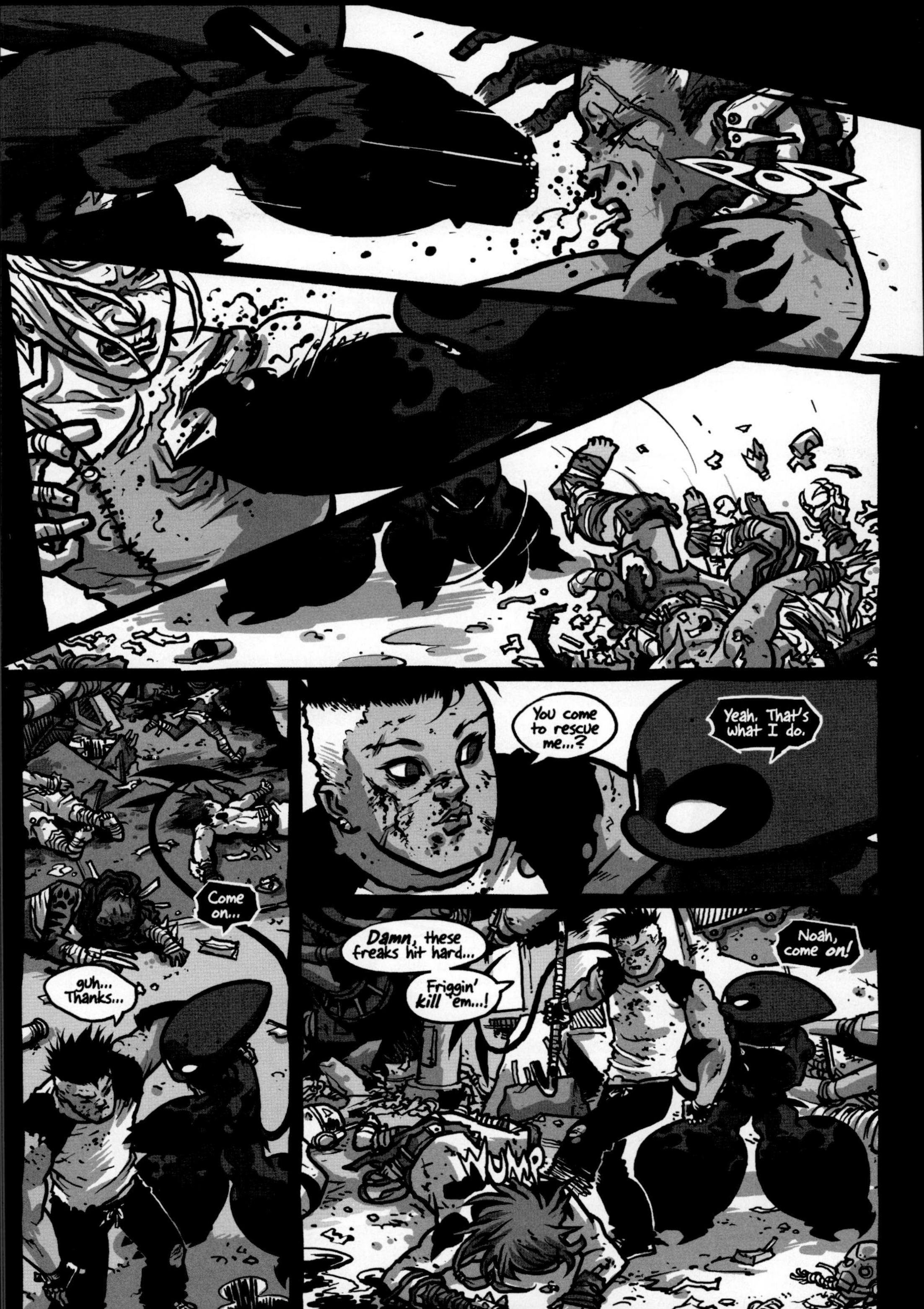

You come to rescue me...?
Yeah. That's what I do.
Come on...
guh... Thanks...
Damn, these freaks hit hard...
Friggin' kill 'em...!
Noah, come on!
WUMP

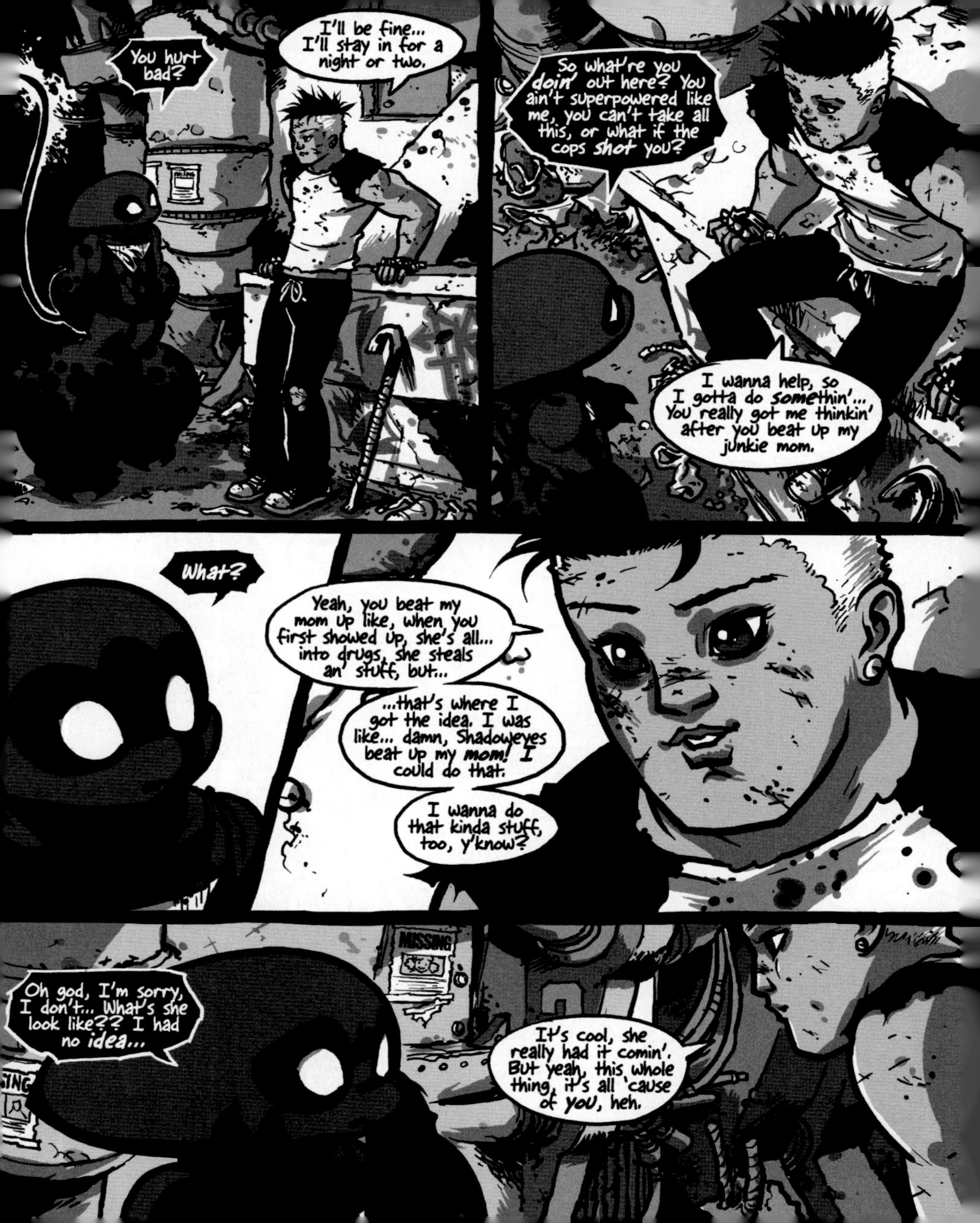
You hurt bad?
I'll be fine... I'll stay in for a night or two.
So what're you doin' out here? You ain't superpowered like me, you can't take all this, or what if the cops shot you?
I wanna help, so I gotta do somethin'... You really got me thinkin' after you beat up my junkie mom.
What?
Yeah, you beat my mom up like, when you first showed up, she's all... into drugs, she steals an' stuff, but...
...that's where I got the idea. I was like... damn, Shadoweyes beat up my mom! I could do that.
I wanna do that kinda stuff, too, y'know?
MISSING
Oh god, I'm sorry, I don't... What's she look like?? I had no idea...
It's cool, she really had it comin'. But yeah, this whole thing, it's all 'cause of you, heh.

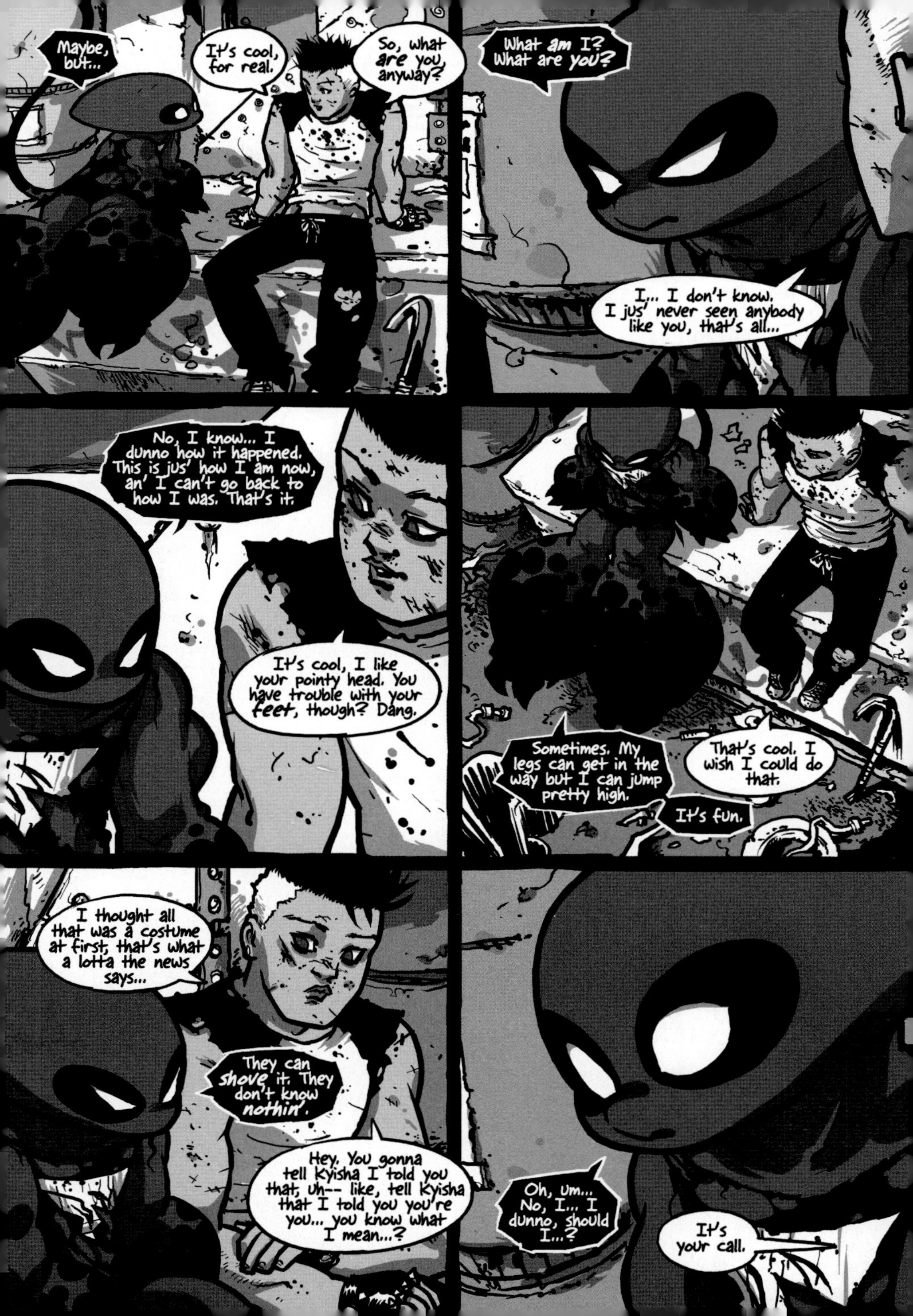
Maybe, but...
It's cool, for real.
So, what are you, anyway?
What am I? What are you?
I... I don't know. I jus' never seen anybody like you, that's all...
No, I know... I dunno how it happened. This is jus' how I am now, an' I can't go back to how I was. That's it.
It's cool, I like your pointy head. You have trouble with your feet, though? Dang.
Sometimes. My legs can get in the way but I can jump pretty high.
It's fun.
That's cool. I wish I could do that.
I thought all that was a costume at first, that's what a lotta the news says...
They can shove it. They don't know nothin'.
Hey, You gonna tell Kyisha I told you that, uh-- like, tell Kyisha that I told you you're you... you know what I mean...?
Oh, um... No, I... I dunno, should I...?
It's your call.

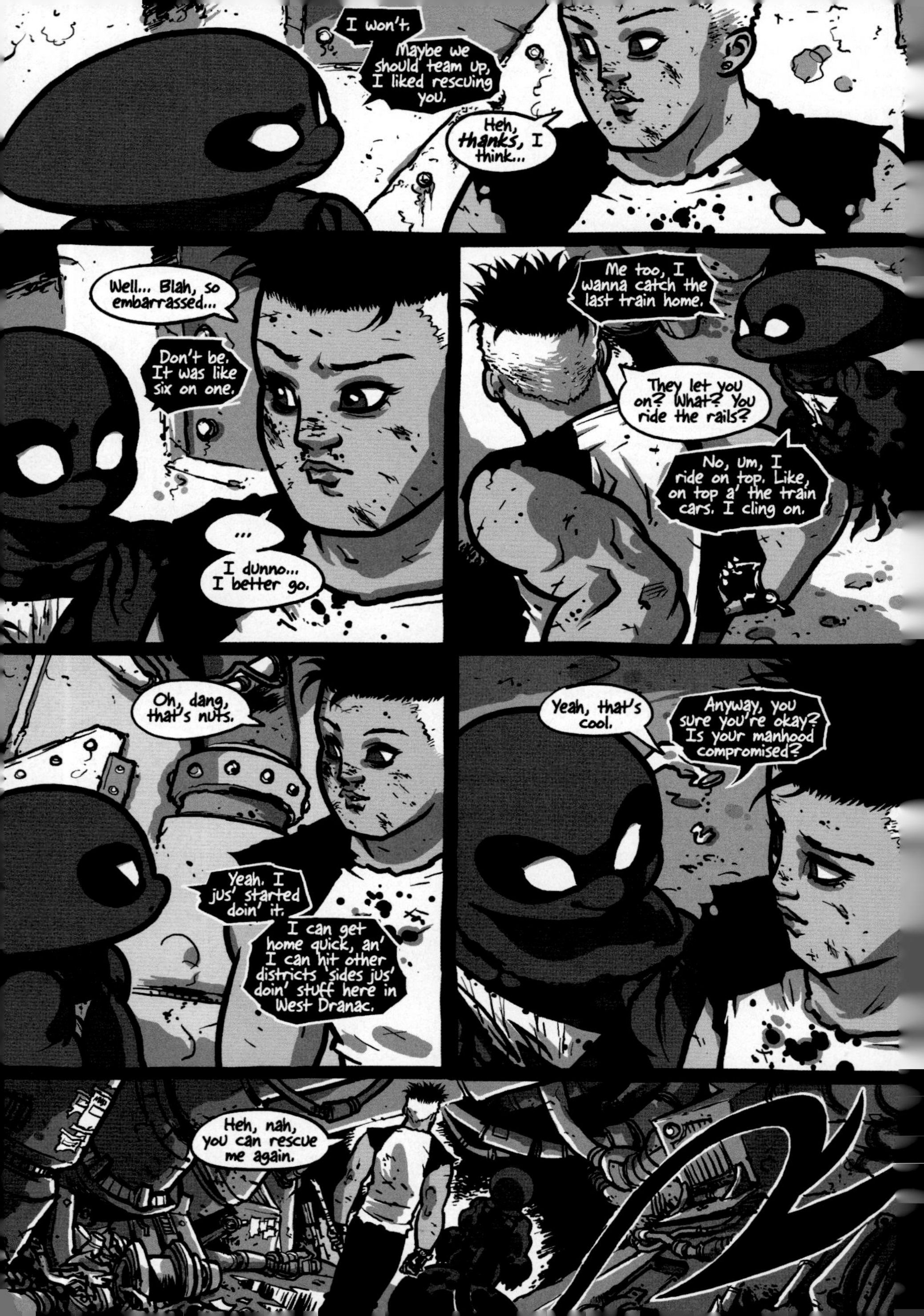

I won't.
Maybe we should team up, I liked rescuing you.
Heh, *thanks*, I think...
Well... Blah, so embarrassed...
Don't be. It was like six on one.
...
I dunno... I better go.
Me too, I wanna catch the last train home.
They let you on? What? You ride the rails?
No, um, I ride on top. Like, on top a' the train cars. I cling on.
Oh, dang, that's nuts.
Yeah. I jus' started doin' it.
I can get home quick, an' I can hit other districts 'sides jus' doin' stuff here in West Dranac.
Yeah, that's cool.
Anyway, you sure you're okay? Is your manhood compromised?
Heh, nah, you can rescue me again.

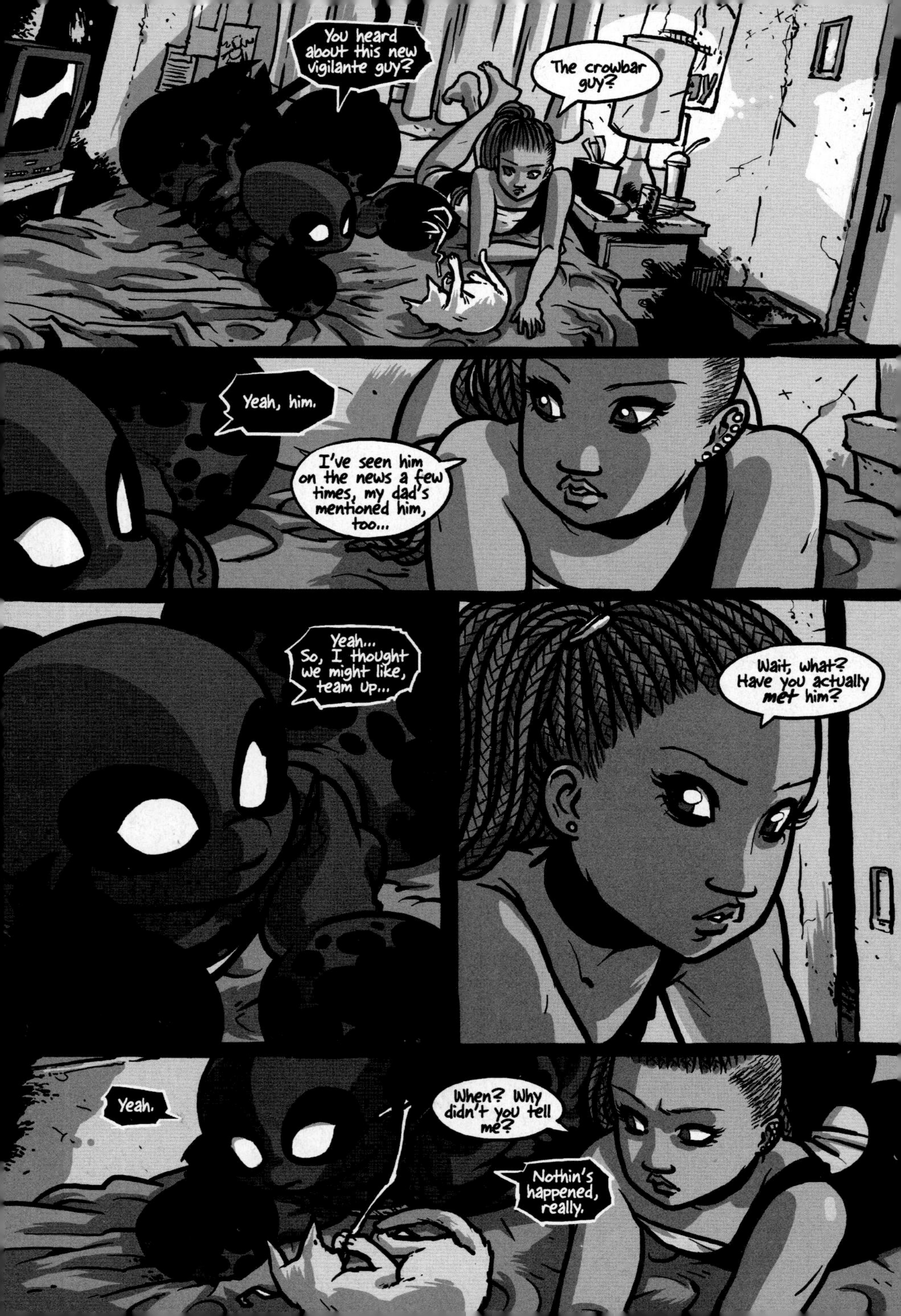
You heard about this new vigilante guy?
The crowbar guy?
Yeah, him.
I've seen him on the news a few times, my dad's mentioned him, too...
Yeah... So, I thought we might like, team up...
Wait, what? Have you actually *met* him?
Yeah.
When? Why didn't you tell me?
Nothin's happened, really.

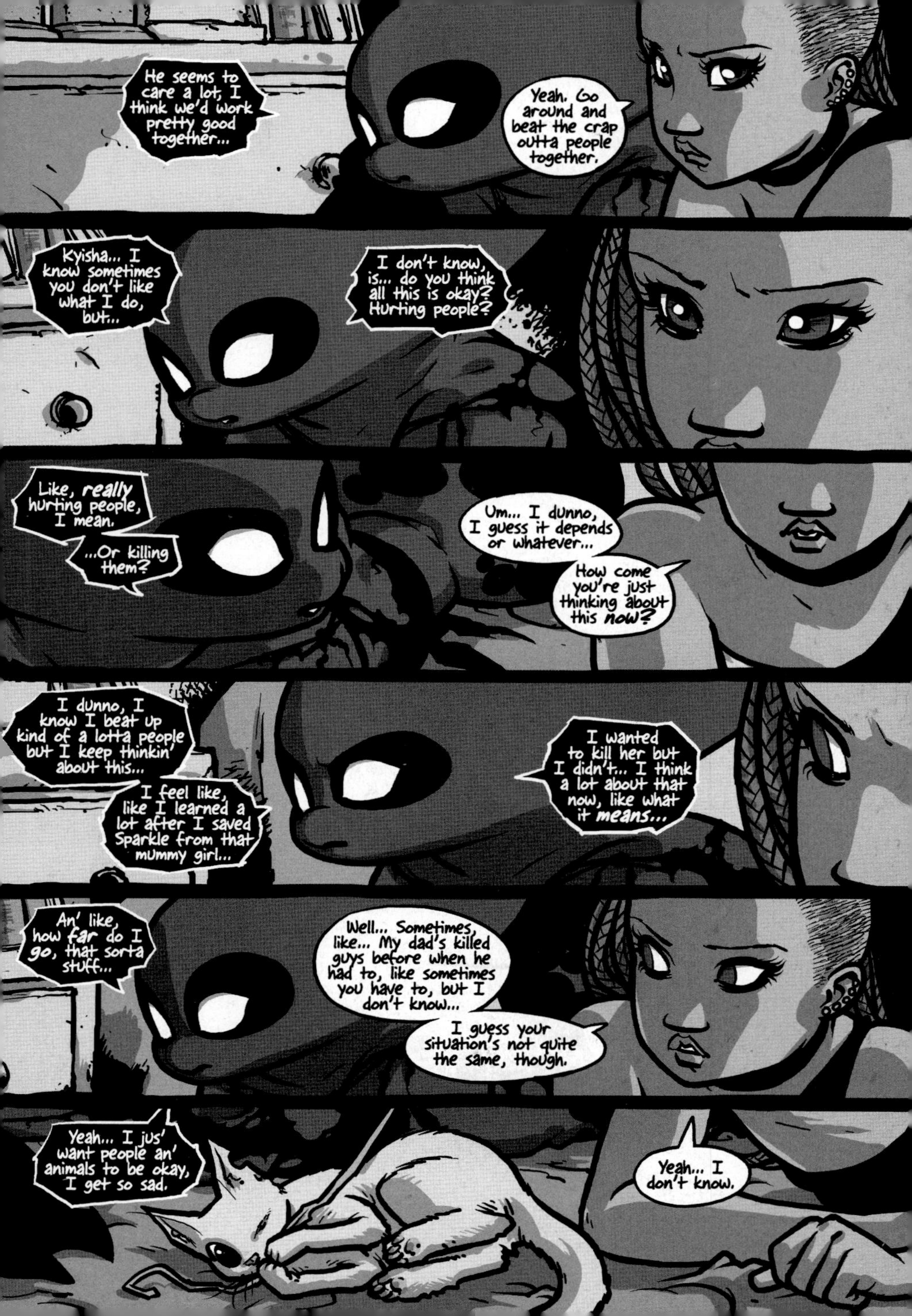
He seems to care a lot, I think we'd work pretty good together...
Yeah. Go around and beat the crap outta people together.
Kyisha... I know sometimes you don't like what I do, but...
I don't know, is... do you think all this is okay? Hurting people?
Like, really hurting people, I mean.
...Or killing them?
Um... I dunno, I guess it depends or whatever...
How come you're just thinking about this now?
I dunno, I know I beat up kind of a lotta people but I keep thinkin' about this...
I feel like, like I learned a lot after I saved Sparkle from that mummy girl...
I wanted to kill her but I didn't... I think a lot about that now, like what it means...
An' like, how far do I go, that sorta stuff...
Well... Sometimes, like... My dad's killed guys before when he had to, like sometimes you have to, but I don't know...
I guess your situation's not quite the same, though.
Yeah... I jus' want people an' animals to be okay, I get so sad.
Yeah... I don't know.

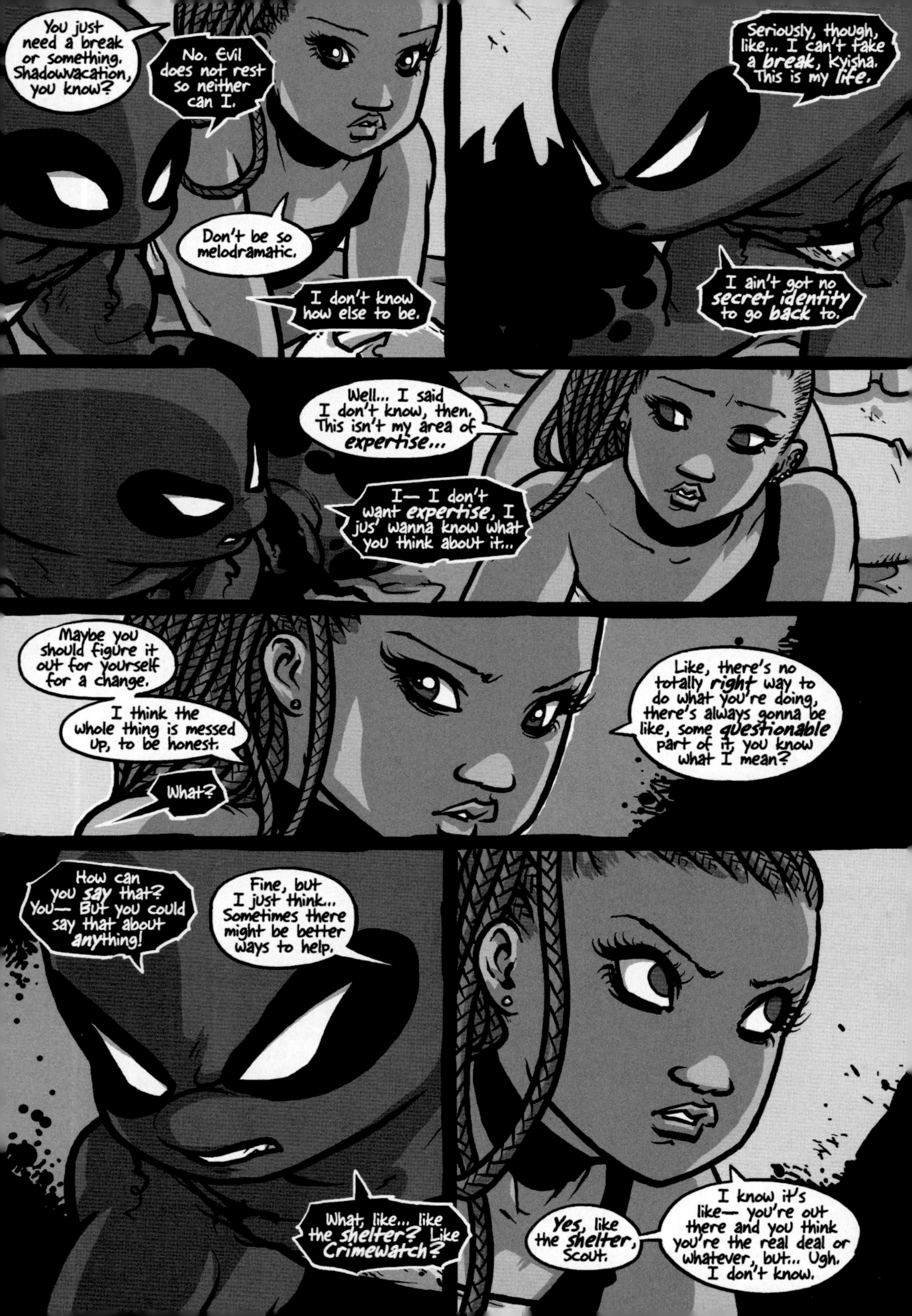
You just need a break or something. Shadowvacation, you know?
No. Evil does not rest so neither can I.
Don't be so melodramatic.
I don't know how else to be.
Seriously, though, like... I can't take a break, Kyisha. This is my life.
I ain't got no secret identity to go back to.
Well... I said I don't know, then. This isn't my area of expertise...
I— I don't want expertise, I jus' wanna know what you think about it...
Maybe you should figure it out for yourself for a change.
I think the whole thing is messed up, to be honest.
What?
Like, there's no totally right way to do what you're doing, there's always gonna be like, some questionable part of it, you know what I mean?
How can you say that? You— But you could say that about anything!
Fine, but I just think... Sometimes there might be better ways to help.
What, like... like the shelter? Like Crimewatch?
Yes, like the shelter, Scout.
I know it's like— you're out there and you think you're the real deal or whatever, but... Ugh. I don't know.

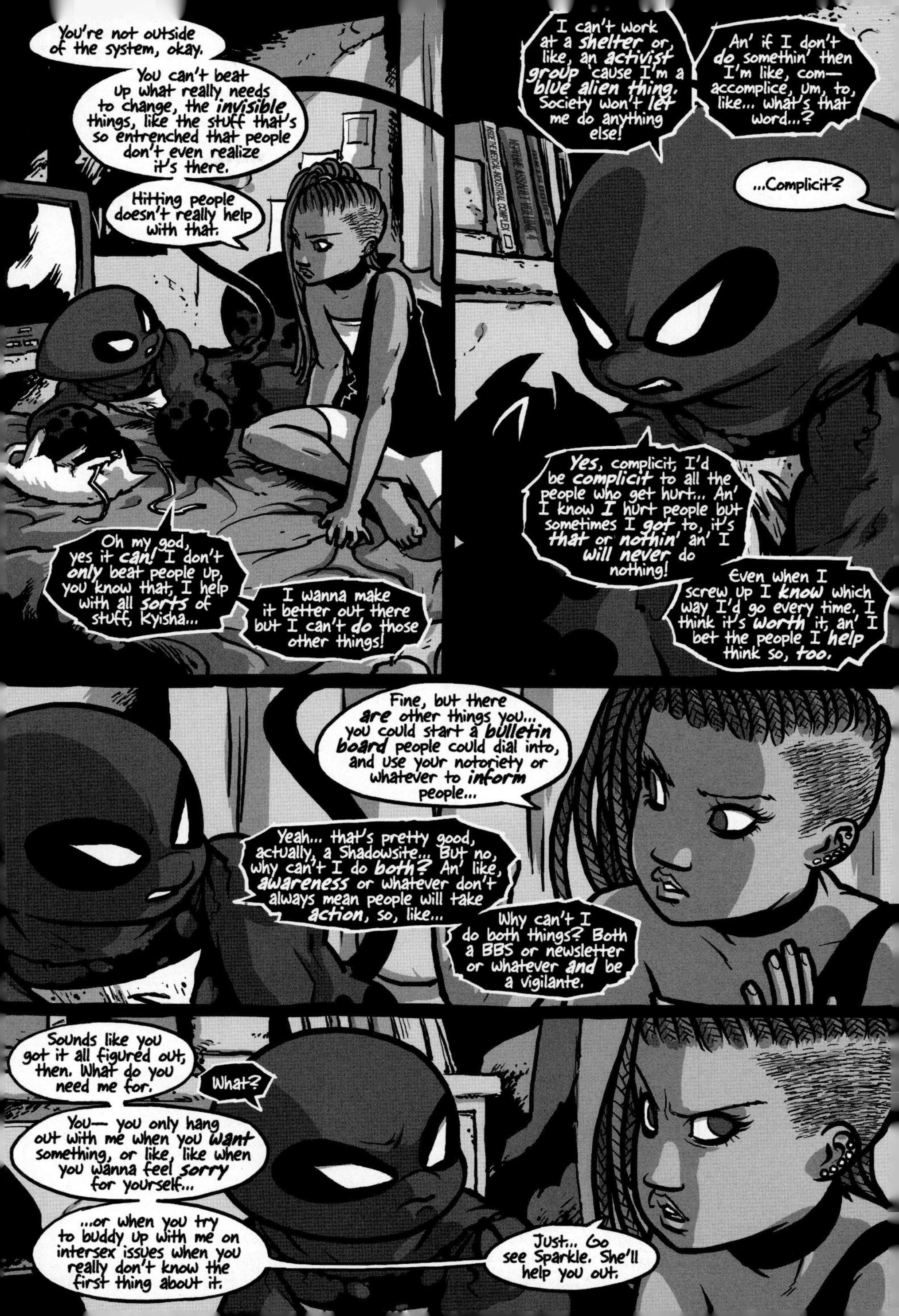
You're not outside of the system, okay.
You can't beat up what really needs to change, the invisible things, like the stuff that's so entrenched that people don't even realize it's there.
Hitting people doesn't really help with that.
Oh my god, yes it can! I don't only beat people up, you know that, I help with all sorts of stuff, Kyisha...
I wanna make it better out there but I can't do those other things!
I can't work at a shelter or, like, an activist group 'cause I'm a blue alien thing. Society won't let me do anything else!
An' if I don't do somethin' then I'm like, com— accomplice, um, to, like... what's that word...?
...Complicit?
Yes, complicit, I'd be complicit to all the people who get hurt... An' I know I hurt people but sometimes I got to, it's that or nothin' an' I will never do nothing!
Even when I screw up I know which way I'd go every time. I think it's worth it, an' I bet the people I help think so, too.
Fine, but there are other things you... you could start a bulletin board people could dial into, and use your notoriety or whatever to inform people...
Yeah... that's pretty good, actually, a Shadowsite... But no, why can't I do both? An' like, awareness or whatever don't always mean people will take action, so, like...
Why can't I do both things? Both a BBS or newsletter or whatever and be a vigilante.
Sounds like you got it all figured out, then. What do you need me for.
What?
You— you only hang out with me when you want something, or like, like when you wanna feel sorry for yourself...
...or when you try to buddy up with me on intersex issues when you really don't know the first thing about it.
Just... Go see Sparkle. She'll help you out.

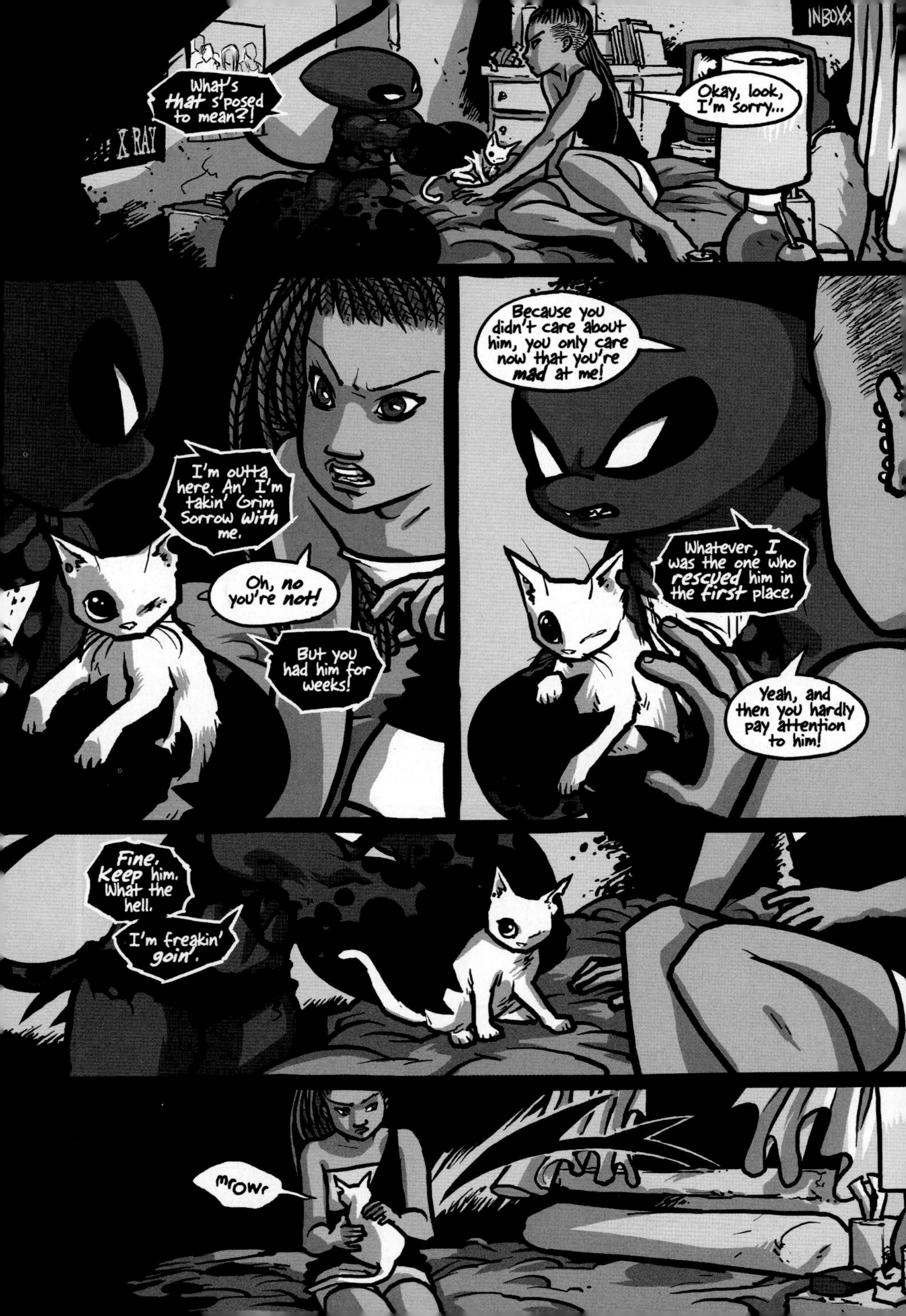
What's that s'posed to mean?!
Okay, look, I'm sorry...
X RAY
INBOXx
I'm outta here. An' I'm takin' Grim Sorrow with me.
Oh, no you're not!
But you had him for weeks!
Because you didn't care about him, you only care now that you're mad at me!
Whatever, I was the one who rescued him in the first place.
Yeah, and then you hardly pay attention to him!
Fine, keep him. What the hell.
I'm freakin' goin'.
mrowr

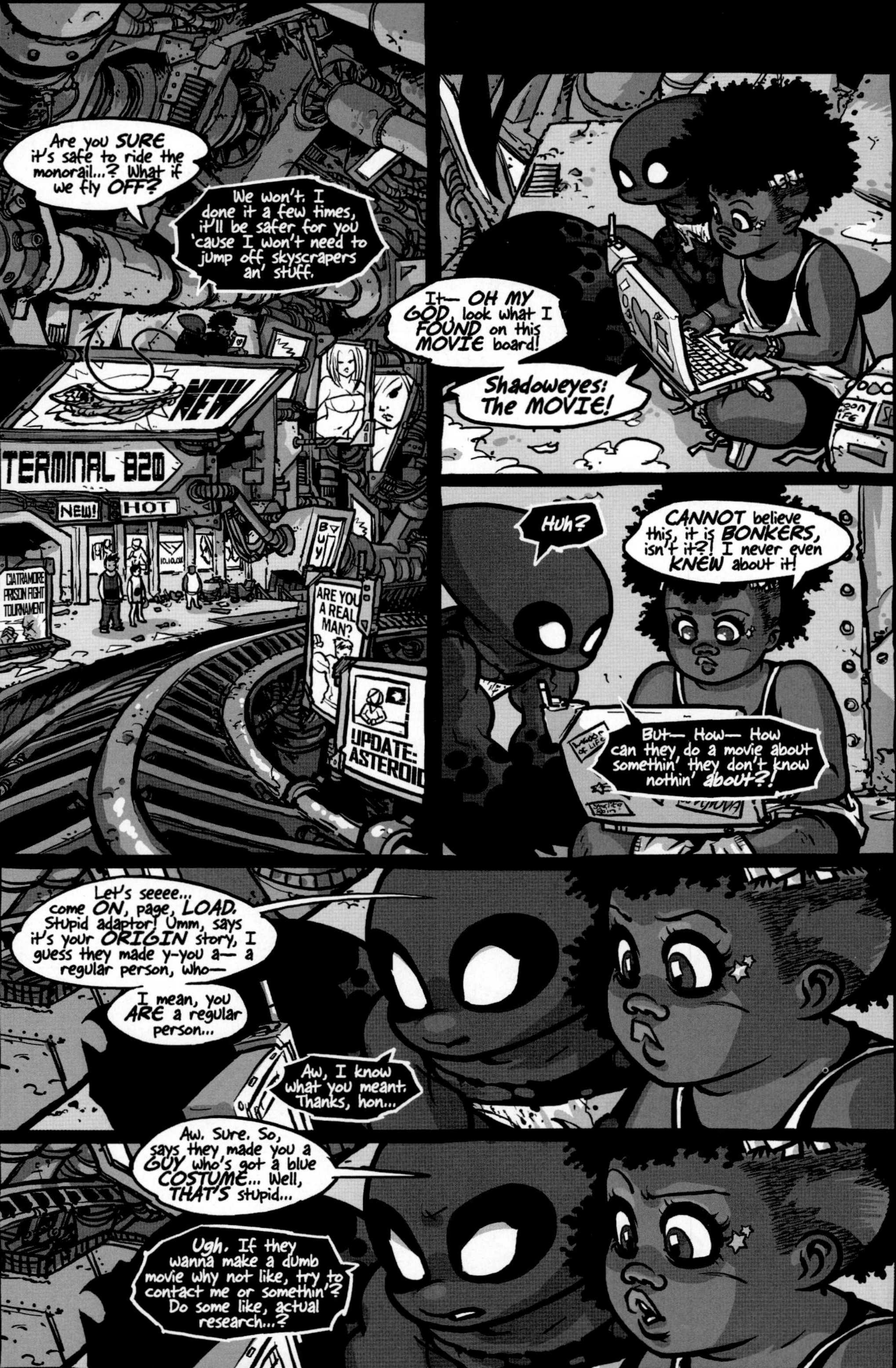
Are you SURE it's safe to ride the monorail...? What if we fly OFF?
We won't. I done it a few times, it'll be safer for you 'cause I won't need to jump off skyscrapers an' stuff.
NEW
TERMINAL B20
NEW!
HOT
CIATRAMORE PRISON FIGHT TOURNAMENT
BUY
ARE YOU A REAL MAN?
UPDATE: ASTEROID
It— OH MY GOD, look what I FOUND on this MOVIE board!
Shadoweyes: The MOVIE!
Huh?
CANNOT believe this, it is BONKERS, isn't it?! I never even KNEW about it!
But— How— How can they do a movie about somethin' they don't know nothin' about?!
Let's seeee... come ON, page, LOAD. Stupid adaptor! Umm, says it's your ORIGIN story, I guess they made y-you a— a regular person, who—
I mean, you ARE a regular person...
Aw, I know what you meant. Thanks, hon...
Aw. Sure. So, says they made you a GUY who's got a blue COSTUME... Well, THAT'S stupid...
Ugh. If they wanna make a dumb movie why not like, try to contact me or somethin'? Do some like, actual research...?

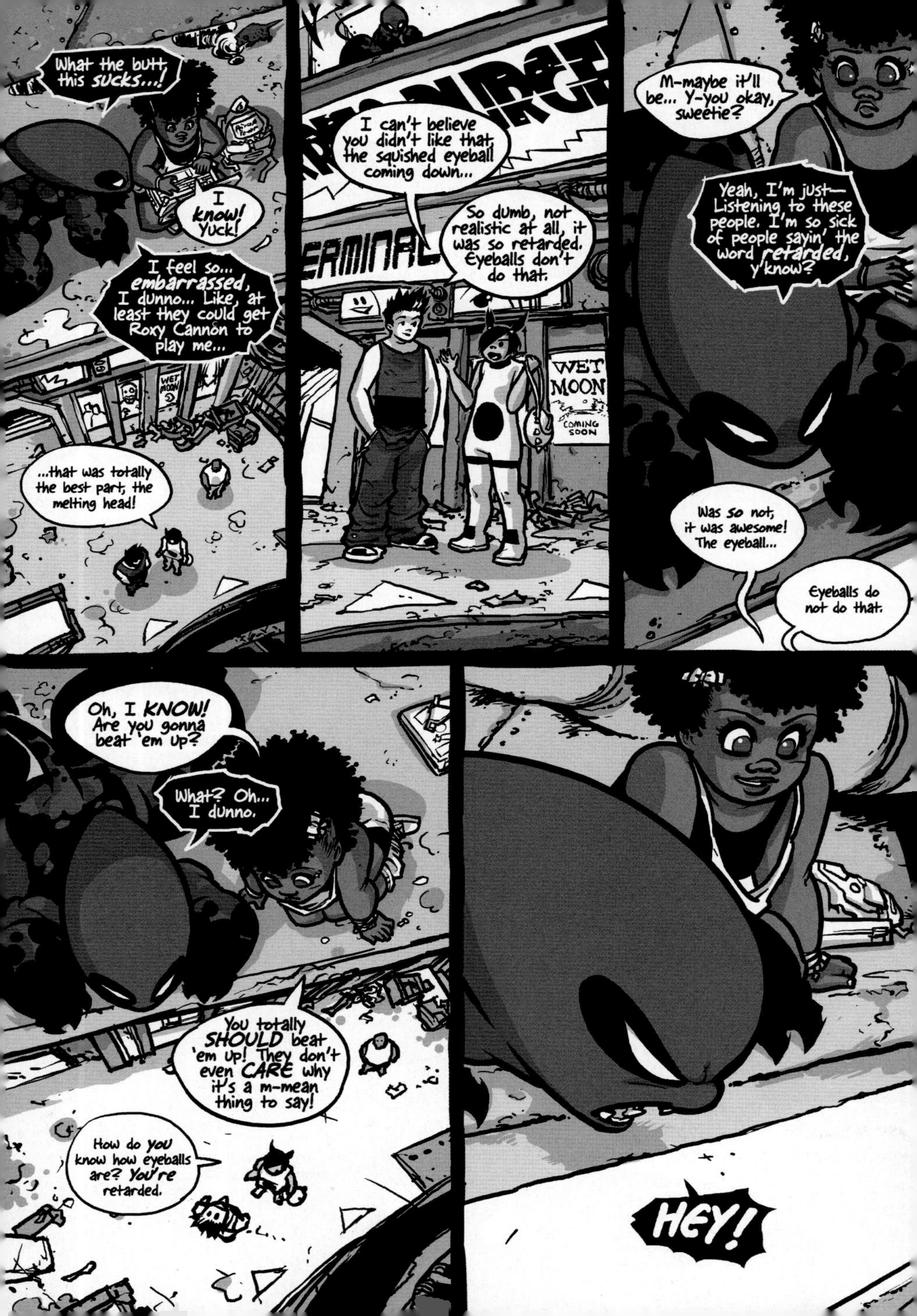

What the butt, this *SUCKS*...!
I *know!* Yuck!
I feel so... *embarrassed*, I dunno... Like, at least they could get Roxy Cannon to play me...
...that was totally the best part, the melting head!
I can't believe you didn't like that the squished eyeball coming down...
So dumb, not realistic at all, it was so retarded. Eyeballs don't do that.
WET MOON
COMING SOON
M-maybe it'll be... Y-you okay, sweetie?
Yeah, I'm just— Listening to these people. I'm so sick of people sayin' the word *retarded*, y'know?
Was *so* not, it was awesome! The eyeball...
Eyeballs do not do that.
Oh, I *KNOW!* Are you gonna beat 'em up?
What? Oh... I dunno.
You totally *SHOULD* beat 'em up! They don't even *CARE* why it's a m-mean thing to say!
How do *you* know how eyeballs are? *You're* retarded.
HEY!

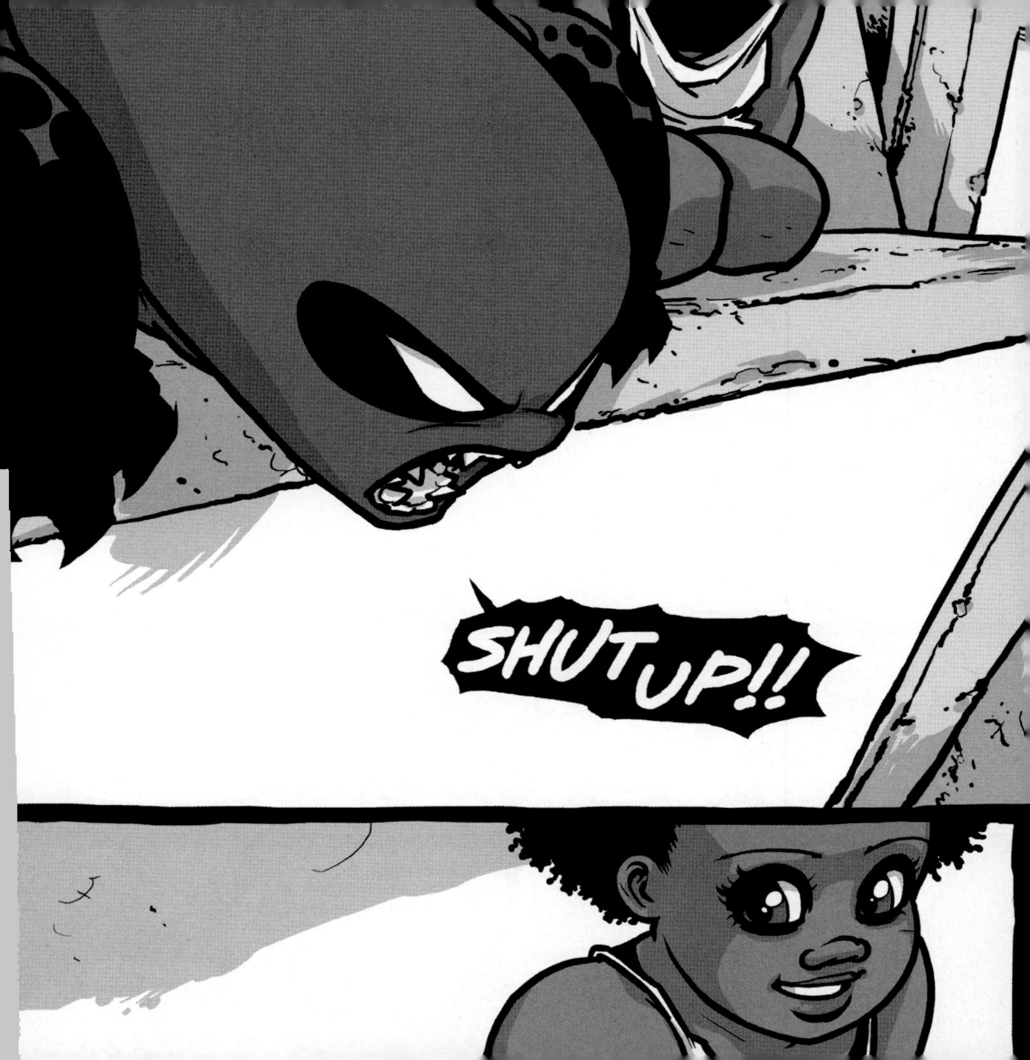
SHUT UP!!

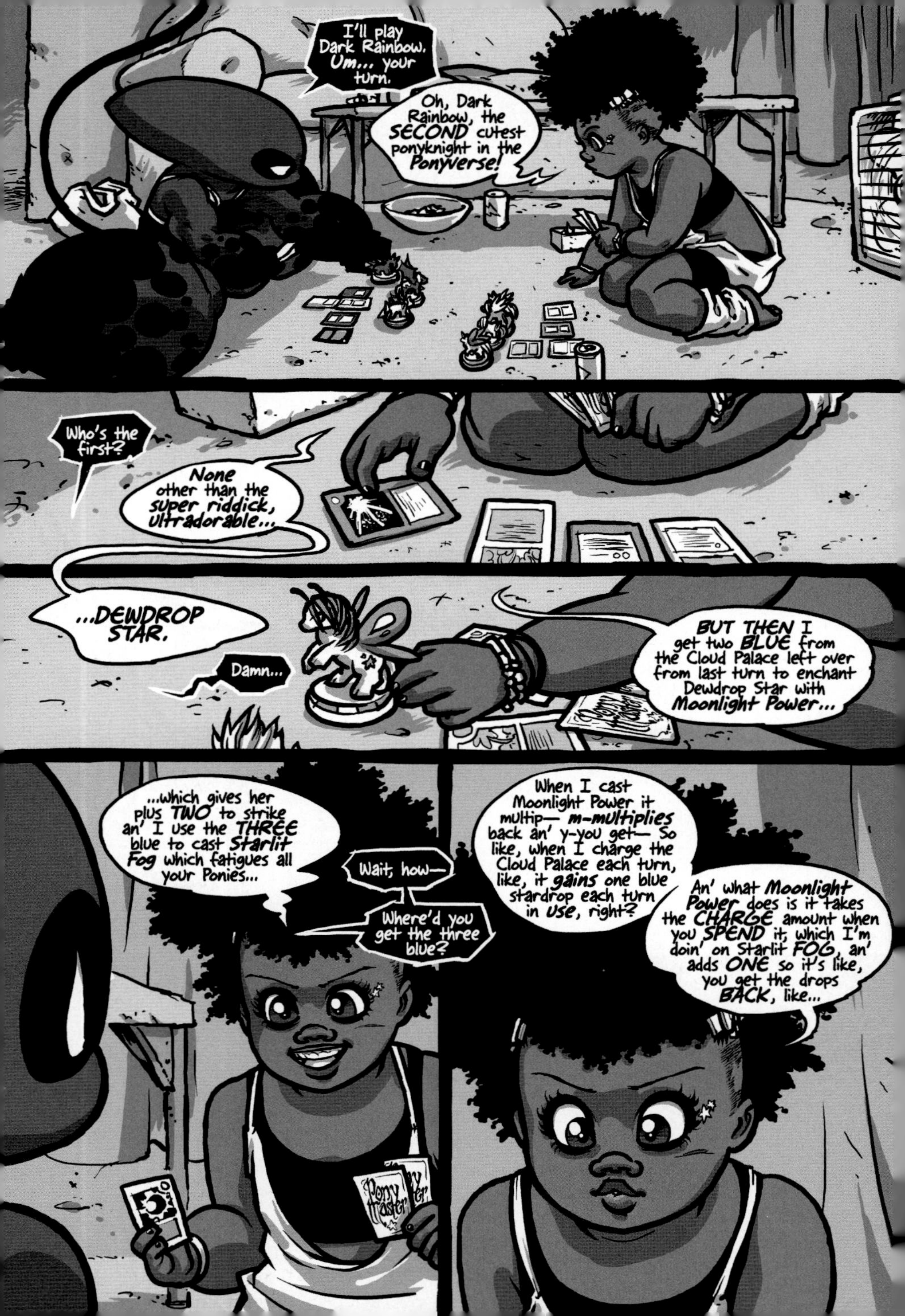
I'll play Dark Rainbow. Um... your turn.
Oh, Dark Rainbow, the SECOND cutest ponyknight in the Ponyverse!
Who's the first?
None other than the super riddick, ultradorable...
...DEWDROP STAR.
Damn...
BUT THEN I get two BLUE from the Cloud Palace left over from last turn to enchant Dewdrop Star with Moonlight Power...
...which gives her plus TWO to strike an' I use the THREE blue to cast Starlit Fog which fatigues all your Ponies...
Wait, how—
Where'd you get the three blue?
When I cast Moonlight Power it multip— m-multiplies back an' y-you get— So like, when I charge the Cloud Palace each turn, like, it gains one blue stardrop each turn in USE, right?
An' what Moonlight Power does is it takes the CHARGE amount when you SPEND it, which I'm doin' on Starlit FOG, an' adds ONE so it's like, you get the drops BACK, like...

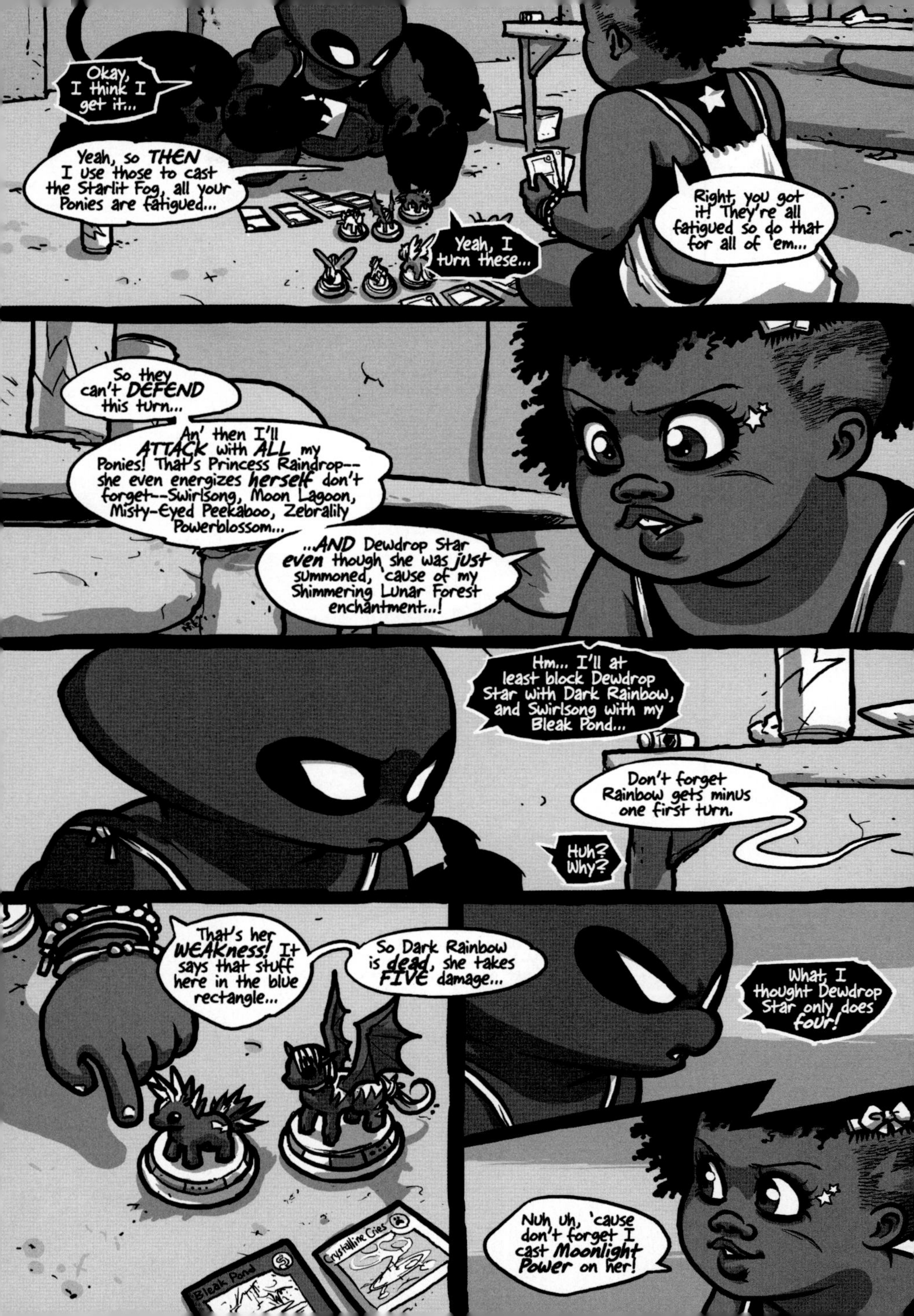
Okay, I think I get it...
Yeah, so THEN I use those to cast the Starlit Fog, all your Ponies are fatigued...
Yeah, I turn these...
Right, you got it! They're all fatigued so do that for all of 'em...
So they can't DEFEND this turn...
An' then I'll ATTACK with ALL my Ponies! That's Princess Raindrop-- she even energizes herself don't forget--Swirlsong, Moon Lagoon, Misty-Eyed Peekaboo, Zebralily Powerblossom...
...AND Dewdrop Star even though she was just summoned, 'cause of my Shimmering Lunar Forest enchantment...!
Hm... I'll at least block Dewdrop Star with Dark Rainbow, and Swirlsong with my Bleak Pond...
Don't forget Rainbow gets minus one first turn.
Huh? Why?
That's her WEAKness! It says that stuff here in the blue rectangle...
So Dark Rainbow is dead, she takes FIVE damage...
What, I thought Dewdrop Star only does four!
Nuh uh, 'cause don't forget I cast Moonlight Power on her!
Crystalline Cries
Bleak Pond

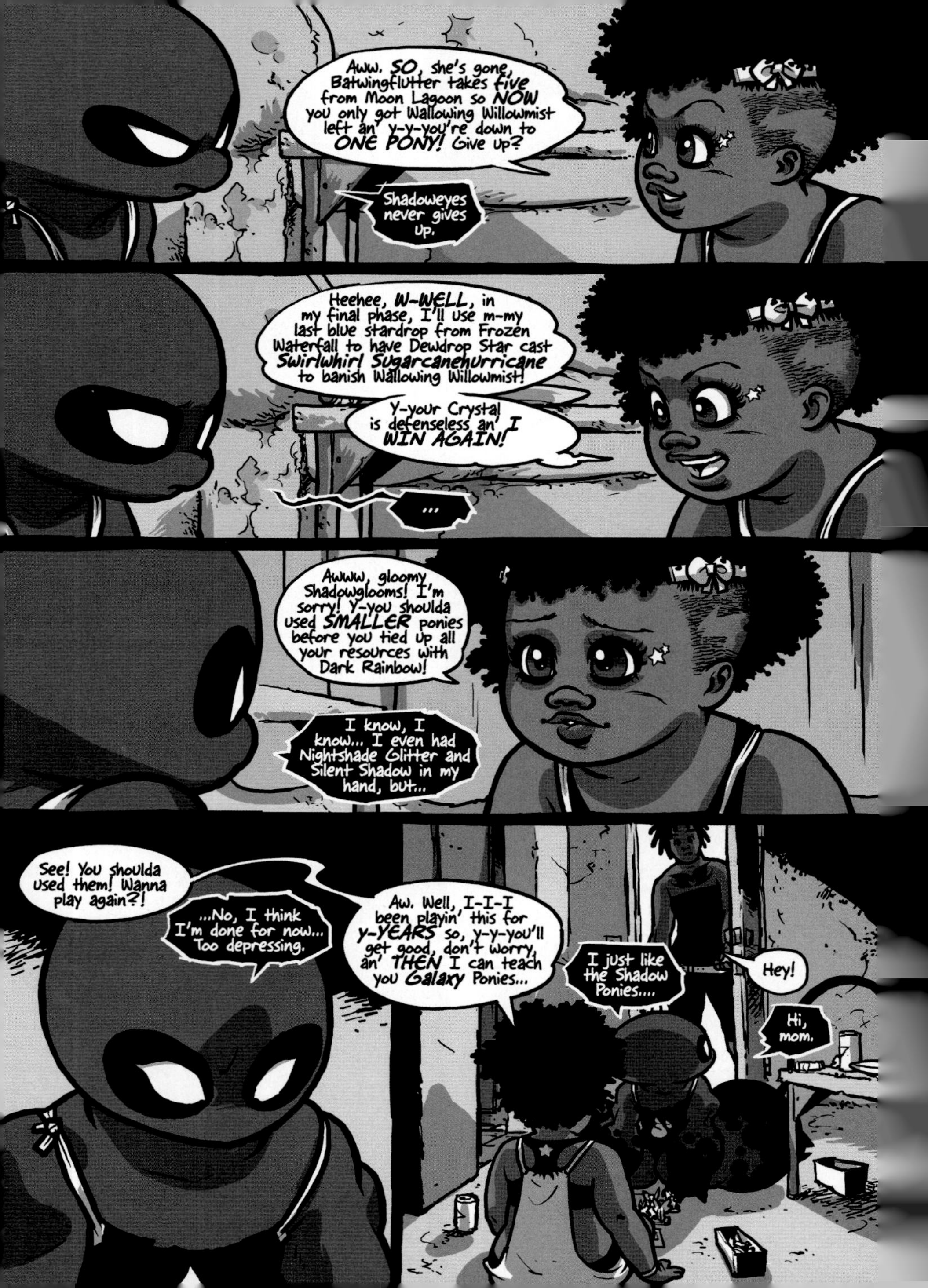

Aww. SO, she's gone, Batwingflutter takes five from Moon Lagoon so NOW you only got Wallowing Willowmist left an' y-y-you're down to ONE PONY! Give up?
Shadoweyes never gives up.
Heehee, W-WELL, in my final phase, I'll use m-my last blue stardrop from Frozen Waterfall to have Dewdrop Star cast Swirlwhirl Sugarcanehurricane to banish Wallowing Willowmist!
Y-your Crystal is defenseless an' I WIN AGAIN!
...
Awww, gloomy Shadowglooms! I'm sorry! Y-you shoulda used SMALLER ponies before you tied up all your resources with Dark Rainbow!
I know, I know... I even had Nightshade Glitter and Silent Shadow in my hand, but...
See! You shoulda used them! Wanna play again?!
...No, I think I'm done for now... Too depressing.
Aw. Well, I-I-I been playin' this for y-YEARS so, y-y-you'll get good, don't worry, an' THEN I can teach you Galaxy Ponies...
I just like the Shadow Ponies....
Hey!
Hi, mom.

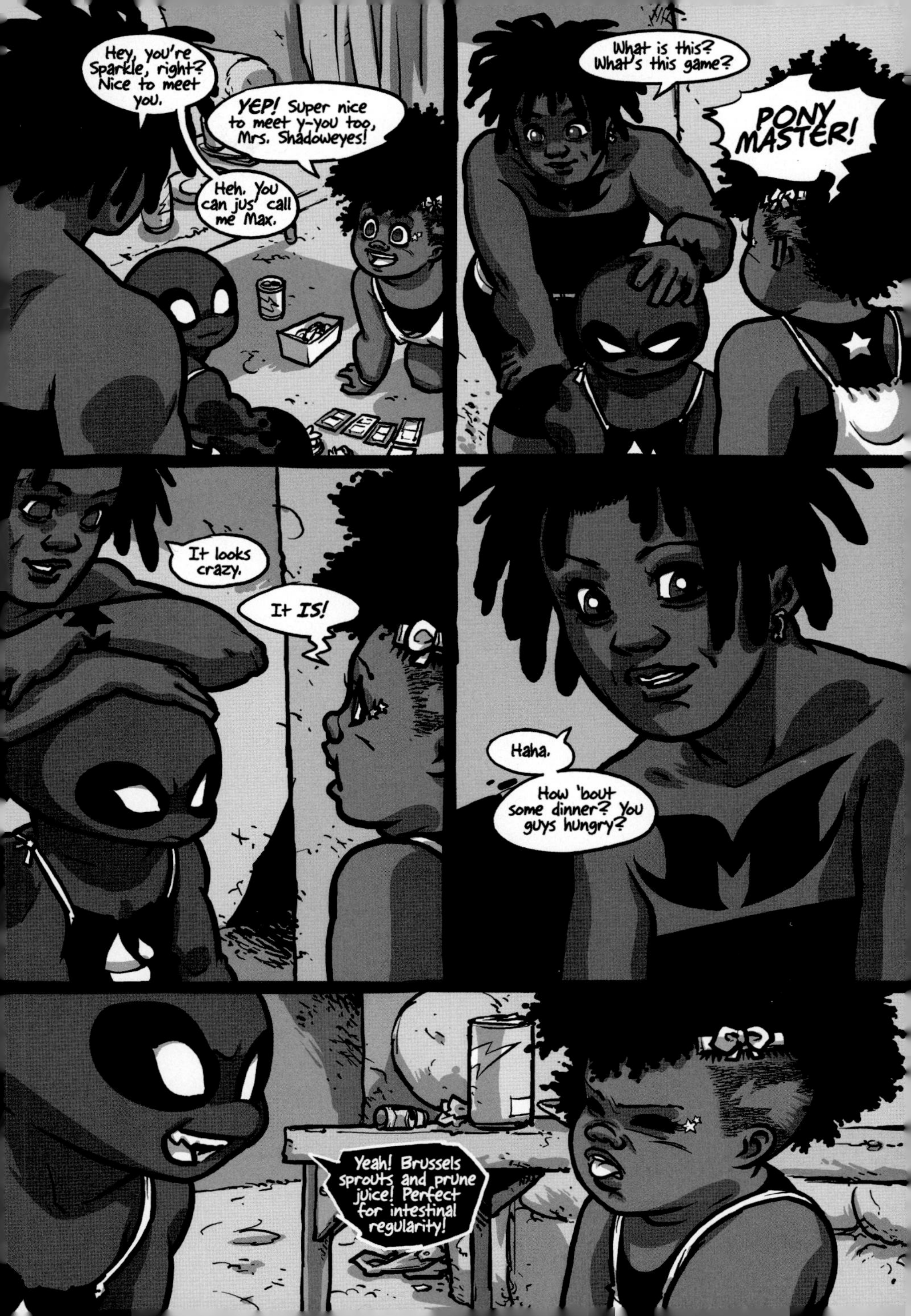

Hey, you're Sparkle, right? Nice to meet you.
YEP! Super nice to meet y-you too, Mrs. Shadoweyes!
Heh. You can jus' call me Max.
What is this? What's this game?
PONY MASTER!
It looks crazy.
It IS!
Haha.
How 'bout some dinner? You guys hungry?
Yeah! Brussels sprouts and prune juice! Perfect for intestinal regularity!

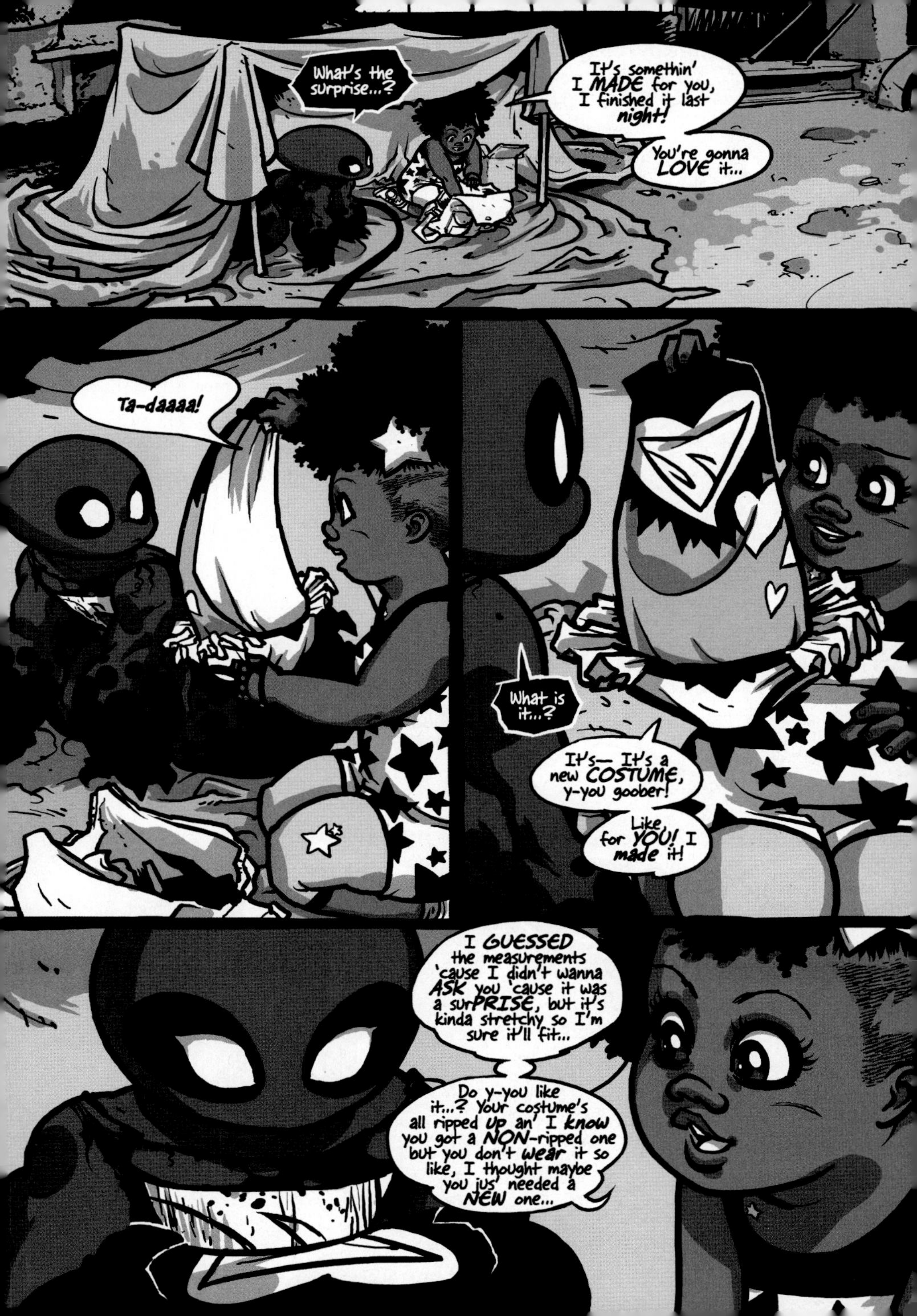
What's the surprise...?
It's somethin' I MADE for you, I finished it last night!
You're gonna LOVE it...
Ta-daaaa!
What is it...?
It's— It's a new COSTUME, y-you goober!
Like, for YOU! I made it!
I GUESSED the measurements 'cause I didn't wanna ASK you 'cause it was a surPRISE, but it's kinda stretchy so I'm sure it'll fit...
Do y-you like it...? Your costume's all ripped UP an' I KNOW you got a NON-ripped one but you don't WEAR it so like, I thought maybe you jus' needed a NEW one...

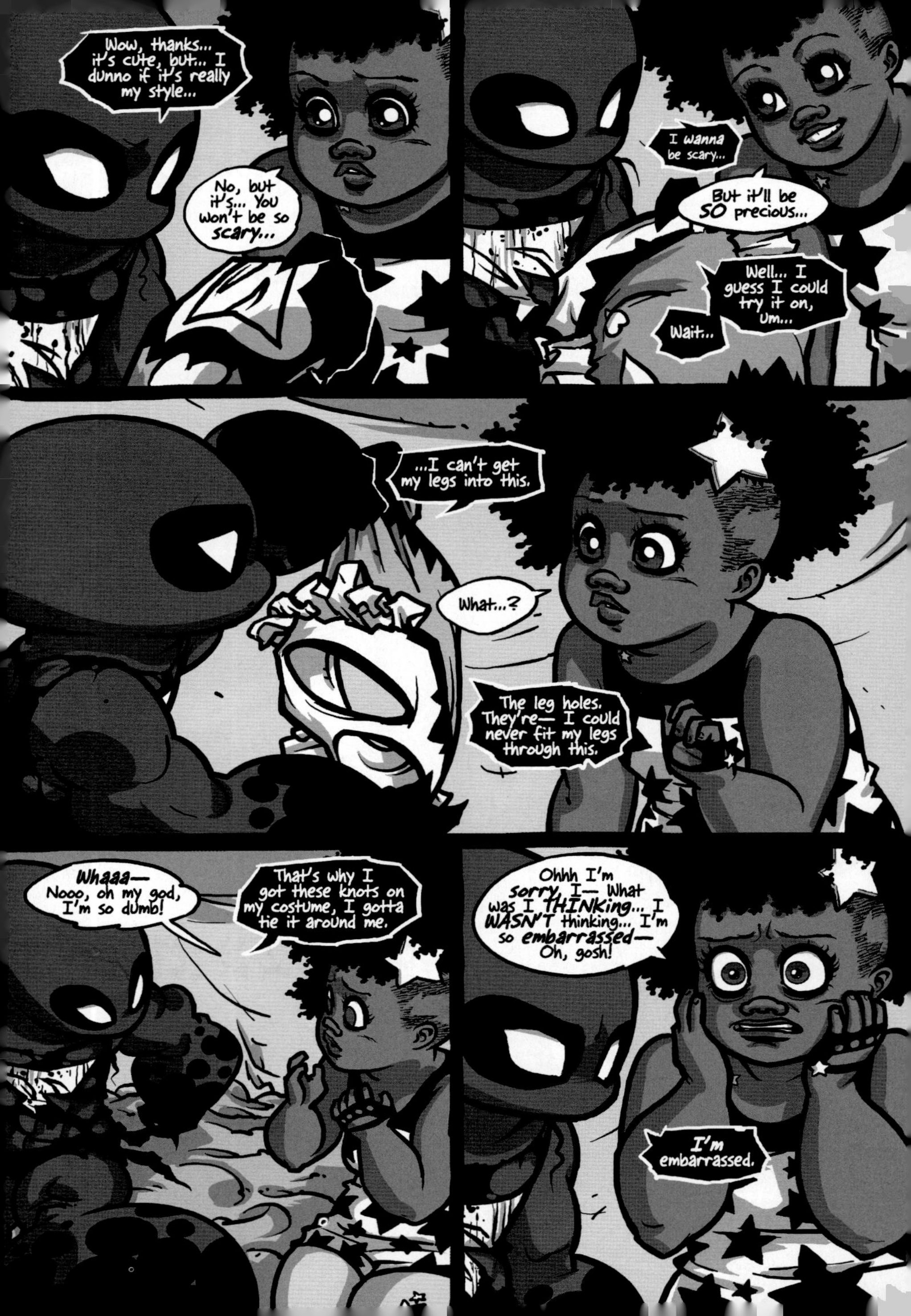
Wow, thanks... it's cute, but... I dunno if it's really my style...
No, but it's... You won't be so scary...
I wanna be scary...
But it'll be SO precious...
Well... I guess I could try it on, um...
Wait...
...I can't get my legs into this.
What...?
The leg holes. They're— I could never fit my legs through this.
Whaaa— Nooo, oh my god, I'm so dumb!
That's why I got these knots on my costume, I gotta tie it around me.
Ohhh I'm sorry, I— What was I THINKING... I WASN'T thinking... I'm so embarrassed— Oh, gosh!
I'm embarrassed.

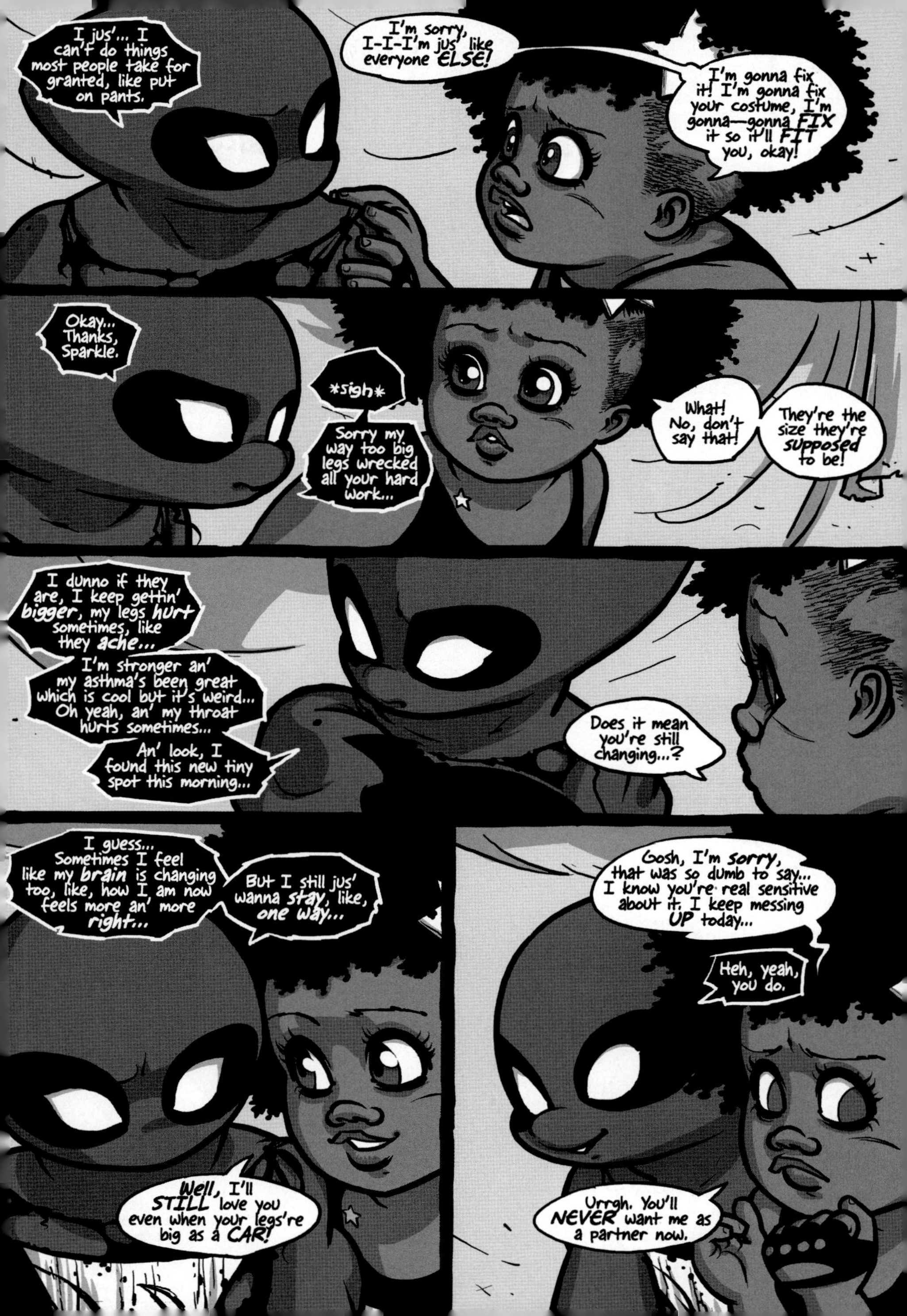

I jus'... I can't do things most people take for granted, like put on pants.
I'm sorry, I-I-I'm jus' like everyone ELSE!
I'm gonna fix it! I'm gonna fix your costume, I'm gonna—gonna FIX it so it'll FIT you, okay!
Okay... Thanks, Sparkle.
sigh
Sorry my way too big legs wrecked all your hard work...
What! No, don't say that!
They're the size they're supposed to be!
I dunno if they are, I keep gettin' bigger, my legs hurt sometimes, like they ache...
I'm stronger an' my asthma's been great which is cool but it's weird... Oh yeah, an' my throat hurts sometimes...
An' look, I found this new tiny spot this morning...
Does it mean you're still changing...?
I guess... Sometimes I feel like my brain is changing too, like, how I am now feels more an' more right...
But I still jus' wanna stay, like, one way...
Well, I'll STILL love you even when your legs're big as a CAR!
Gosh, I'm sorry, that was so dumb to say... I know you're real sensitive about it. I keep messing UP today...
Heh, yeah, you do.
Urrgh. You'll NEVER want me as a partner now.

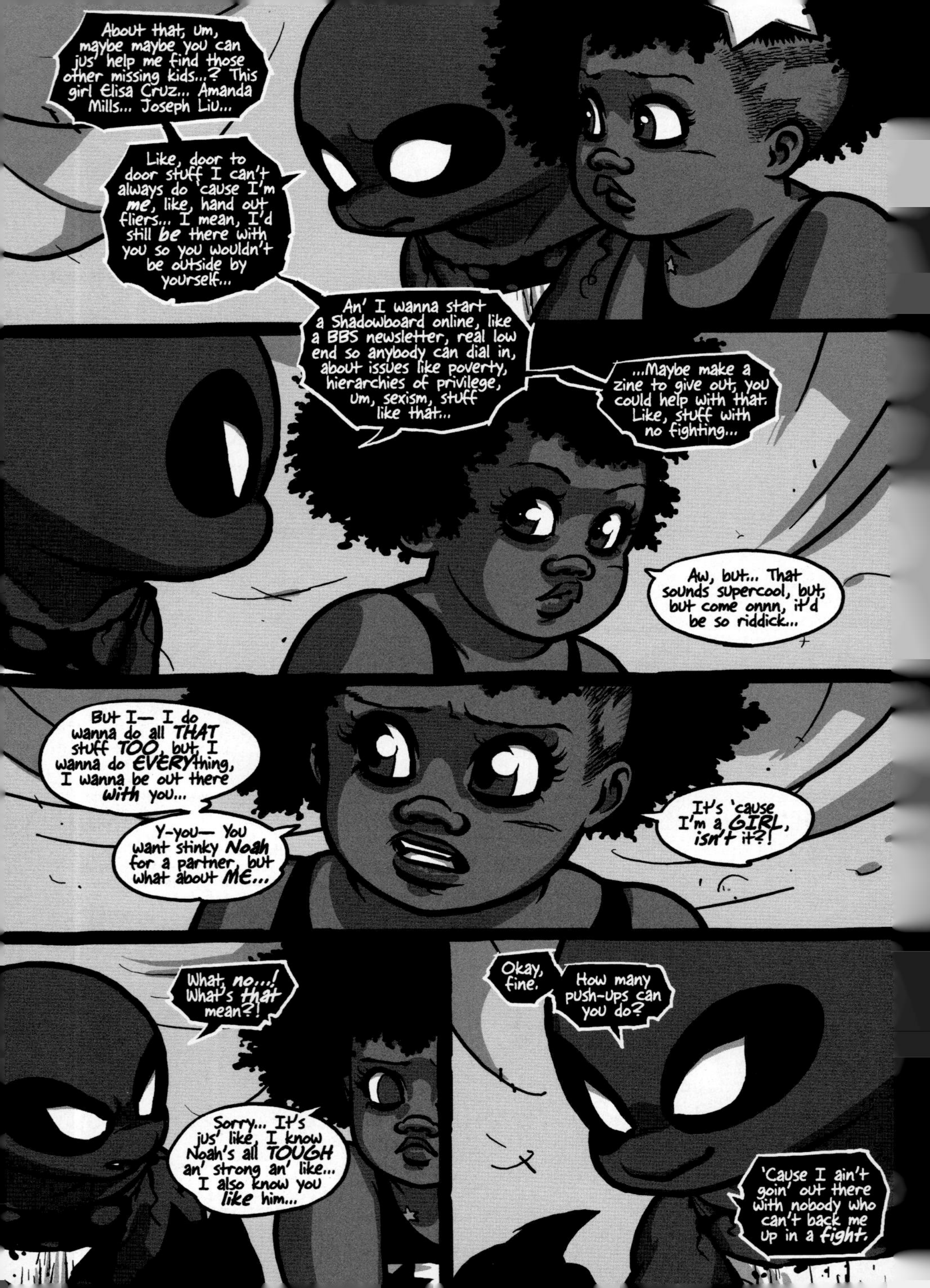
About that, um, maybe maybe you can jus' help me find those other missing kids...? This girl Elisa Cruz... Amanda Mills... Joseph Liu...
Like, door to door stuff I can't always do 'cause I'm me, like, hand out fliers... I mean, I'd still be there with you so you wouldn't be outside by yourself...
An' I wanna start a Shadowboard online, like a BBS newsletter, real low end so anybody can dial in, about issues like poverty, hierarchies of privilege, um, sexism, stuff like that...
...Maybe make a zine to give out, you could help with that. Like, stuff with no fighting...
Aw, but... That sounds supercool, but, but come onnn, it'd be so riddick...
But I— I do wanna do all THAT stuff TOO, but, I wanna do EVERYthing, I wanna be out there with you...
Y-you— You want stinky Noah for a partner, but what about ME...
It's 'cause I'm a GIRL, isn't it?!
What, no...! What's that mean?!
Sorry... It's jus' like, I know Noah's all TOUGH an' strong an' like... I also know you like him...
Okay, fine.
How many push-ups can you do?
'Cause I ain't goin' out there with nobody who can't back me up in a fight.

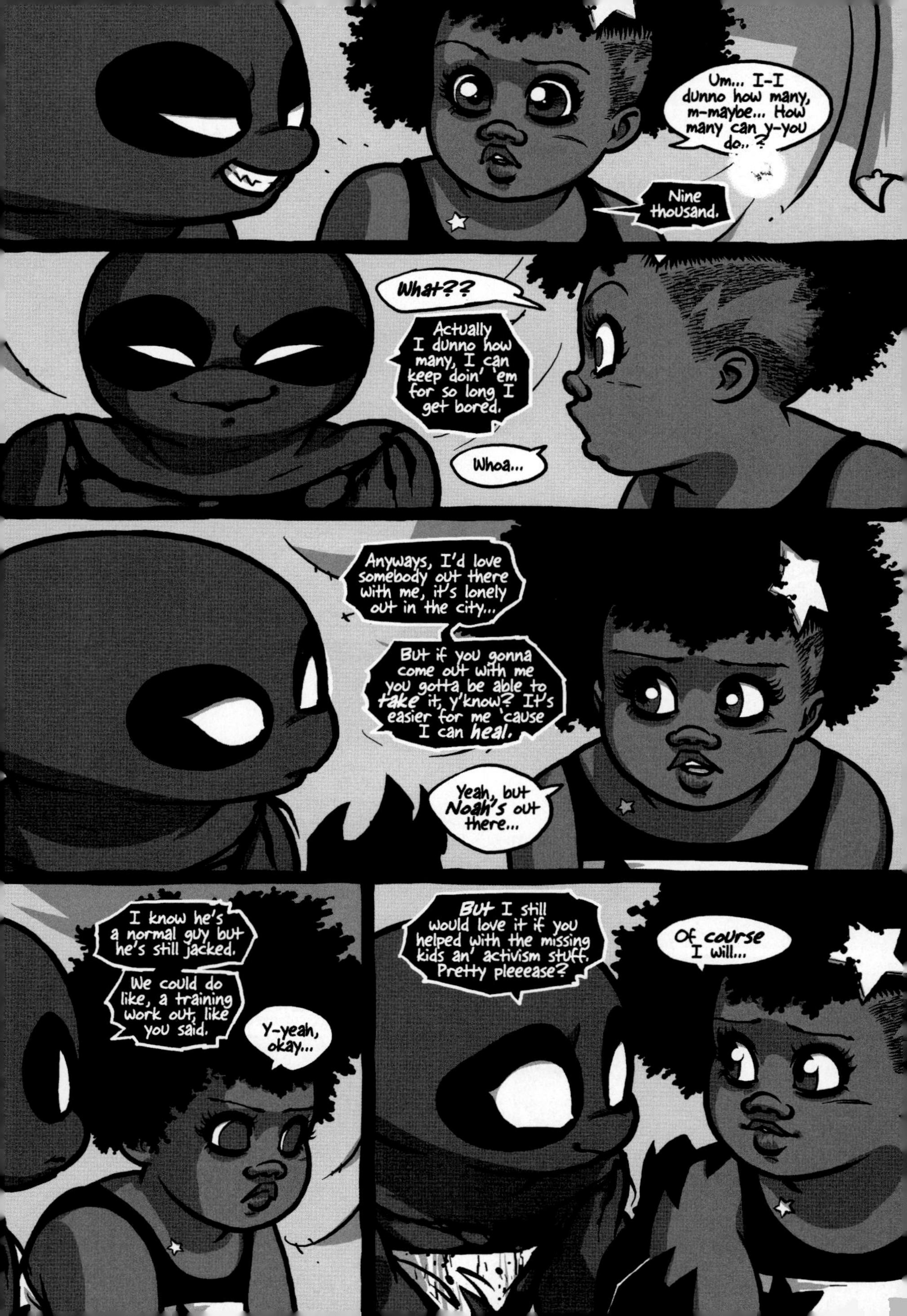
Um... I-I dunno how many, m-maybe... How many can y-you do..?
Nine thousand.
What??
Actually I dunno how many, I can keep doin' 'em for so long I get bored.
Whoa...
Anyways, I'd love somebody out there with me, it's lonely out in the city...
But if you gonna come out with me you gotta be able to take it, y'know? It's easier for me 'cause I can heal.
Yeah, but Noah's out there...
I know he's a normal guy but he's still jacked.
We could do like, a training work out, like you said.
Y-yeah, okay...
But I still would love it if you helped with the missing kids an' activism stuff. Pretty pleeease?
Of course I will...

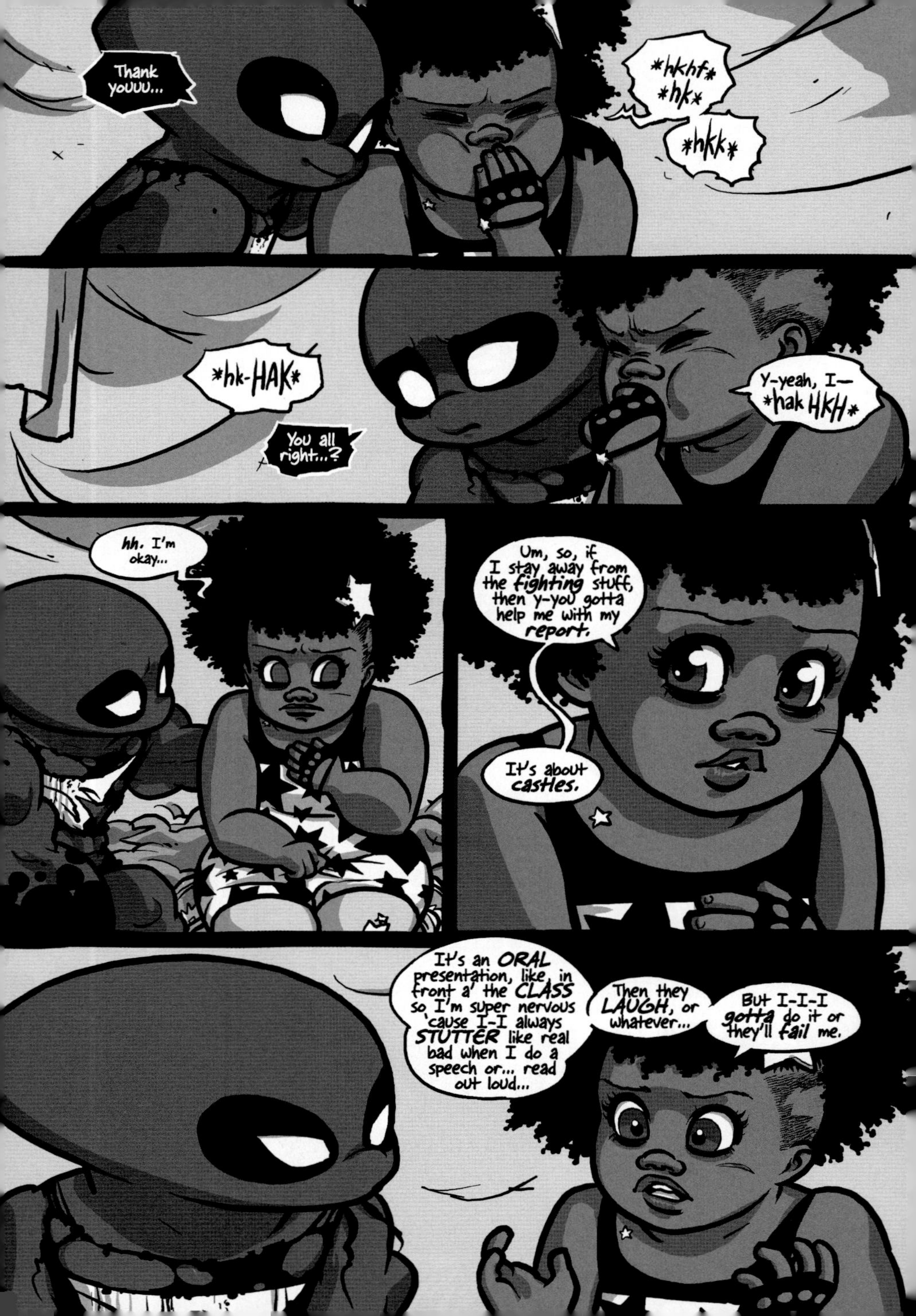
Thank youuu...
hkhf *hk*
hkk
hk-HAK
You all right...?
Y-yeah, I— *hak HKH*
hh. I'm okay...
Um, so, if I stay away from the fighting stuff, then y-you gotta help me with my report.
It's about castles.
It's an ORAL presentation, like, in front a' the CLASS so I'm super nervous 'cause I-I always STUTTER like real bad when I do a speech or... read out loud...
Then they LAUGH, or whatever...
But I-I-I gotta do it or they'll fail me.

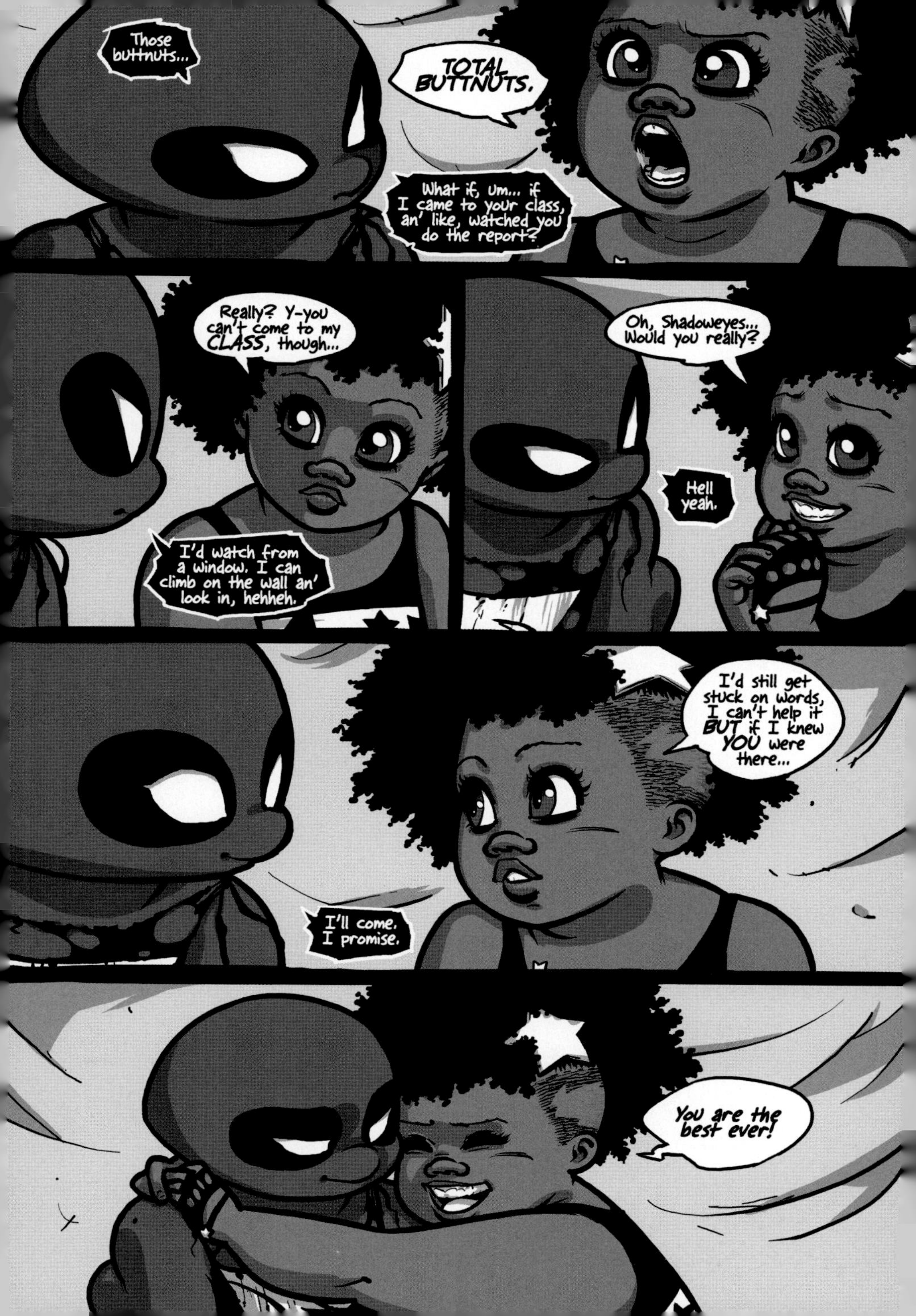

Those buttnuts...
TOTAL BUTTNUTS.
What if, um... if I came to your class, an' like, watched you do the report?
Really? Y-you can't come to my CLASS, though...
I'd watch from a window. I can climb on the wall an' look in, hehheh.
Oh, Shadoweyes... Would you really?
Hell yeah.
I'd still get stuck on words, I can't help it BUT if I knew YOU were there...
I'll come. I promise.
You are the best ever!

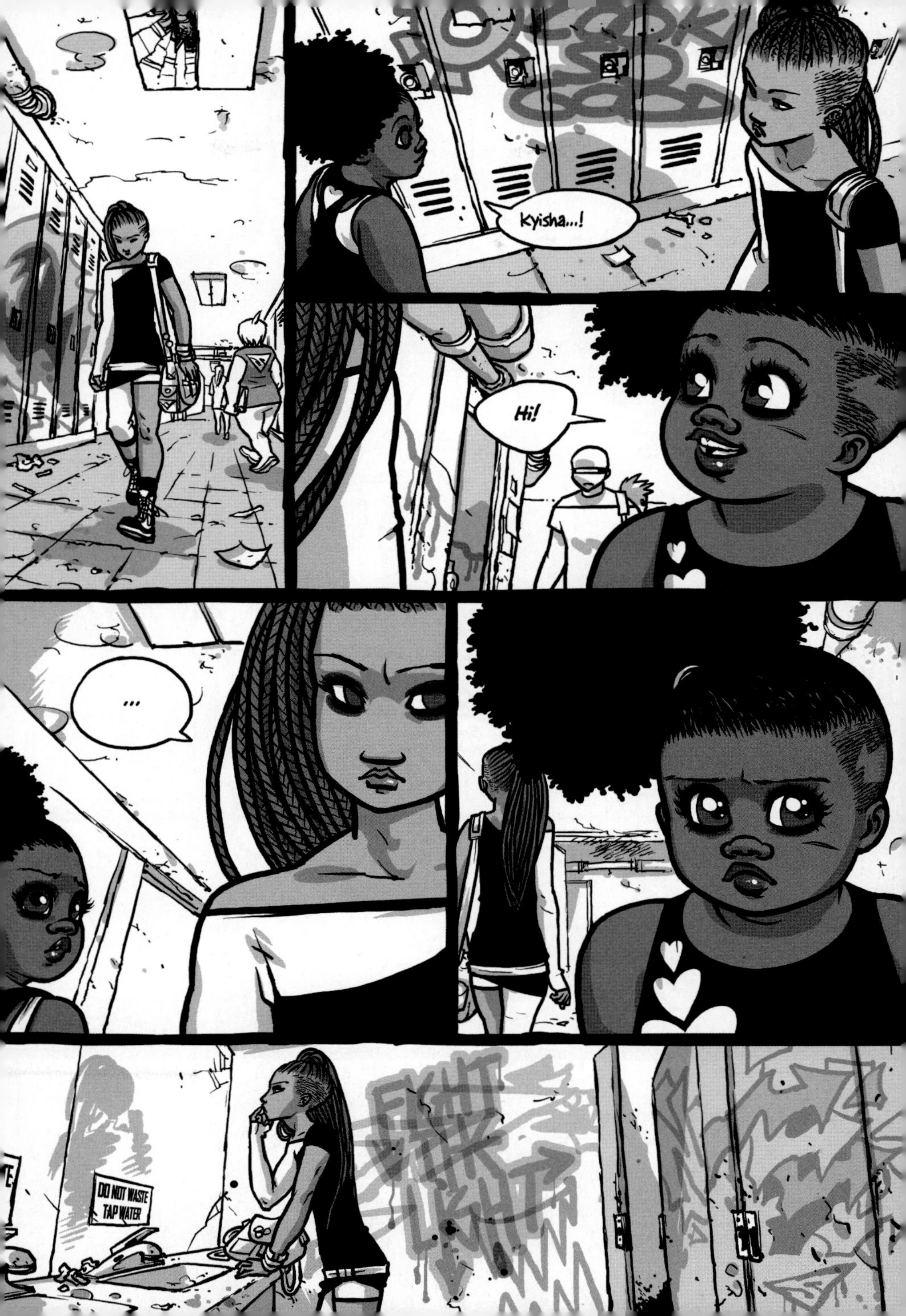
Kyisha...!
Hi!
...
DO NOT WASTE
TAP WATER

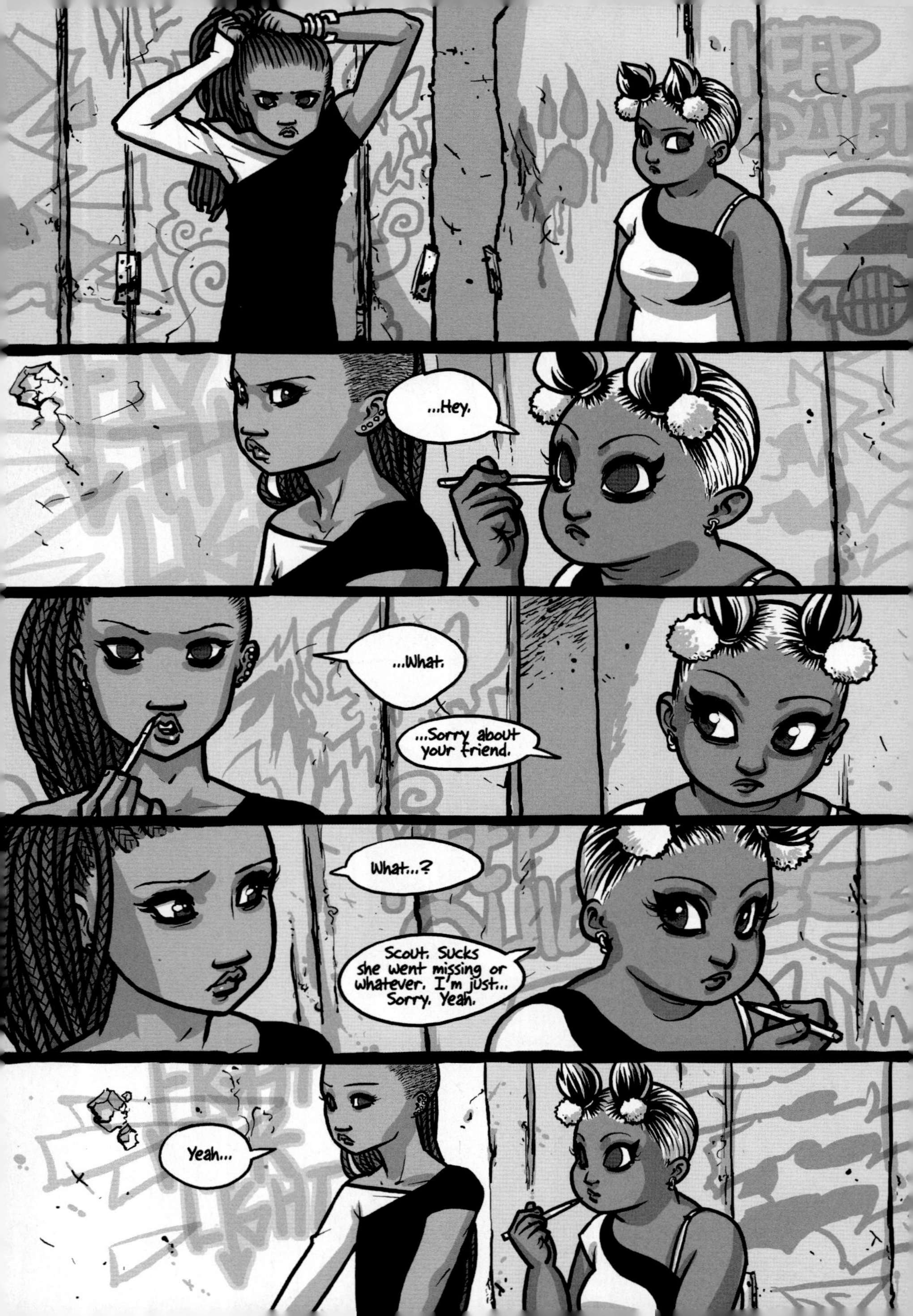
...Hey.
...What.
...Sorry about your friend.
What...?
Scout. Sucks she went missing or whatever. I'm just... Sorry. Yeah.
Yeah...

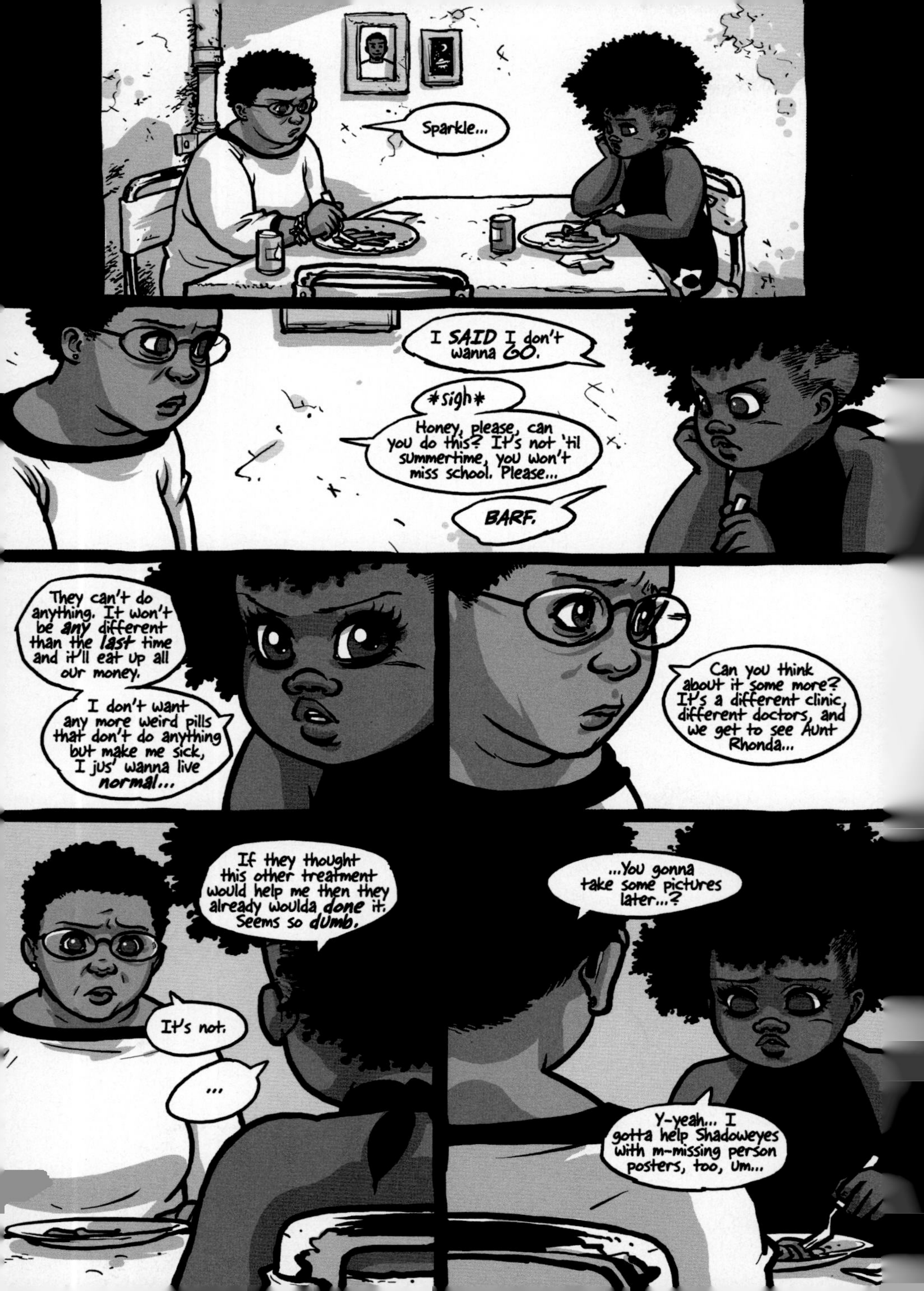
Sparkle...
I SAID I don't wanna GO.
sigh
Honey, please, can you do this? It's not 'til summertime, you won't miss school. Please...
BARF.
They can't do anything. It won't be any different than the last time and it'll eat up all our money.
I don't want any more weird pills that don't do anything but make me sick, I jus' wanna live normal...
Can you think about it some more? It's a different clinic, different doctors, and we get to see Aunt Rhonda...
If they thought this other treatment would help me then they already woulda done it. Seems so dumb.
It's not.
...
...You gonna take some pictures later...?
Y-yeah... I gotta help Shadoweyes with m-missing person posters, too, um...

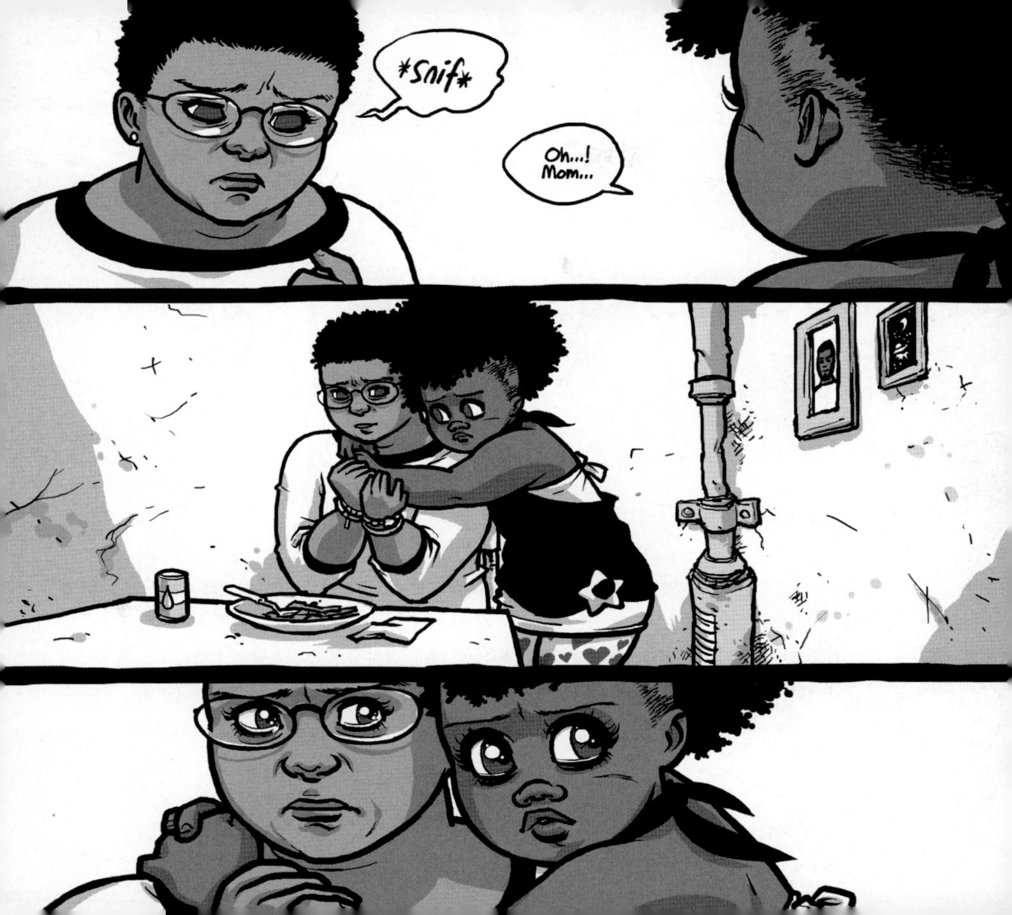
Snif
Oh...! Mom...

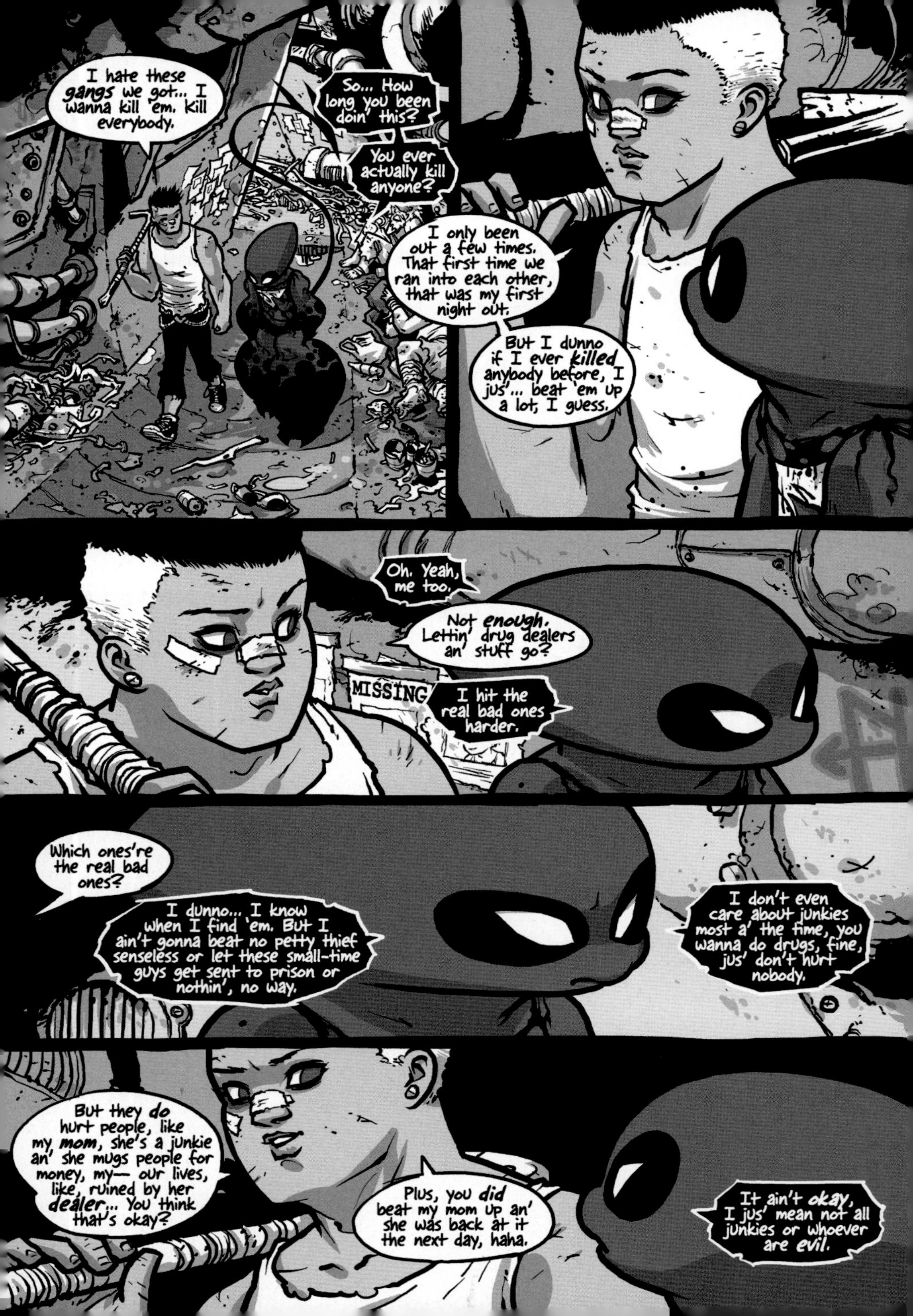
I hate these gangs we got... I wanna kill 'em. Kill everybody.
So... How long you been doin' this?
You ever actually kill anyone?
I only been out a few times. That first time we ran into each other, that was my first night out.
But I dunno if I ever killed anybody before, I jus'... beat 'em up a lot, I guess.
Oh. Yeah, me too.
Not enough. Lettin' drug dealers an' stuff go?
MISSING
I hit the real bad ones harder.
Which ones're the real bad ones?
I dunno... I know when I find 'em. But I ain't gonna beat no petty thief senseless or let these small-time guys get sent to prison or nothin', no way.
I don't even care about junkies most a' the time, you wanna do drugs, fine, jus' don't hurt nobody.
But they do hurt people, like my mom, she's a junkie an' she mugs people for money, my— our lives, like, ruined by her dealer... You think that's okay?
Plus, you did beat my mom up an' she was back at it the next day, haha.
It ain't okay, I jus' mean not all junkies or whoever are evil.

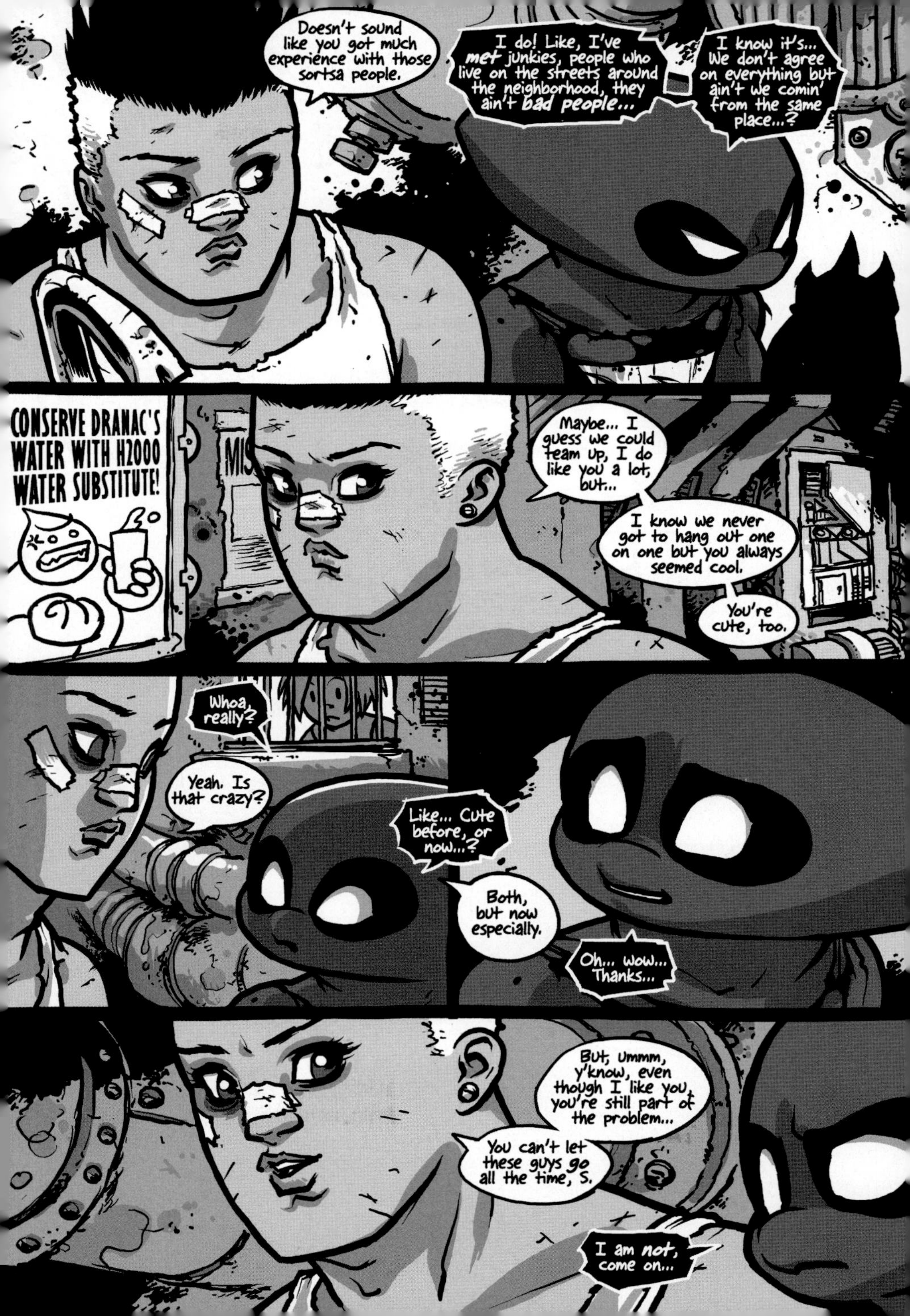

Doesn't sound like you got much experience with those sortsa people.
I do! Like, I've met junkies, people who live on the streets around the neighborhood, they ain't bad people...
I know it's... We don't agree on everything but ain't we comin' from the same place...?
CONSERVE DRANAC'S WATER WITH H2000 WATER SUBSTITUTE!
Maybe... I guess we could team up, I do like you a lot, but...
I know we never got to hang out one on one but you always seemed cool.
You're cute, too.
Whoa, really?
Yeah. Is that crazy?
Like... Cute before, or now...?
Both, but now especially.
Oh... wow... Thanks...
But, ummm, y'know, even though I like you, you're still part of the problem...
You can't let these guys go all the time, S.
I am not, come on...

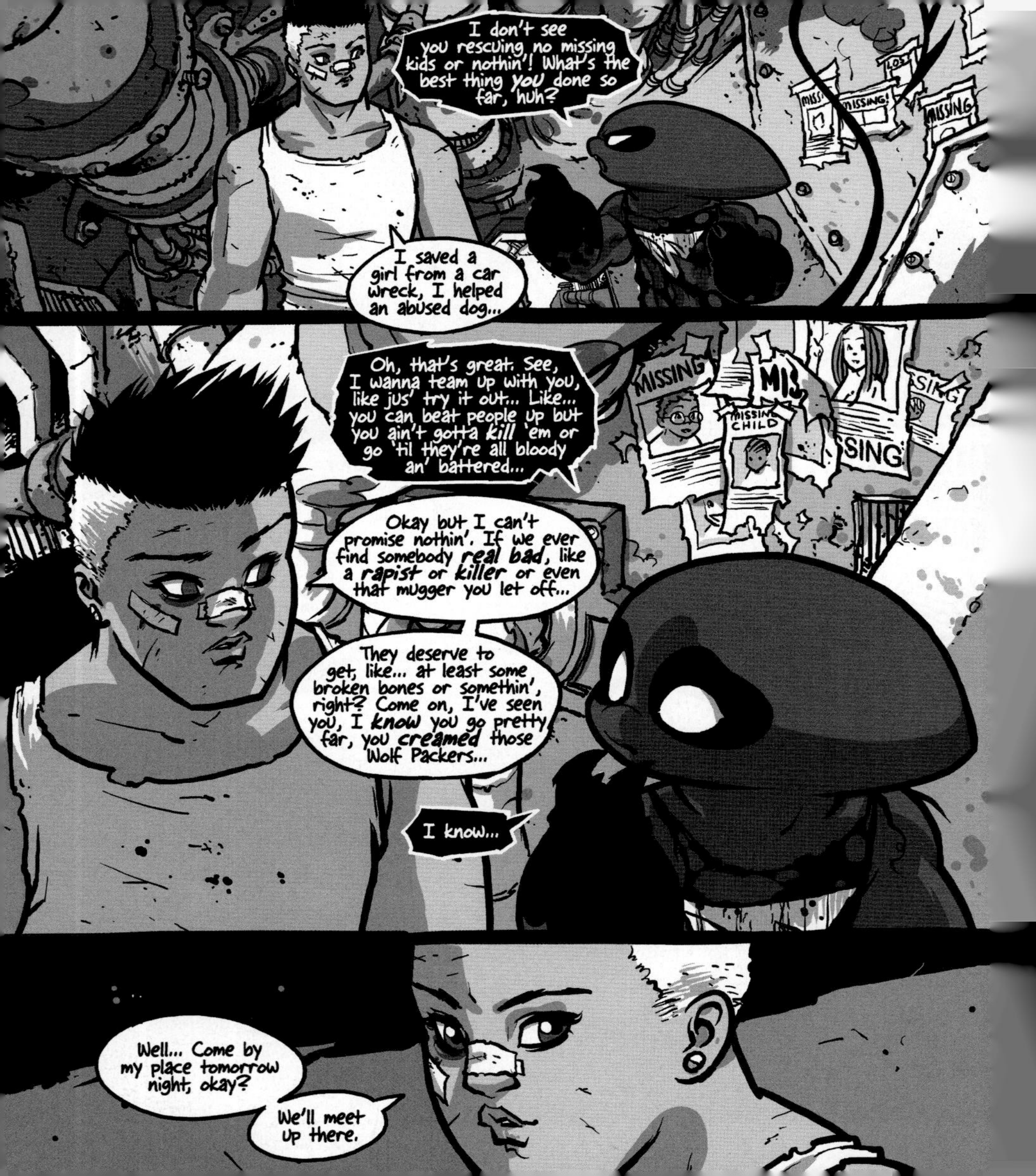
I don't see you rescuing no missing kids or nothin'! What's the best thing you done so far, huh?
MISSING
MISSING!
MISSING
I saved a girl from a car wreck, I helped an abused dog...
Oh, that's great. See, I wanna team up with you, like jus' try it out... Like... you can beat people up but you ain't gotta kill 'em or go 'til they're all bloody an' battered...
MISSING
MISSING CHILD
SSING
Okay but I can't promise nothin'. If we ever find somebody real bad, like a rapist or killer or even that mugger you let off...
They deserve to get, like... at least some broken bones or somethin', right? Come on, I've seen you, I know you go pretty far, you creamed those Wolf Packers...
I know...
Well... Come by my place tomorrow night, okay?
We'll meet up there.

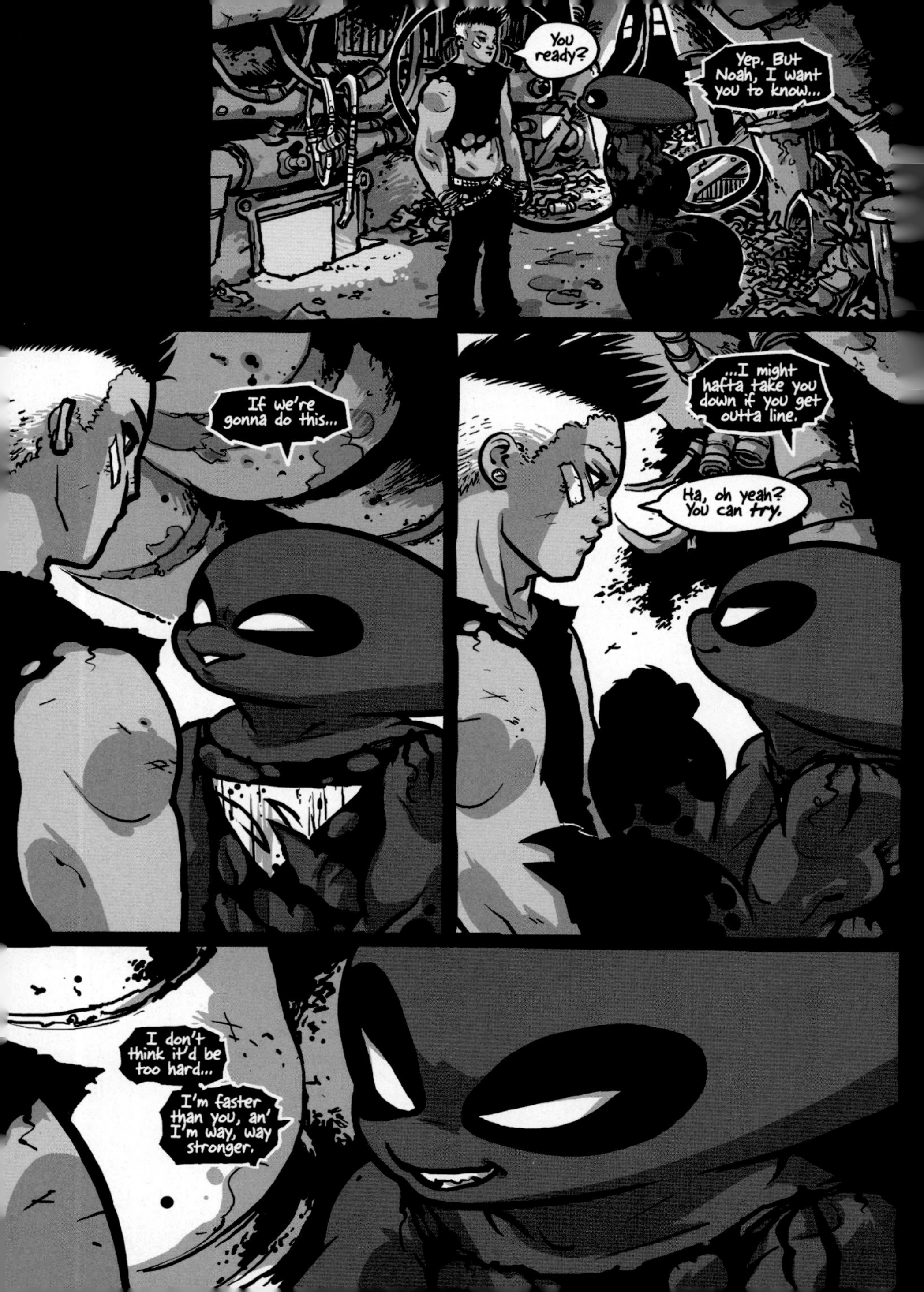

You ready?
Yep. But Noah, I want you to know...
If we're gonna do this...
...I might hafta take you down if you get outta line.
Ha, oh yeah? You can try.
I don't think it'd be too hard...
I'm faster than you, an' I'm way, way stronger.

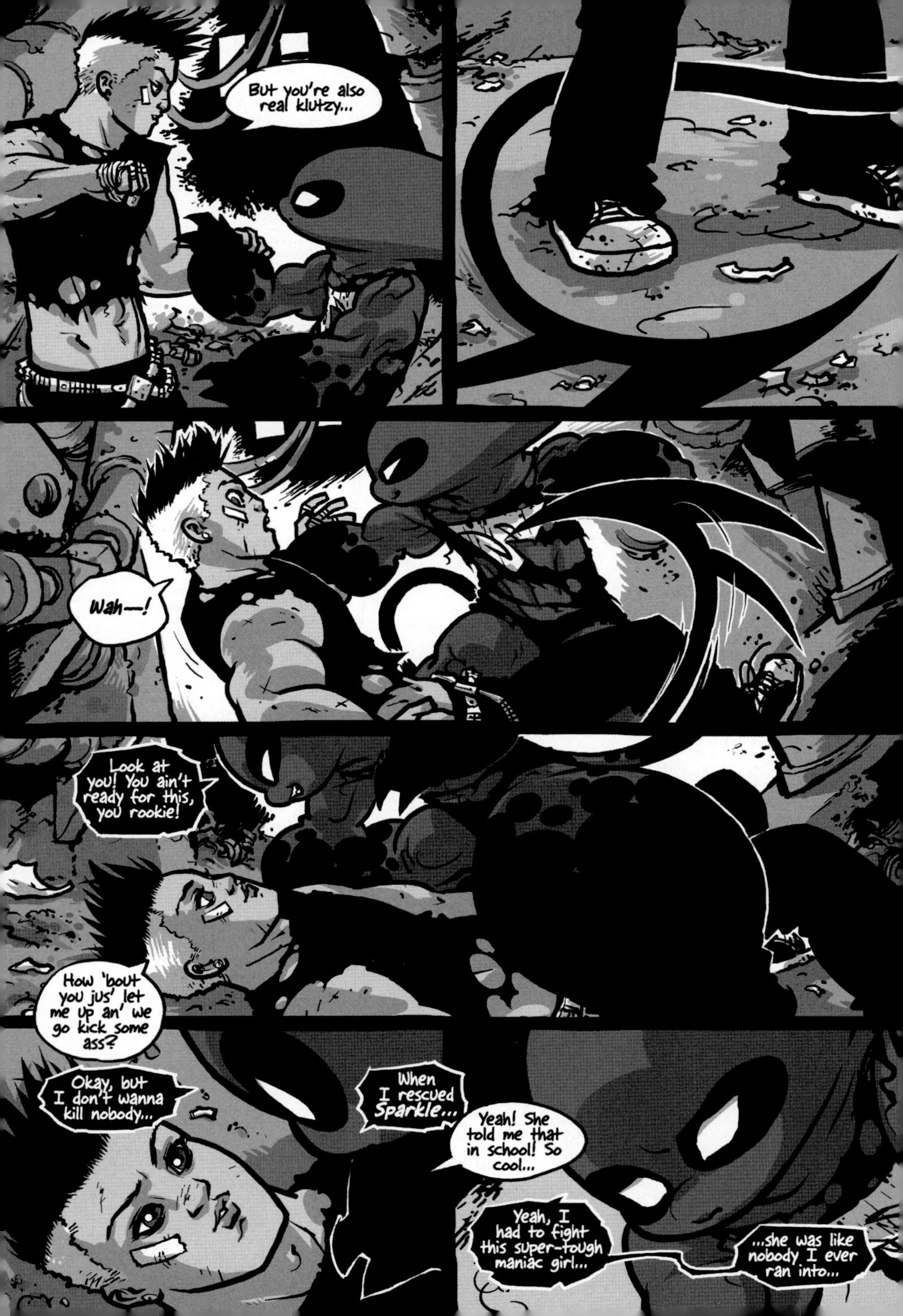
But you're also real klutzy...
Wah—!
Look at you! You ain't ready for this, you rookie!
How 'bout you jus' let me up an' we go kick some ass?
Okay, but I don't wanna kill nobody...
When I rescued Sparkle...
Yeah! She told me that in school! So cool...
Yeah, I had to fight this super-tough maniac girl...
...she was like nobody I ever ran into...

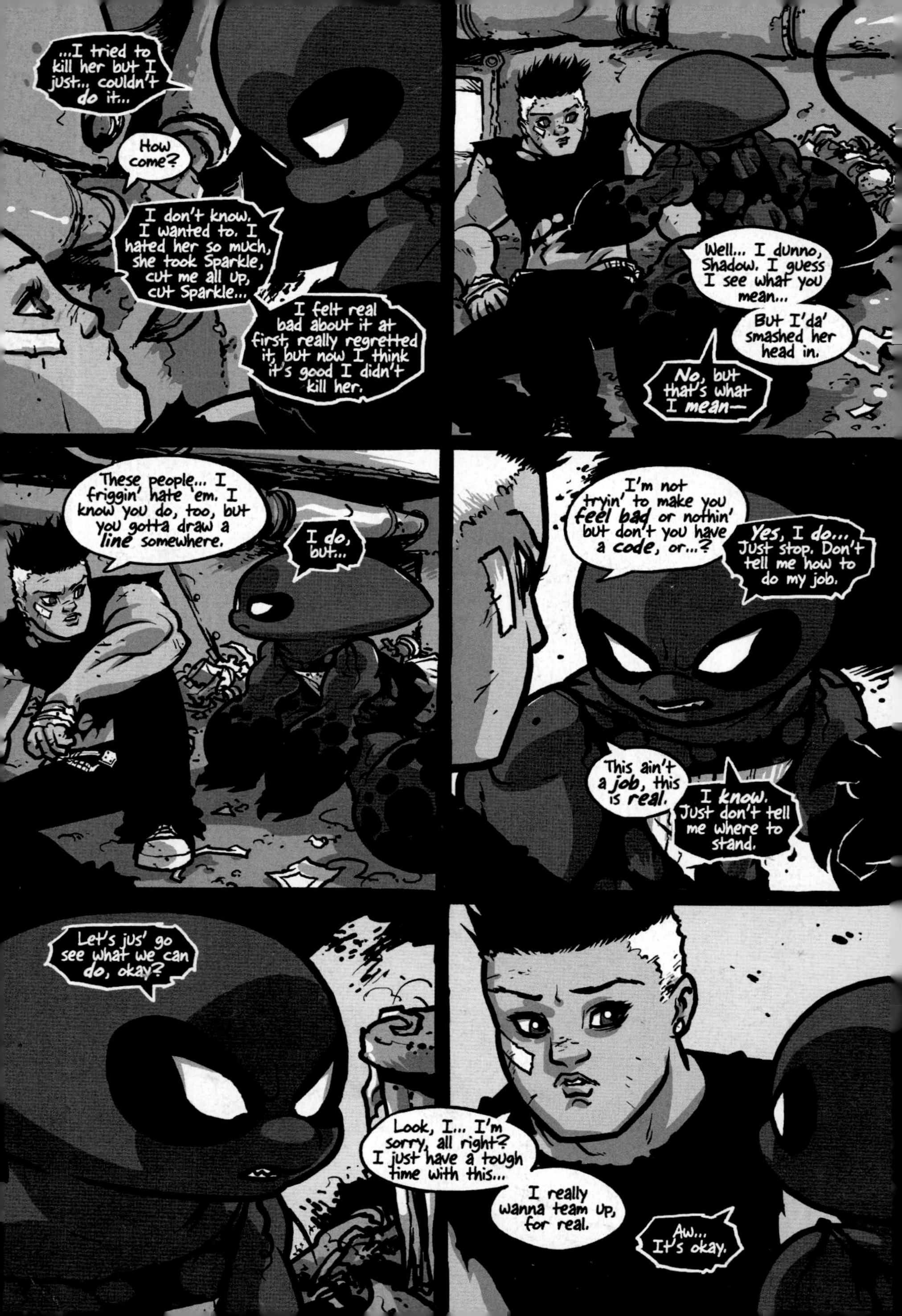
...I tried to kill her but I just... couldn't do it...
How come?
I don't know. I wanted to. I hated her so much, she took Sparkle, cut me all up, cut Sparkle...
I felt real bad about it at first, really regretted it, but now I think it's good I didn't kill her.
Well... I dunno, Shadow. I guess I see what you mean...
But I'da' smashed her head in.
No, but that's what I mean—
These people... I friggin' hate 'em. I know you do, too, but you gotta draw a line somewhere.
I do, but...
I'm not tryin' to make you feel bad or nothin' but don't you have a code, or...?
Yes, I do... Just stop. Don't tell me how to do my job.
This ain't a job, this is real.
I know. Just don't tell me where to stand.
Let's jus' go see what we can do, okay?
Look, I... I'm sorry, all right? I just have a tough time with this...
I really wanna team up, for real.
Aw... It's okay.

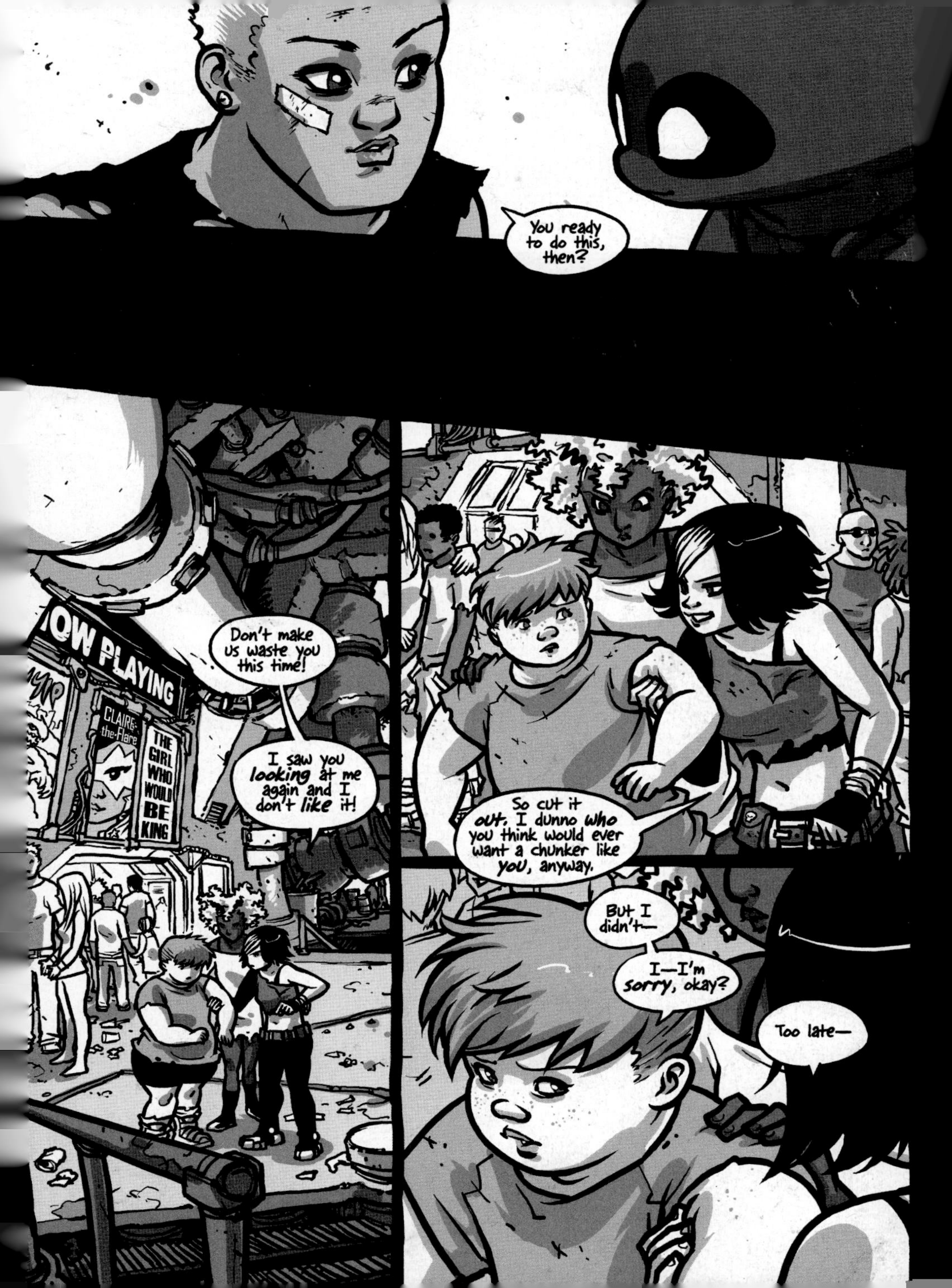
You ready to do this, then?
NOW PLAYING
CLAIRE-the-Flare
THE GIRL WHO WOULD BE KING
Don't make us waste you this time!
I saw you *looking* at me again and I don't *like* it!
So cut it *out*. I dunno *who* you think would ever want a chunker like *you*, anyway.
But I didn't—
I—I'm *sorry*, okay?
Too late—

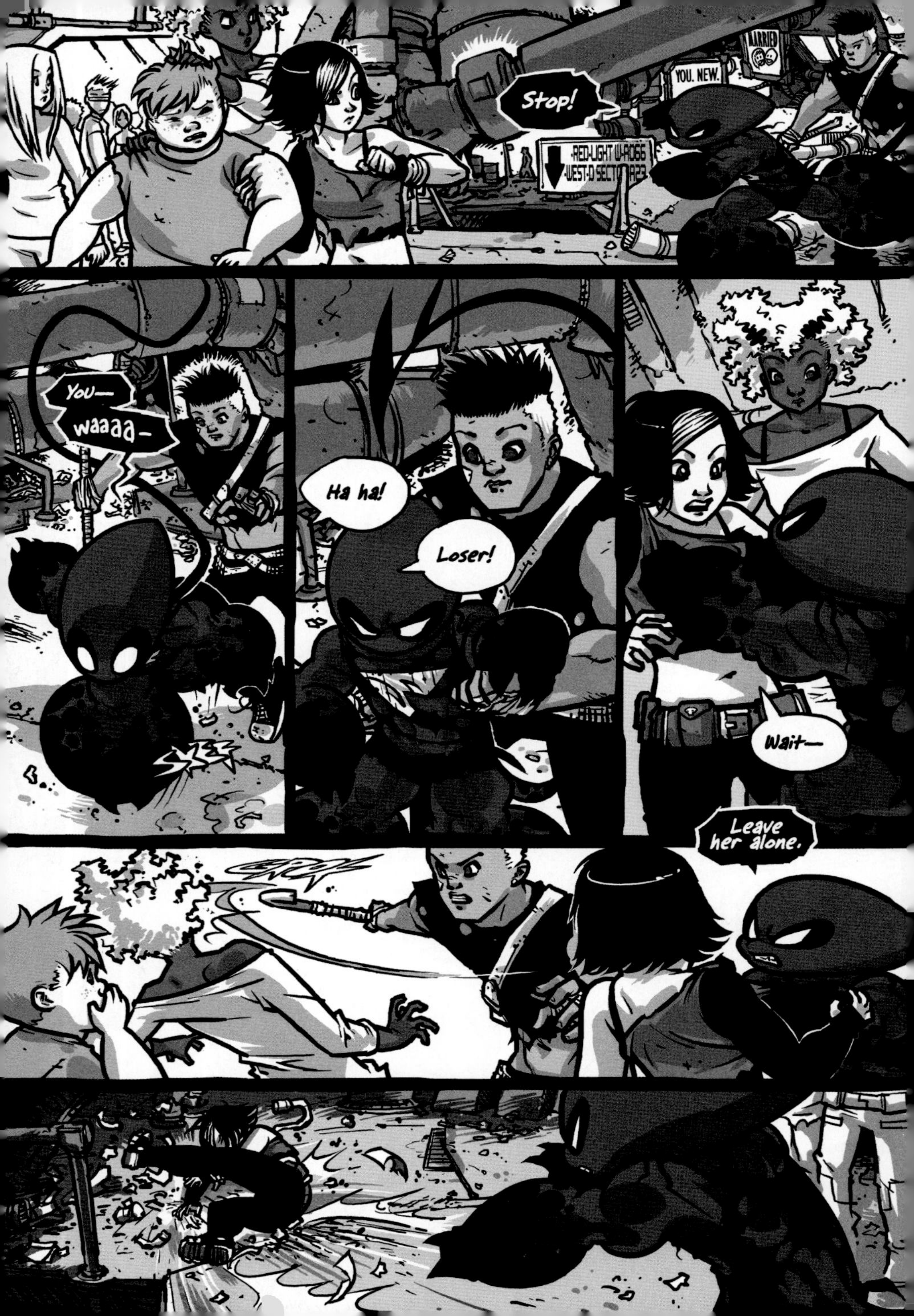
YOU. NEW.
MARRIED
Stop!
-RED-LIGHT W-RO66
-WEST-D SECT
You—
waaaa-
Ha ha!
Loser!
Wait—
Leave her alone.

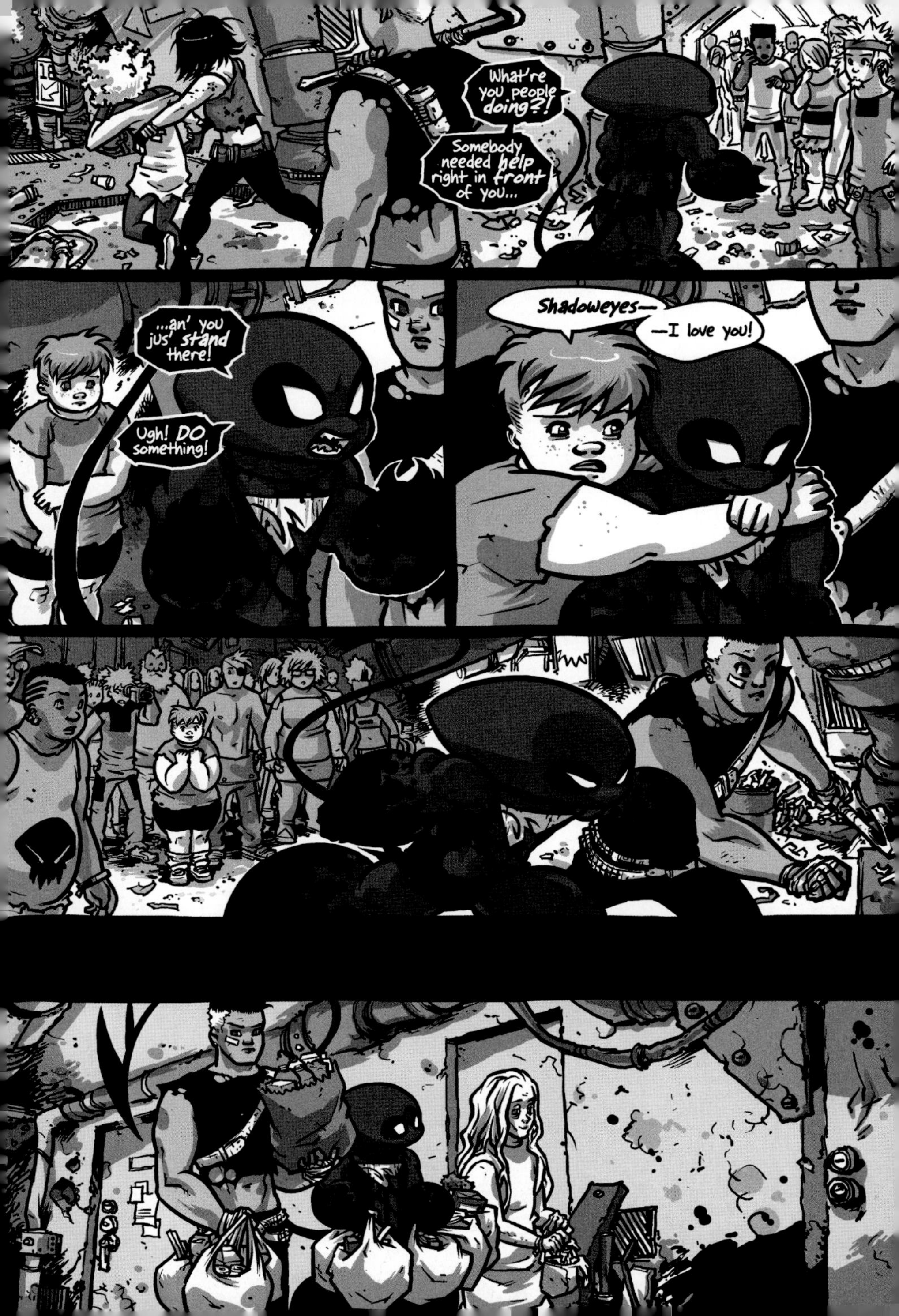
What're you people doing?!
Somebody needed help right in front of you...
...an' you jus' stand there!
Ugh! DO something!
Shadoweyes—
—I love you!

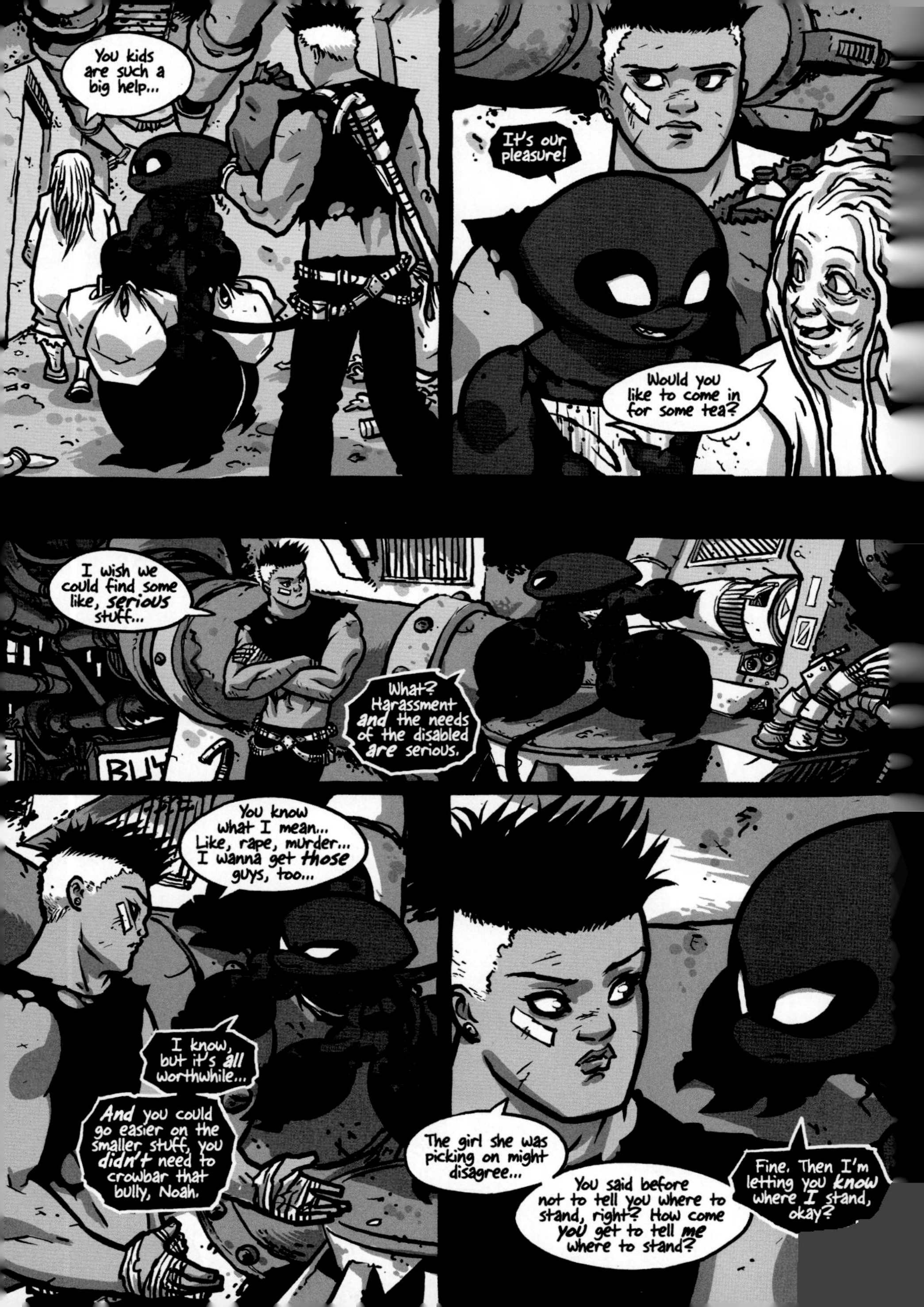

You kids are such a big help...
It's our pleasure!
Would you like to come in for some tea?
I wish we could find some like, serious stuff...
What? Harassment and the needs of the disabled are serious.
BU
You know what I mean... Like, rape, murder... I wanna get those guys, too...
I know, but it's all worthwhile...
And you could go easier on the smaller stuff, you didn't need to crowbar that bully, Noah.
The girl she was picking on might disagree...
You said before not to tell you where to stand, right? How come you get to tell me where to stand?
Fine. Then I'm letting you know where I stand, okay?

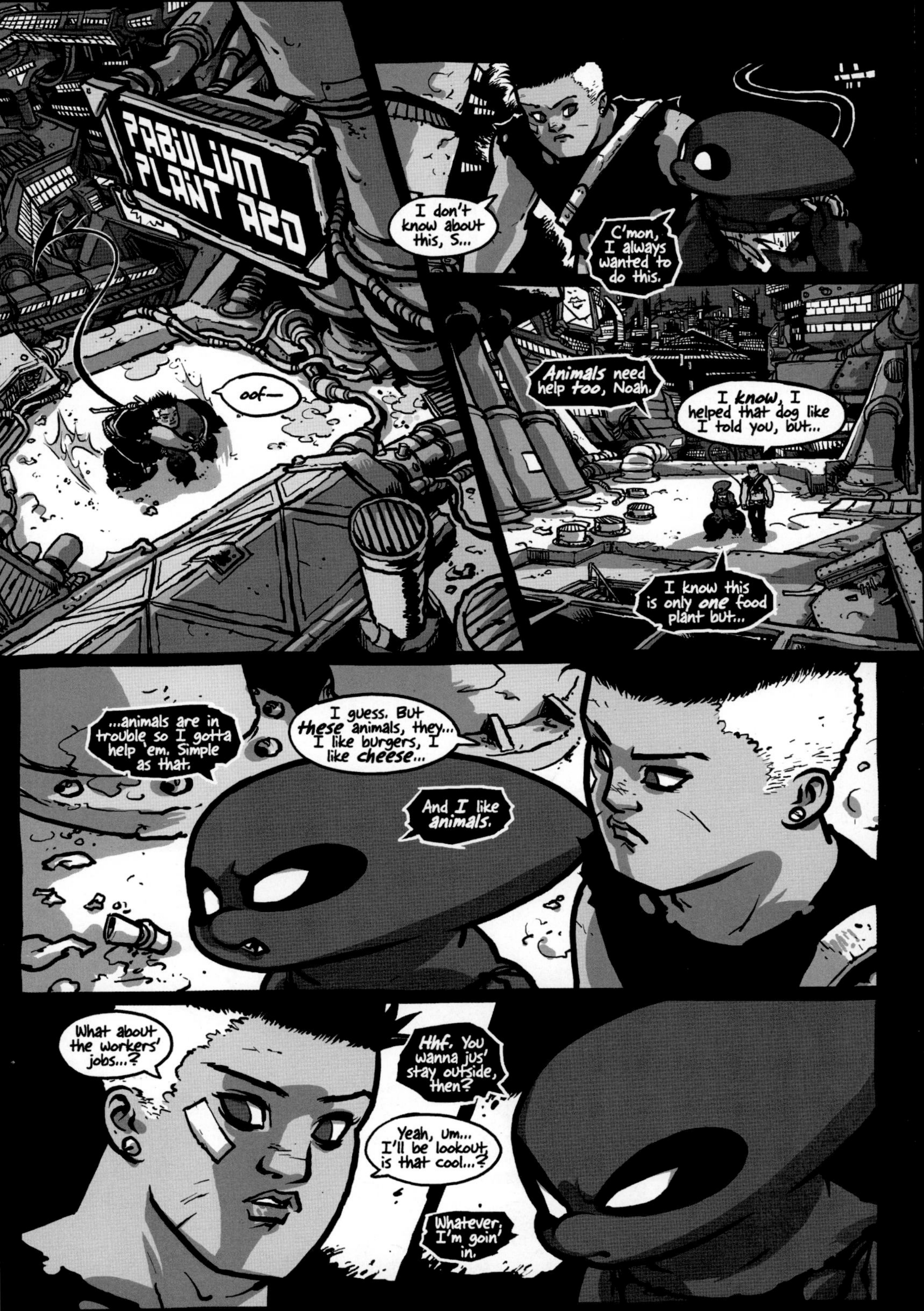
PABULUM PLANT A20
I don't know about this, S...
C'mon, I always wanted to do this.
oof—
Animals need help too, Noah.
I know, I helped that dog like I told you, but...
I know this is only one food plant but...
...animals are in trouble so I gotta help 'em. Simple as that.
I guess. But these animals, they... I like burgers, I like cheese...
And I like animals.
What about the workers' jobs...?
Hhf. You wanna jus' stay outside, then?
Yeah, um... I'll be lookout, is that cool...?
Whatever, I'm goin' in.

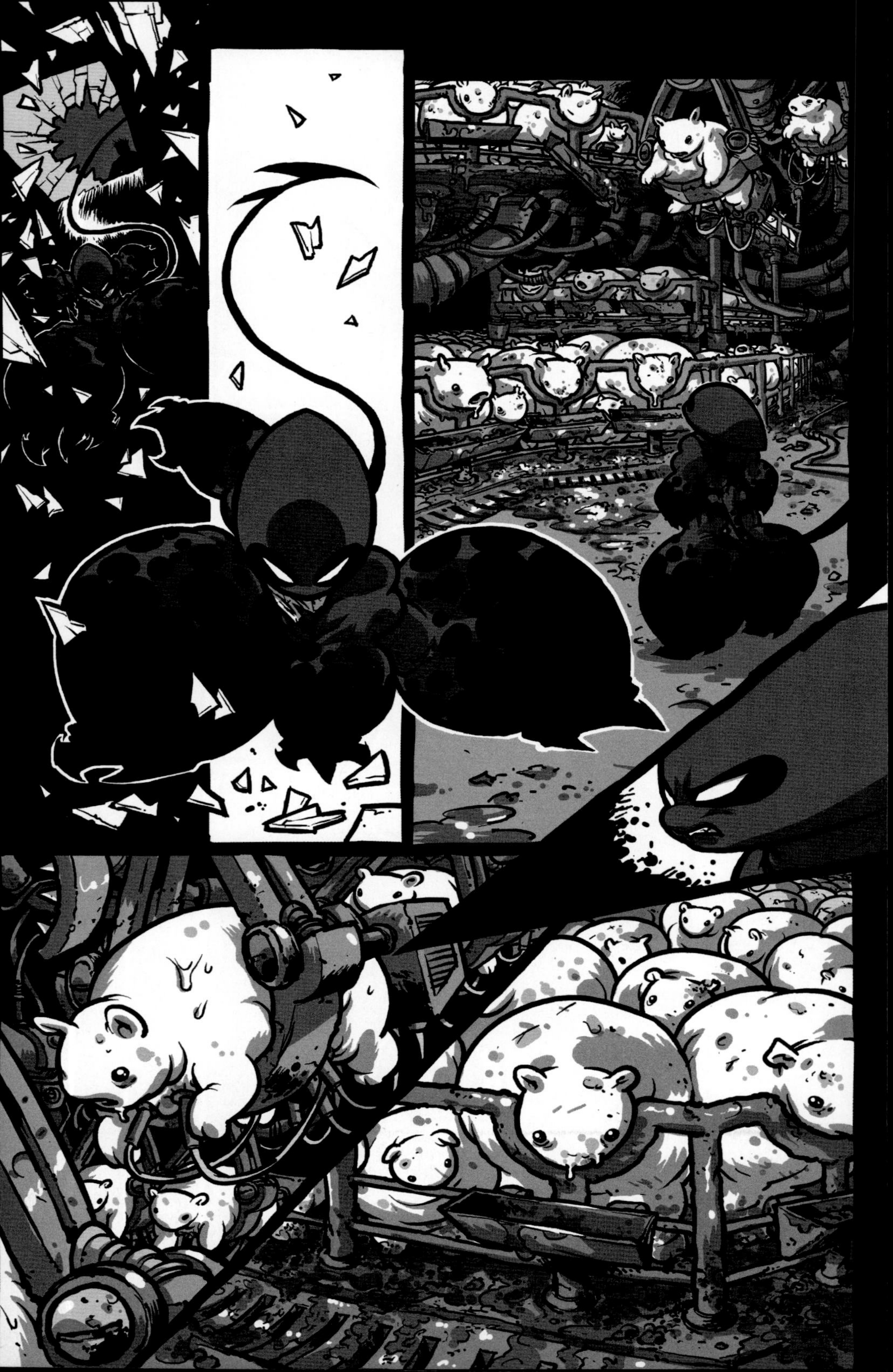

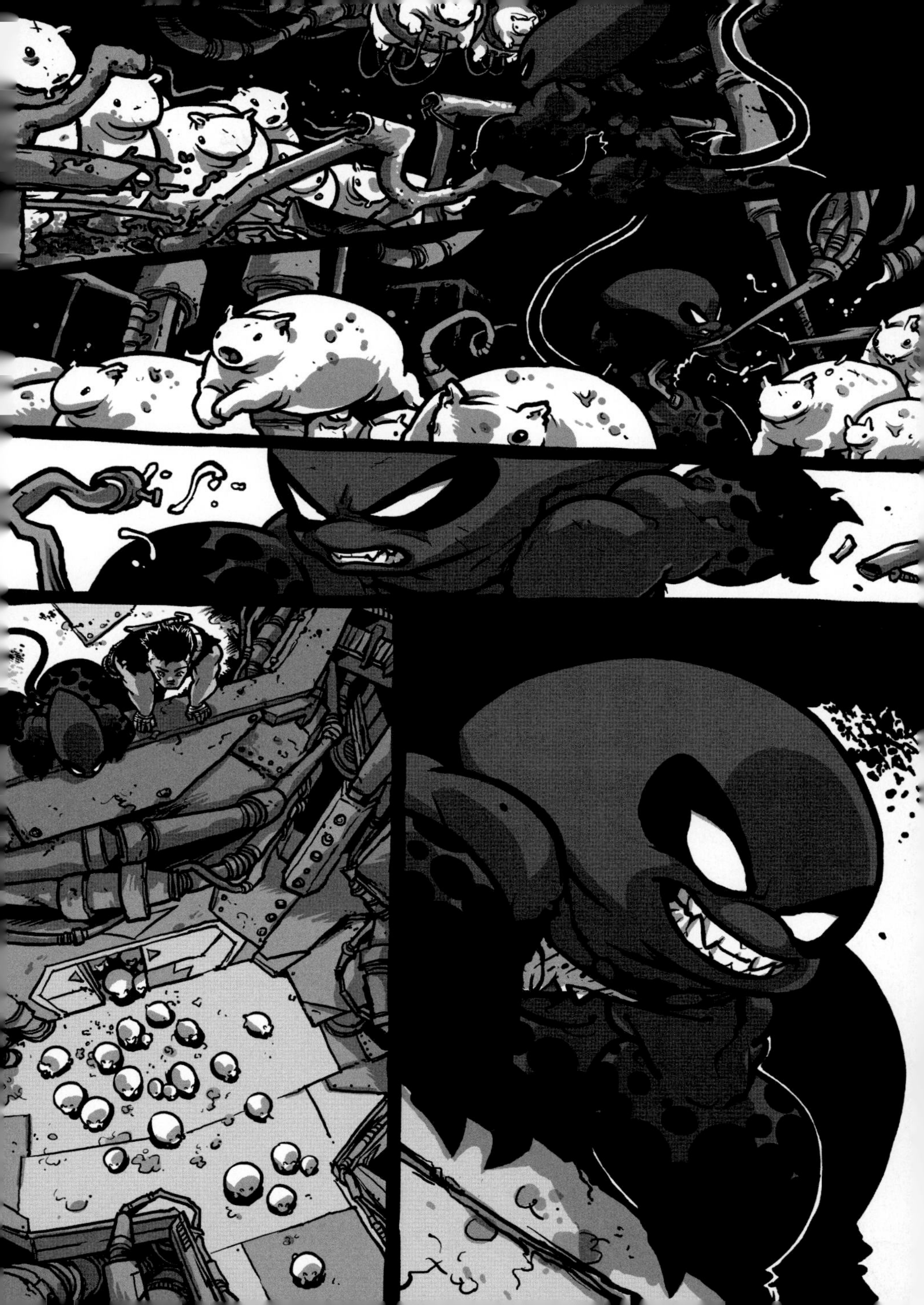

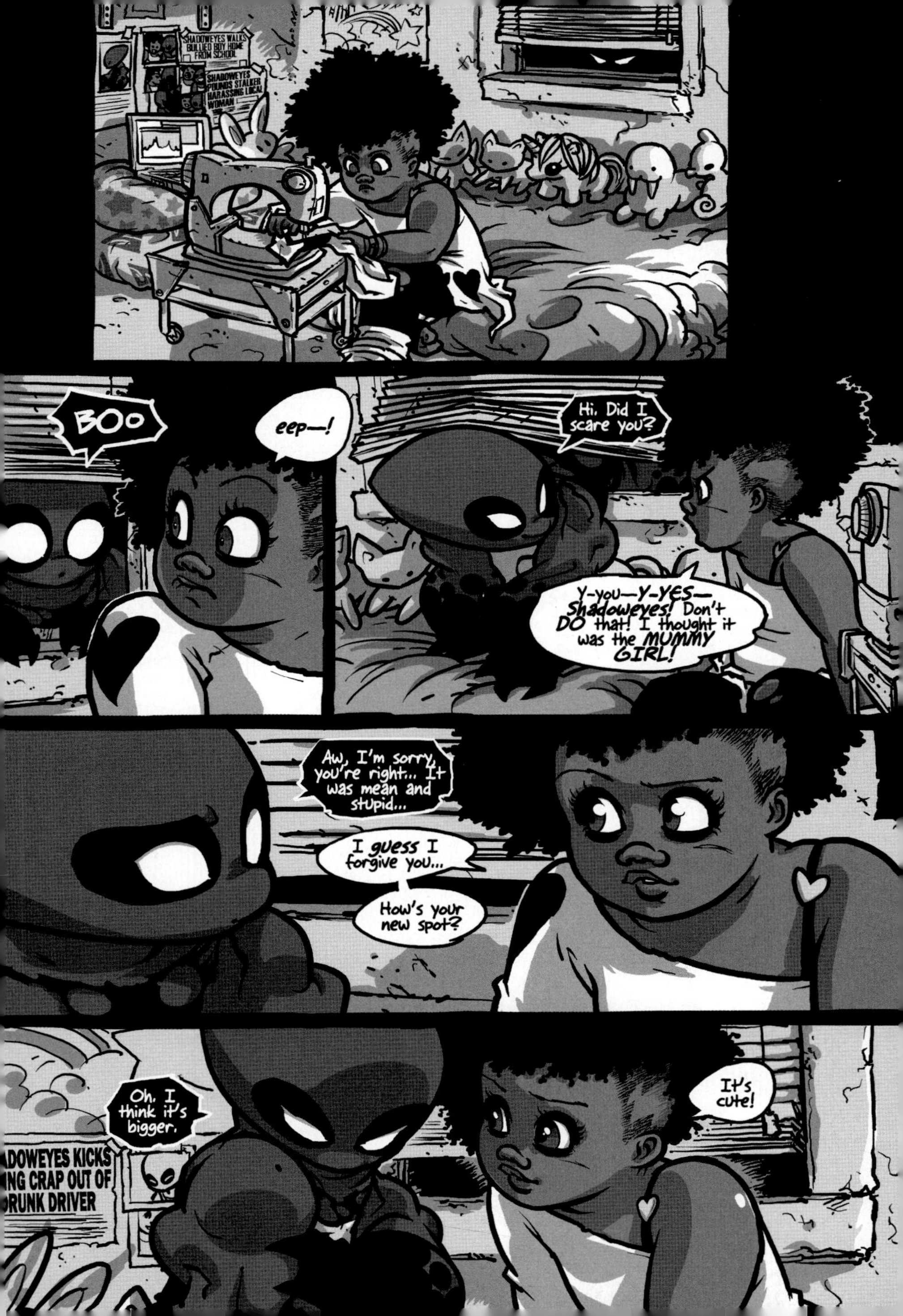
SHADOWEYES WALKS BULLIED BOY HOME FROM SCHOOL
SHADOWEYES POUNDS STALKER HARASSING LOCAL WOMAN
BOO
eep—!
Hi. Did I scare you?
Y-you—Y-YES—Shadoweyes! Don't DO that! I thought it was the MUMMY GIRL!
Aw, I'm sorry, you're right... It was mean and stupid...
I guess I forgive you...
How's your new spot?
Oh. I think it's bigger.
It's cute!
ADOWEYES KICKS
NG CRAP OUT OF
DRUNK DRIVER

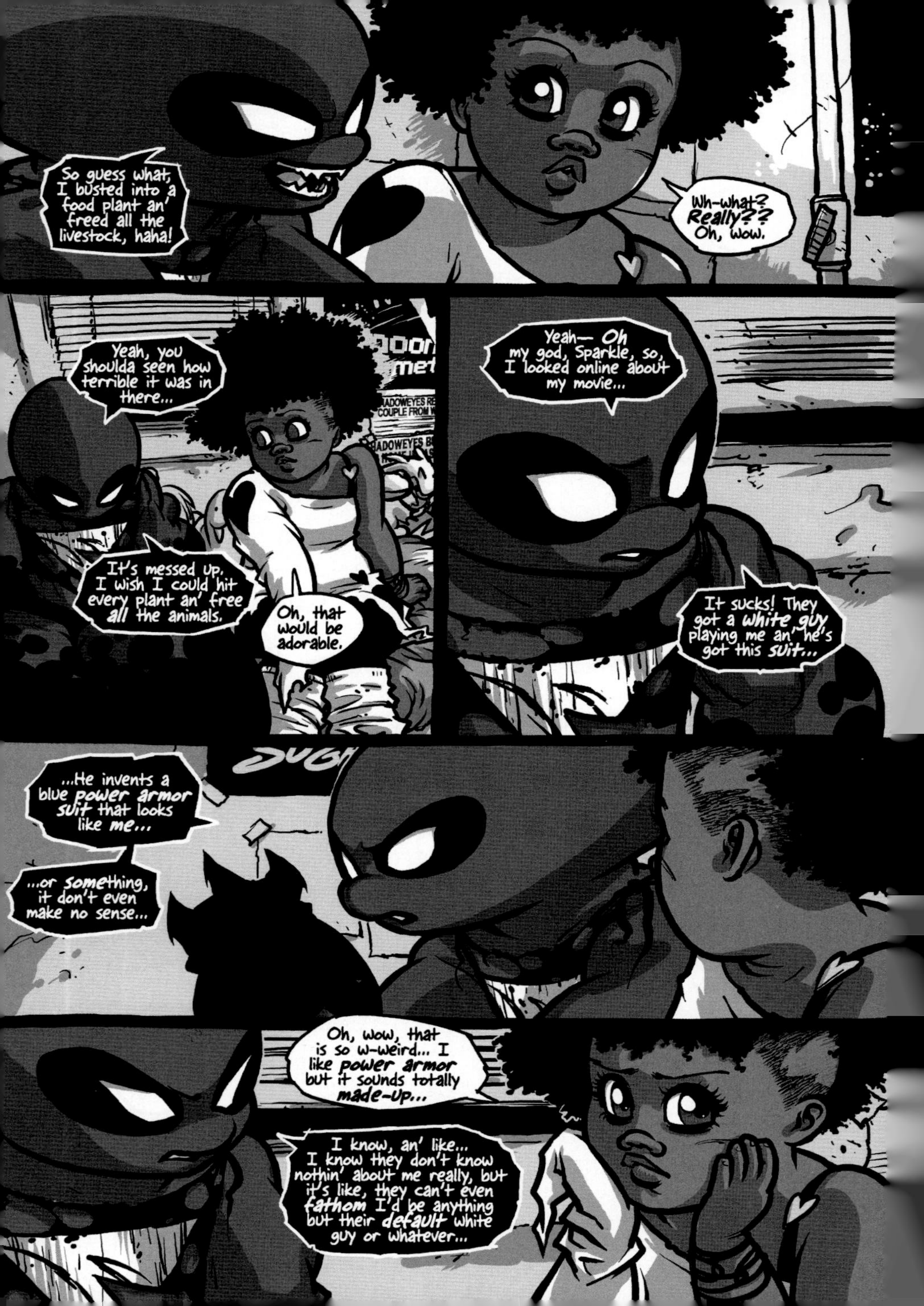
So guess what, I busted into a food plant an' freed all the livestock, haha!
Wh-what? Really?? Oh, wow.
Yeah, you shoulda seen how terrible it was in there...
It's messed up. I wish I could hit every plant an' free all the animals.
Oh, that would be adorable.
Yeah— Oh my god, Sparkle, so, I looked online about my movie...
It sucks! They got a white guy playing me an' he's got this suit...
...He invents a blue power armor suit that looks like me...
...or something, it don't even make no sense...
Oh, wow, that is so w-weird... I like power armor but it sounds totally made-up...
I know, an' like... I know they don't know nothin' about me really, but it's like, they can't even fathom I'd be anything but their default white guy or whatever...

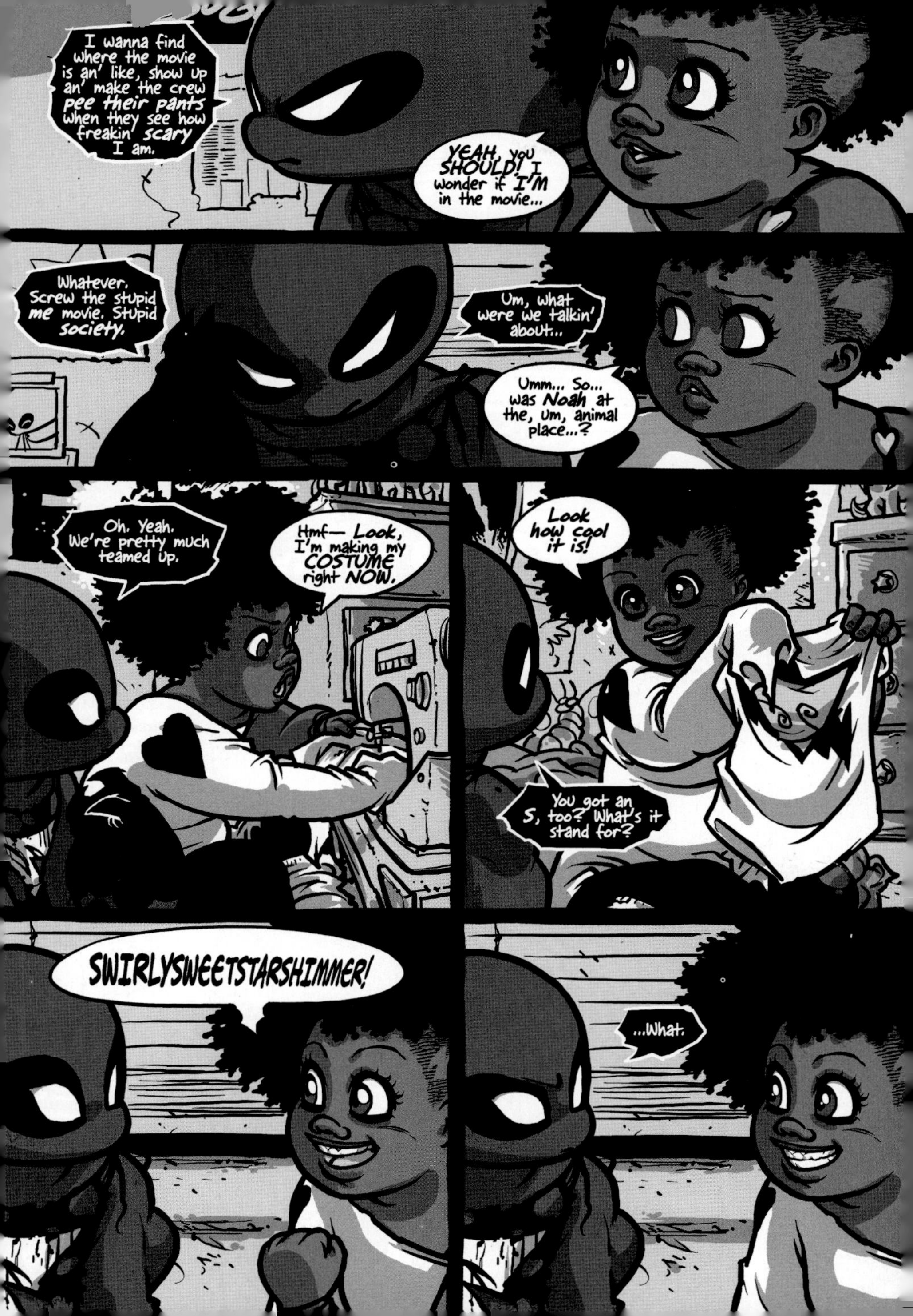
I wanna find where the movie is an' like, show up an' make the crew pee their pants when they see how freakin' scary I am.
YEAH, you SHOULD! I wonder if I'M in the movie...
Whatever. Screw the stupid me movie. Stupid society.
Um, what were we talkin' about...
Umm... So... was Noah at the, um, animal place...?
Oh. Yeah. We're pretty much teamed up.
Hmf— Look, I'm making my COSTUME right NOW.
Look how cool it is!
You got an S, too? What's it stand for?
SWIRLYSWEETSTARSHIMMER!
...What.

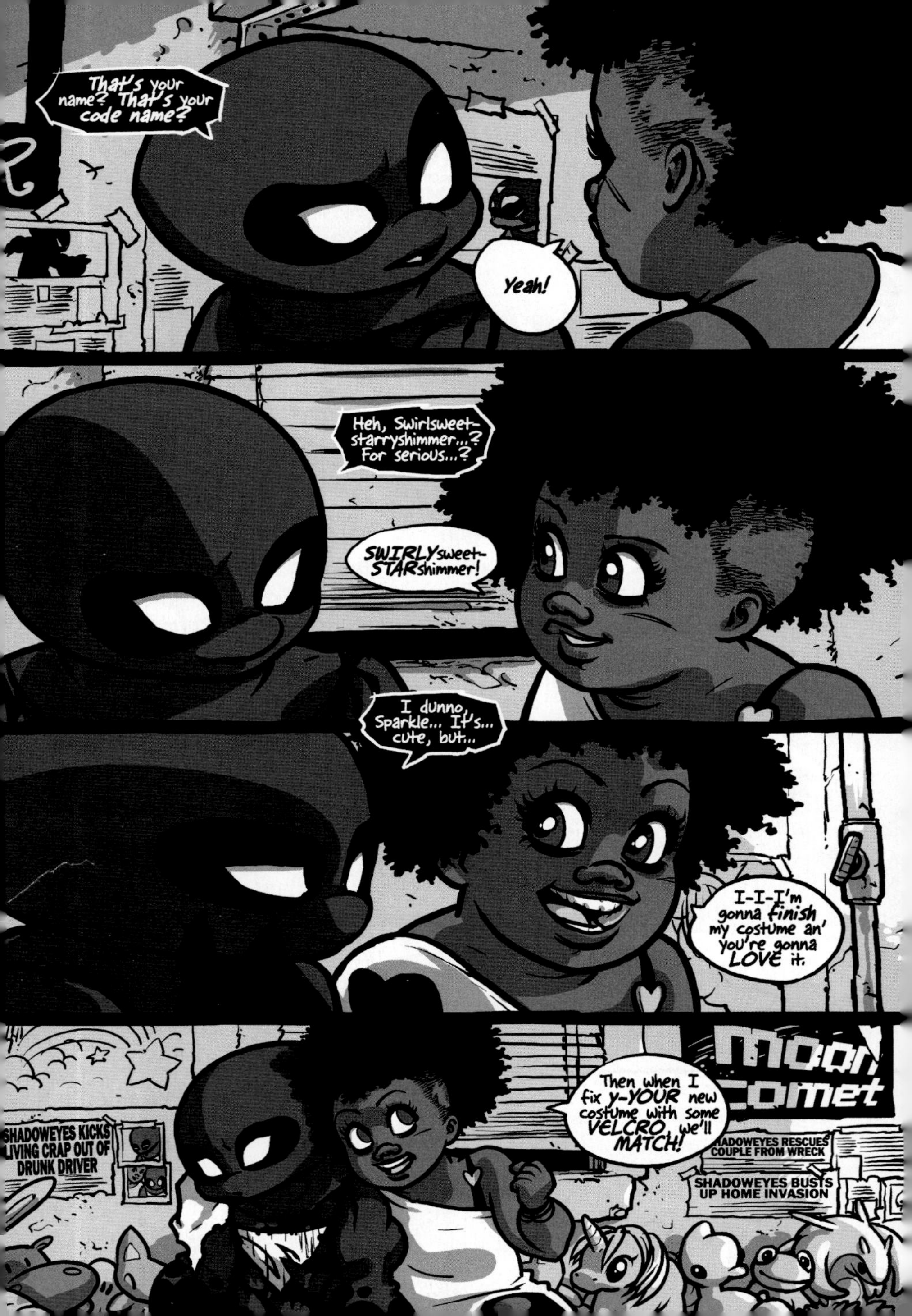

That's your name? That's your code name?
Yeah!
Heh, Swirlsweet-starryshimmer...? For serious...?
SWIRLYsweet-STARshimmer!
I dunno, Sparkle... It's... cute, but...
I-I-I'm gonna finish my costume an' you're gonna LOVE it.
moon comet
SHADOWEYES KICKS LIVING CRAP OUT OF DRUNK DRIVER
Then when I fix y-YOUR new costume with some VELCRO, we'll MATCH!
SHADOWEYES RESCUES COUPLE FROM WRECK
SHADOWEYES BUSTS UP HOME INVASION

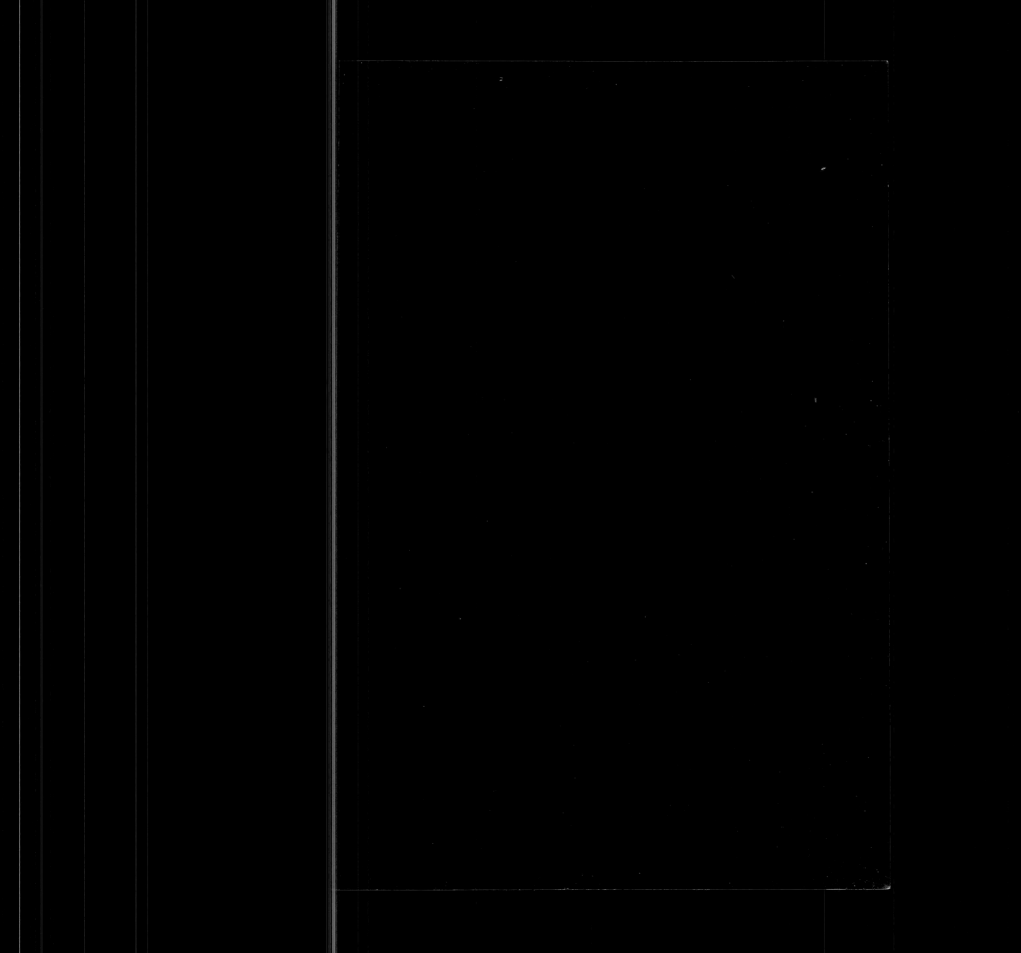

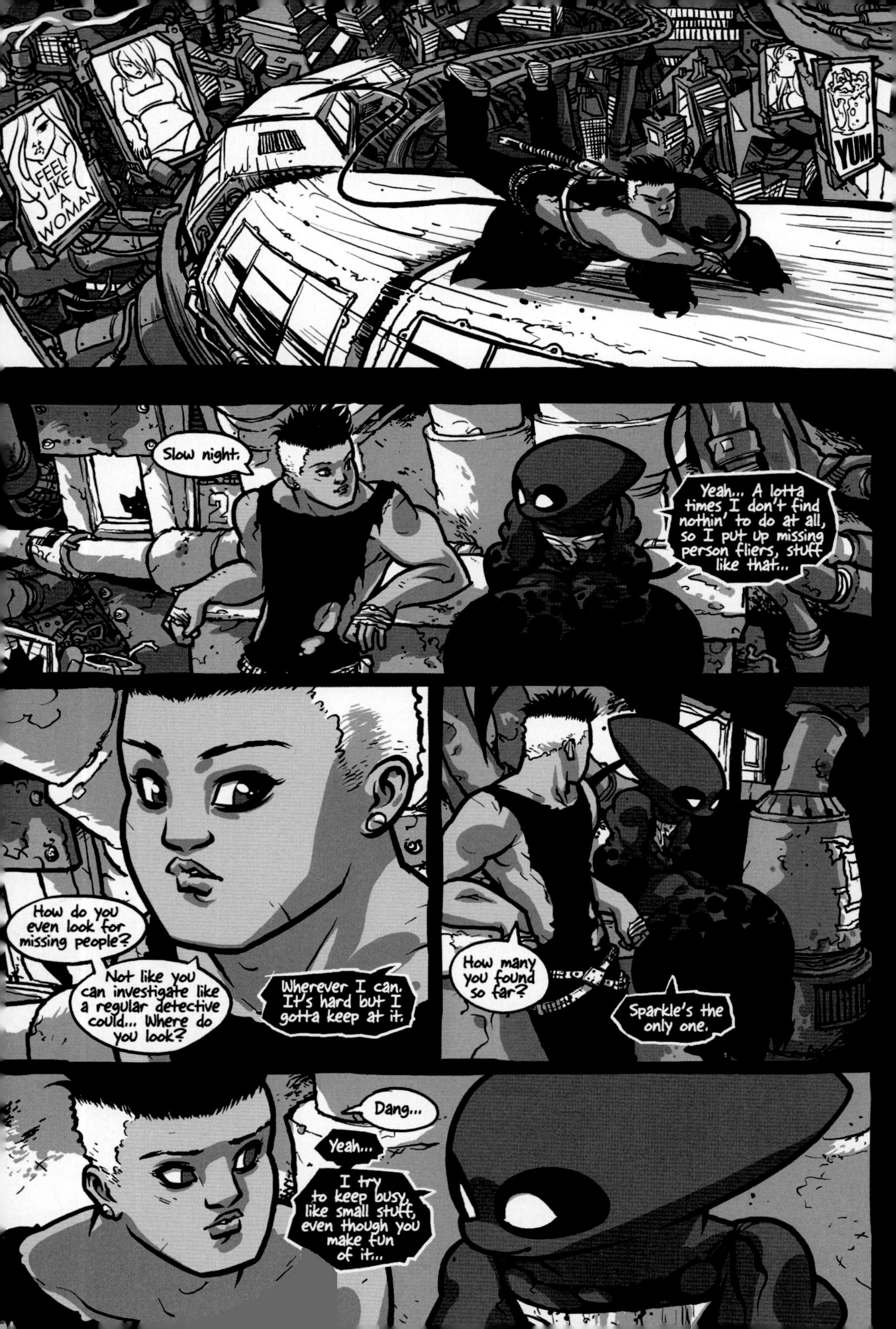
FEEL LIKE A WOMAN
YUM
Slow night.
Yeah... A lotta times I don't find nothin' to do at all, so I put up missing person fliers, stuff like that...
How do you even look for missing people?
Not like you can investigate like a regular detective could... Where do you look?
Wherever I can. It's hard but I gotta keep at it.
How many you found so far?
Sparkle's the only one.
Dang...
Yeah...
I try to keep busy, like small stuff, even though you make fun of it...

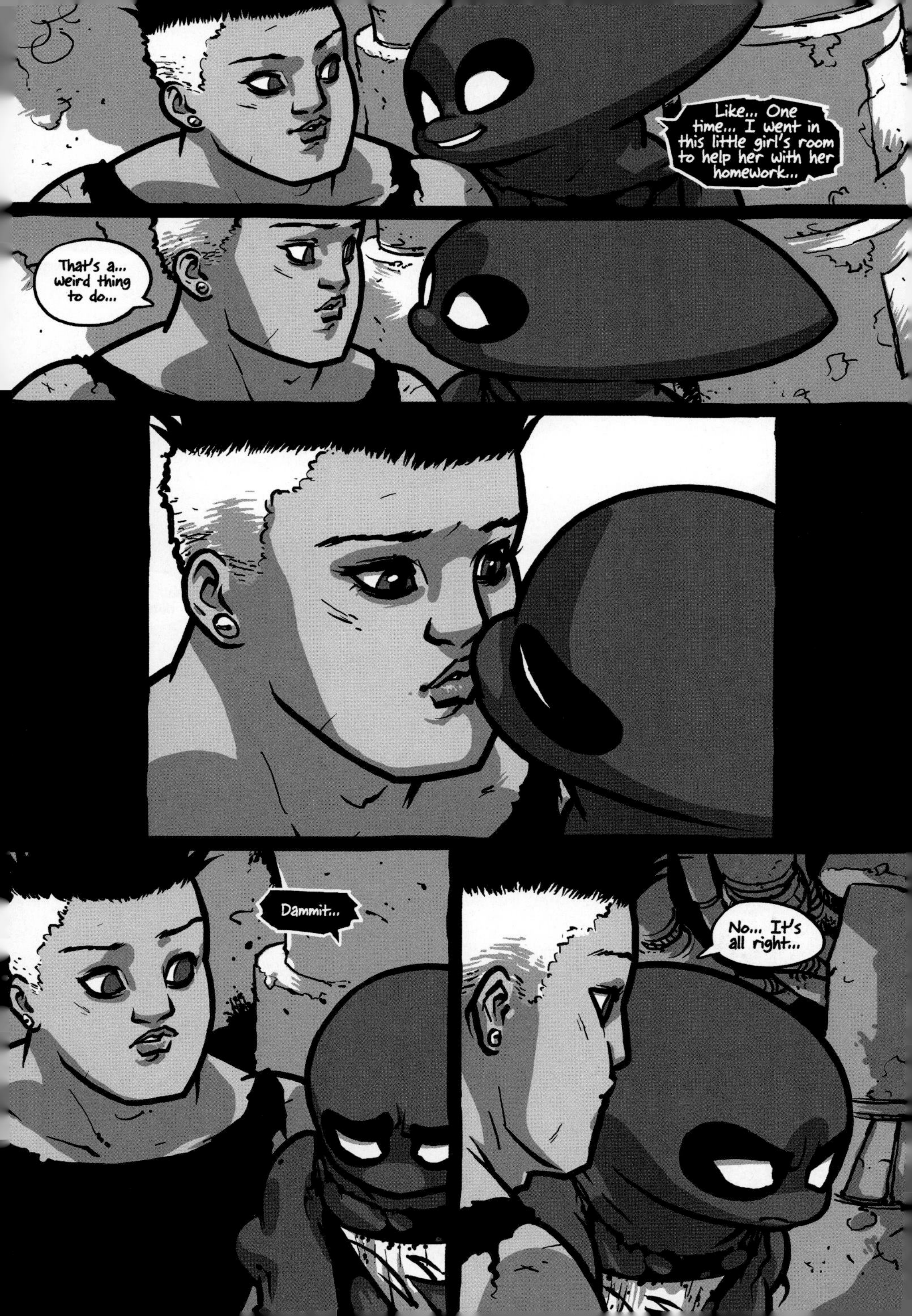
Like... One time... I went in this little girl's room to help her with her homework...
That's a... weird thing to do...
Dammit...
No... It's all right...

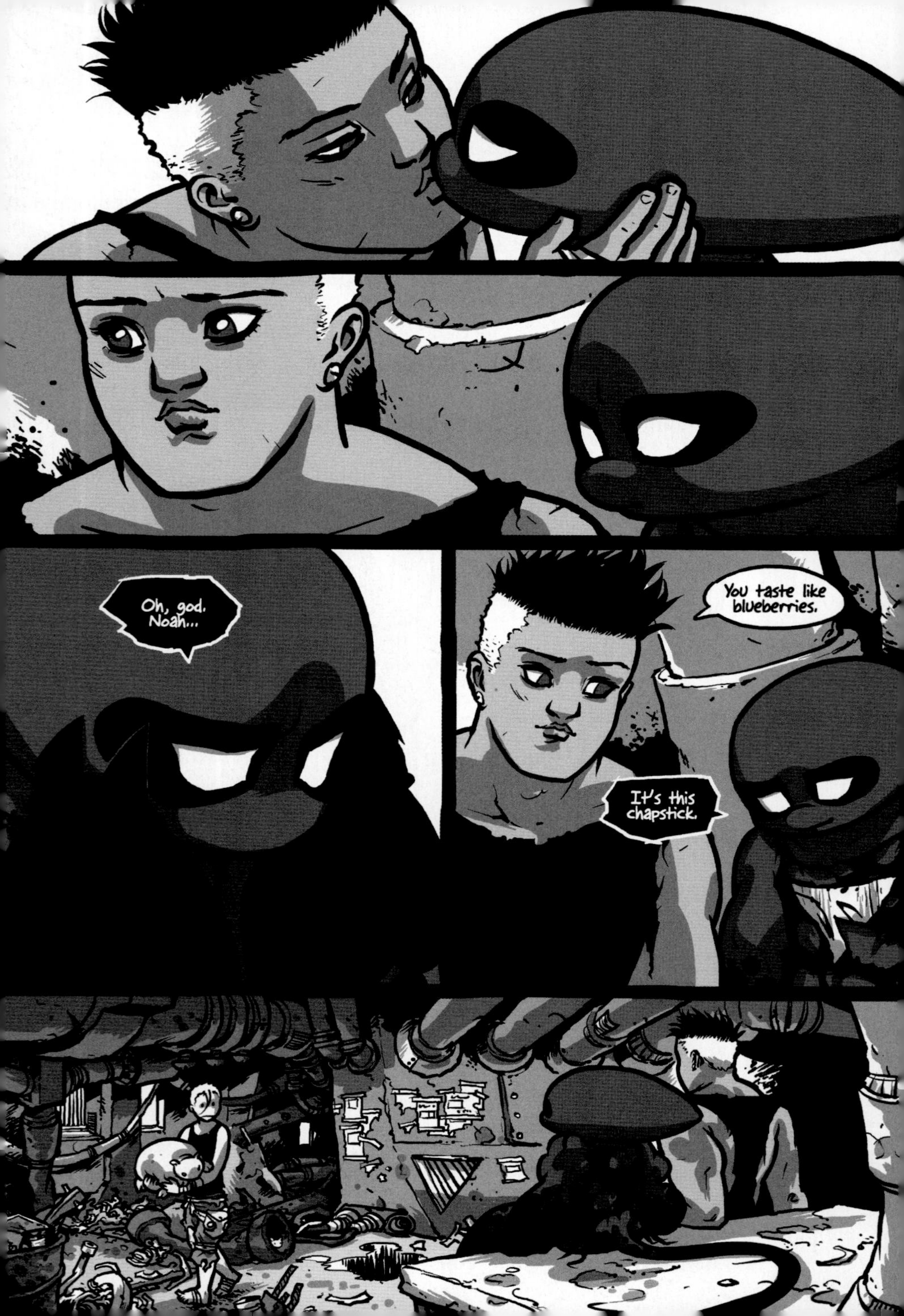
Oh, god. Noah...
You taste like blueberries.
It's this chapstick.

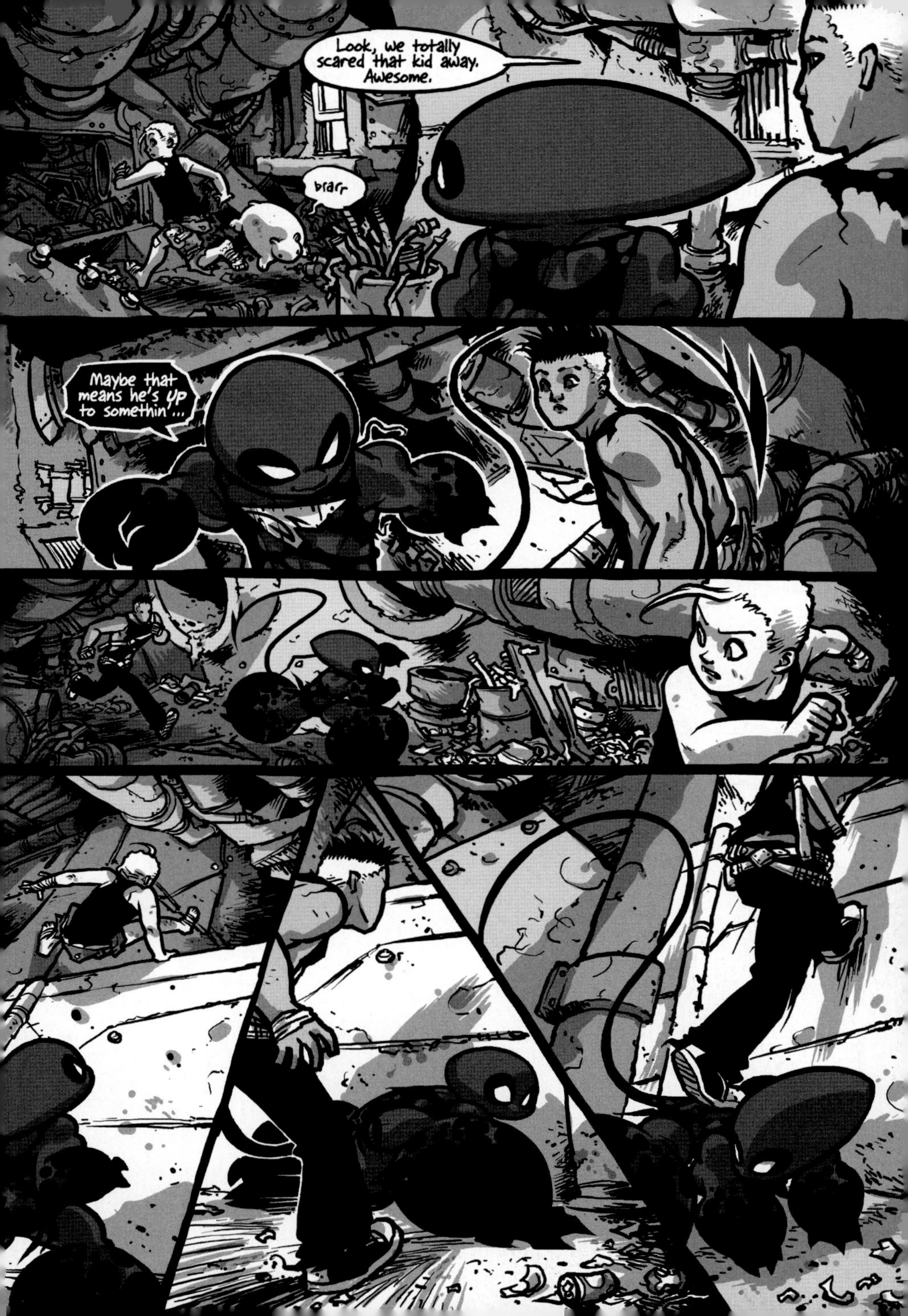
Look, we totally scared that kid away. Awesome.
brarr
Maybe that means he's UP to somethin'...

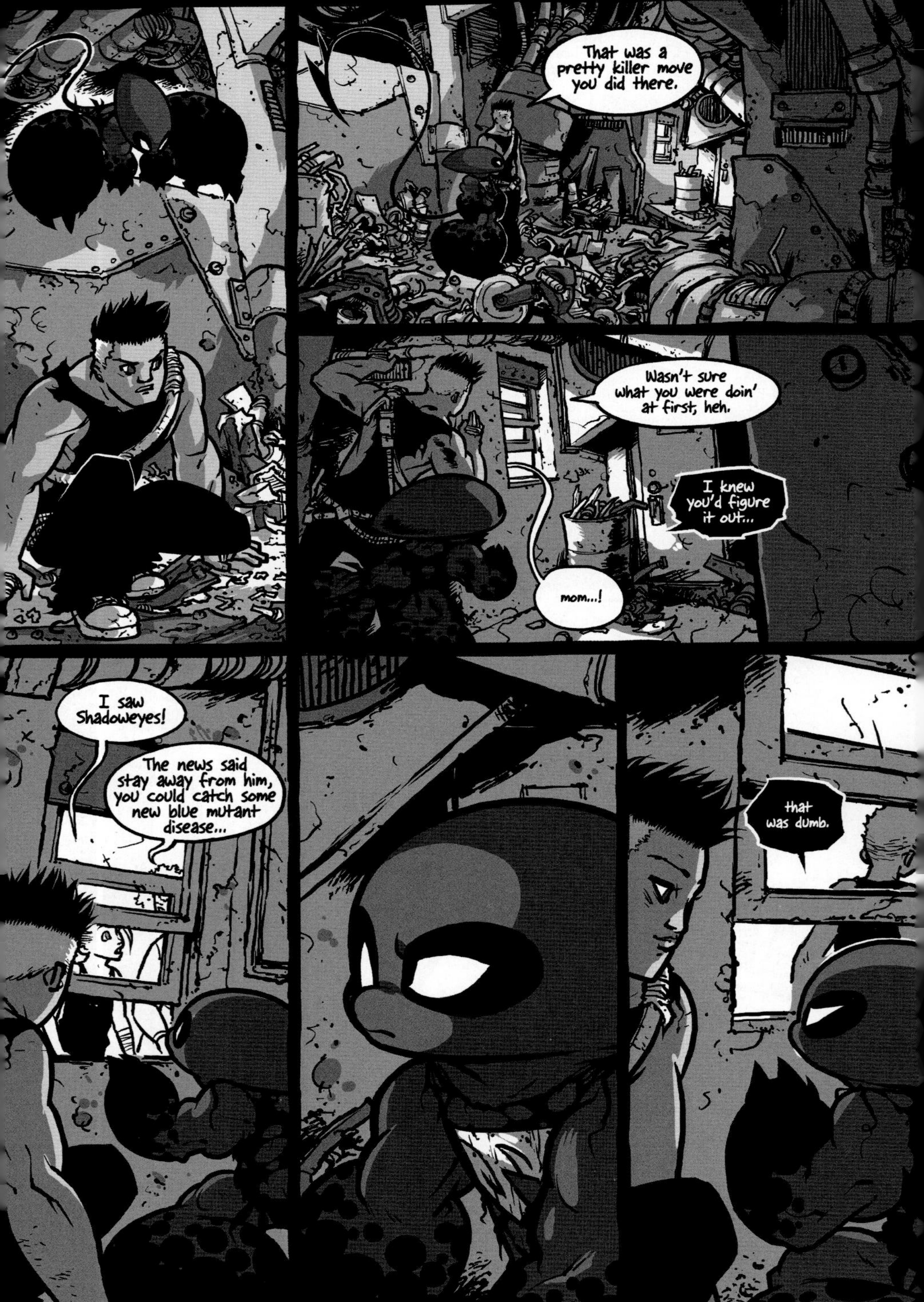
That was a pretty killer move you did there.
Wasn't sure what you were doin' at first, heh.
I knew you'd figure it out...
mom...!
I saw Shadoweyes!
The news said stay away from him, you could catch some new blue mutant disease...
that was dumb.

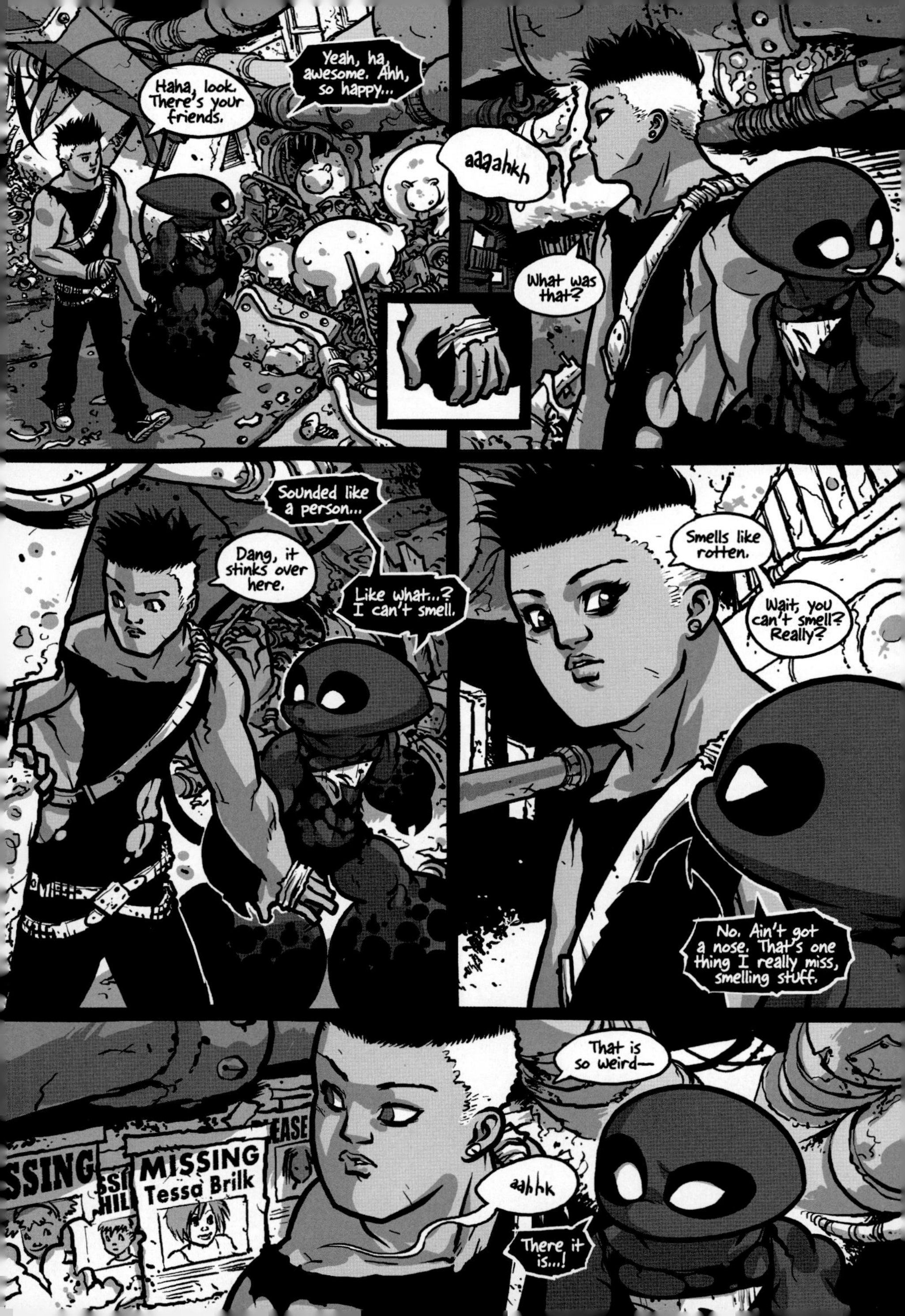

Haha, look. There's your friends.
Yeah, ha, awesome. Ahh, so happy...
aaaahkh
What was that?
Sounded like a person...
Dang, it stinks over here.
Like what...? I can't smell.
Smells like rotten.
Wait, you can't smell? Really?
No. Ain't got a nose. That's one thing I really miss, smelling stuff.
That is so weird—
aahhk
There it is...!
SSING
MISSING
Tessa Brilk
EASE

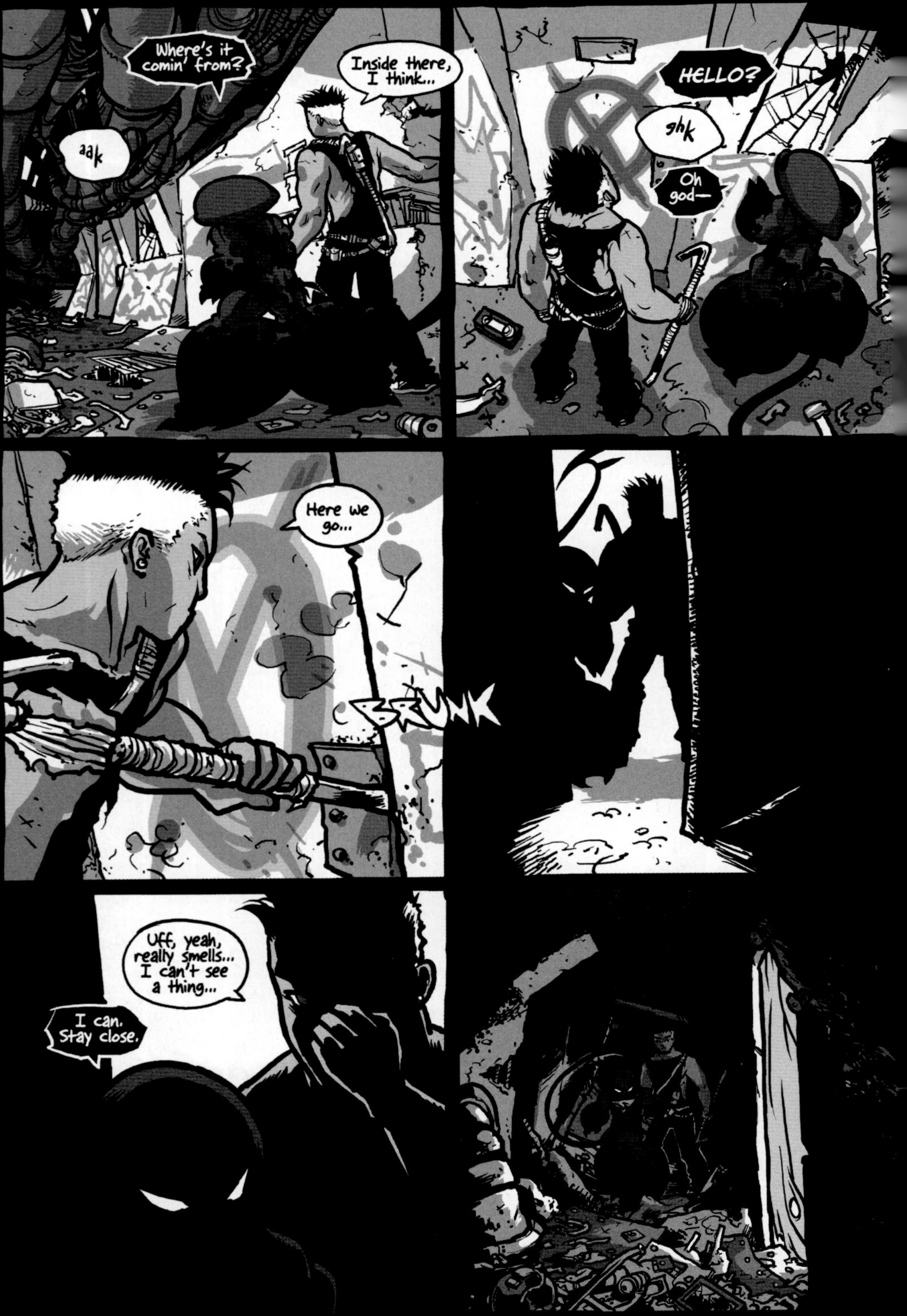
Where's it comin' from?
Inside there, I think...
aak
HELLO?
ghk
Oh god—
Here we go...
BRUNK
Uff, yeah, really smells... I can't see a thing...
I can. Stay close.

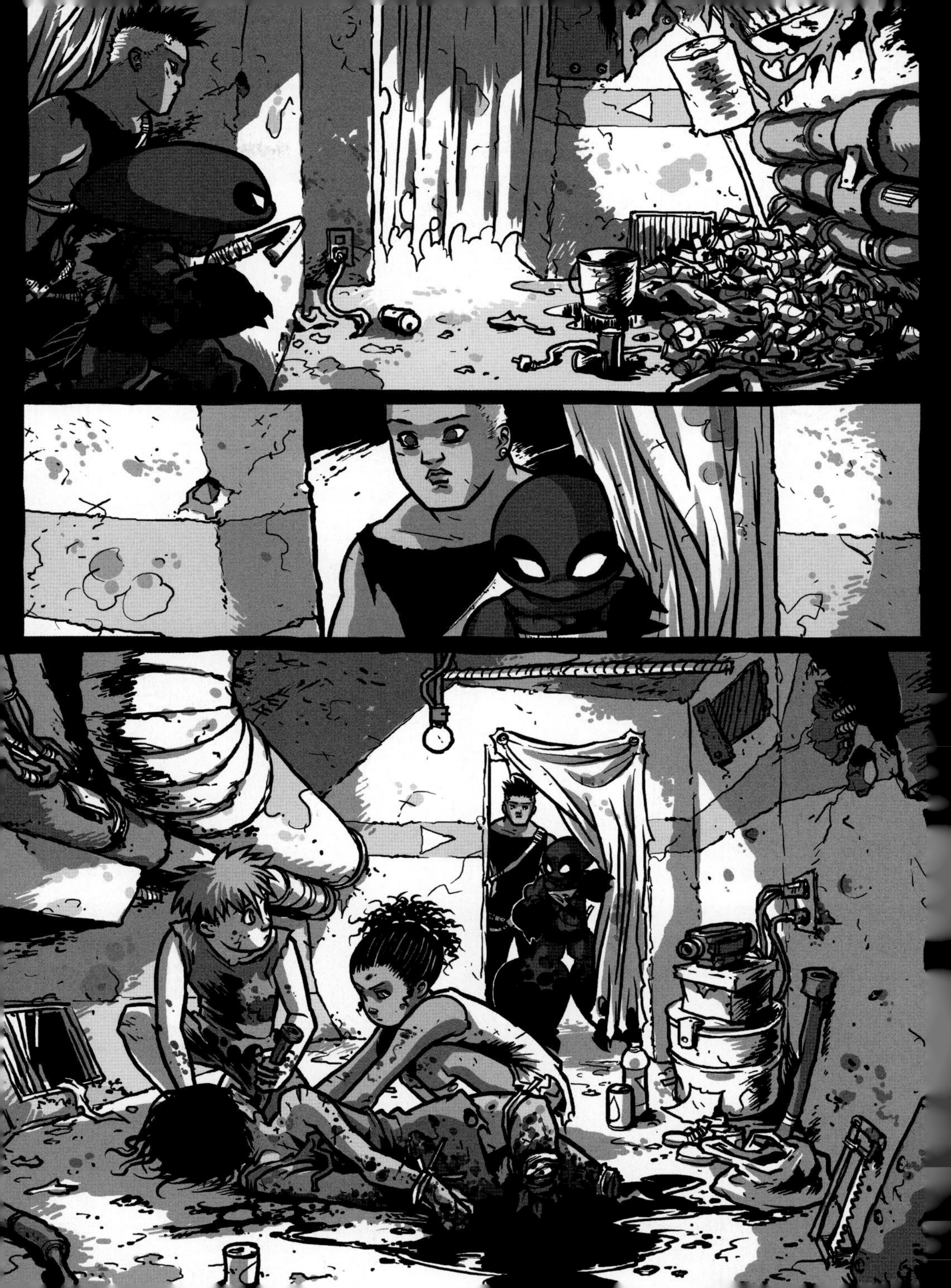

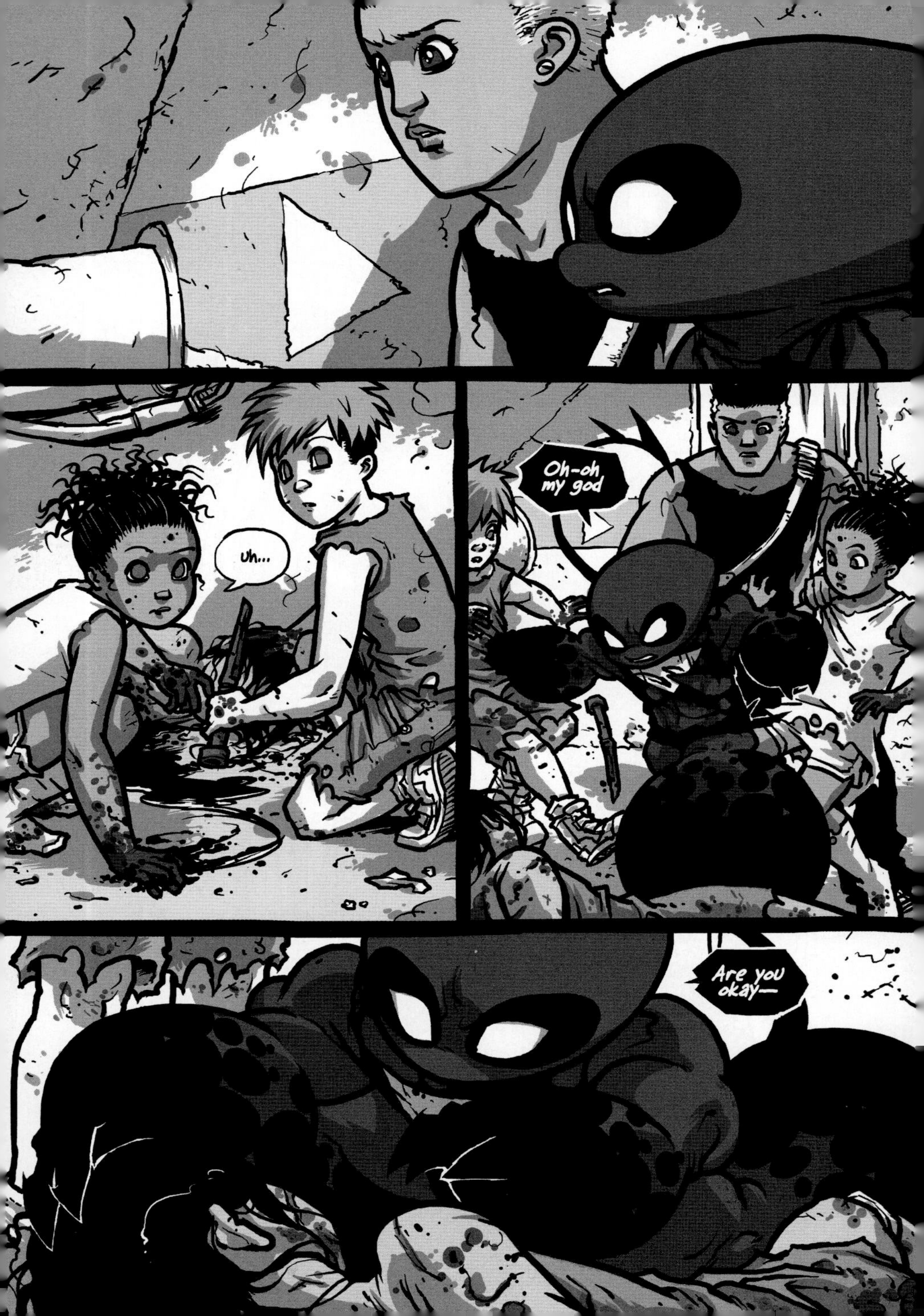
Uh...
Oh-oh my god
Are you okay—

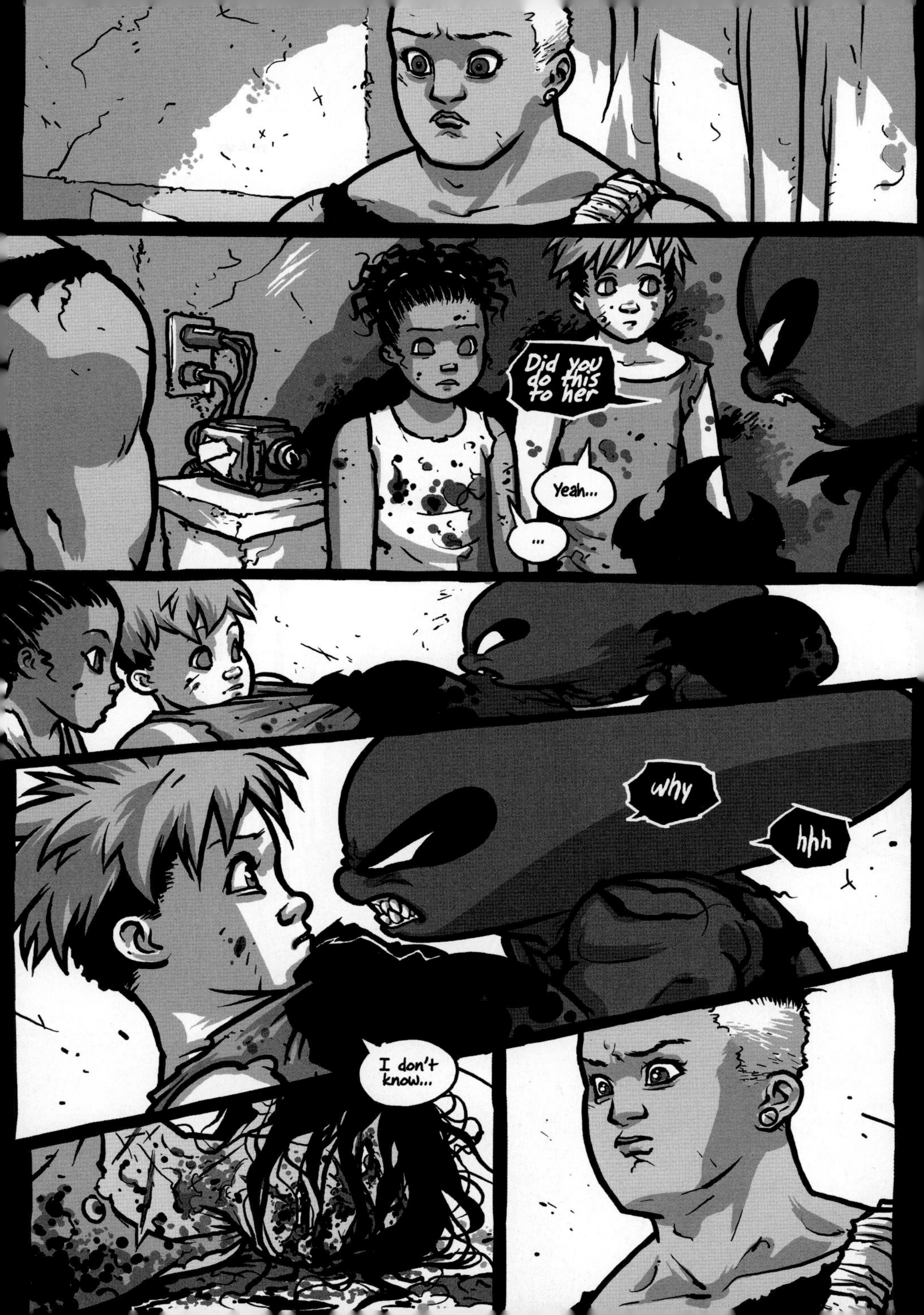

Did you do this to her
Yeah...
...
why
hhh
I don't know...

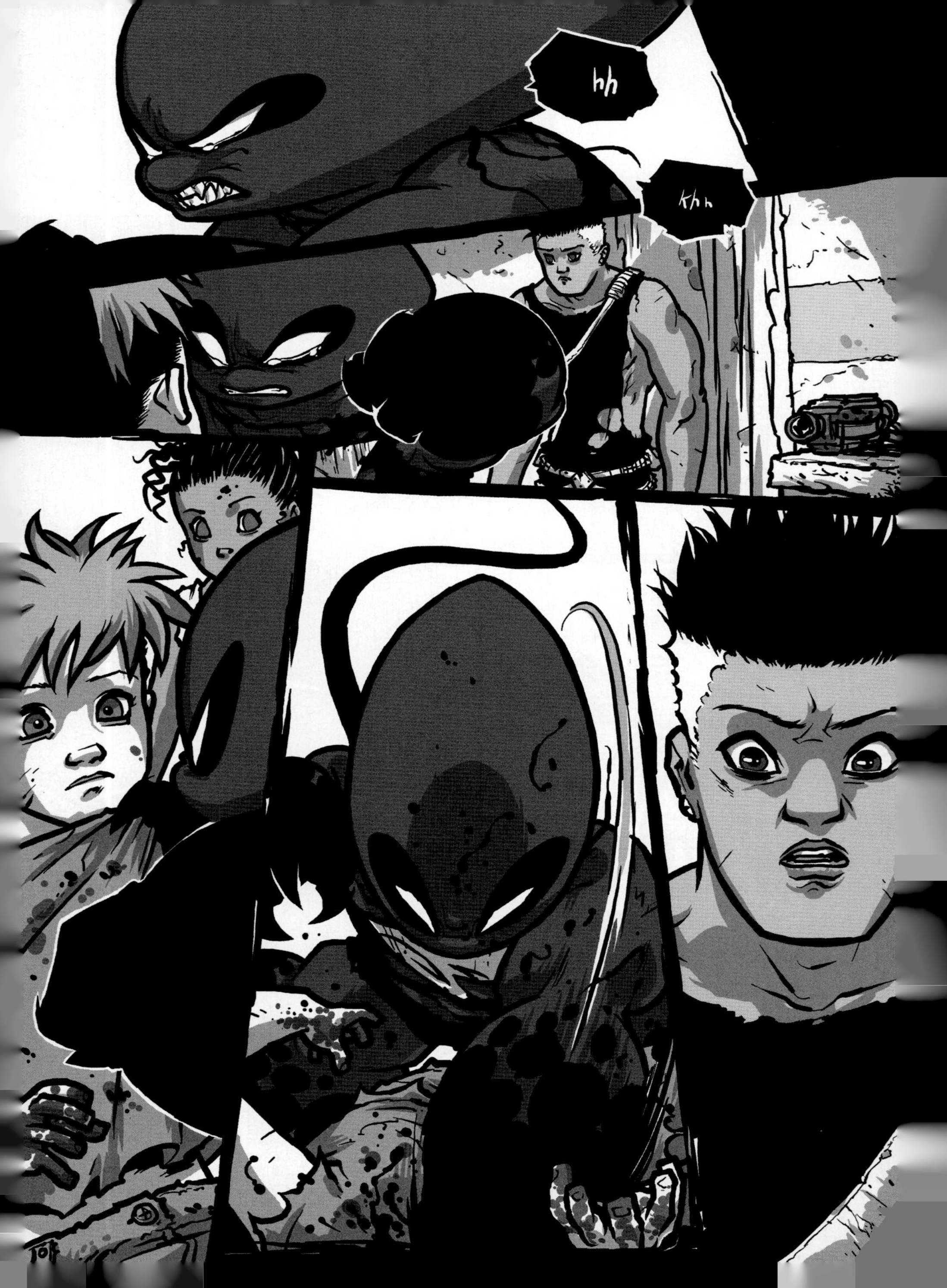
hh
khh

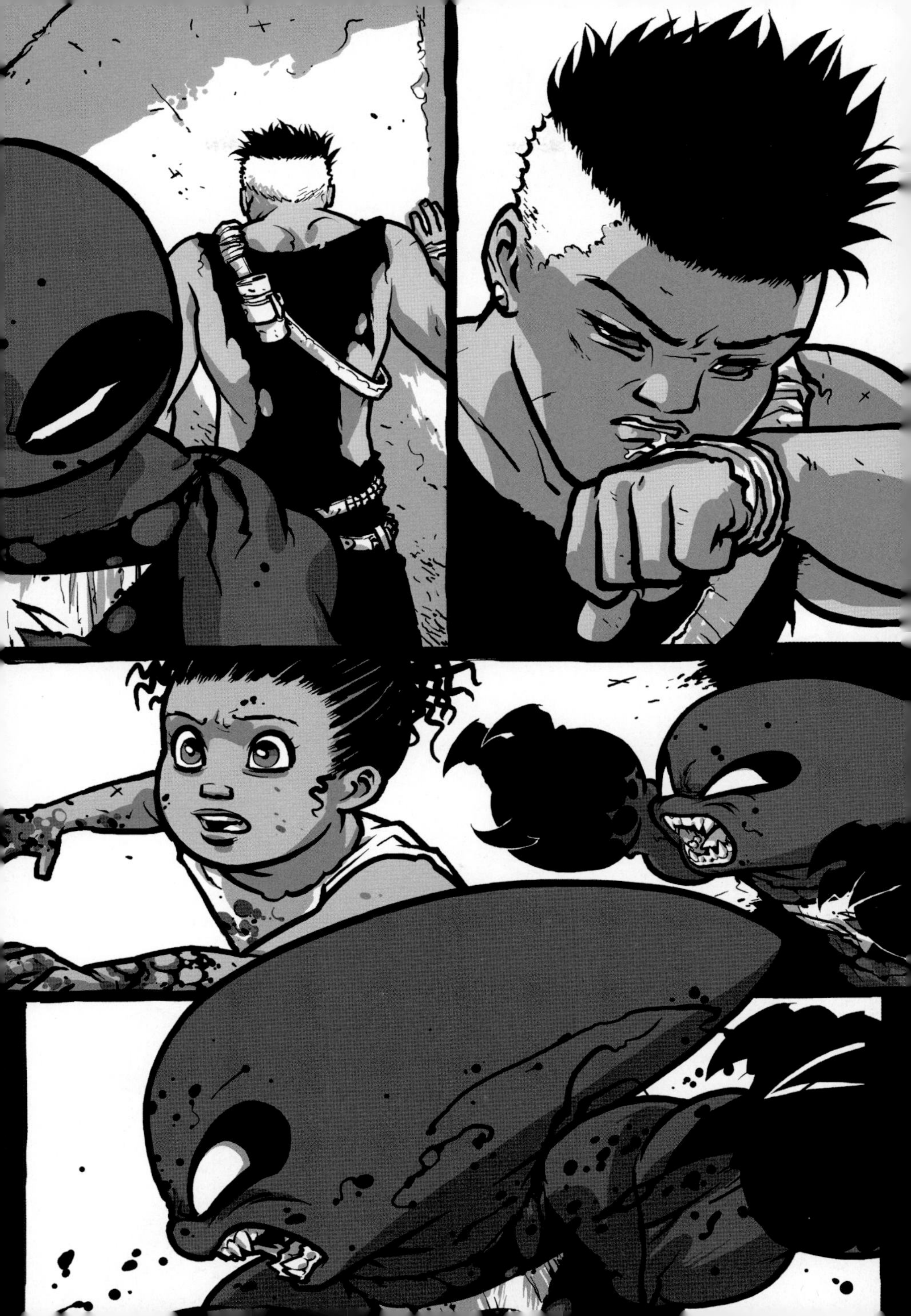

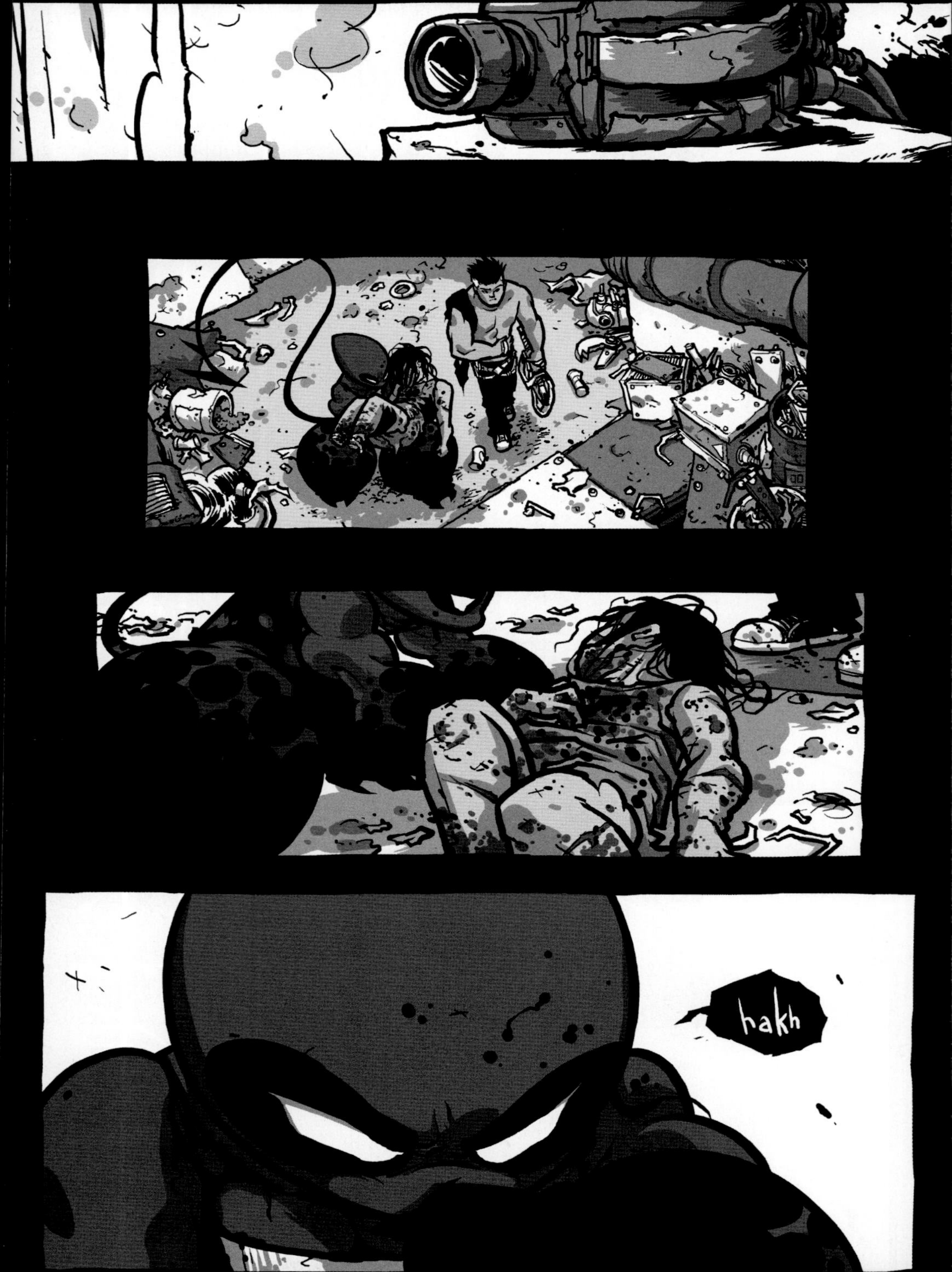
hakh

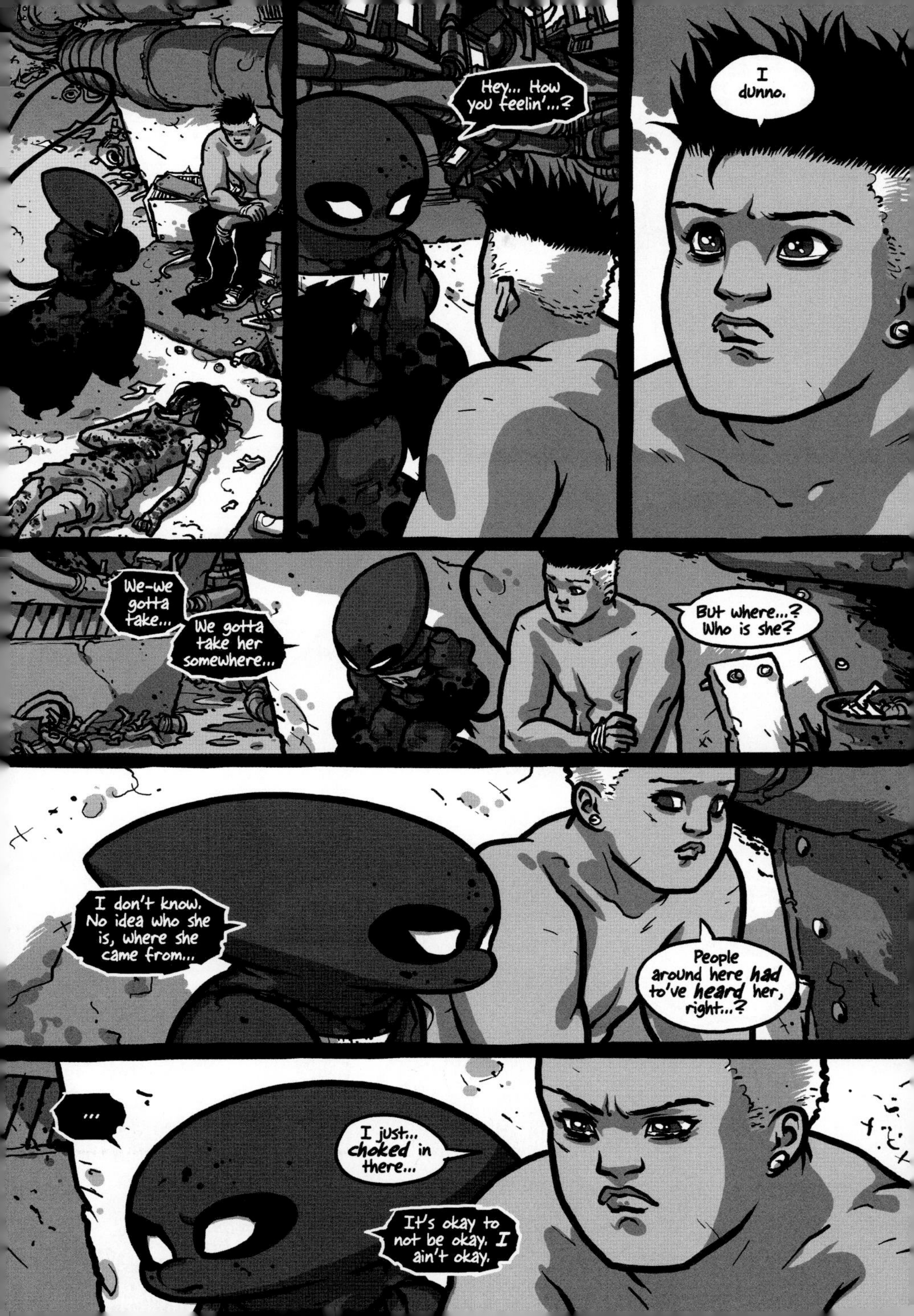
Hey... How you feelin'...?
I dunno.
We-we gotta take...
We gotta take her somewhere...
But where...? Who is she?
I don't know. No idea who she is, where she came from...
People around here **had** to've **heard** her, right...?
...
I just... **choked** in there...
It's okay to not be okay. I ain't okay.

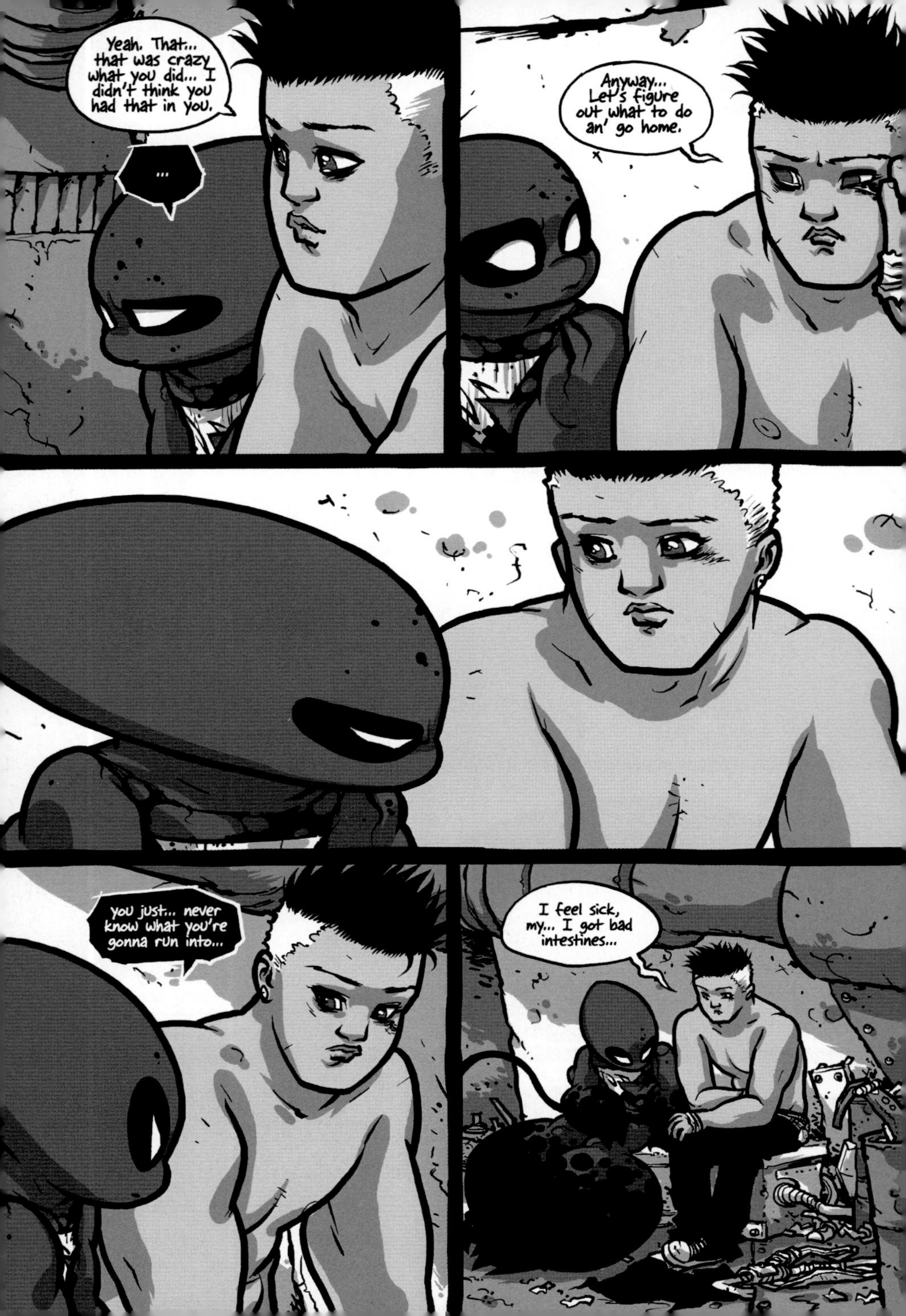
Yeah. That... that was crazy what you did... I didn't think you had that in you.
...
Anyway... Let's figure out what to do an' go home.
you just... never know what you're gonna run into...
I feel sick, my... I got bad intestines...

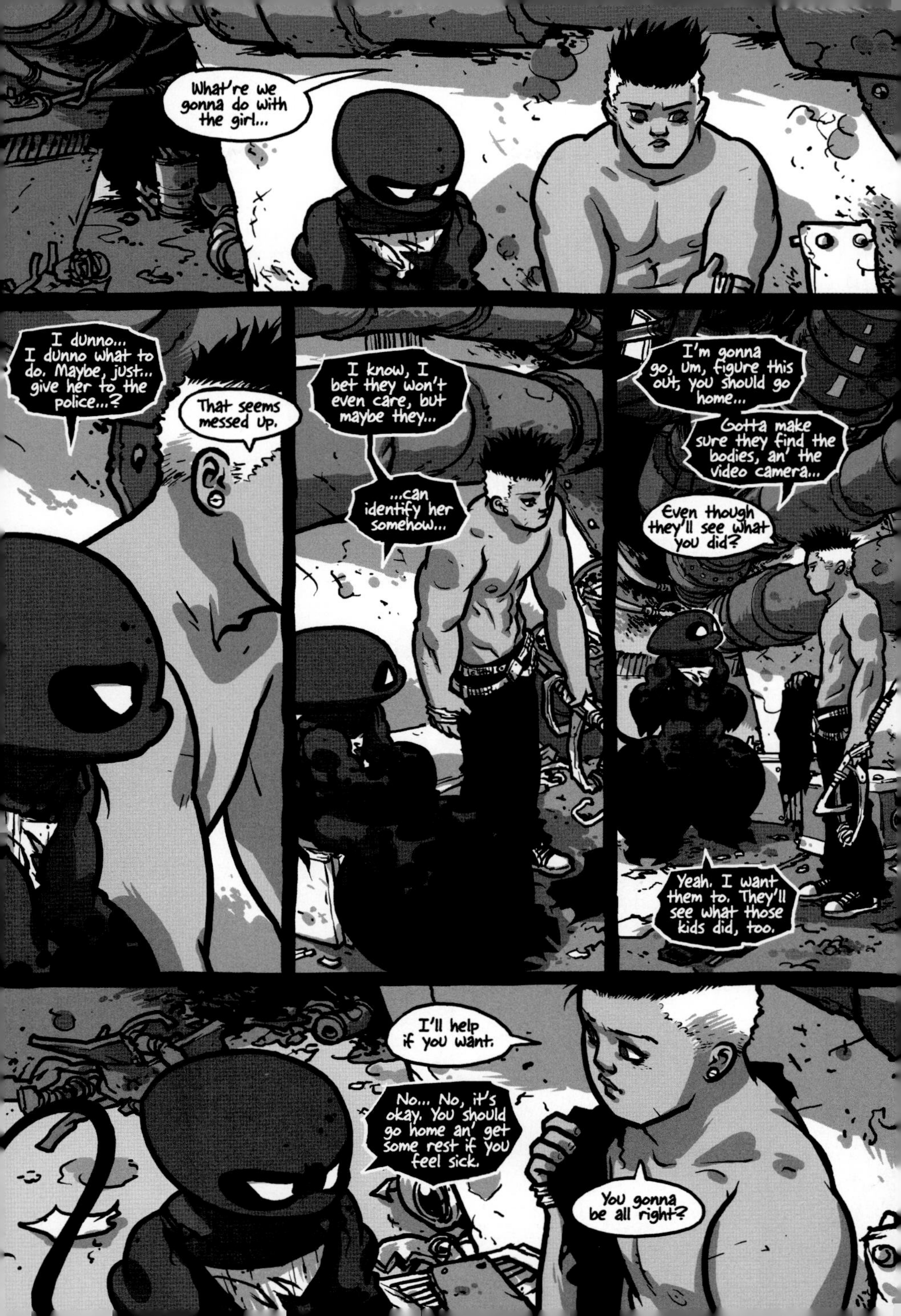

What're we gonna do with the girl...
I dunno... I dunno what to do. Maybe, just... give her to the police...?
That seems messed up.
I know, I bet they won't even care, but maybe they...
...can identify her somehow...
I'm gonna go, um, figure this out, you should go home...
Gotta make sure they find the bodies, an' the video camera...
Even though they'll see what you did?
Yeah. I want them to. They'll see what those kids did, too.
I'll help if you want.
No... No, it's okay. You should go home an' get some rest if you feel sick.
You gonna be all right?

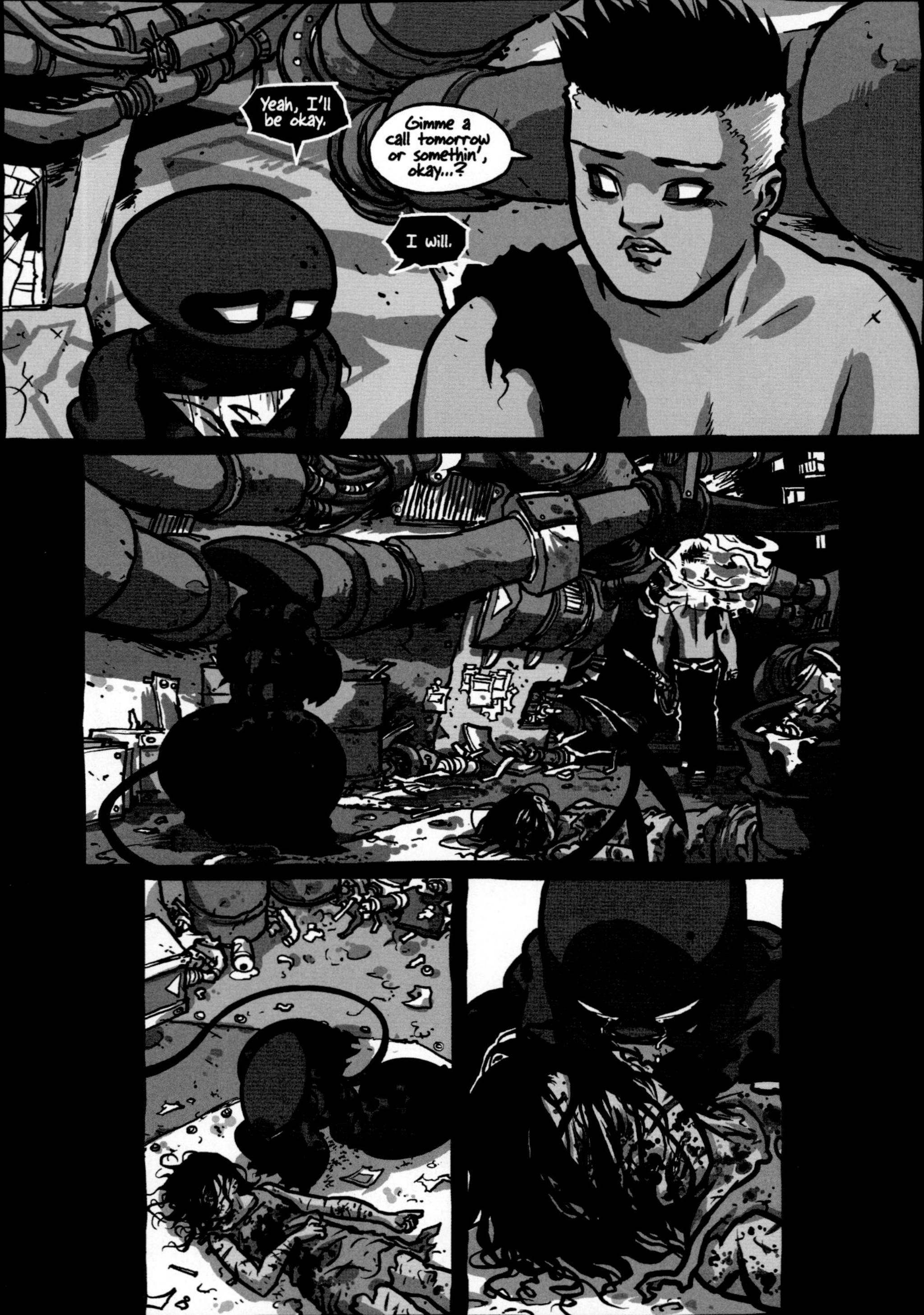
Yeah, I'll be okay.
Gimme a call tomorrow or somethin', okay...?
I will.

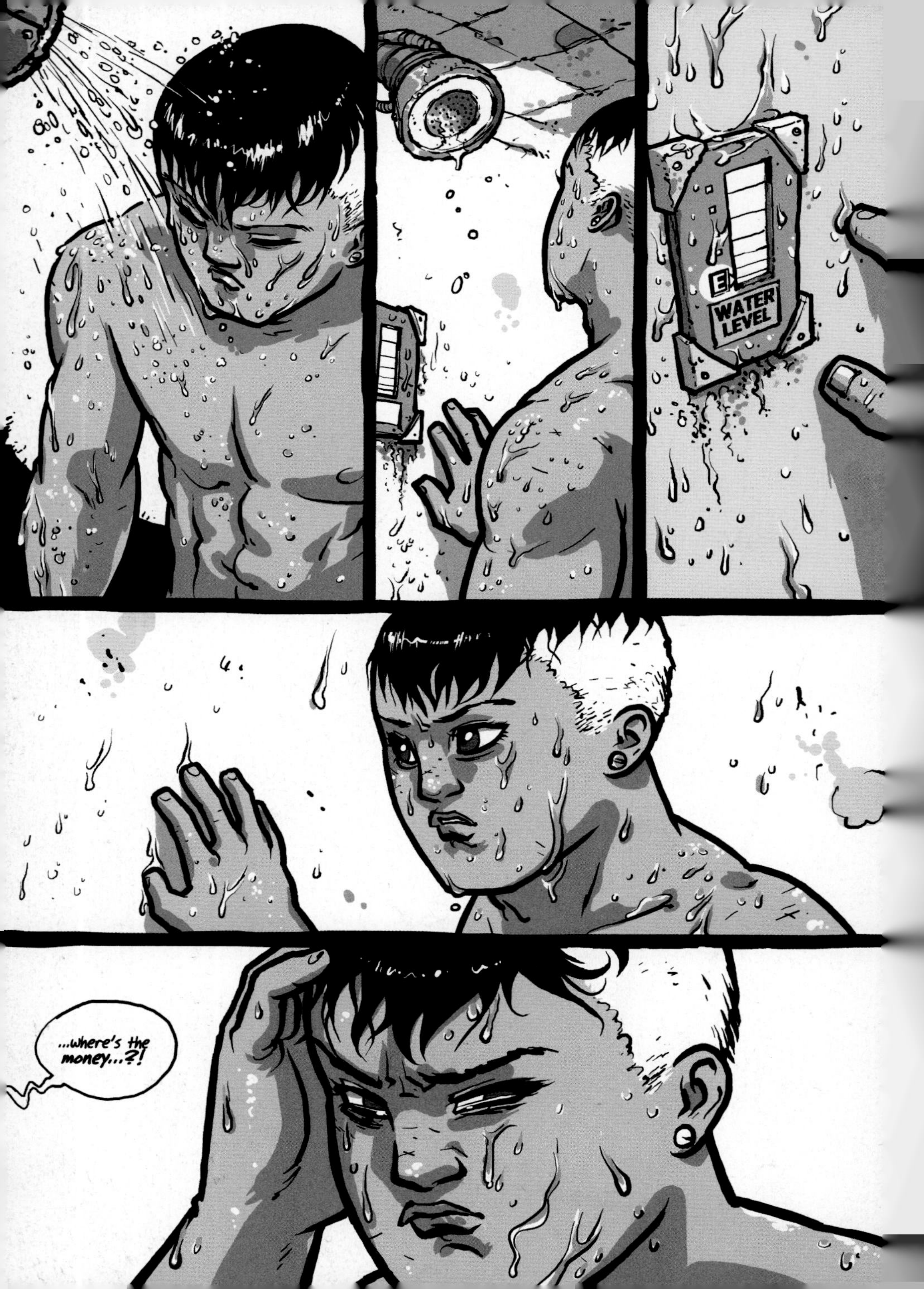
E
WATER LEVEL
...where's the money...?!

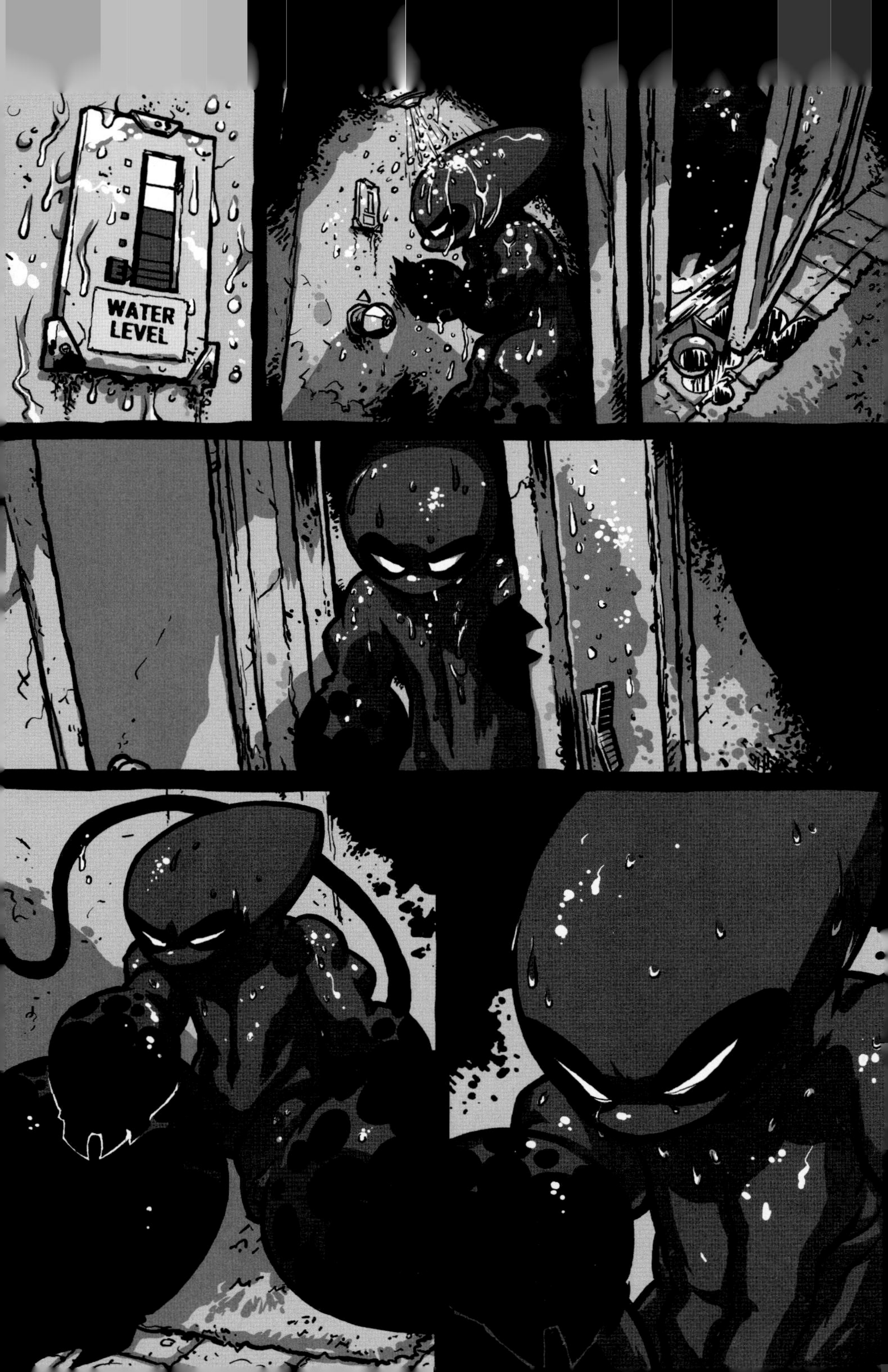
WATER LEVEL

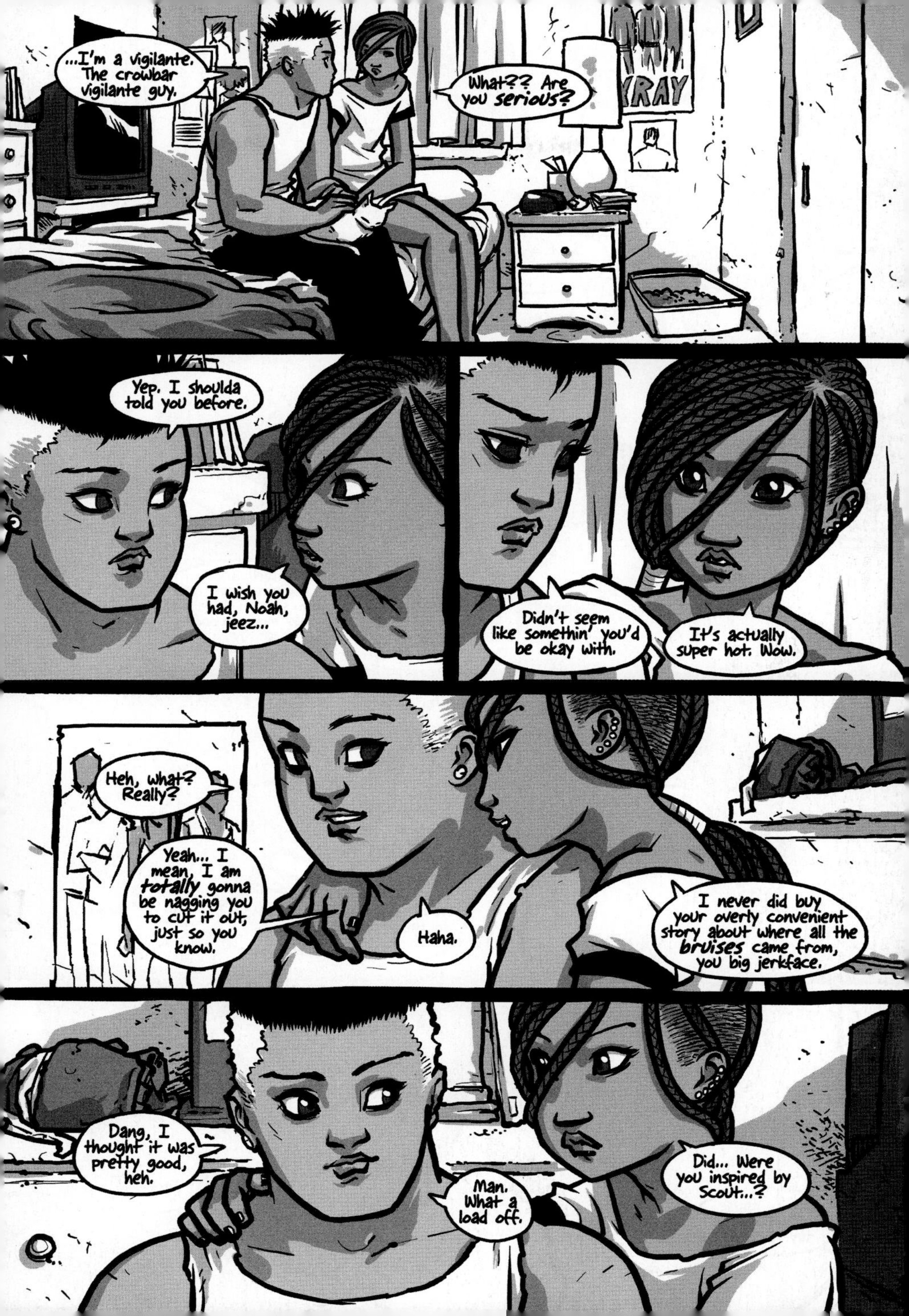

...I'm a vigilante. The crowbar vigilante guy.
What?? Are you serious?
XRAY
Yep. I shoulda told you before.
I wish you had, Noah, jeez...
Didn't seem like somethin' you'd be okay with.
It's actually super hot. Wow.
Heh, what? Really?
Yeah... I mean, I am totally gonna be nagging you to cut it out, just so you know.
Haha.
I never did buy your overly convenient story about where all the bruises came from, you big jerkface.
Dang, I thought it was pretty good, heh.
Man. What a load off.
Did... Were you inspired by Scout...?

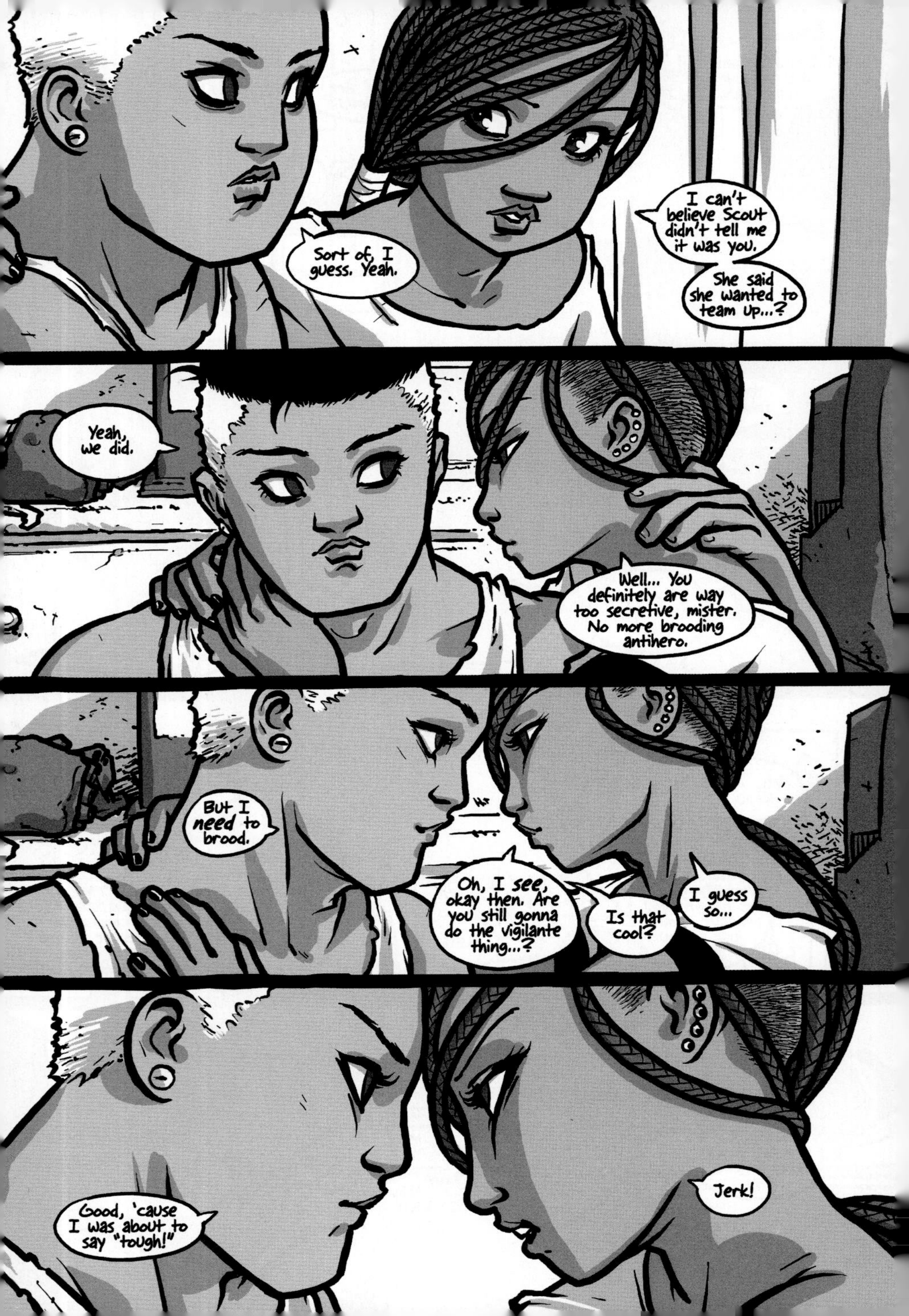
Sort of, I guess. Yeah.
I can't believe Scout didn't tell me it was you.
She said she wanted to team up...?
Yeah, we did.
Well... You definitely are way too secretive, mister. No more brooding antihero.
But I need to brood.
Oh, I see, okay then. Are you still gonna do the vigilante thing...?
Is that cool?
I guess so...
Good, 'cause I was about to say "tough!"
Jerk!

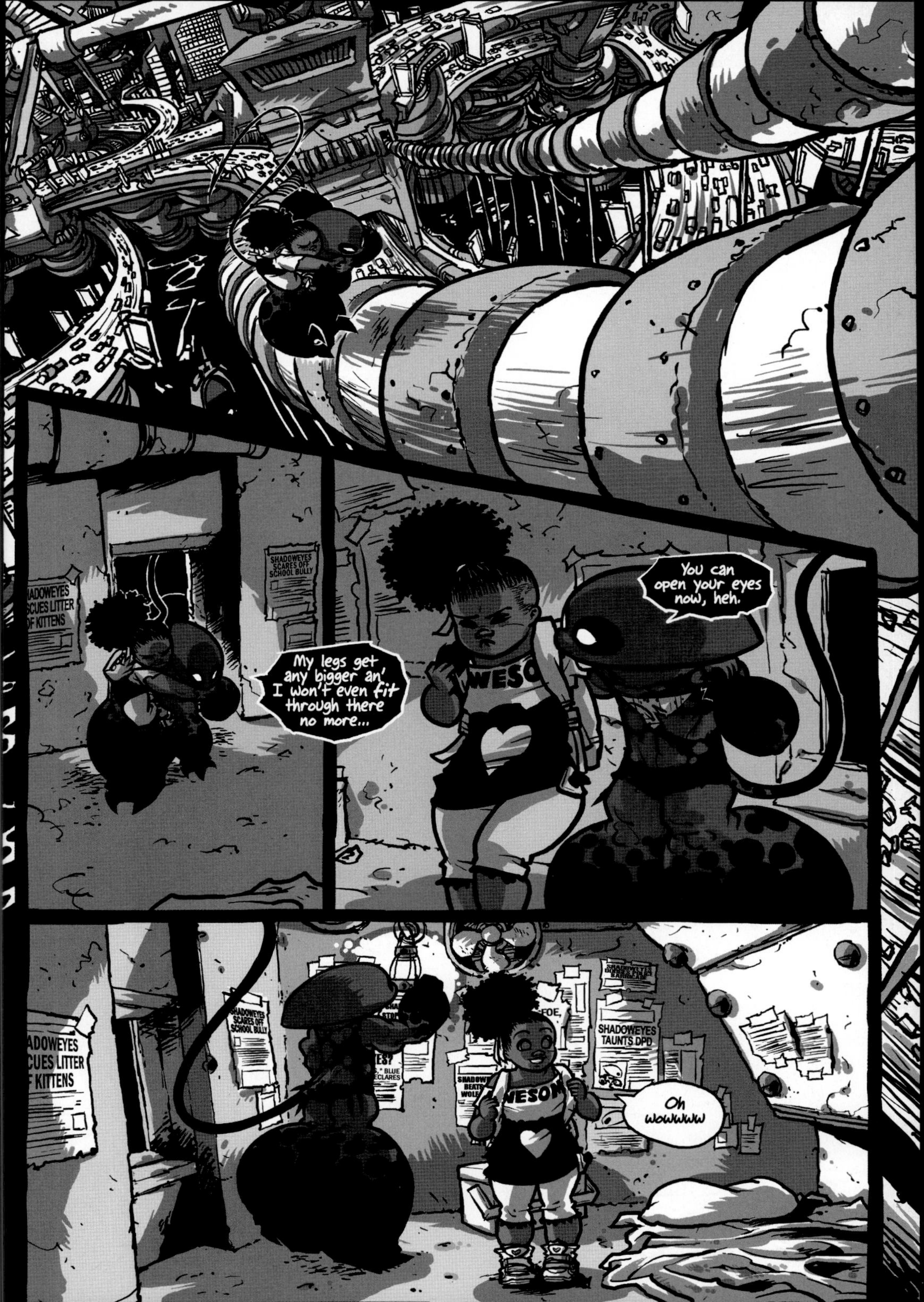
SHADOWEYES SCARES OFF SCHOOL BULLY
My legs get any bigger an' I won't even fit through there no more...
You can open your eyes now, heh.
SHADOWEYES SCARES OFF SCHOOL BULLY
SHADOWEYES TAUNTS DPD
Oh wowwww

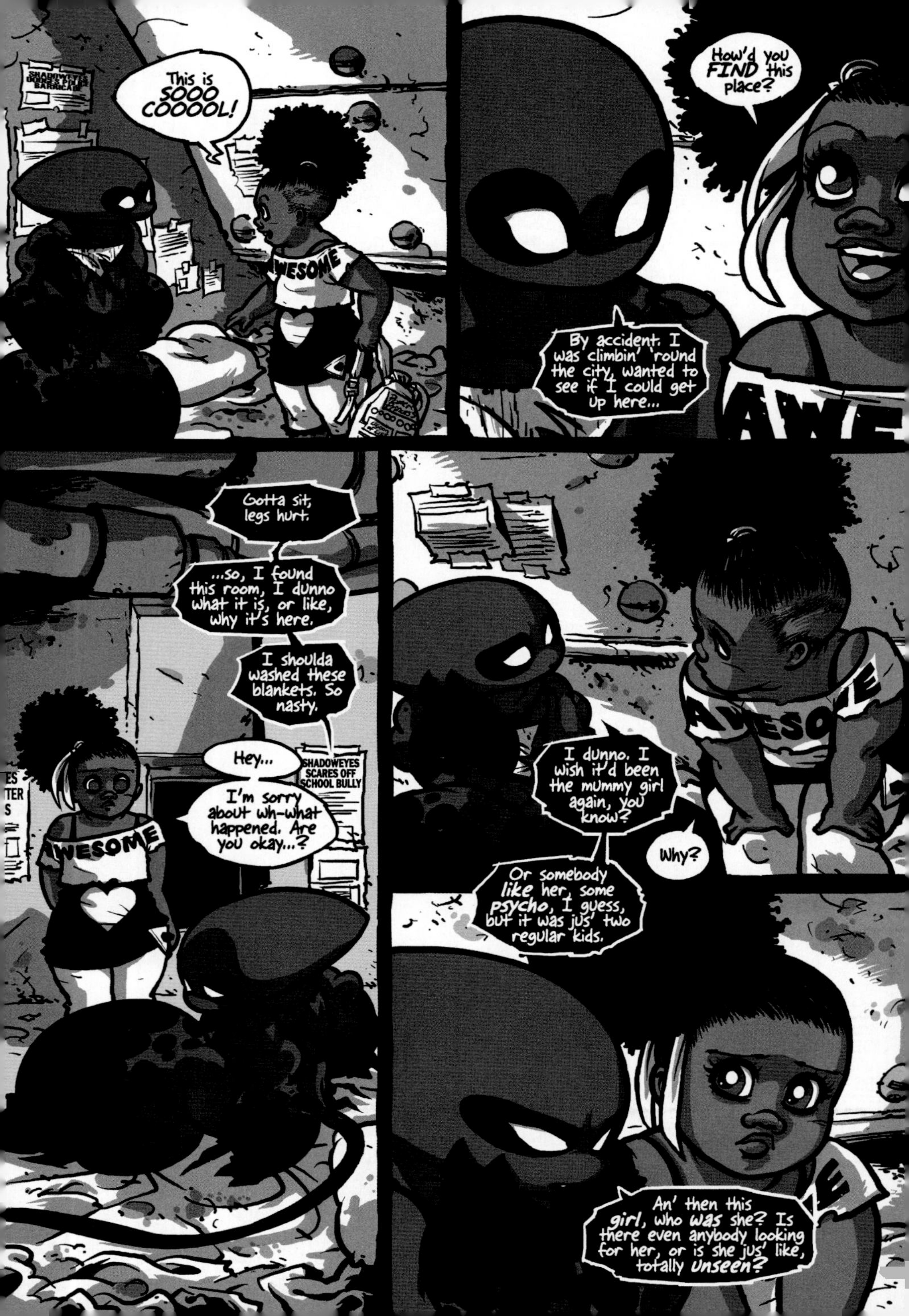
This is SOOO COOOOL!
AWESOME
How'd you FIND this place?
By accident. I was climbin' 'round the city, wanted to see if I could get up here...
Gotta sit, legs hurt.
...so, I found this room, I dunno what it is, or like, why it's here.
I shoulda washed these blankets. So nasty.
SHADOWEYES SCARES OFF SCHOOL BULLY
Hey...
I'm sorry about wh-what happened. Are you okay...?
AWESOME
I dunno. I wish it'd been the mummy girl again, you know?
Why?
Or somebody like her, some psycho, I guess, but it was jus' two regular kids.
An' then this girl, who was she? Is there even anybody looking for her, or is she jus' like, totally unseen?

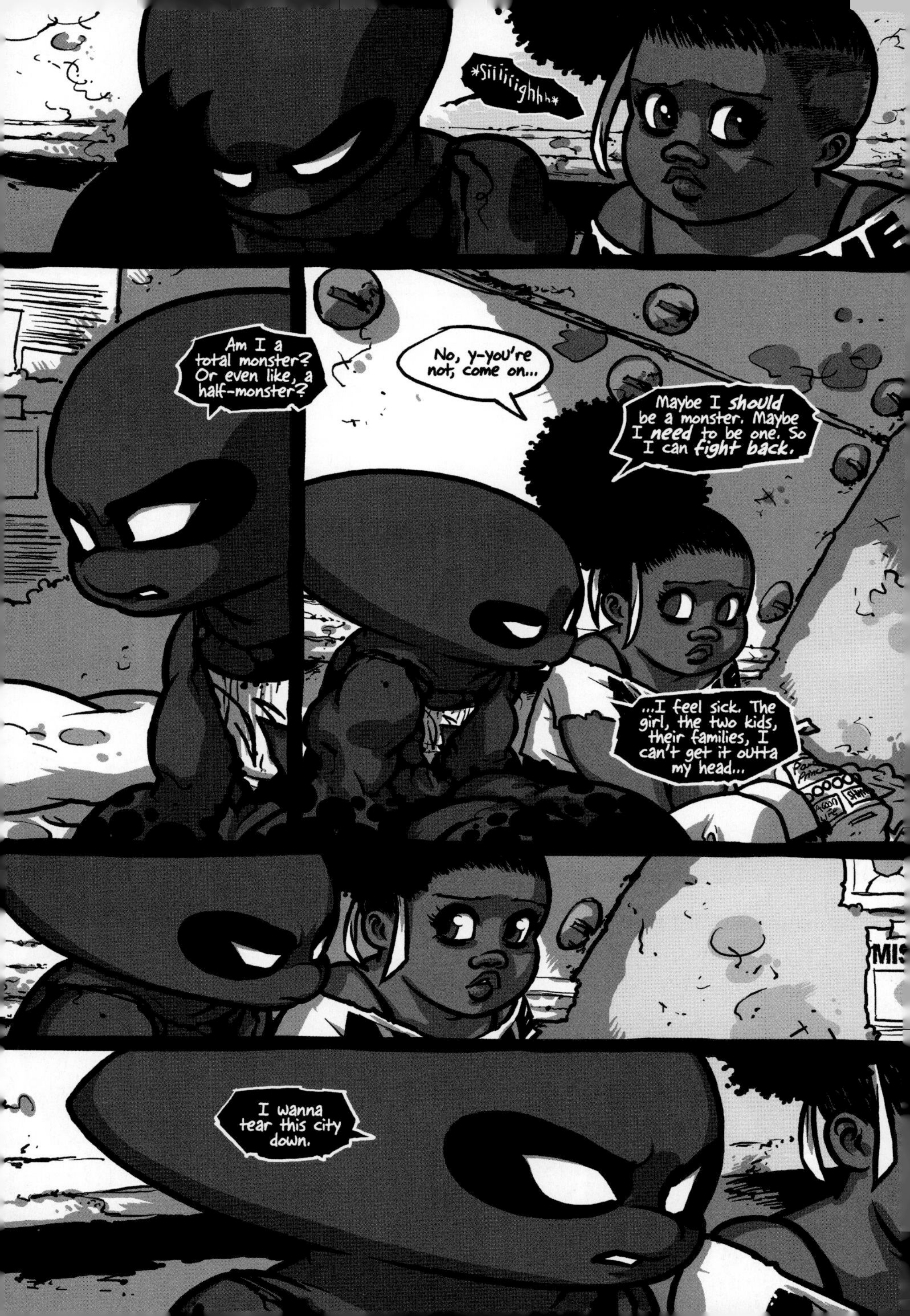
Siiiiighhh
Am I a total monster? Or even like, a half-monster?
No, y-you're not, come on...
Maybe I should be a monster. Maybe I need to be one. So I can fight back.
...I feel sick. The girl, the two kids, their families, I can't get it outta my head...
I wanna tear this city down.

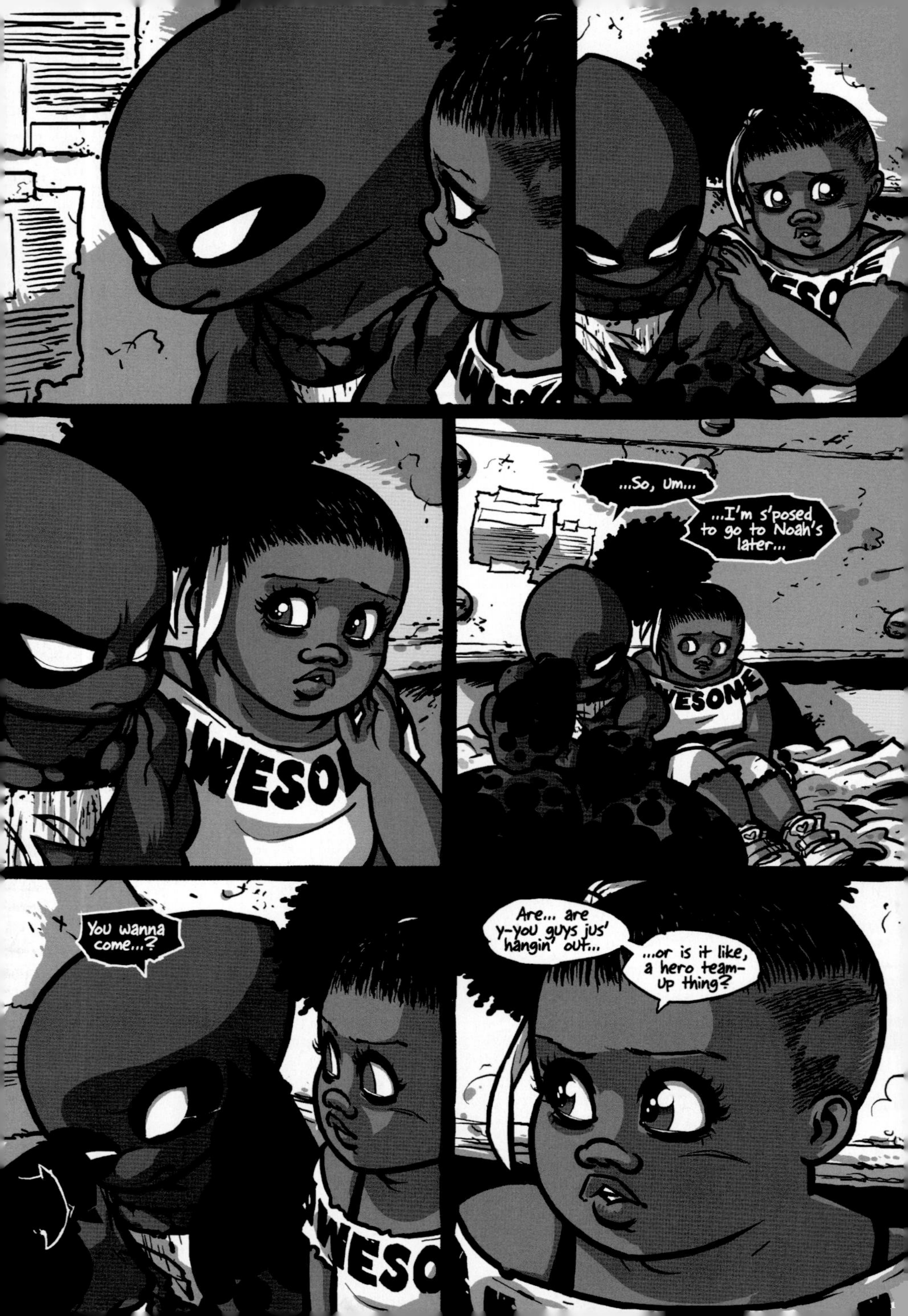
...So, um...
...I'm s'posed to go to Noah's later...
You wanna come...?
Are... are y-you guys jus' hangin' out...
...or is it like, a hero team-up thing?

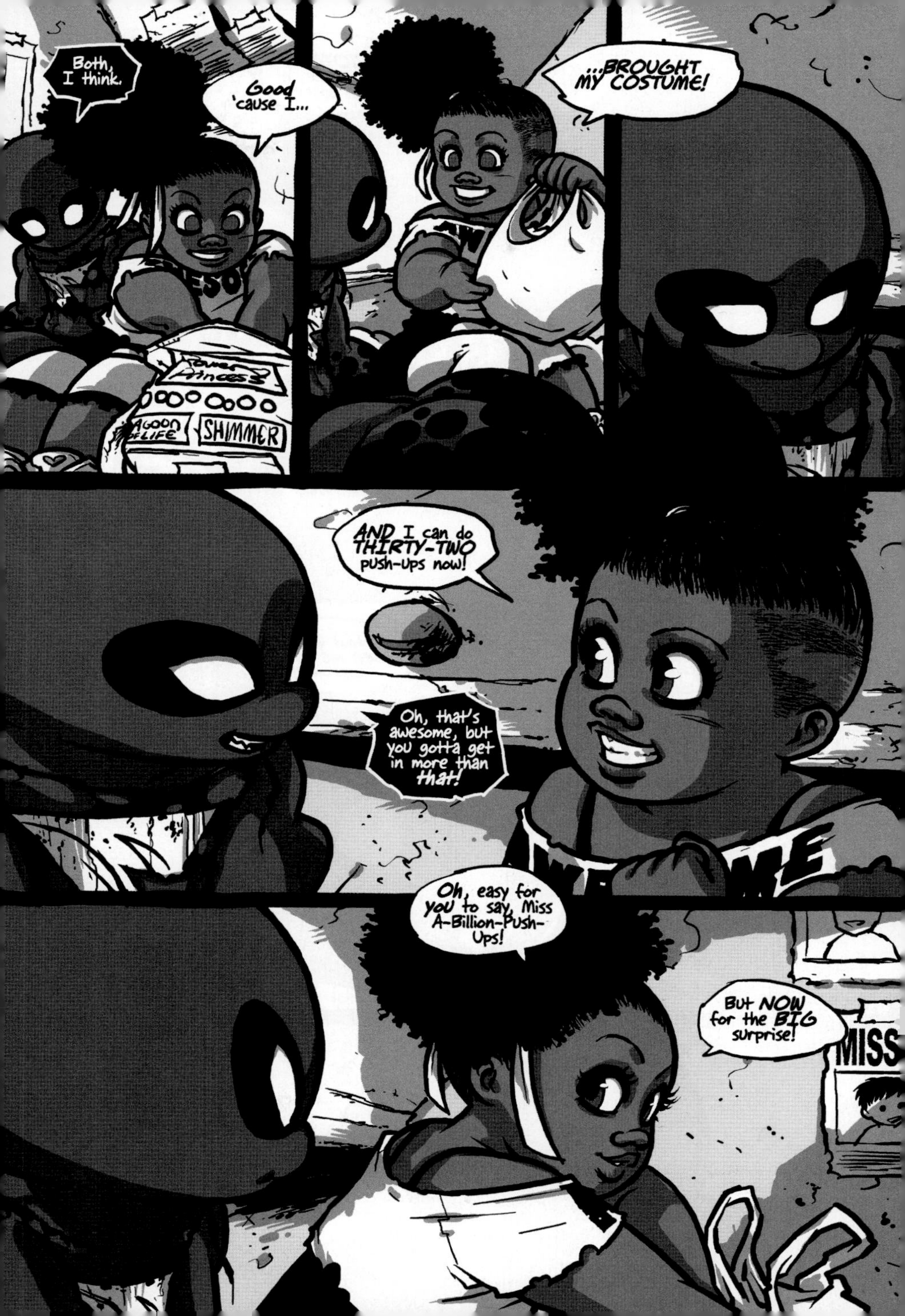
Both, I think.
Good 'cause I...
Power Princess
LAGOON OF LIFE
SHIMMER
...BROUGHT MY COSTUME!
AND I can do THIRTY-TWO push-ups now!
Oh, that's awesome, but you gotta get in more than that!
Oh, easy for you to say, Miss A-Billion-Push-Ups!
But NOW for the BIG surprise!
MISS

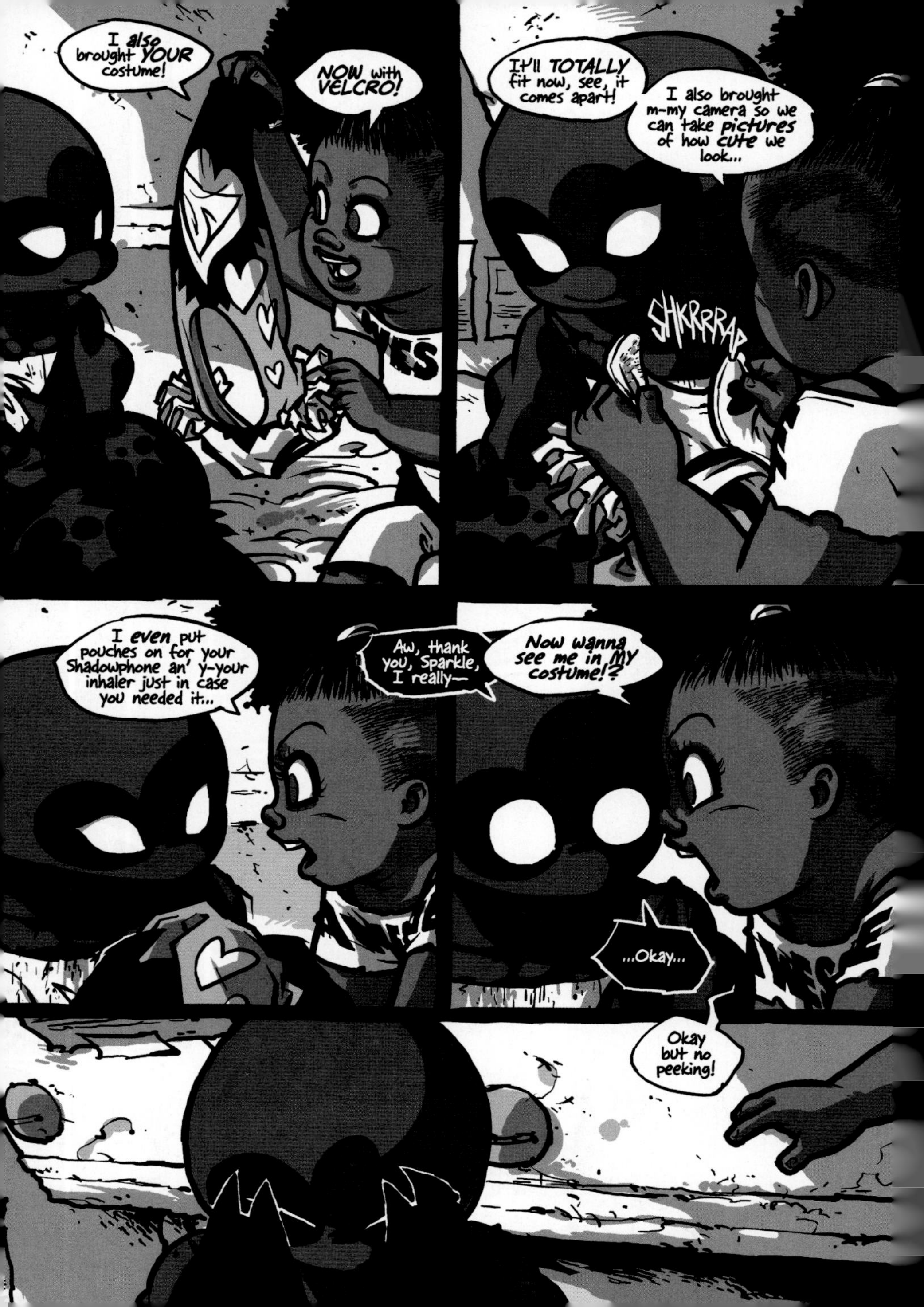
I also brought YOUR costume!
NOW with VELCRO!
It'll TOTALLY fit now, see, it comes apart!
I also brought m-my camera so we can take pictures of how cute we look...
SHKRRRAP
I even put pouches on for your Shadowphone an' y-your inhaler just in case you needed it...
Aw, thank you, Sparkle, I really—
Now wanna see me in MY costume!?
...Okay...
Okay but no peeking!

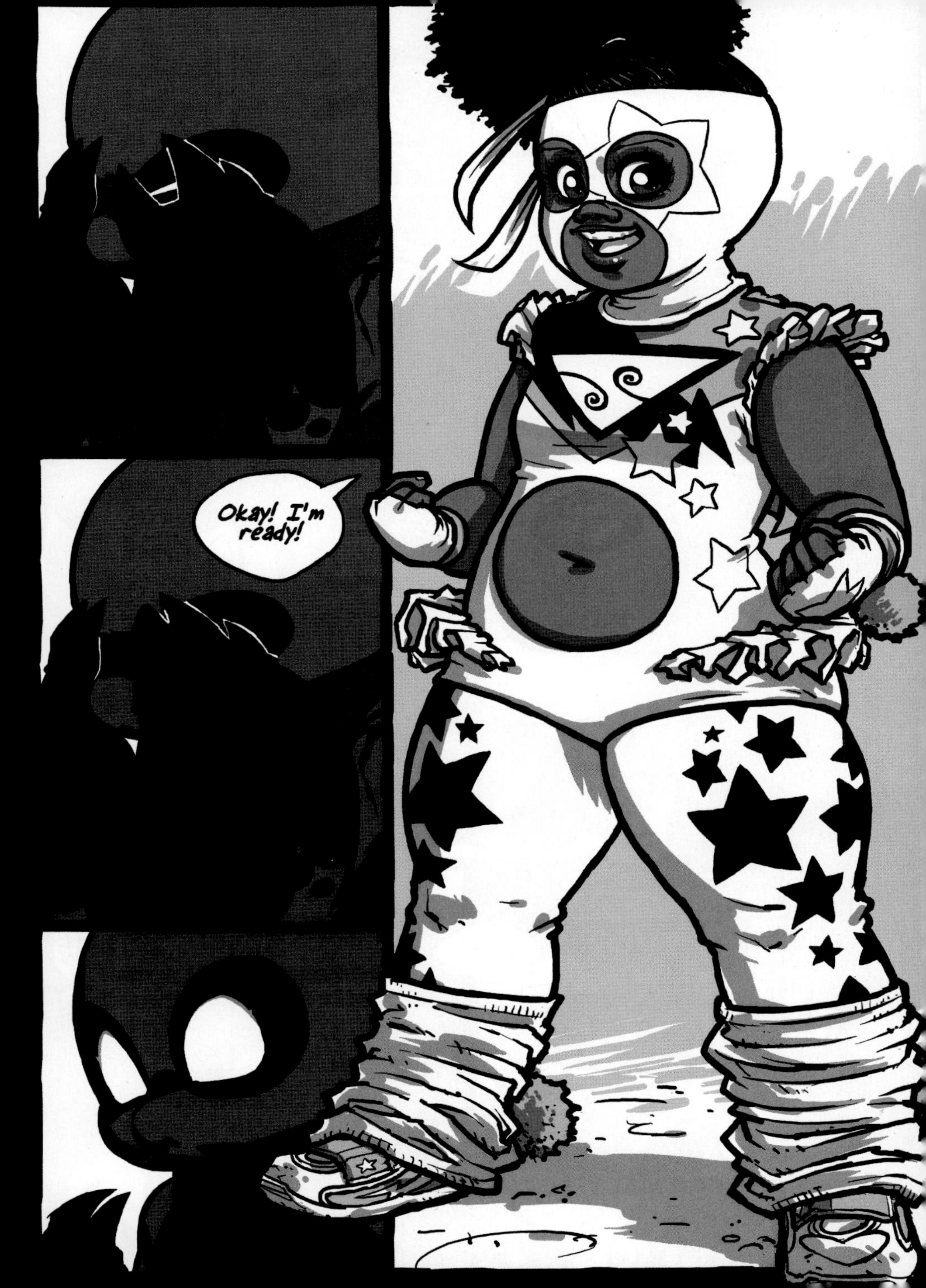
Okay! I'm ready!

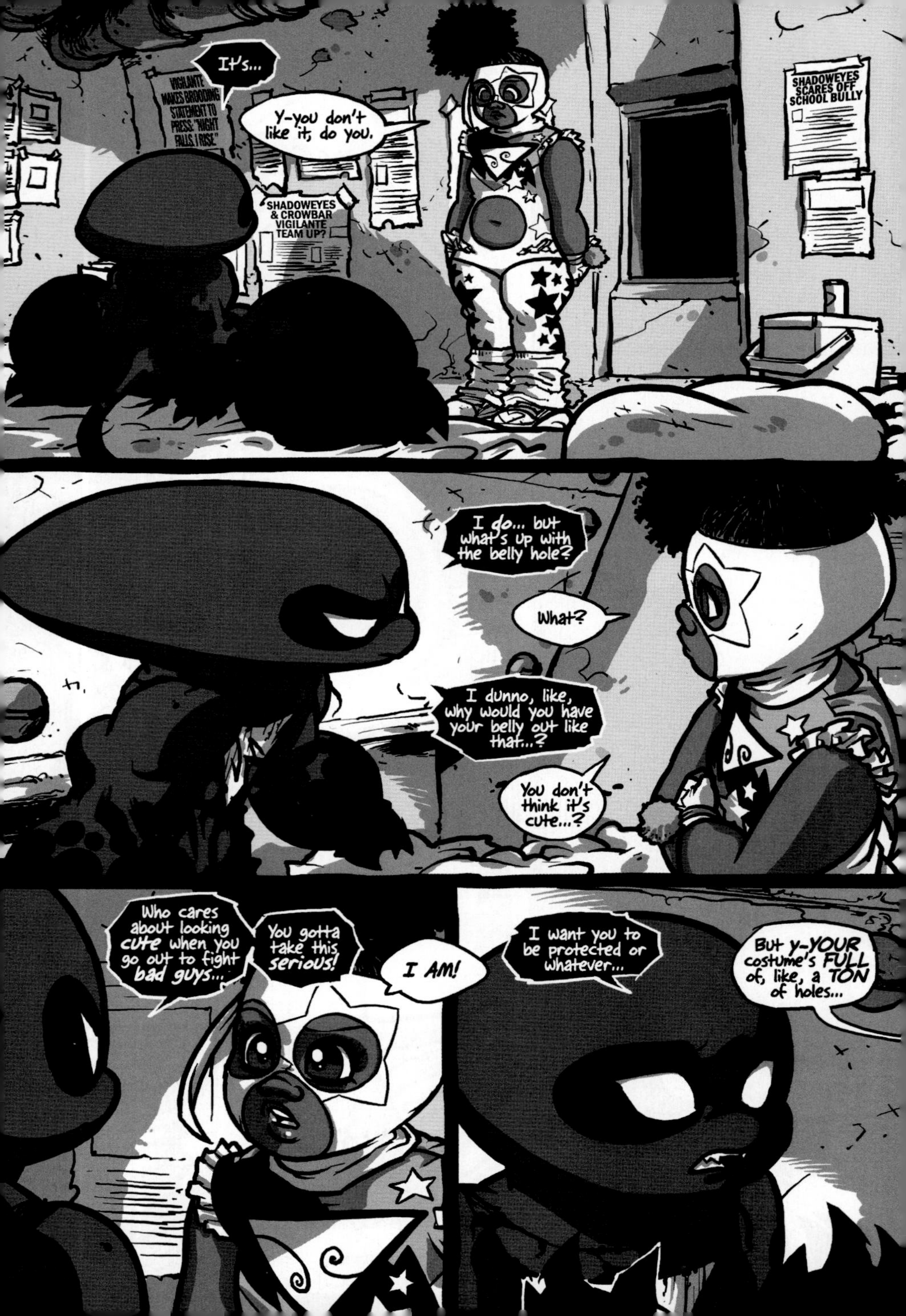

VIGILANTE MAKES BROODING STATEMENT TO PRESS: "NIGHT FALLS, I RISE"
It's...
Y-you don't like it, do you.
SHADOWEYES SCARES OFF SCHOOL BULLY
SHADOWEYES & CROWBAR VIGILANTE TEAM UP?
I do... but what's up with the belly hole?
What?
I dunno, like, why would you have your belly out like that...?
You don't think it's cute...?
Who cares about looking cute when you go out to fight bad guys...
You gotta take this serious!
I AM!
I want you to be protected or whatever...
But y-YOUR costume's FULL of, like, a TON of holes...

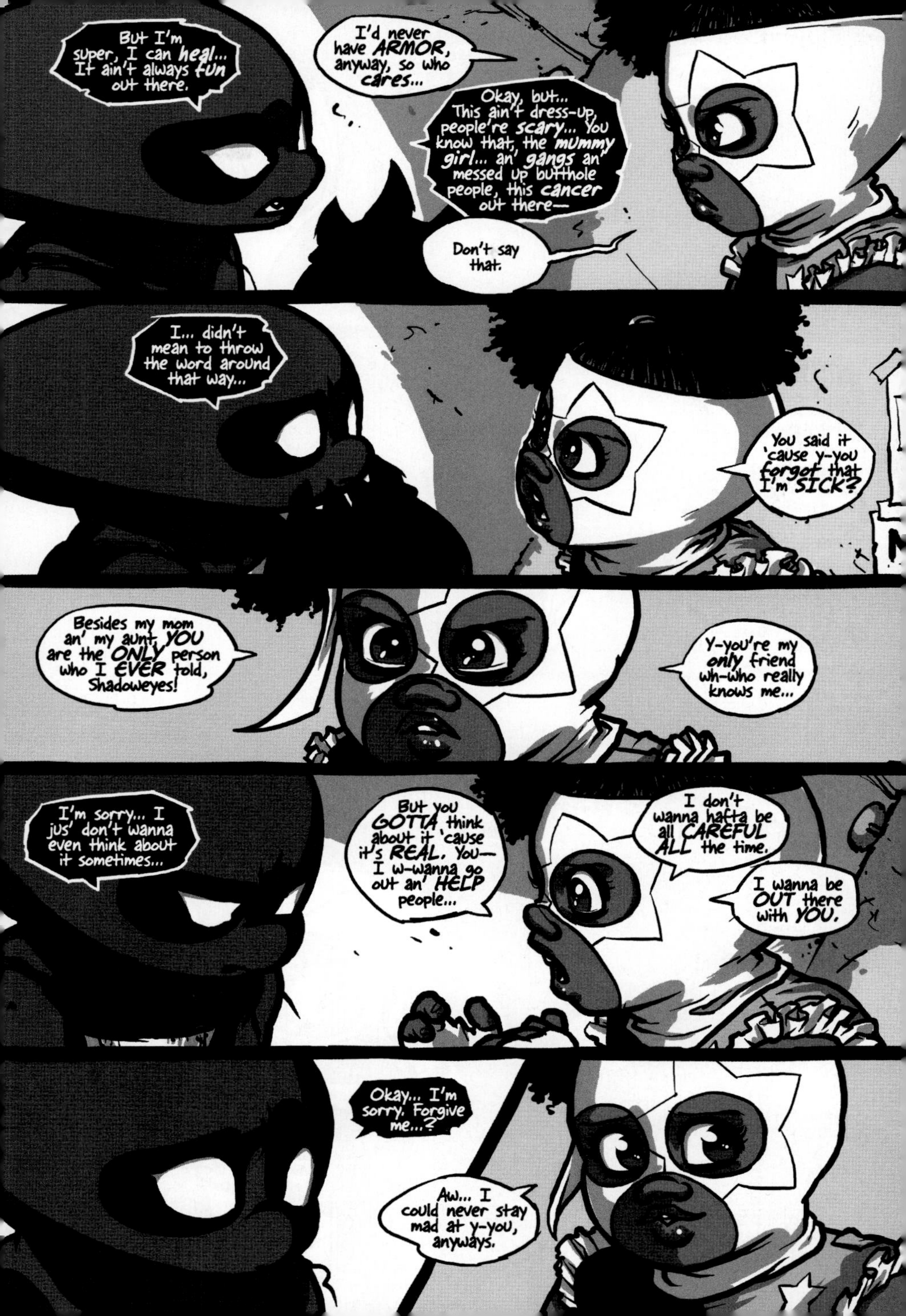
But I'm super, I can heal... It ain't always fun out there.
I'd never have ARMOR, anyway, so who cares...
Okay, but... This ain't dress-up, people're scary... You know that, the mummy girl... an' gangs an' messed up butthole people, this cancer out there—
Don't say that.
I... didn't mean to throw the word around that way...
You said it 'cause y-you forgot that I'm SICK?
Besides my mom an' my aunt, YOU are the ONLY person who I EVER told, Shadoweyes!
Y-you're my only friend wh-who really knows me...
I'm sorry... I jus' don't wanna even think about it sometimes...
But you GOTTA think about it 'cause it's REAL. You— I w-wanna go out an' HELP people...
I don't wanna hafta be all CAREFUL ALL the time.
I wanna be OUT there with YOU.
Okay... I'm sorry. Forgive me...?
Aw... I could never stay mad at y-you, anyways.

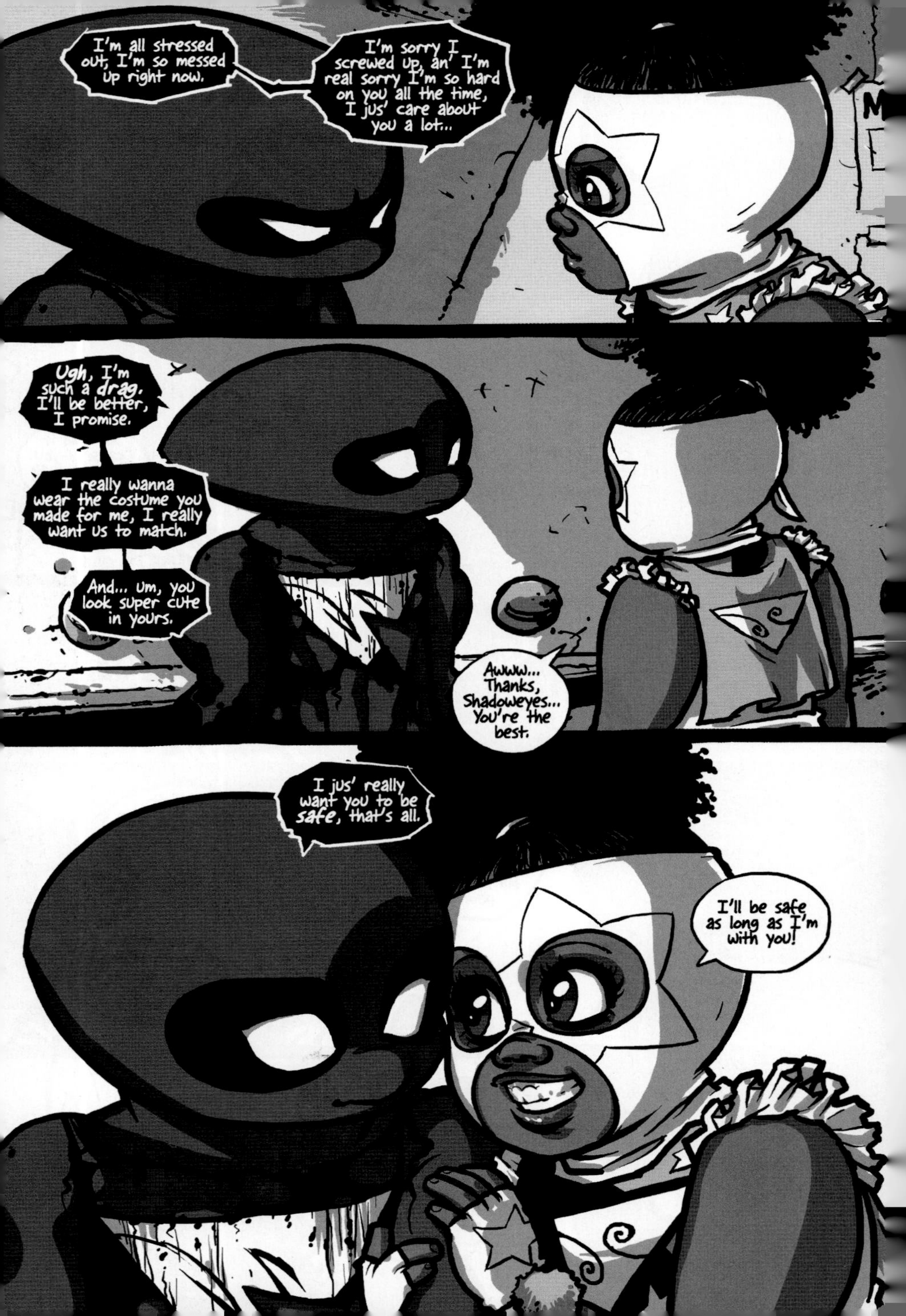

I'm all stressed out, I'm so messed up right now.
I'm sorry I screwed up, an' I'm real sorry I'm so hard on you all the time, I jus' care about you a lot...
Ugh, I'm such a drag. I'll be better, I promise.
I really wanna wear the costume you made for me, I really want us to match.
And... um, you look super cute in yours.
Awww... Thanks, Shadoweyes... You're the best.
I jus' really want you to be safe, that's all.
I'll be safe as long as I'm with you!

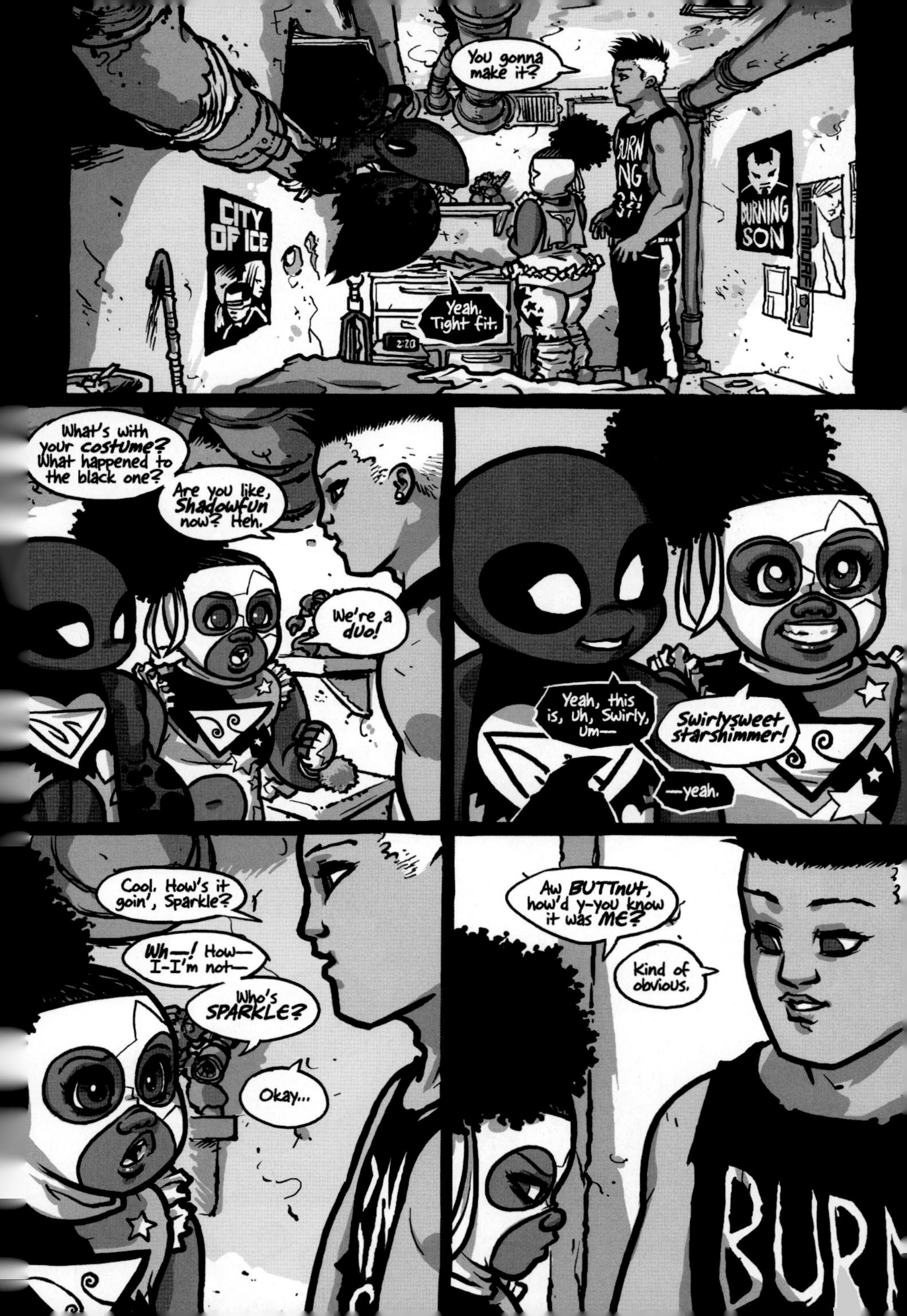
You gonna make it?
Yeah. Tight fit.
CITY OF ICE
BURNING SON
METAMORF
2:20
What's with your costume? What happened to the black one?
Are you like, Shadowfun now? Heh.
We're a duo!
Yeah, this is, uh, Swirly, um—
Swirlysweet starshimmer!
—yeah.
Cool. How's it goin', Sparkle?
Wh—! How— I-I'm not—
Who's SPARKLE?
Okay...
Aw BUTTNUT, how'd y-you know it was ME?
Kind of obvious.
BURN

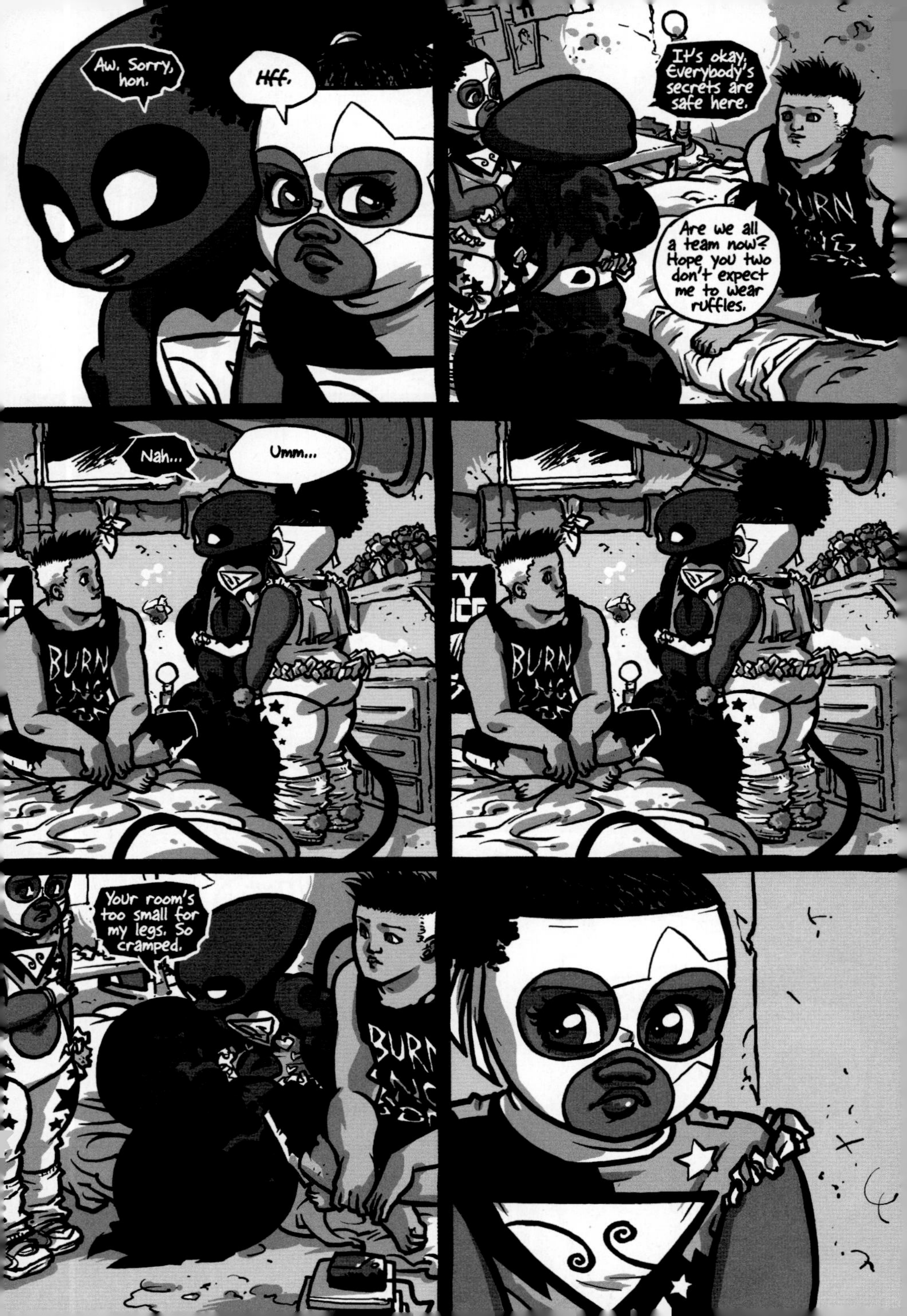
Aw. Sorry, hon.
Hff.
It's okay. Everybody's secrets are safe here.
Are we all a team now? Hope you two don't expect me to wear ruffles.
Nah...
Umm...
Your room's too small for my legs. So cramped.

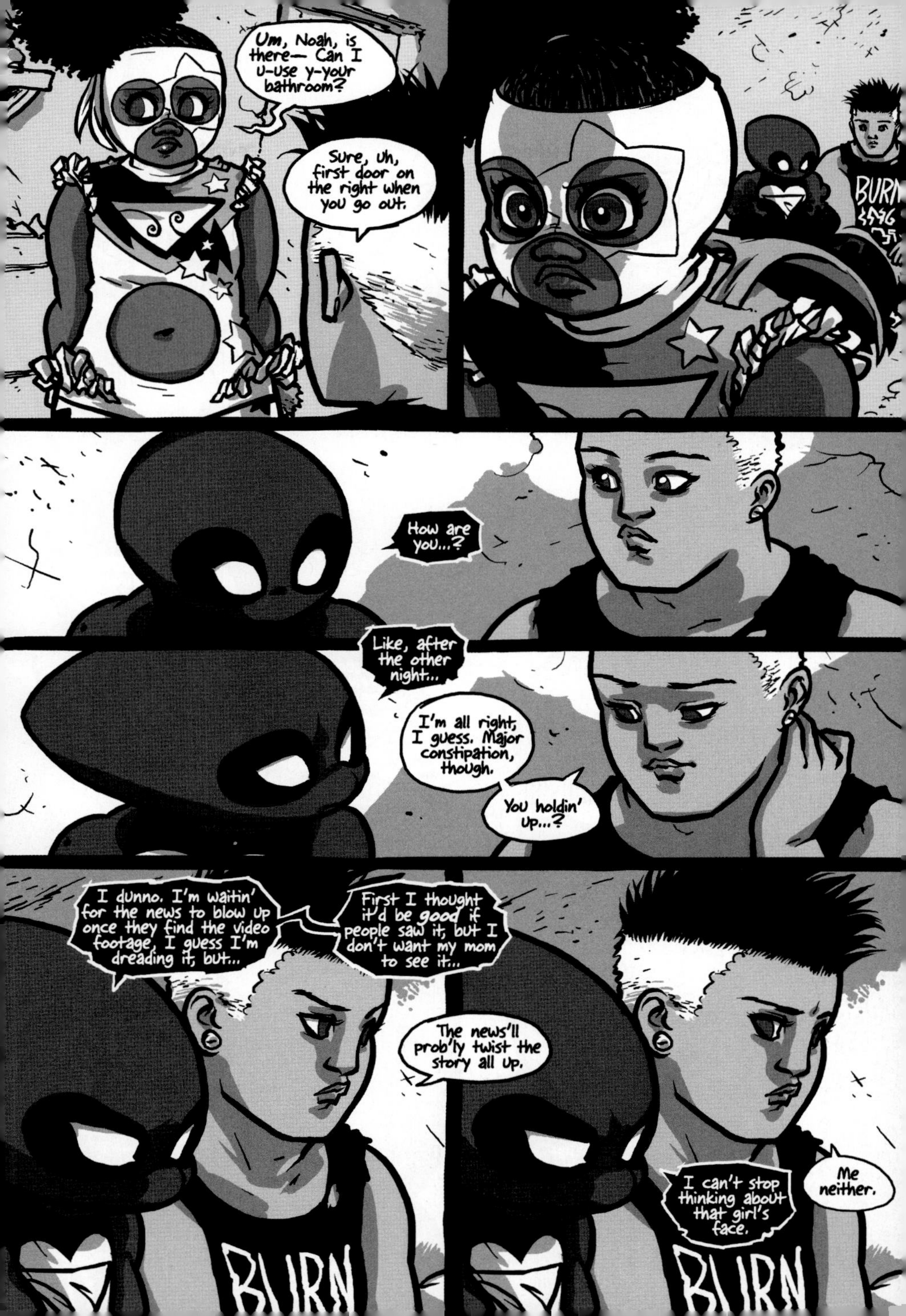
Um, Noah, is there— Can I u-use y-your bathroom?
Sure, uh, first door on the right when you go out.
BURN
How are you...?
Like, after the other night...
I'm all right, I guess. Major constipation, though.
You holdin' up...?
I dunno. I'm waitin' for the news to blow up once they find the video footage, I guess I'm dreading it, but...
First I thought it'd be good if people saw it, but I don't want my mom to see it...
The news'll prob'ly twist the story all up.
BURN
I can't stop thinking about that girl's face.
Me neither.
BURN

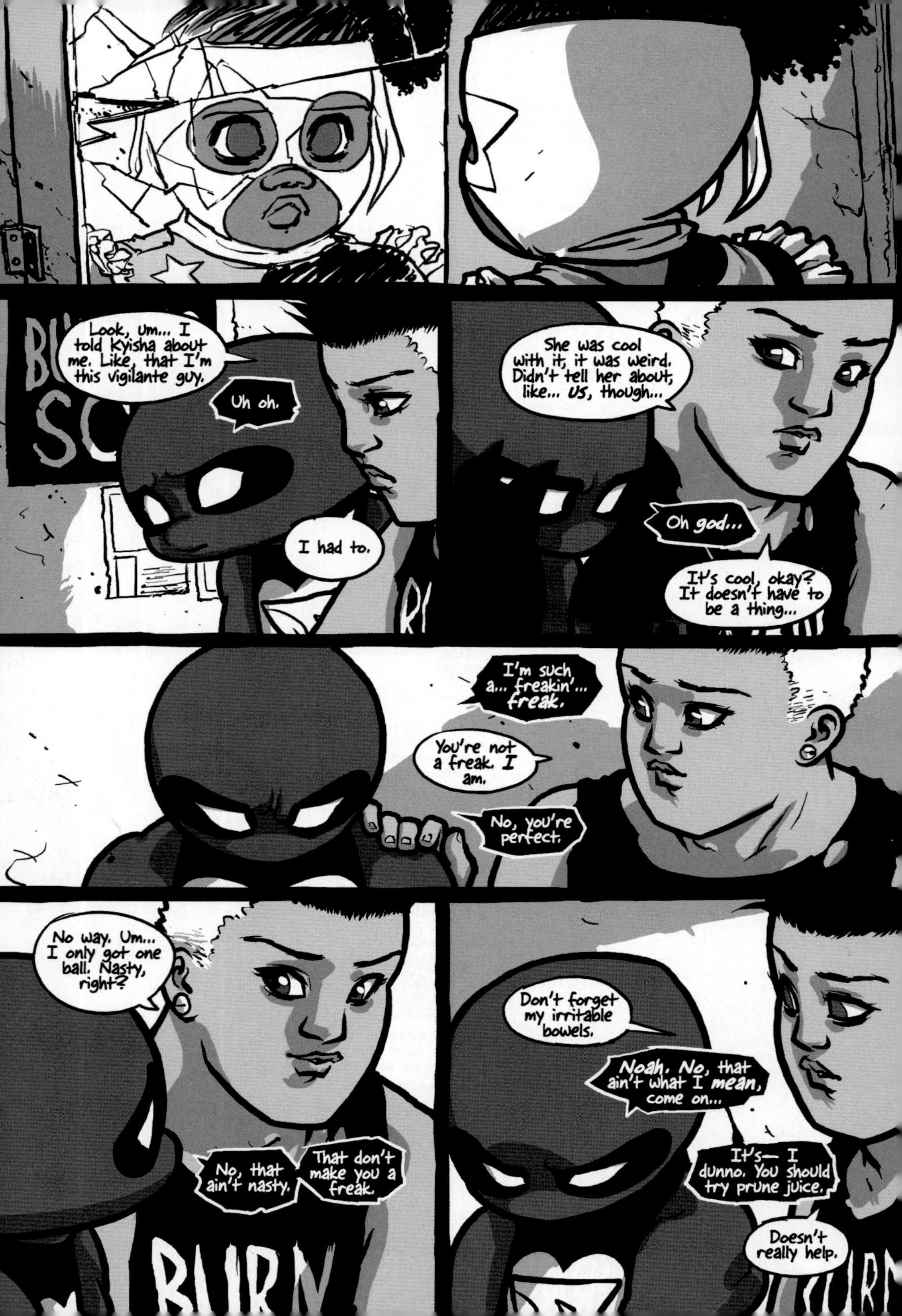
Look, um... I told Kyisha about me. Like, that I'm this vigilante guy.
Uh oh.
I had to.
She was cool with it, it was weird. Didn't tell her about, like... US, though...
Oh god...
It's cool, okay? It doesn't have to be a thing...
I'm such a... freakin'... freak.
You're not a freak. I am.
No, you're perfect.
No way. Um... I only got one ball. Nasty, right?
No, that ain't nasty.
That don't make you a freak.
Don't forget my irritable bowels.
Noah. No, that ain't what I mean, come on...
It's— I dunno. You should try prune juice.
Doesn't really help.

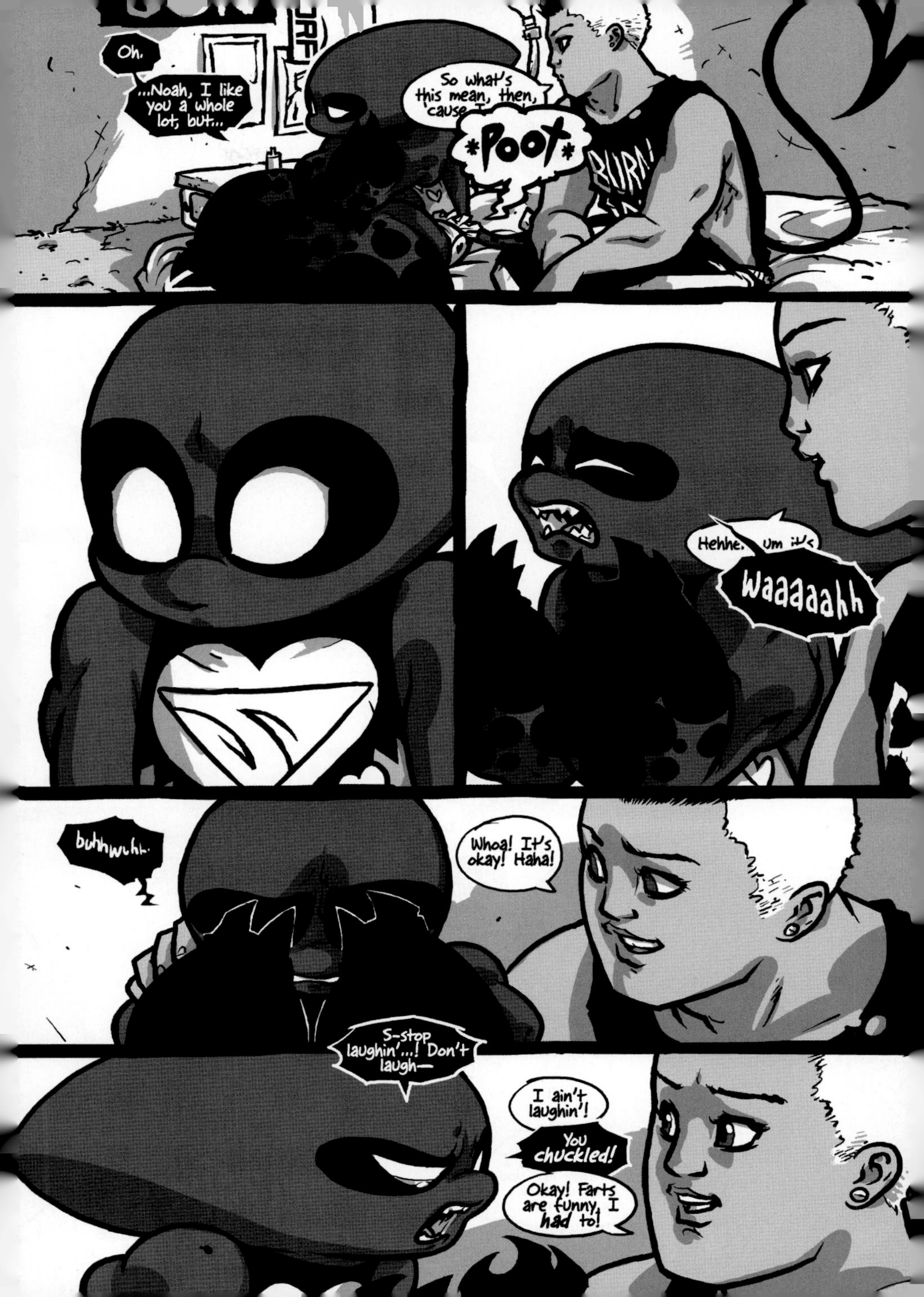

Oh.
...Noah, I like you a whole lot, but...
So what's this mean, then, cause I
POOT
Hehhe. um it's
waaaaahh
buhhwuhh.
Whoa! It's okay! Haha!
S-stop laughin'...! Don't laugh—
I ain't laughin'!
You chuckled!
Okay! Farts are funny, I had to!

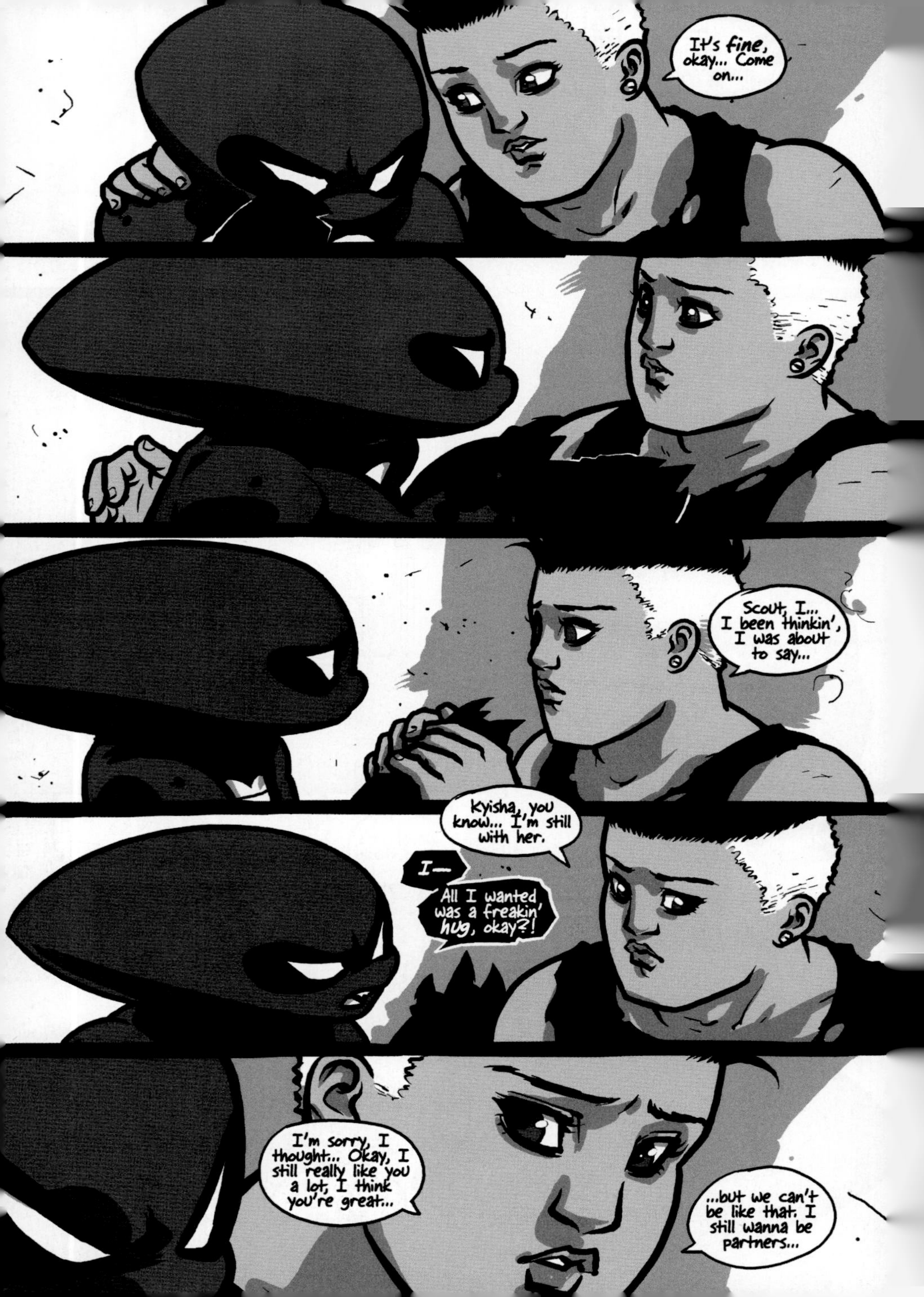

It's fine, okay... Come on...
Scout, I... I been thinkin', I was about to say...
Kyisha, you know... I'm still with her.
I—
All I wanted was a freakin' hug, okay?!
I'm sorry, I thought... Okay, I still really like you a lot, I think you're great...
...but we can't be like that. I still wanna be partners...

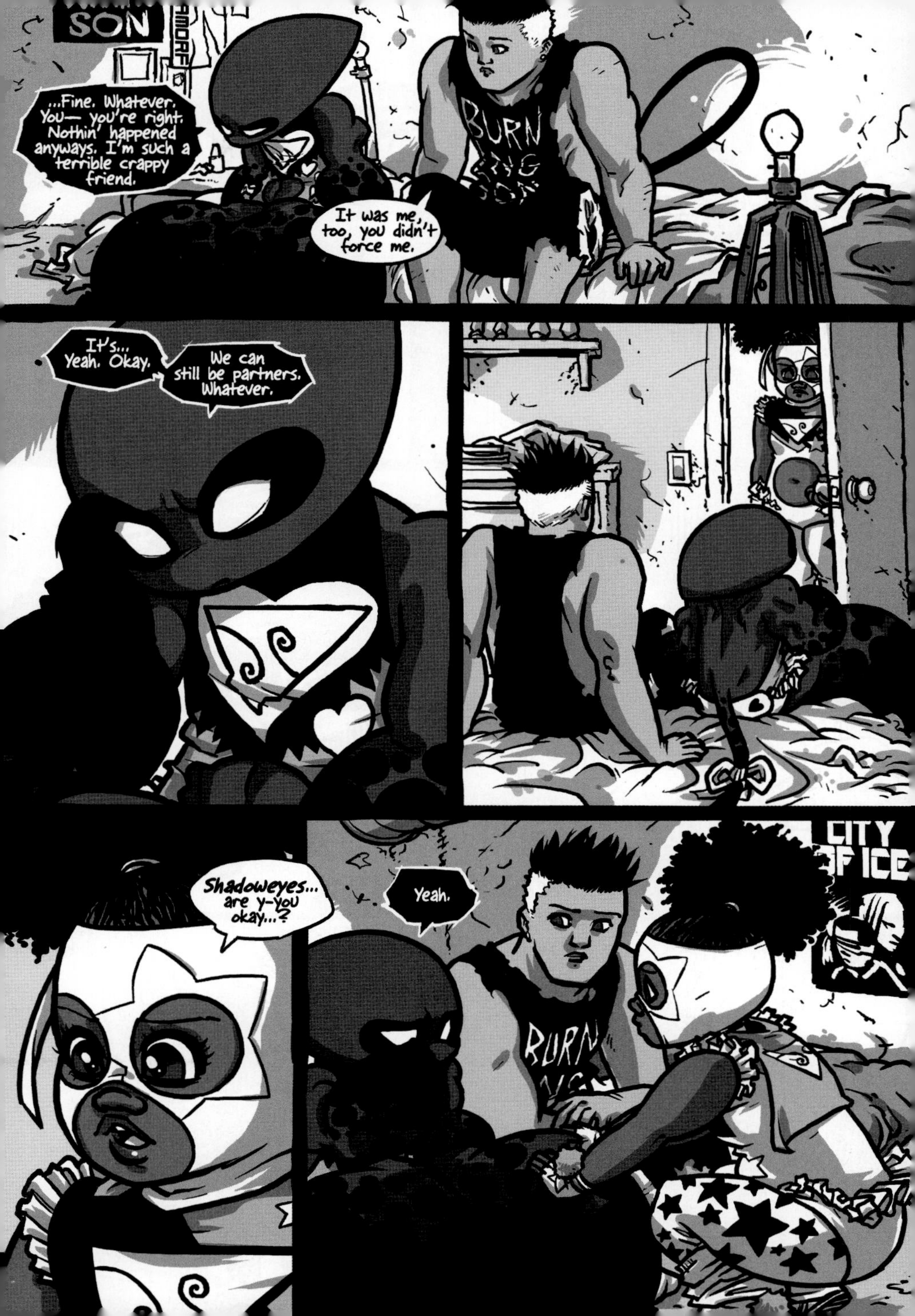
SON
...Fine. Whatever. You— you're right. Nothin' happened anyways. I'm such a terrible crappy friend.
It was me, too, you didn't force me.
It's... Yeah. Okay.
We can still be partners. Whatever.
Shadoweyes... are y-you okay...?
Yeah.
CITY OF ICE

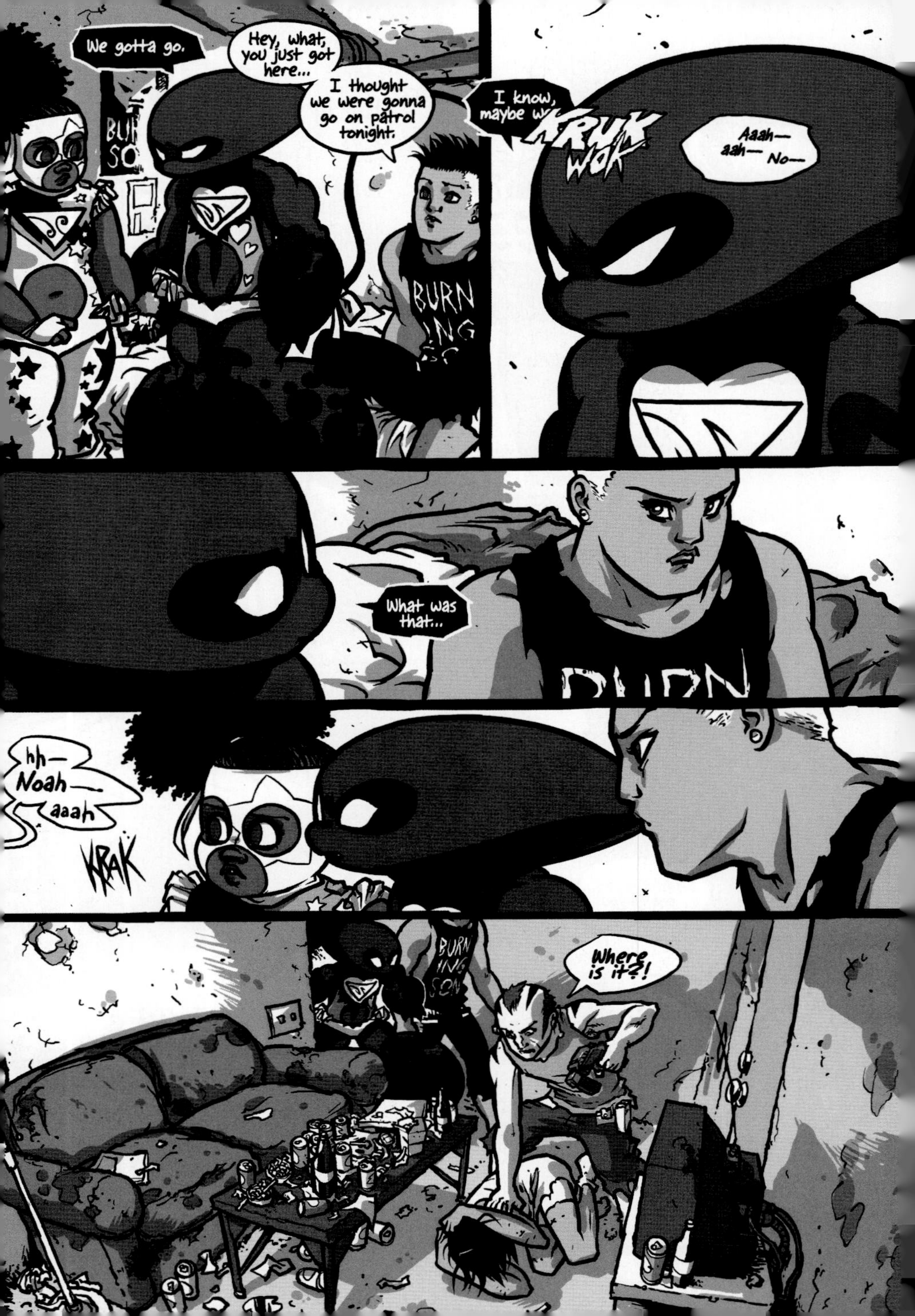

We gotta go.
Hey, what, you just got here...
I thought we were gonna go on patrol tonight.
I know, maybe w
KRUK WOK
Aaah— aah— No—
What was that...
hh— Noah— aaah
KRAK
Where is it?!

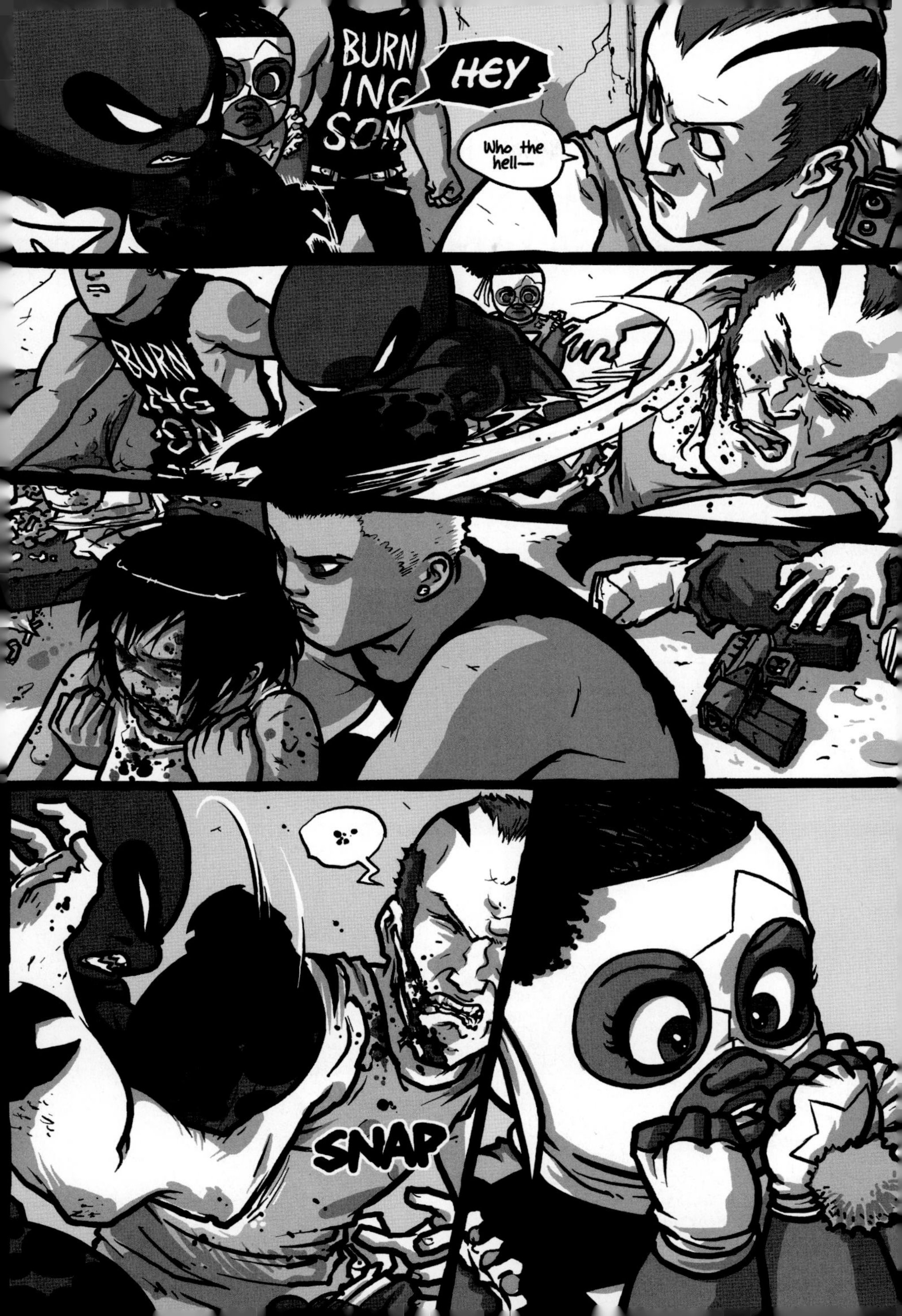
BURNING SON
HEY
Who the hell—
SNAP

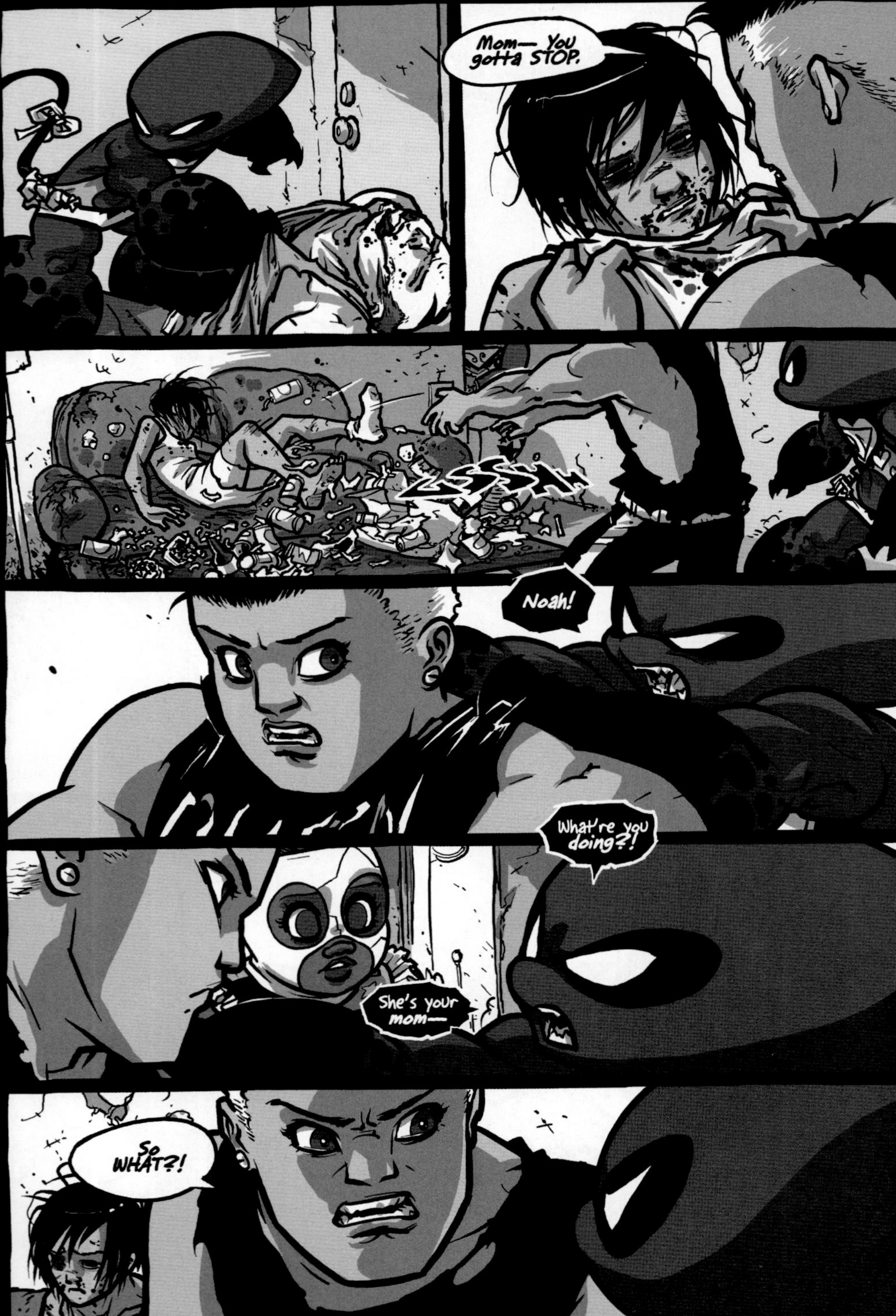
Mom— You gotta STOP.
Noah!
What're you doing?!
She's your mom—
So WHAT?!

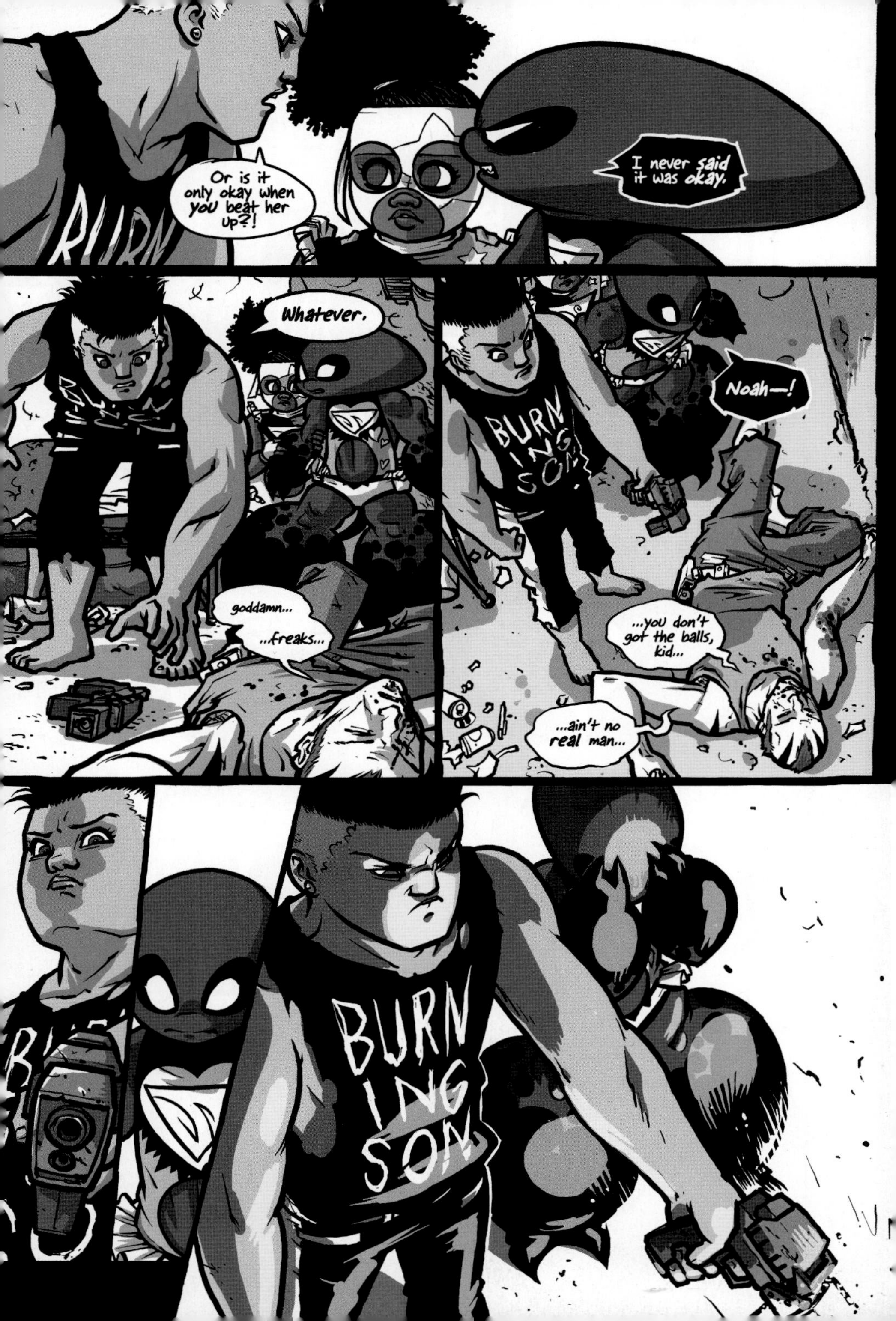
Or is it only okay when you beat her up?!
I never said it was okay.
Whatever.
goddamn...
...freaks...
Noah—!
...you don't got the balls, kid...
...ain't no real man...
BURN ING SON

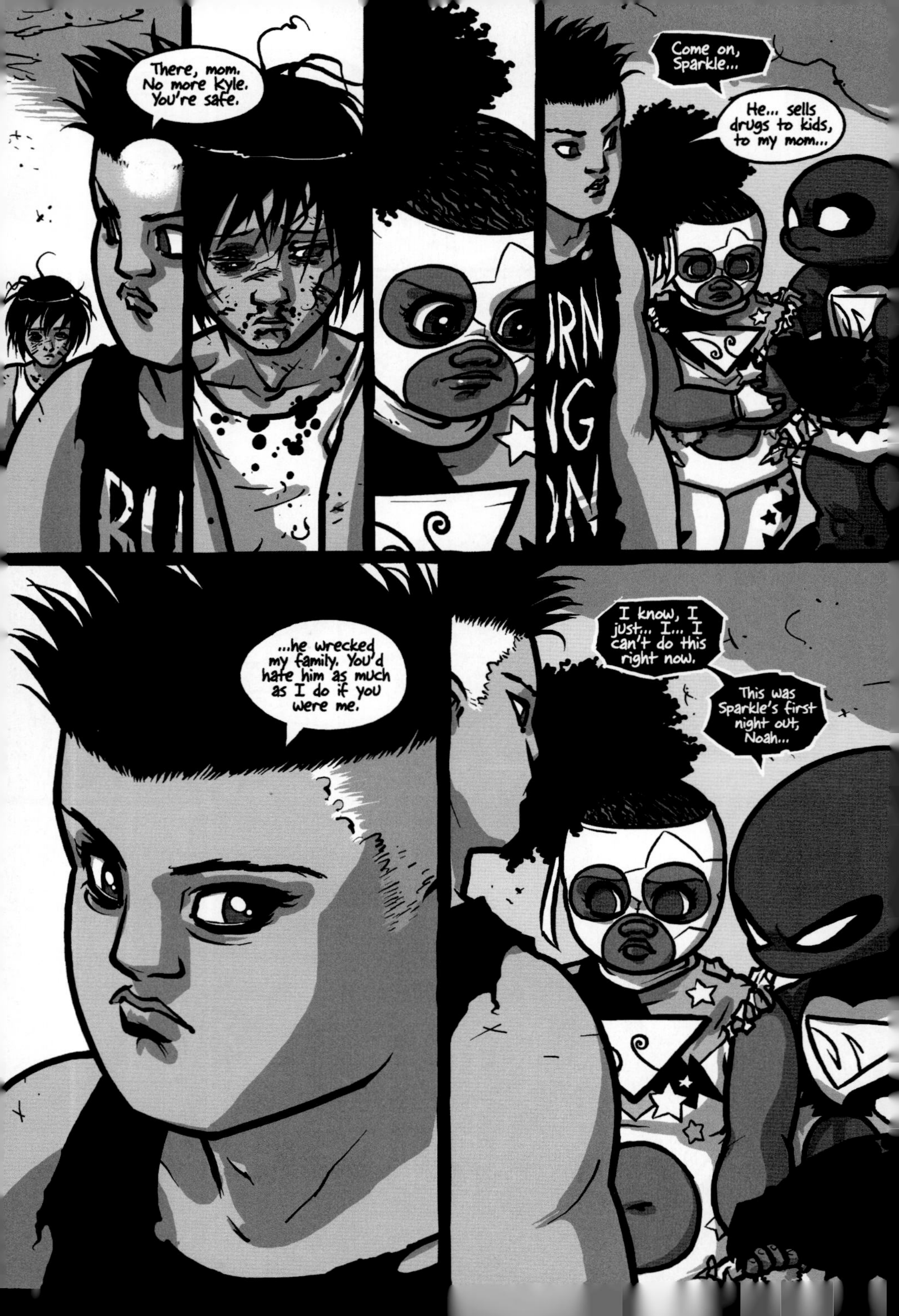
There, mom. No more Kyle. You're safe.
Come on, Sparkle...
He... sells drugs to kids, to my mom...
...he wrecked my family. You'd hate him as much as I do if you were me.
I know, I just... I... I can't do this right now.
This was Sparkle's first night out, Noah...

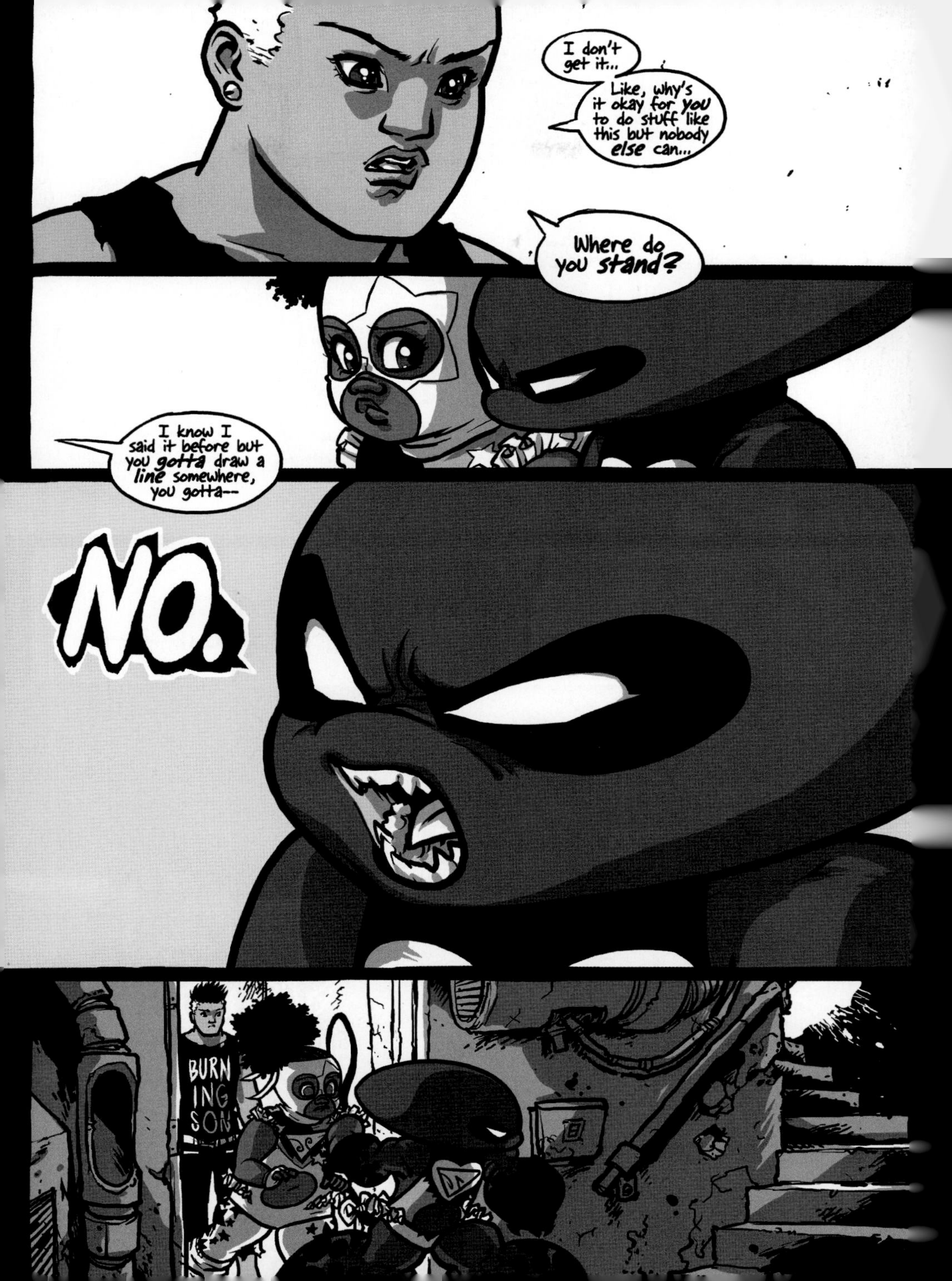

I don't get it...
Like, why's it okay for you to do stuff like this but nobody else can...
Where do you stand?
I know I said it before but you gotta draw a line somewhere, you gotta--
NO.
BURNING SON

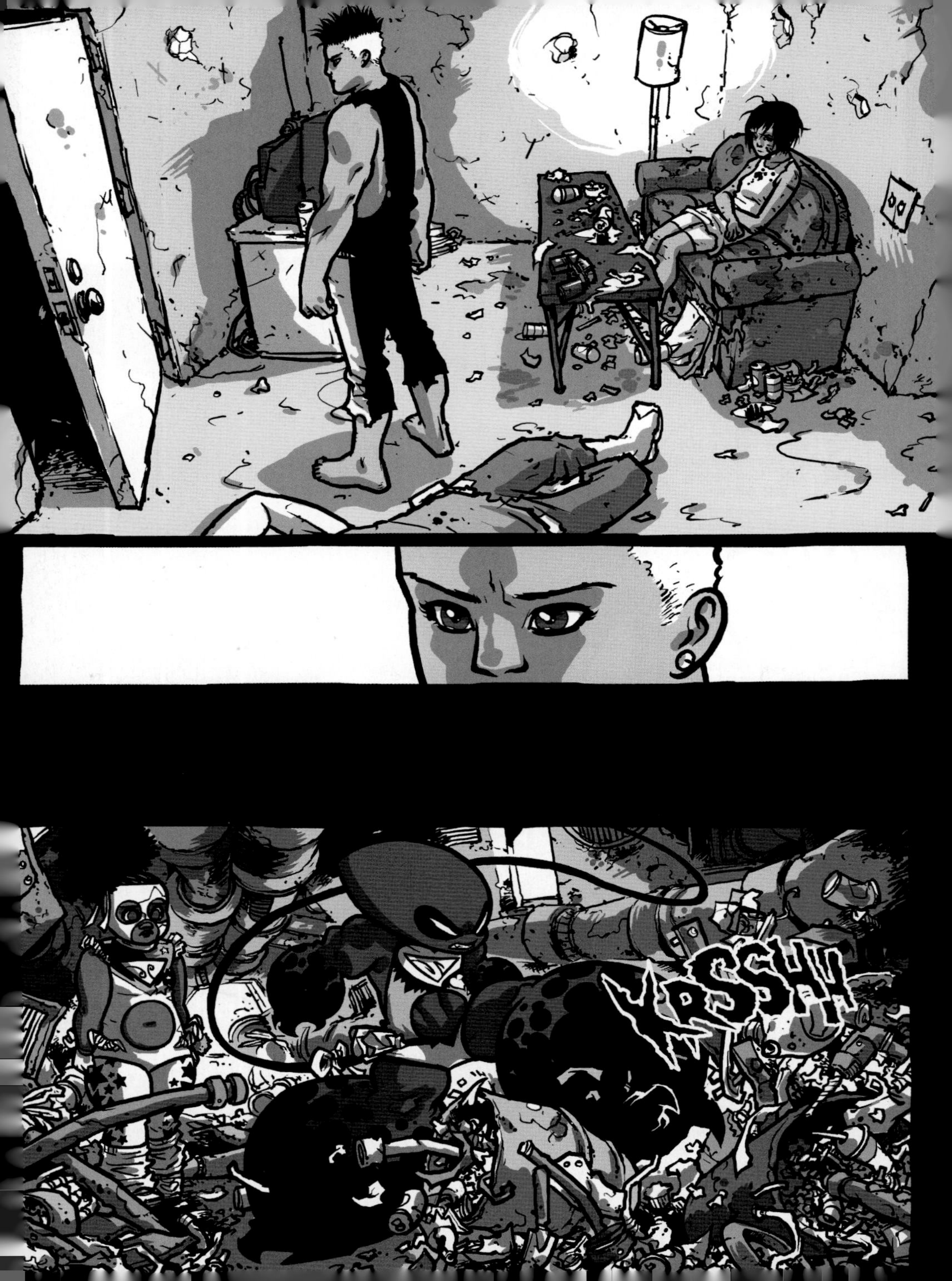
VRSSHH

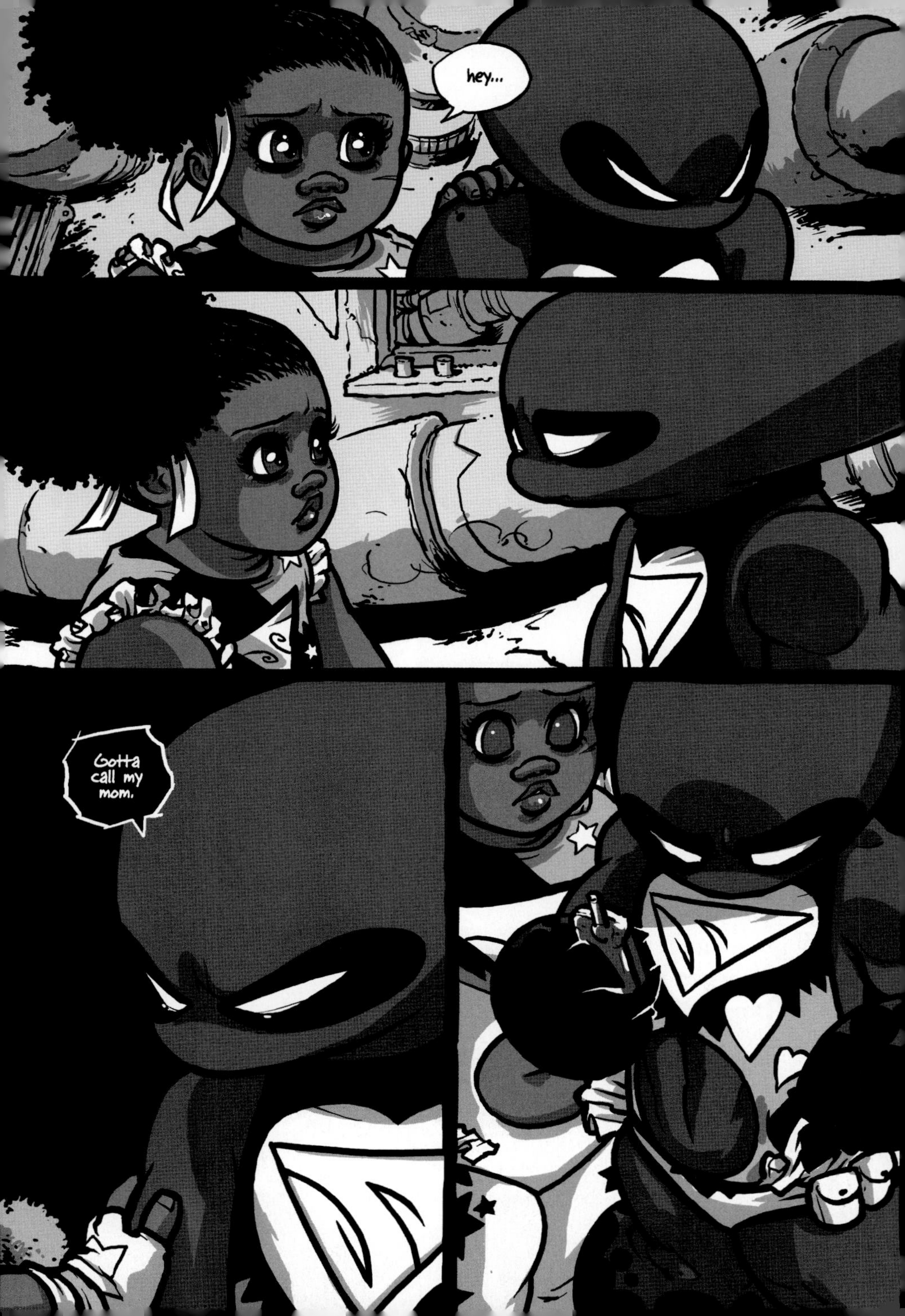
hey...
Gotta call my mom.

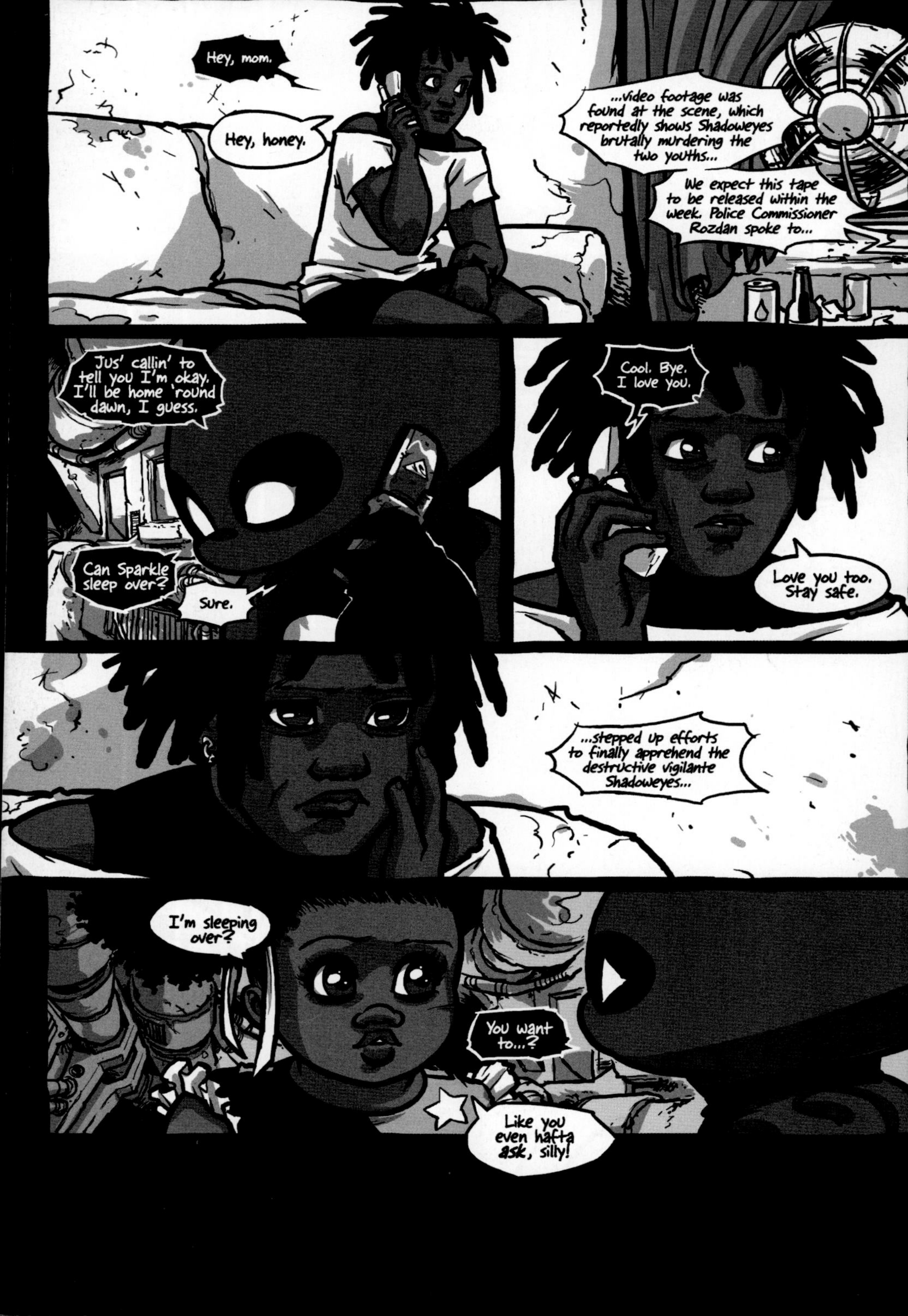
Hey, mom.
Hey, honey.
...video footage was found at the scene, which reportedly shows Shadoweyes brutally murdering the two youths...
We expect this tape to be released within the week. Police Commissioner Rozdan spoke to...
Jus' callin' to tell you I'm okay. I'll be home 'round dawn, I guess.
Can Sparkle sleep over?
Sure.
Cool. Bye. I love you.
Love you too. Stay safe.
...stepped up efforts to finally apprehend the destructive vigilante Shadoweyes...
I'm sleeping over?
You want to...?
Like you even hafta ask, silly!

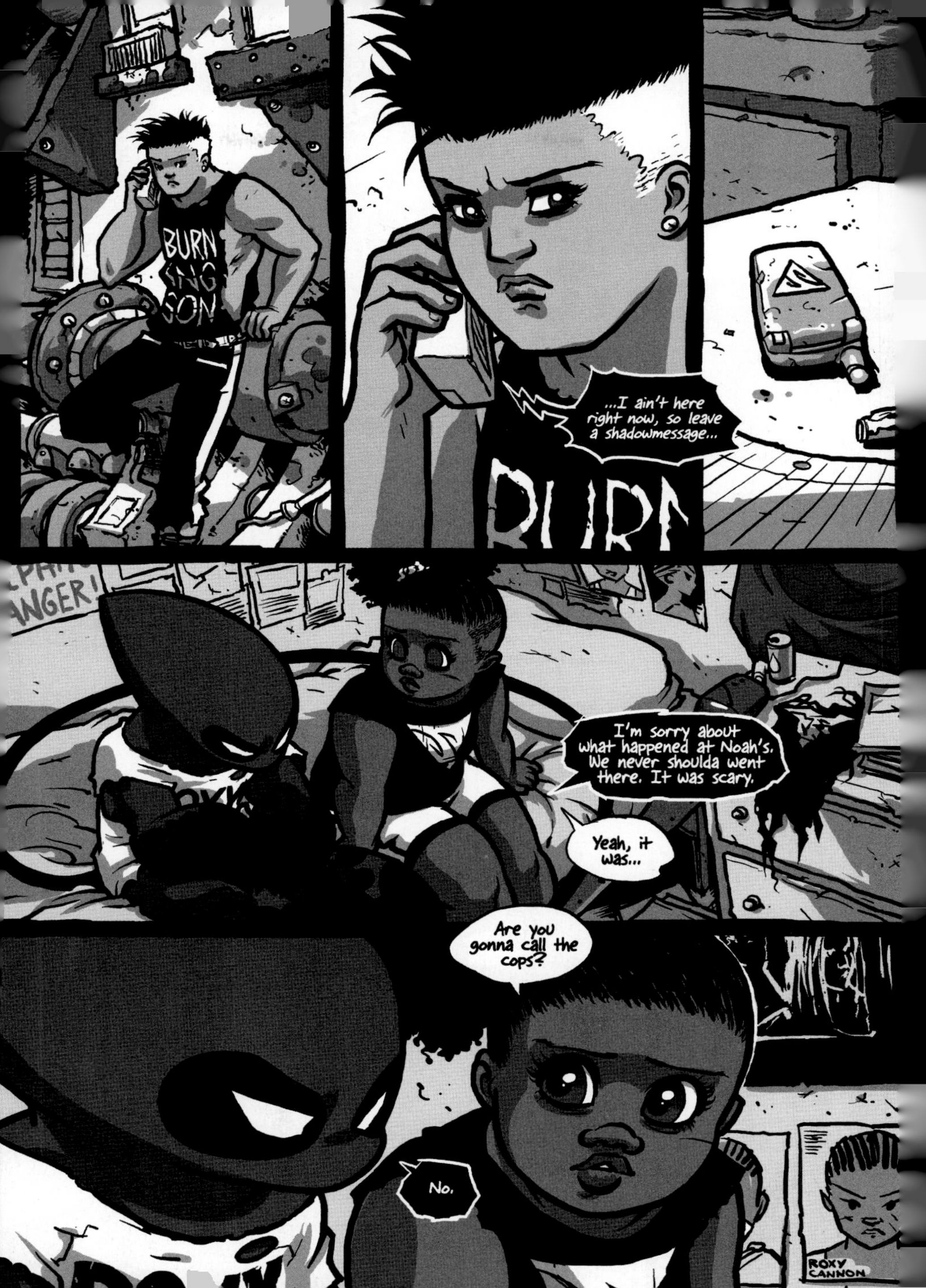
BURNING SON
...I ain't here right now, so leave a shadowmessage...
BURN
I'm sorry about what happened at Noah's. We never shoulda went there. It was scary.
Yeah, it was...
Are you gonna call the cops?
No.
ROXY CANNON

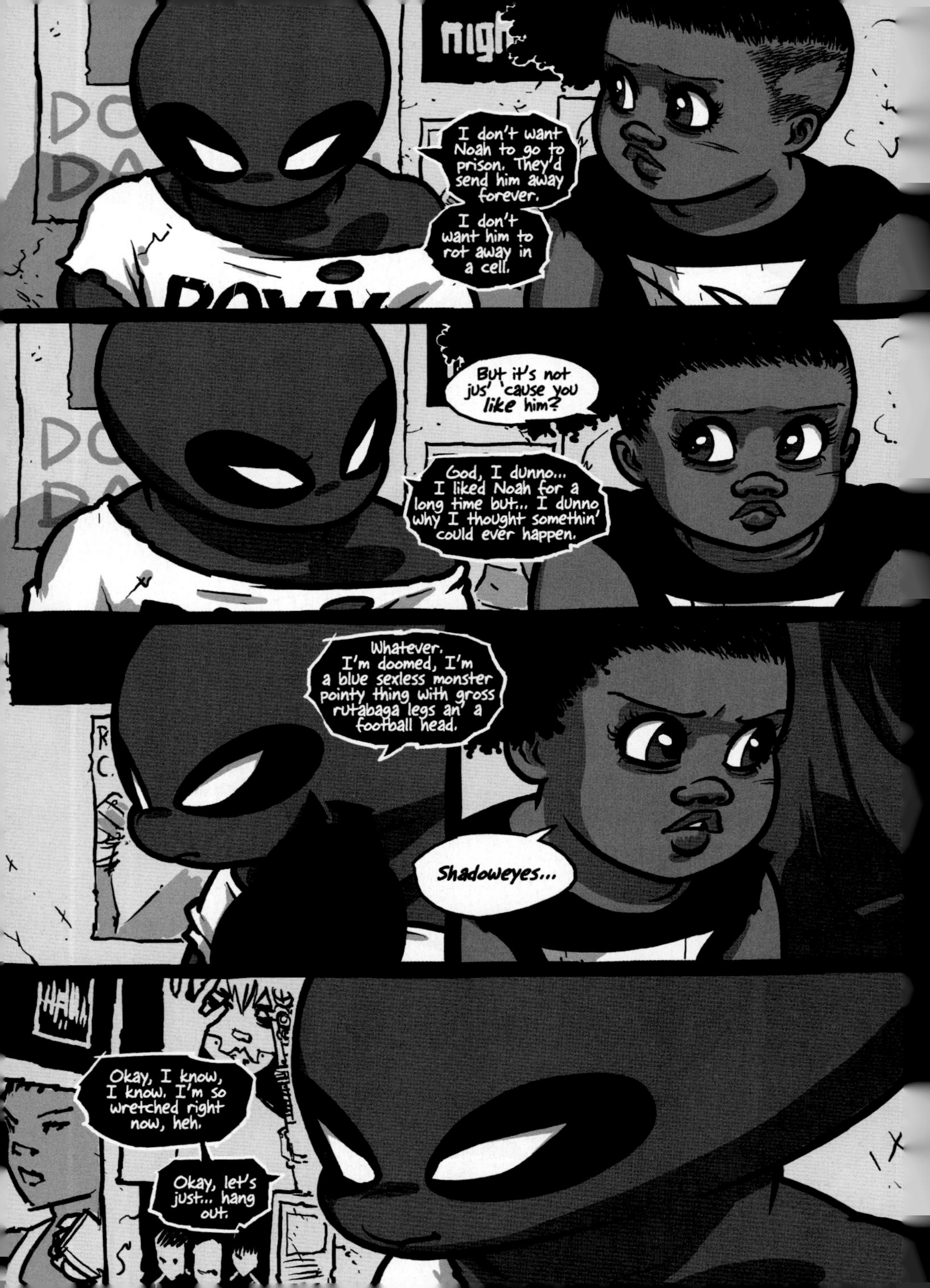
nigh
I don't want Noah to go to prison. They'd send him away forever.
I don't want him to rot away in a cell.
But it's not jus' 'cause you *like* him?
God, I dunno... I liked Noah for a long time but... I dunno why I thought somethin' could ever happen.
Whatever. I'm doomed, I'm a blue sexless monster pointy thing with gross rutabaga legs an' a football head.
Shadoweyes...
Okay, I know, I know. I'm so wretched right now, heh.
Okay, let's just... hang out.

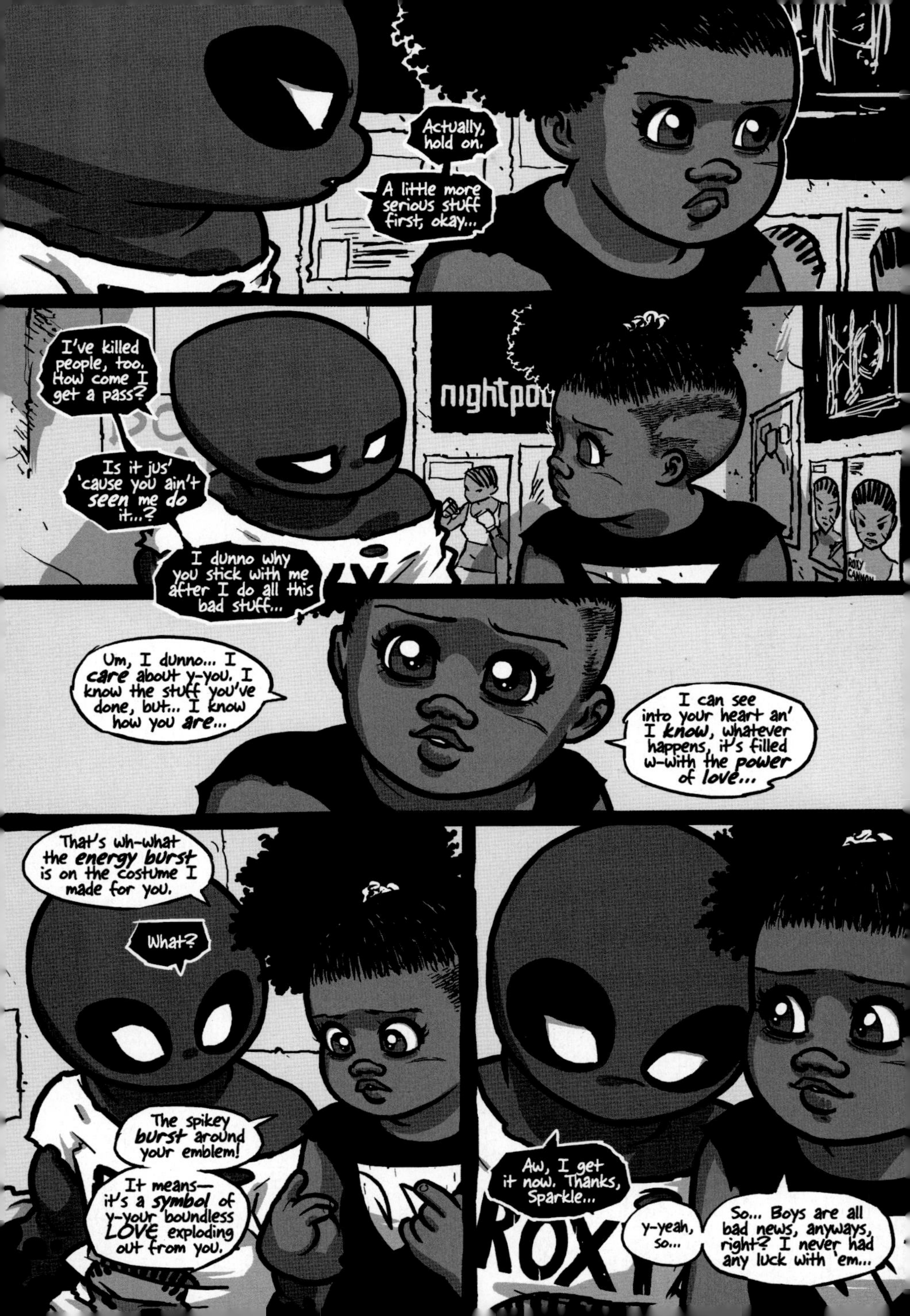

Actually, hold on.
A little more serious stuff first, okay...
I've killed people, too. How come I get a pass?
Is it jus' 'cause you ain't seen me do it...?
I dunno why you stick with me after I do all this bad stuff...
nightpoo
ROXY CANNON
Um, I dunno... I care about y-you. I know the stuff you've done, but... I know how you are...
I can see into your heart an' I know, whatever happens, it's filled w-with the power of love...
That's wh-what the energy burst is on the costume I made for you.
What?
The spikey burst around your emblem!
It means— it's a symbol of y-your boundless LOVE exploding out from you.
Aw, I get it now. Thanks, Sparkle...
Y-yeah, so...
So... Boys are all bad news, anyways, right? I never had any luck with 'em...
ROX

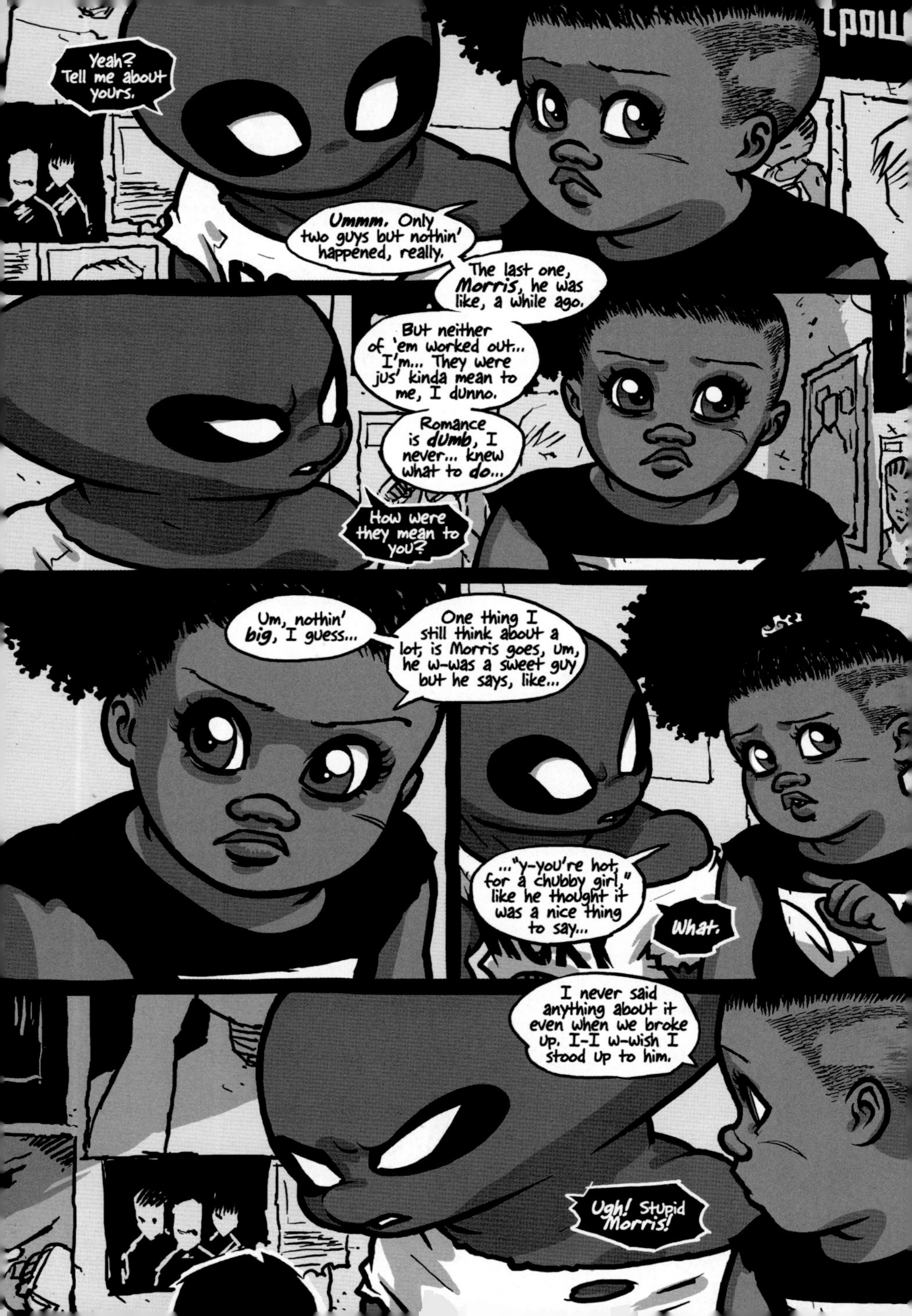
Yeah? Tell me about yours.
Ummm. Only two guys but nothin' happened, really.
The last one, Morris, he was like, a while ago.
But neither of 'em worked out... I'm... They were jus' kinda mean to me, I dunno.
Romance is dumb, I never... knew what to do...
How were they mean to you?
Um, nothin' big, I guess...
One thing I still think about a lot, is Morris goes, um, he w-was a sweet guy but he says, like...
..."y-you're hot, for a chubby girl," like he thought it was a nice thing to say...
What.
I never said anything about it even when we broke up. I-I w-wish I stood up to him.
Ugh! Stupid Morris!

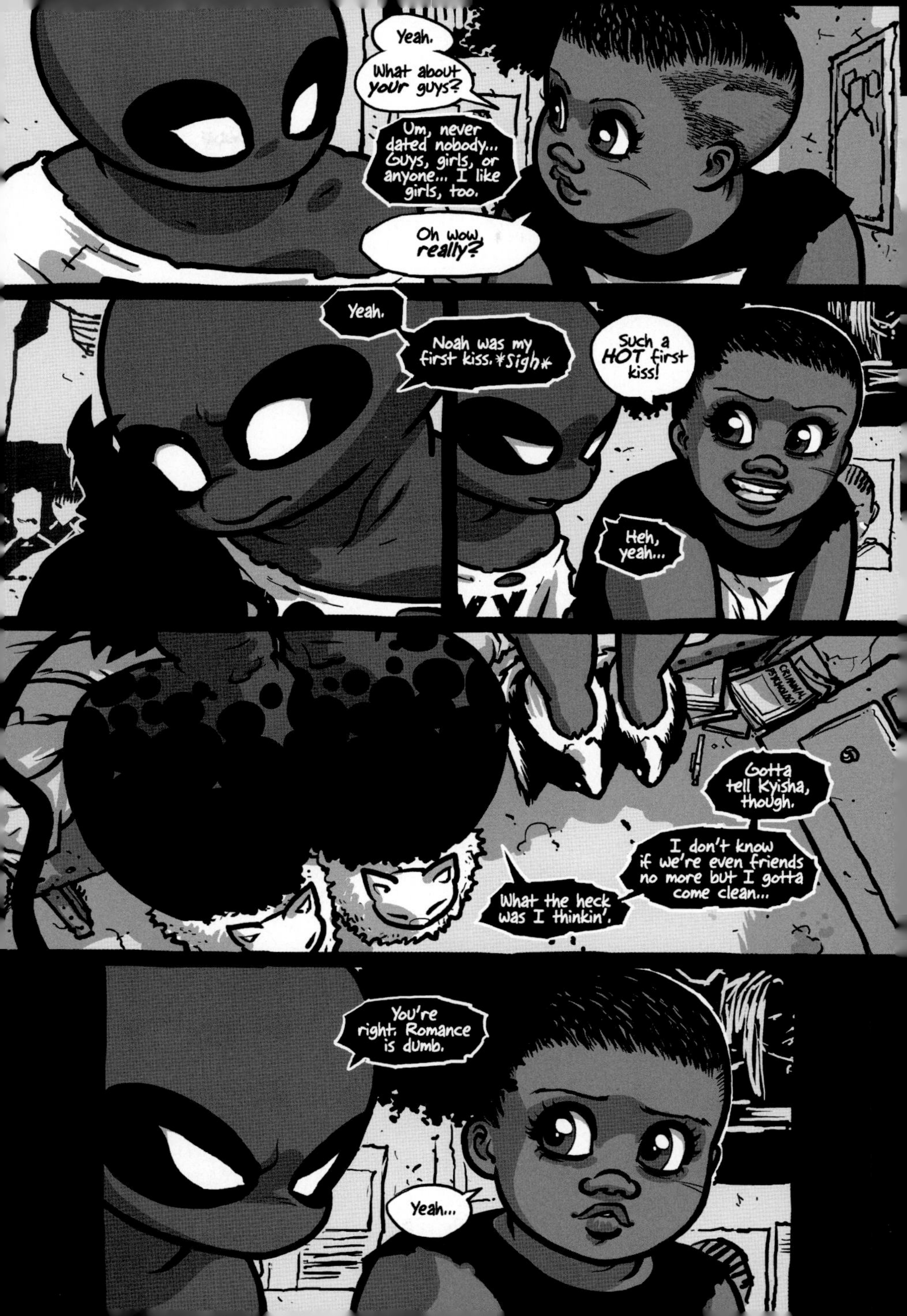
Yeah.
What about your guys?
Um, never dated nobody... Guys, girls, or anyone... I like girls, too.
Oh wow, really?
Yeah.
Noah was my first kiss. *sigh*
Such a HOT first kiss!
Heh, yeah...
CRIMINAL PSYCHOLOGY
Gotta tell Kyisha, though.
I don't know if we're even friends no more but I gotta come clean...
What the heck was I thinkin'.
You're right. Romance is dumb.
Yeah...

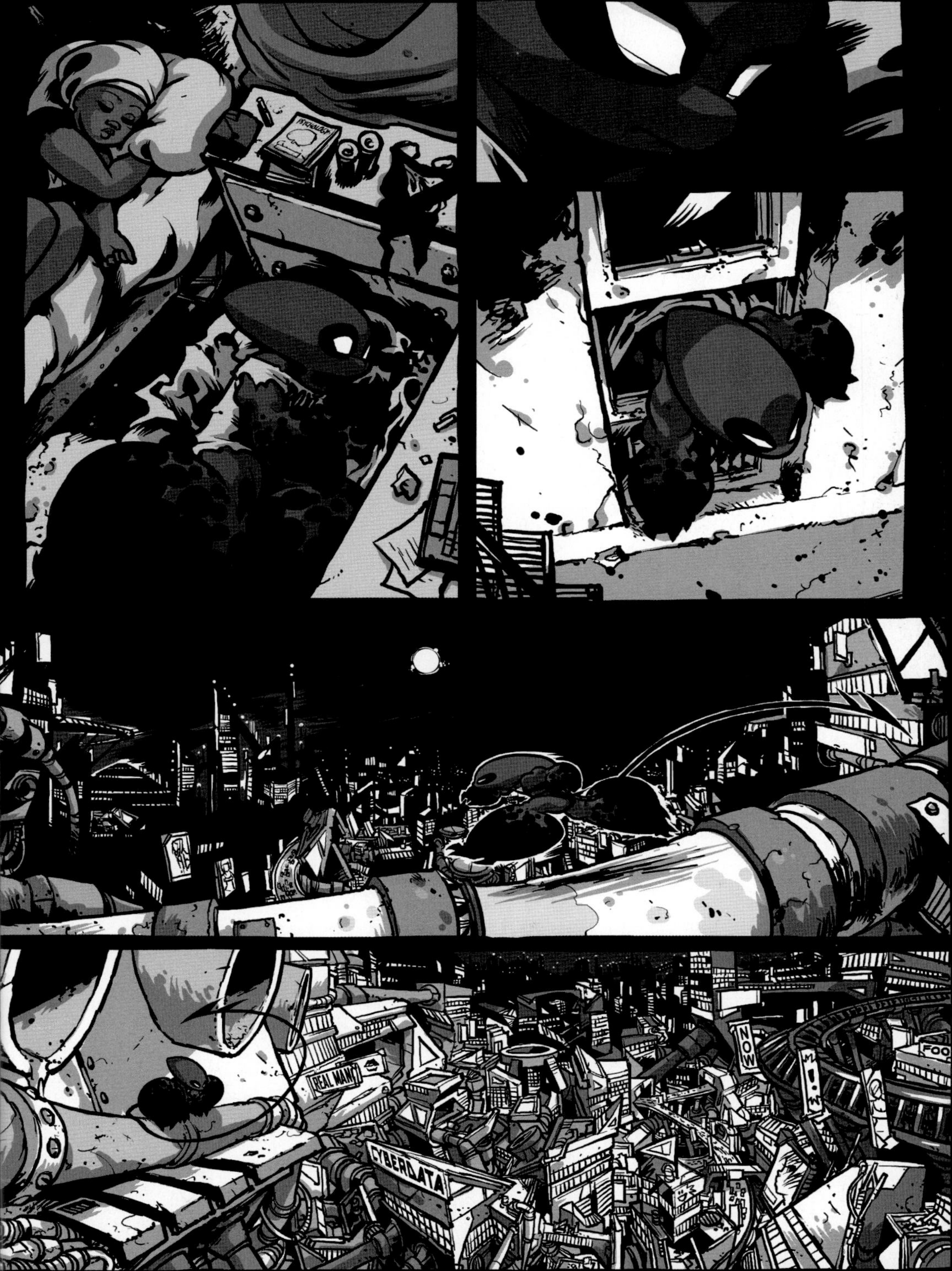
REAL MAN
NOW
CYBERDATA

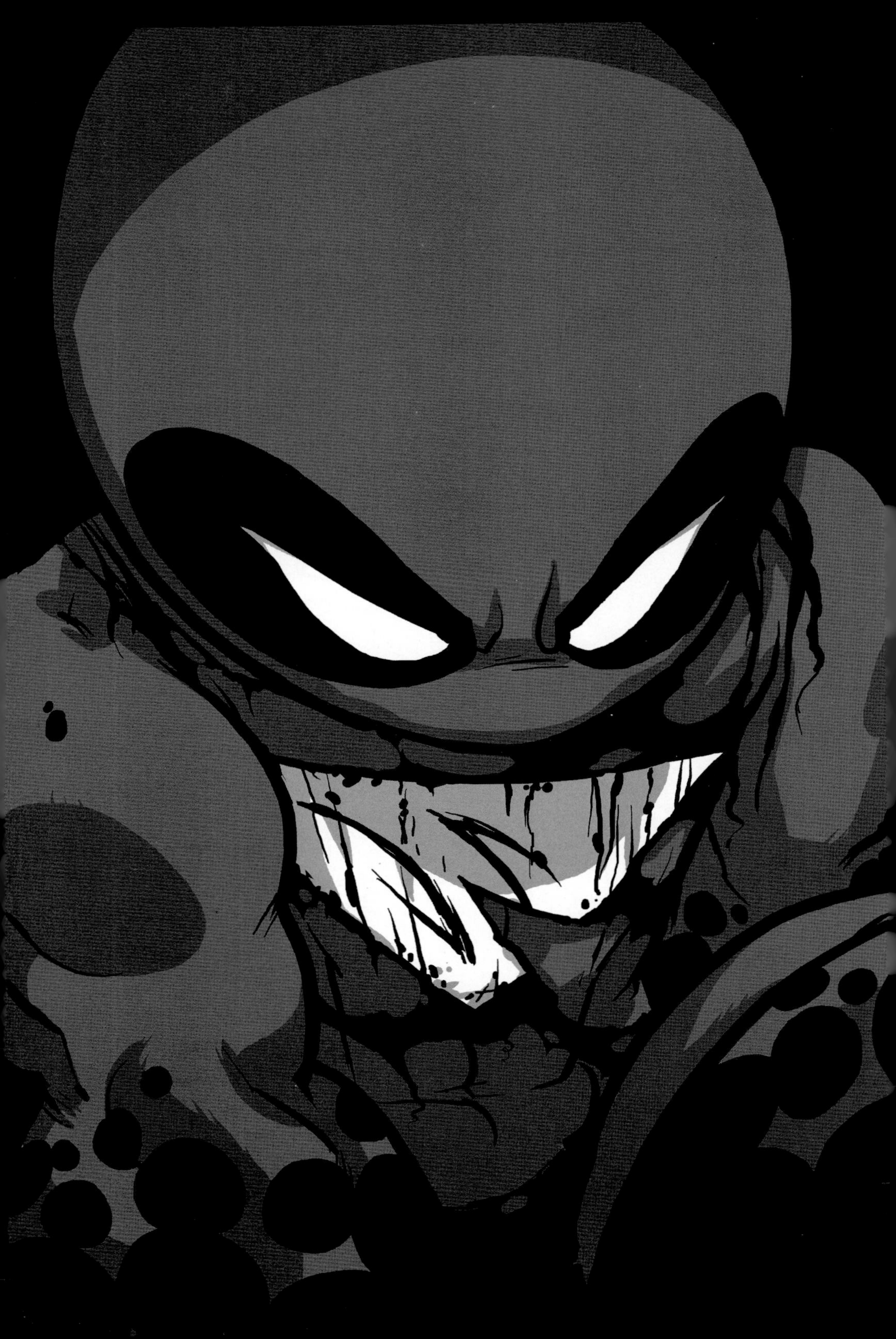

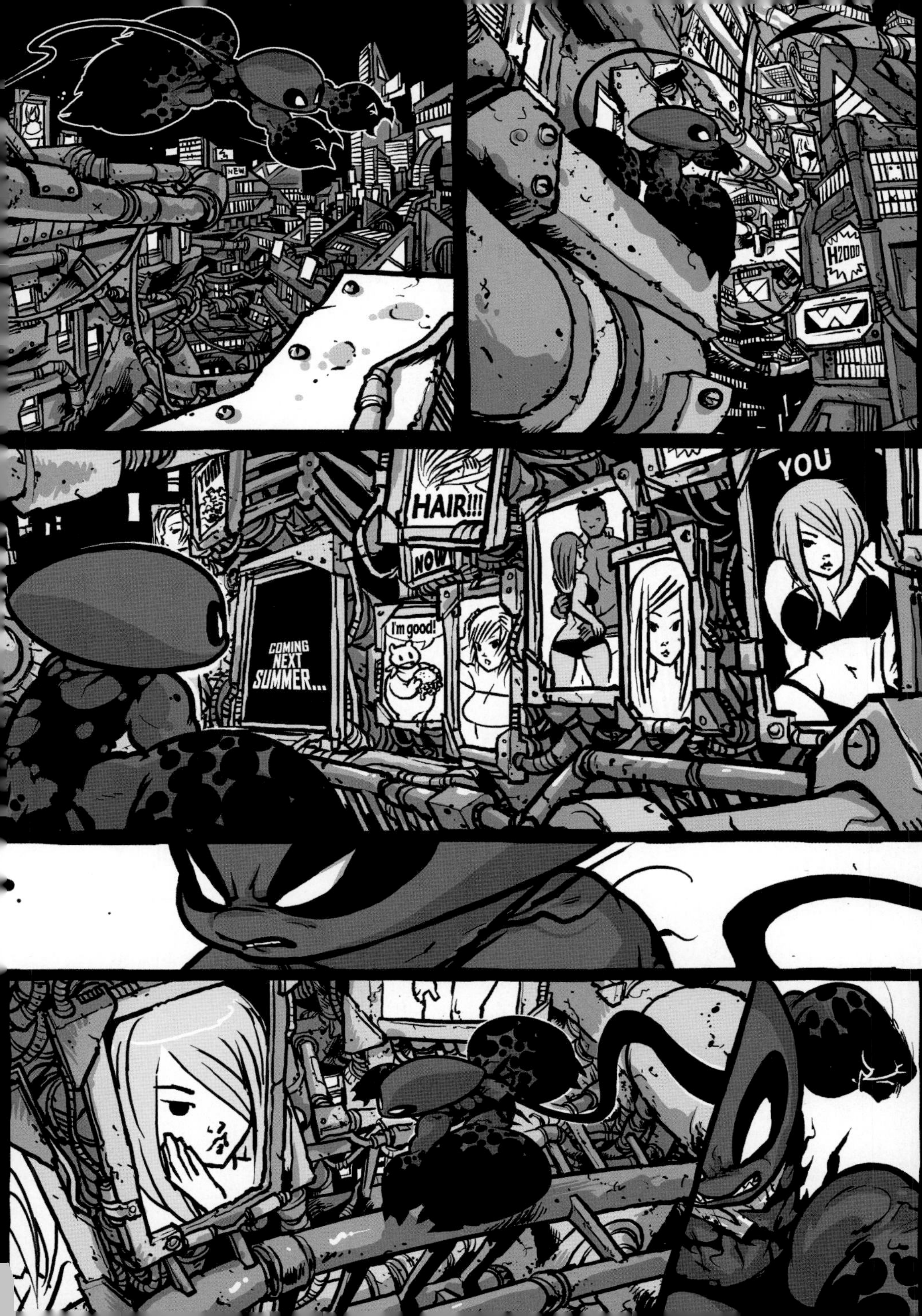
NEW
H2000
HAIR!!!
NOW
YOU
COMING NEXT SUMMER...
I'm good!

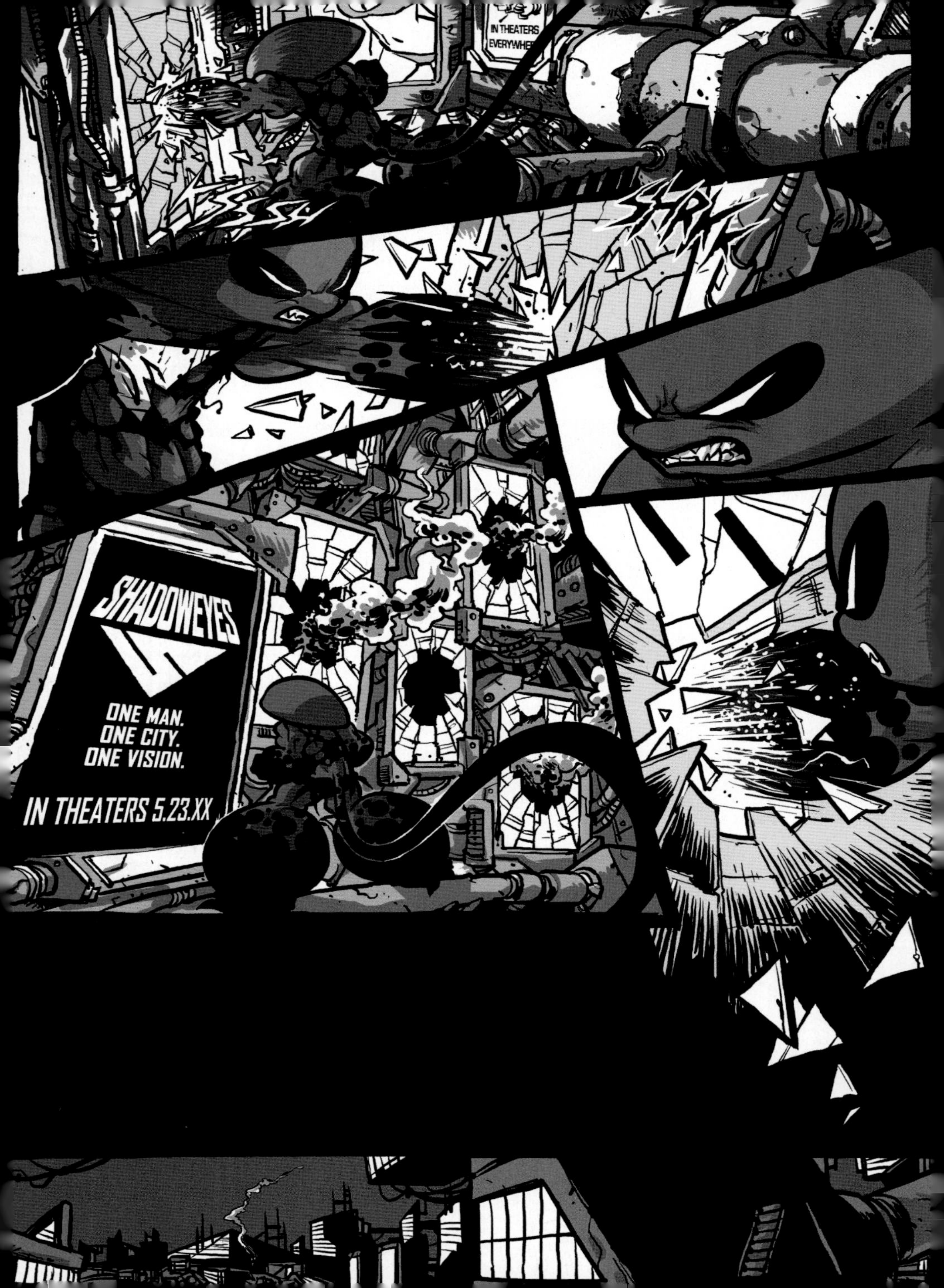
IN THEATERS
EVERYWHER
SHADOWEYES
ONE MAN.
ONE CITY.
ONE VISION.
IN THEATERS 5.23.XX

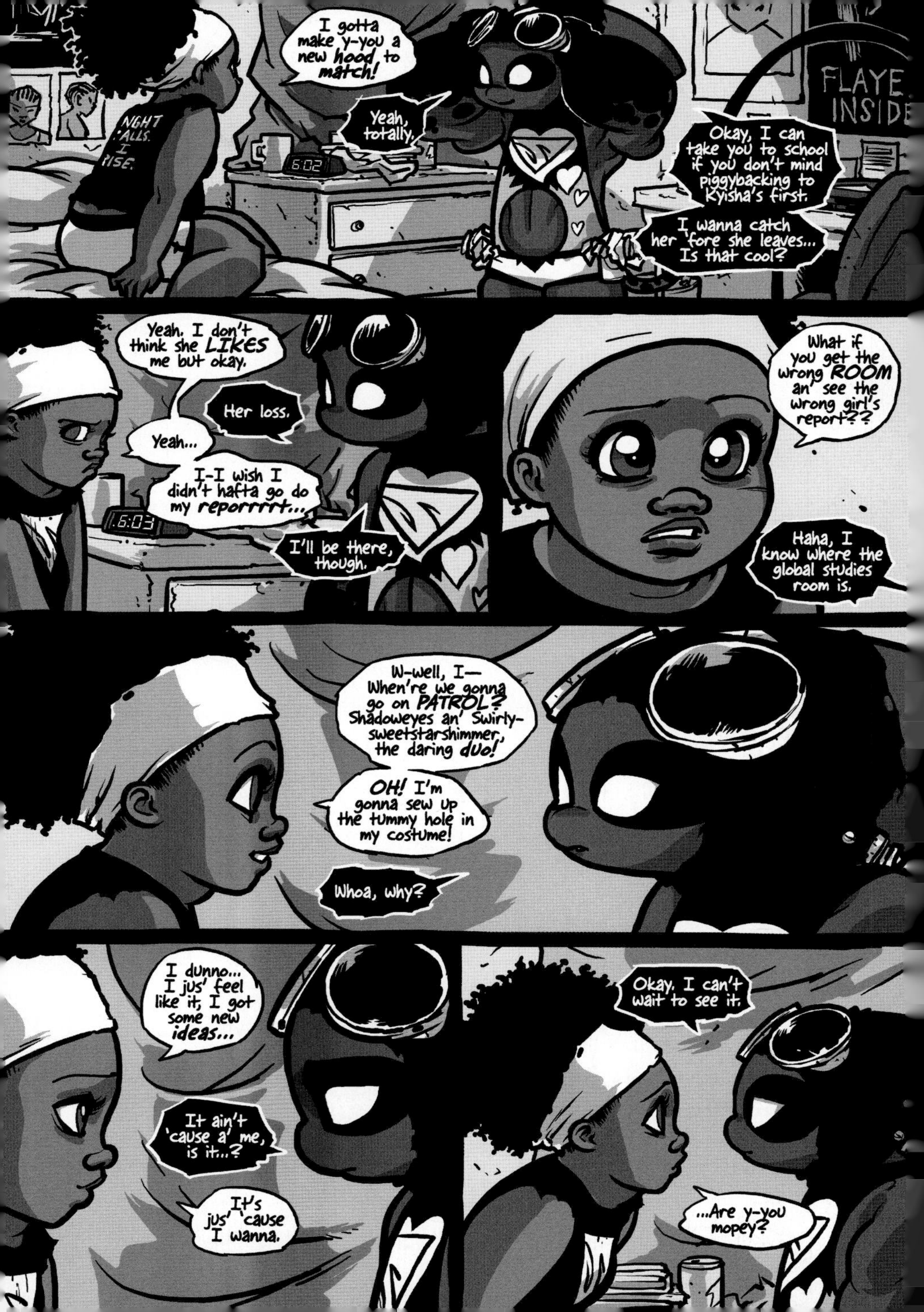
NGHT FALLS. I RISE.
I gotta make y-you a new hood to match!
Yeah, totally.
FLAYE INSIDE
Okay, I can take you to school if you don't mind piggybacking to Kyisha's first.
I wanna catch her 'fore she leaves... Is that cool?
Yeah. I don't think she LIKES me but okay.
Her loss.
Yeah...
I-I wish I didn't hafta go do my reporrrrt...
I'll be there, though.
What if you get the wrong ROOM an' see the wrong girl's report??
Haha, I know where the global studies room is.
W-well, I— When're we gonna go on PATROL? Shadoweyes an' Swirlysweetstarshimmer, the daring duo!
OH! I'm gonna sew up the tummy hole in my costume!
Whoa, why?
I dunno... I jus' feel like it, I got some new ideas...
It ain't 'cause a' me, is it...?
It's jus' 'cause I wanna.
Okay, I can't wait to see it.
...Are y-you mopey?

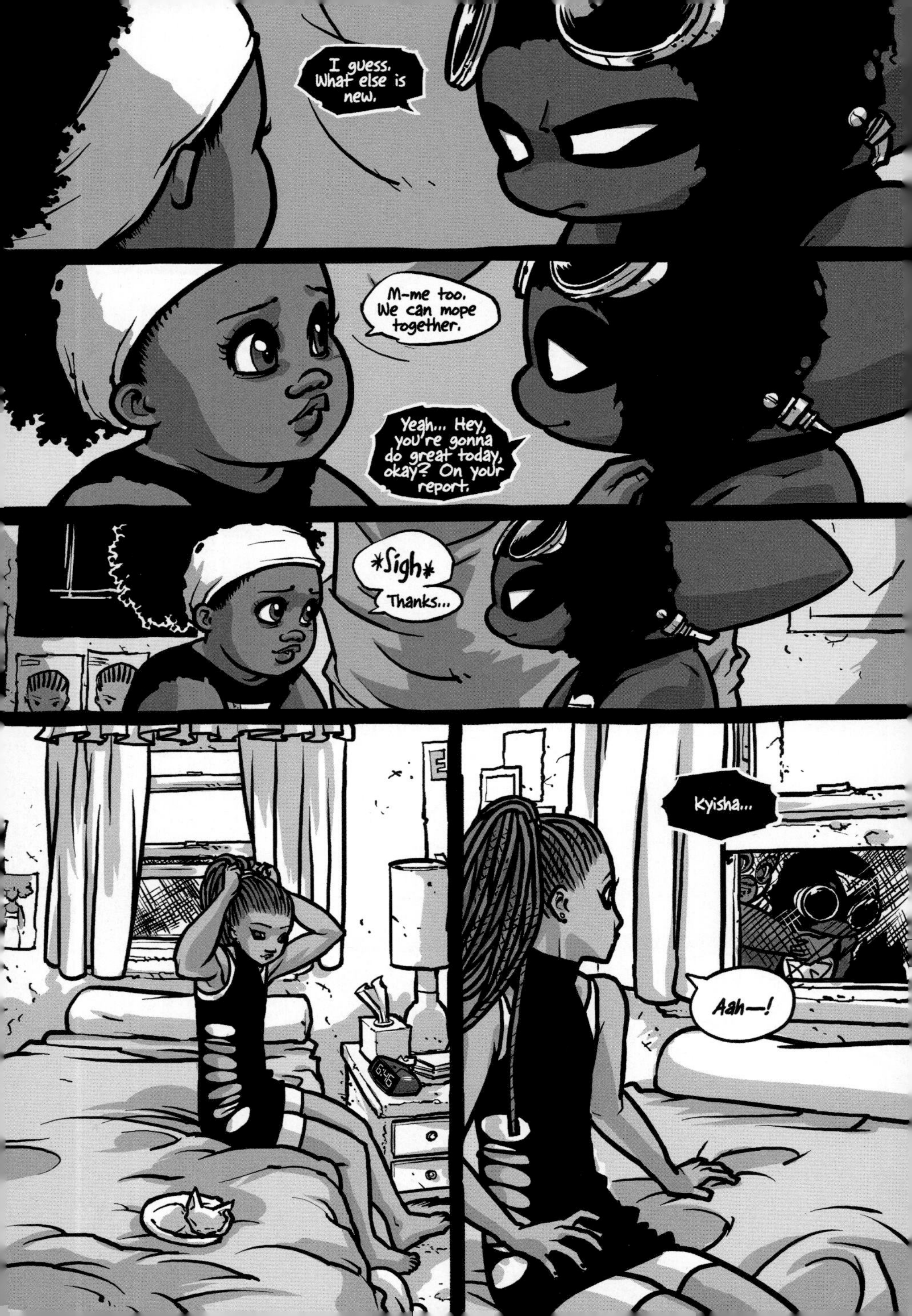
I guess. What else is new.
M-me too. We can mope together.
Yeah... Hey, you're gonna do great today, okay? On your report.
Sigh
Thanks...
Kyisha...
Aah—!

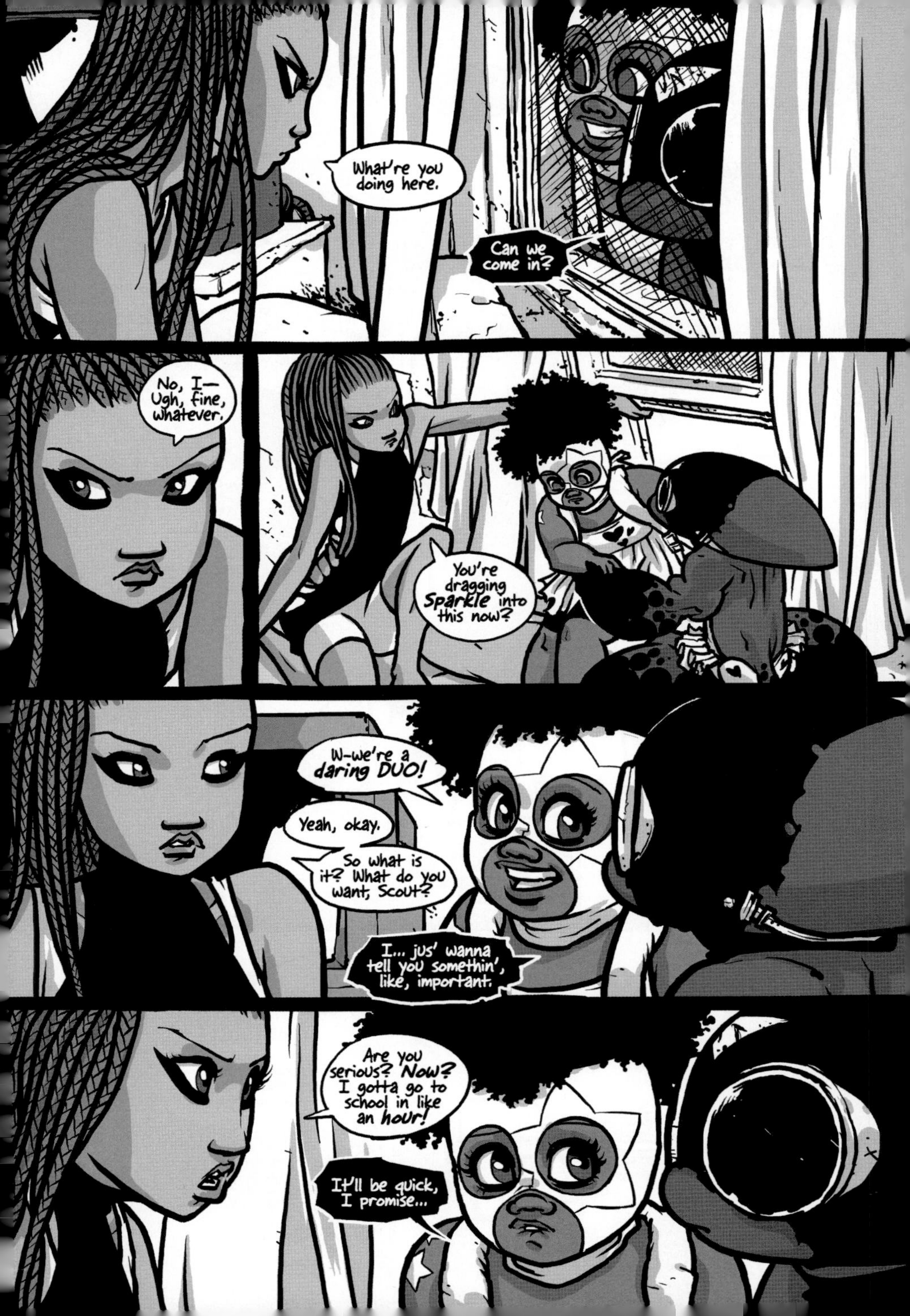
What're you doing here.
Can we come in?
No, I— Ugh, fine, whatever.
You're dragging Sparkle into this now?
W-we're a daring DUO!
Yeah, okay.
So what is it? What do you want, Scout?
I... jus' wanna tell you somethin', like, important.
Are you serious? Now? I gotta go to school in like an hour!
It'll be quick, I promise...

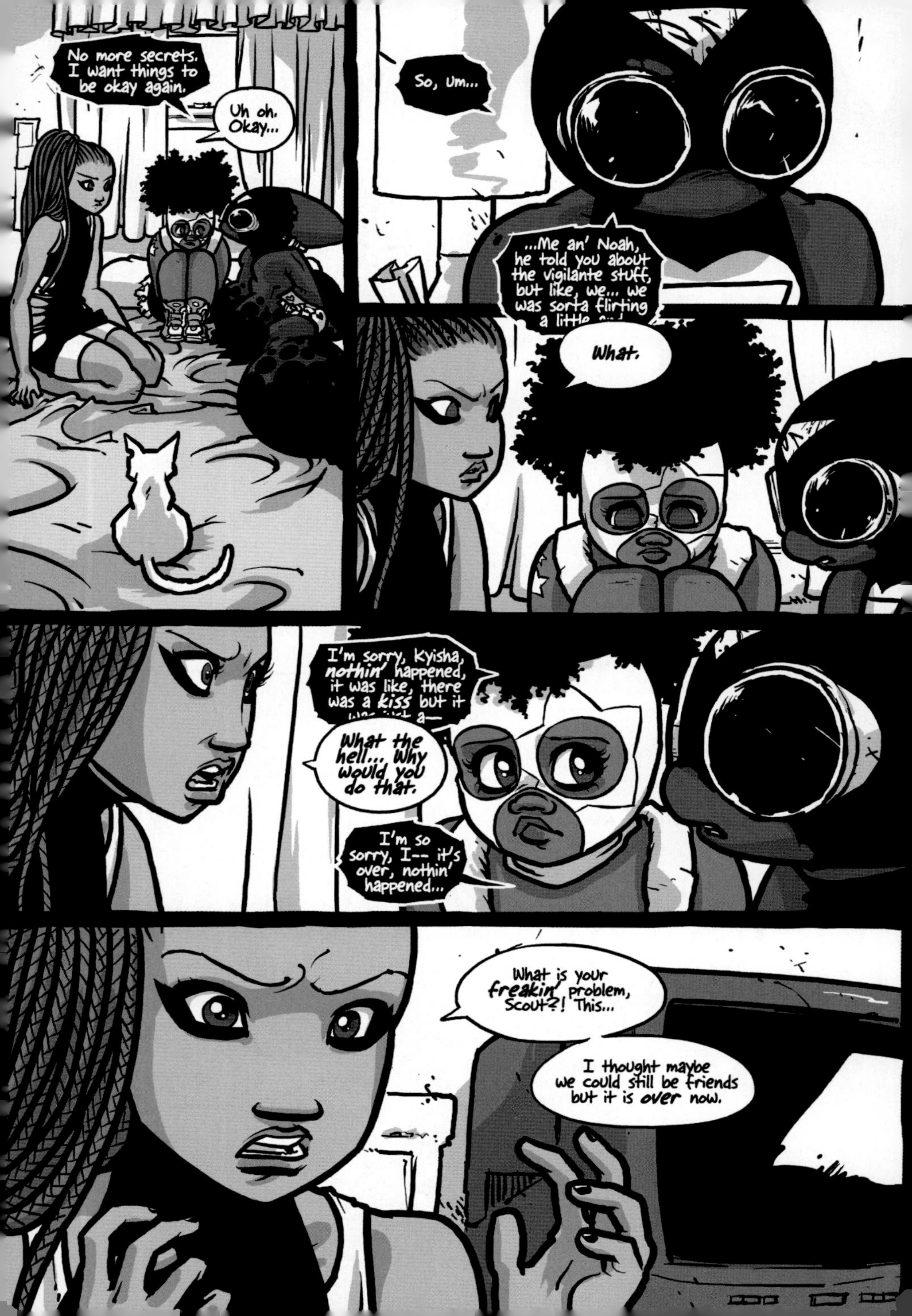
No more secrets. I want things to be okay again.
Uh oh. Okay...
So, um...
...Me an' Noah, he told you about the vigilante stuff, but like, we... we was sorta flirting a little
What.
I'm sorry, Kyisha, nothin' happened, it was like, there was a kiss but it
What the hell... Why would you do that.
I'm so sorry, I-- it's over, nothin' happened...
What is your freakin' problem, Scout?! This...
I thought maybe we could still be friends but it is over now.

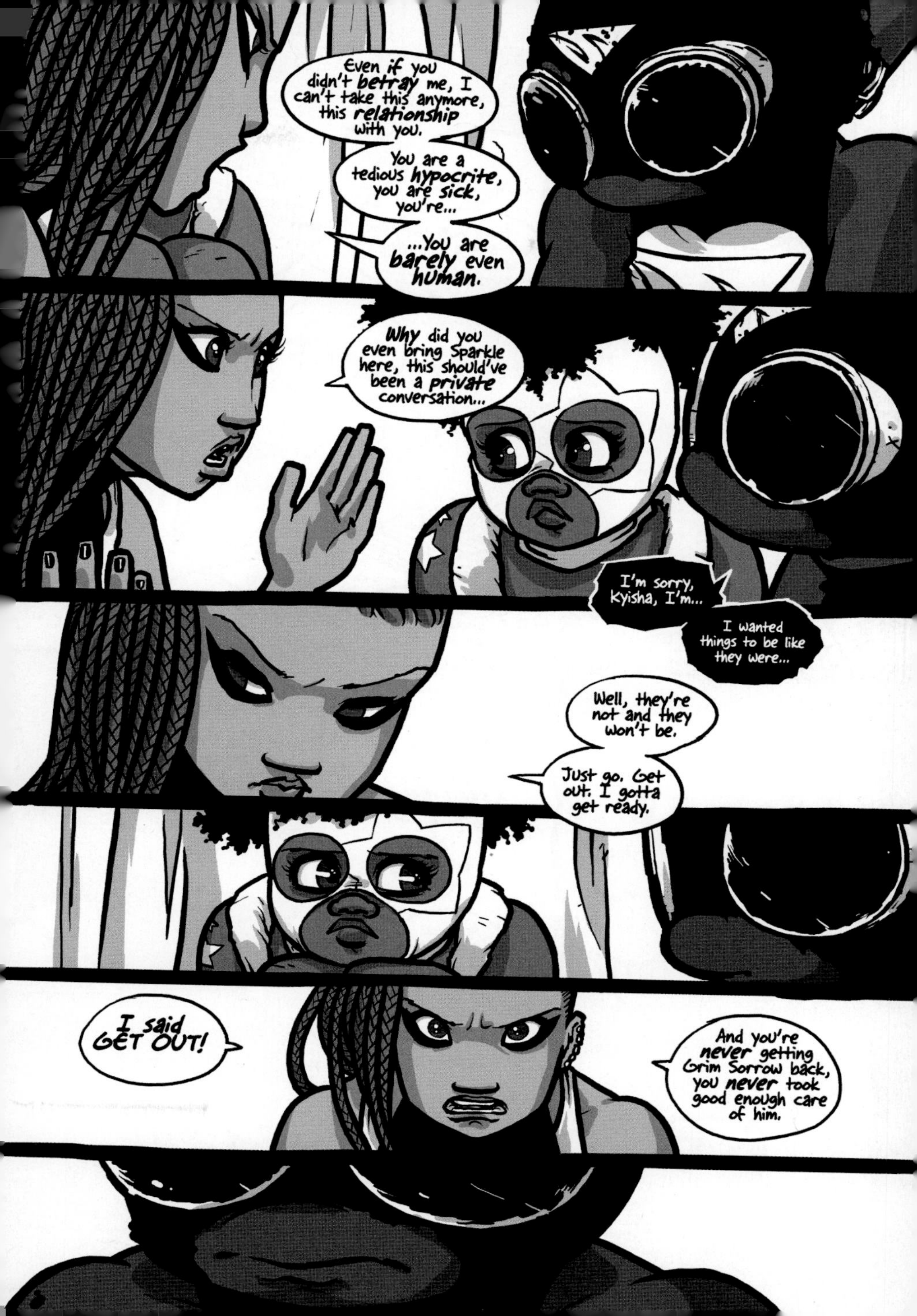
Even if you didn't betray me, I can't take this anymore, this relationship with you.
You are a tedious hypocrite, you are sick, you're...
...You are barely even human.
Why did you even bring Sparkle here, this should've been a private conversation...
I'm sorry, Kyisha, I'm...
I wanted things to be like they were...
Well, they're not and they won't be.
Just go. Get out. I gotta get ready.
I said GET OUT!
And you're never getting Grim Sorrow back, you never took good enough care of him.

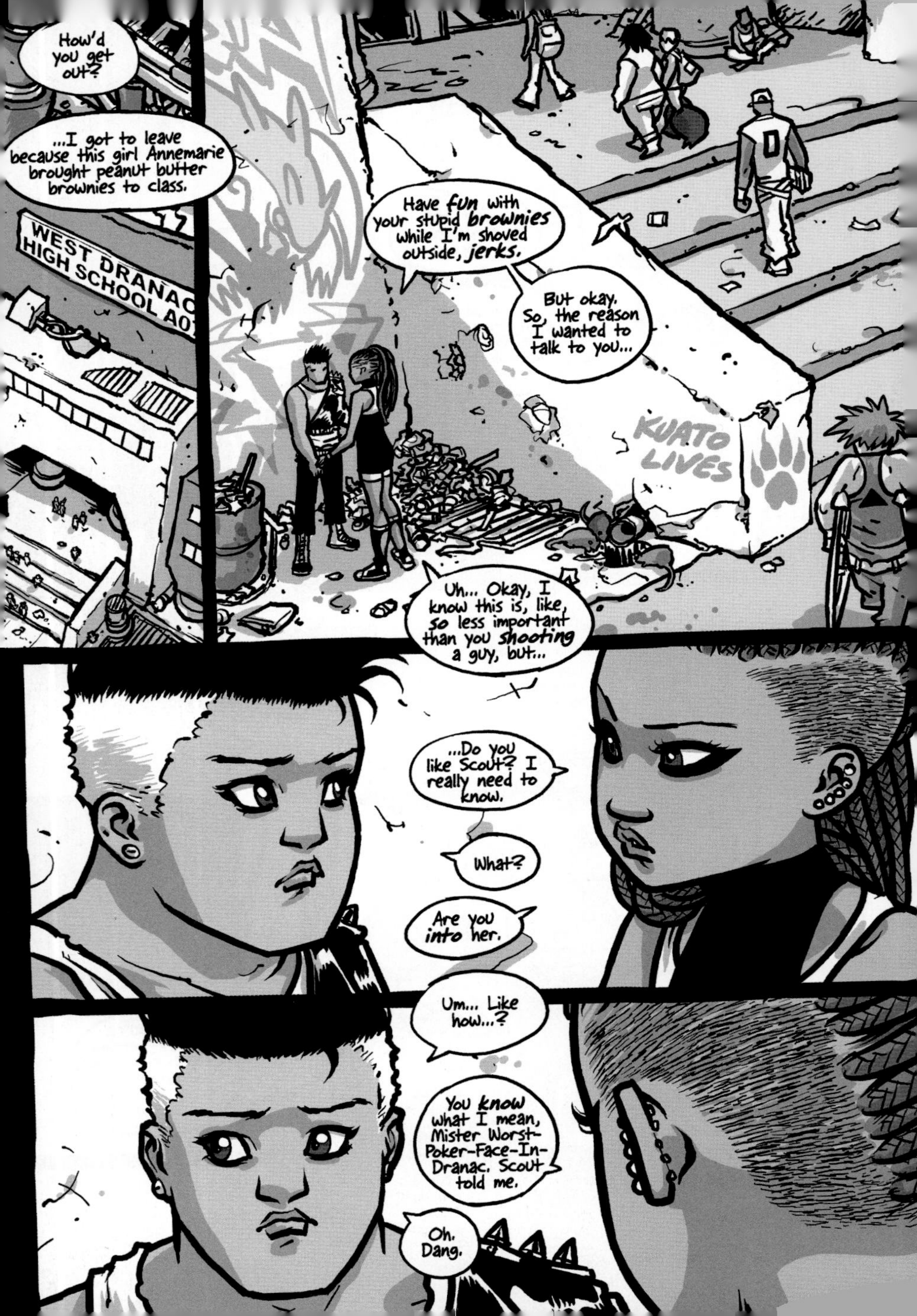
How'd you get out?
...I got to leave because this girl Annemarie brought peanut butter brownies to class.
WEST DRANAC HIGH SCHOOL A07
Have fun with your stupid brownies while I'm shoved outside, jerks.
But okay. So, the reason I wanted to talk to you...
KUATO LIVES
Uh... Okay, I know this is, like, so less important than you shooting a guy, but...
...Do you like Scout? I really need to know.
What?
Are you into her.
Um... Like how...?
You know what I mean, Mister Worst-Poker-Face-In-Dranac. Scout told me.
Oh. Dang.

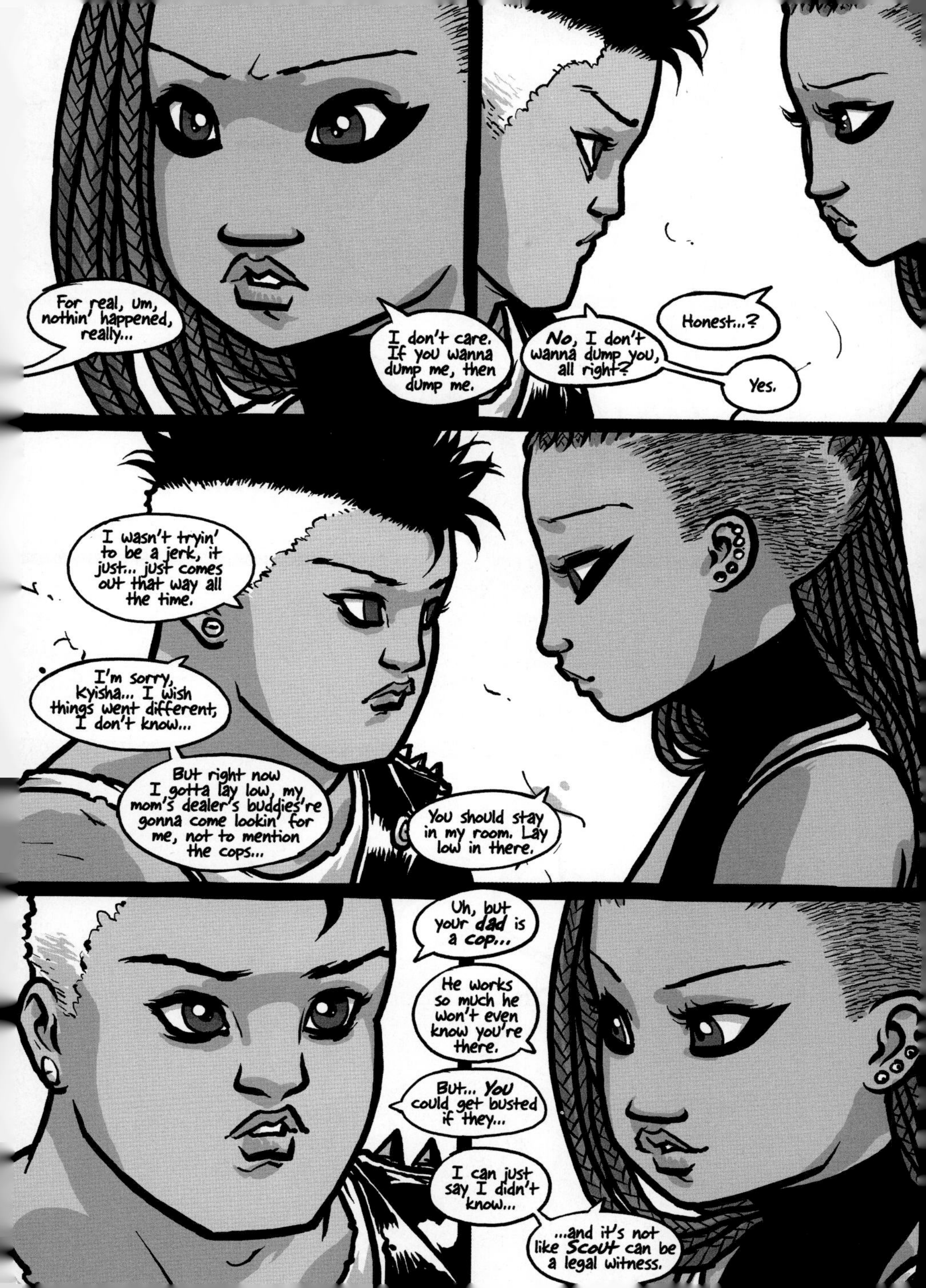
For real, um, nothin' happened, really...
I don't care. If you wanna dump me, then dump me.
No, I don't wanna dump you, all right?
Honest...?
Yes.
I wasn't tryin' to be a jerk, it just... just comes out that way all the time.
I'm sorry, Kyisha... I wish things went different, I don't know...
But right now I gotta lay low, my mom's dealer's buddies're gonna come lookin' for me, not to mention the cops...
You should stay in my room. Lay low in there.
Uh, but your dad is a cop...
He works so much he won't even know you're there.
But... You could get busted if they...
I can just say I didn't know...
...and it's not like Scout can be a legal witness.

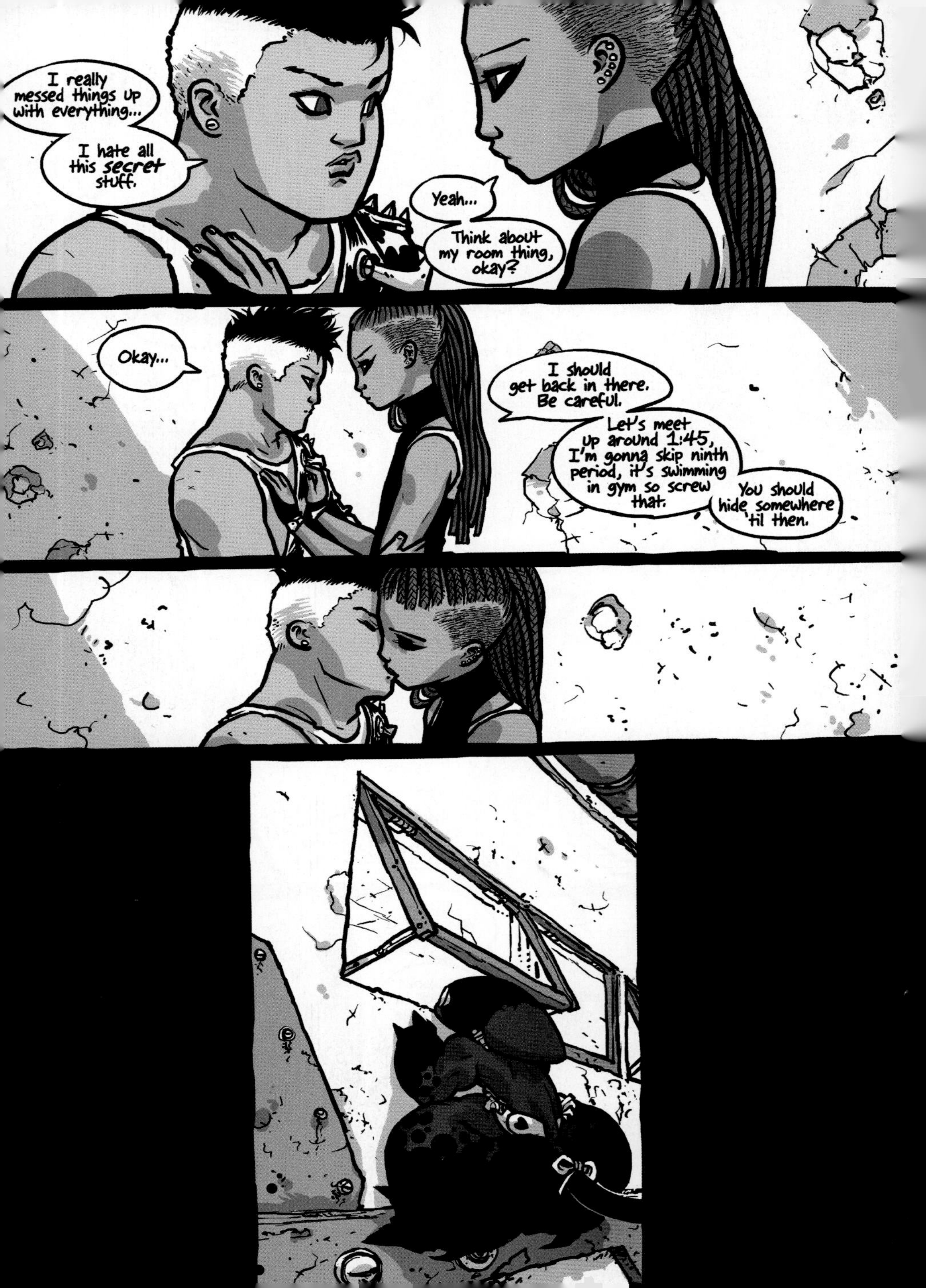
I really messed things up with everything...
I hate all this secret stuff.
Yeah...
Think about my room thing, okay?
Okay...
I should get back in there. Be careful.
Let's meet up around 1:45, I'm gonna skip ninth period, it's swimming in gym so screw that.
You should hide somewhere 'til then.

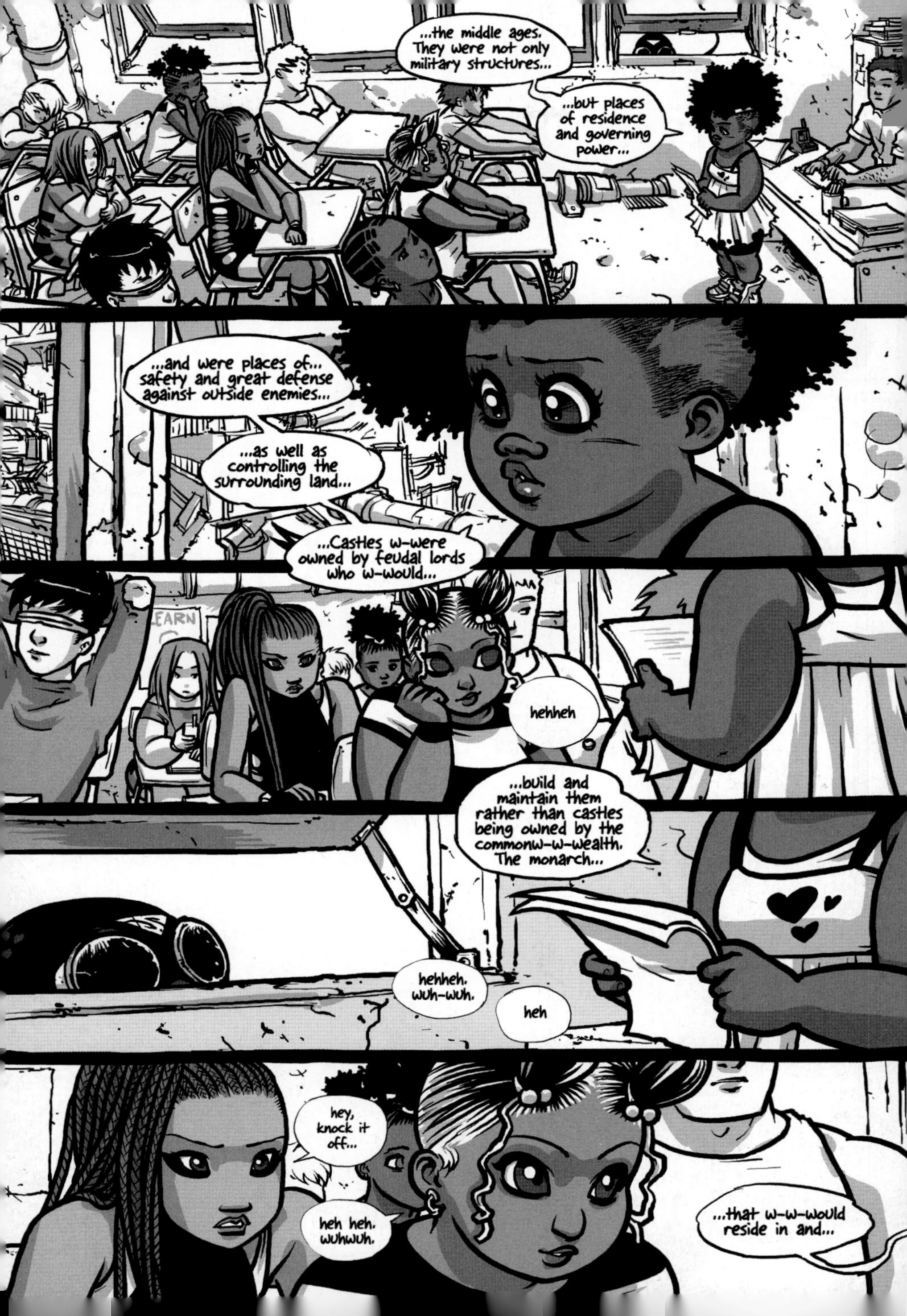
...the middle ages. They were not only military structures...
...but places of residence and governing power...
...and were places of... safety and great defense against outside enemies...
...as well as controlling the surrounding land...
...Castles w-were owned by feudal lords who w-would...
LEARN
hehheh
...build and maintain them rather than castles being owned by the commonw-w-wealth. The monarch...
hehheh. wuh-wuh.
heh
hey, knock it off...
heh heh. wuhwuh.
...that w-w-would reside in and...

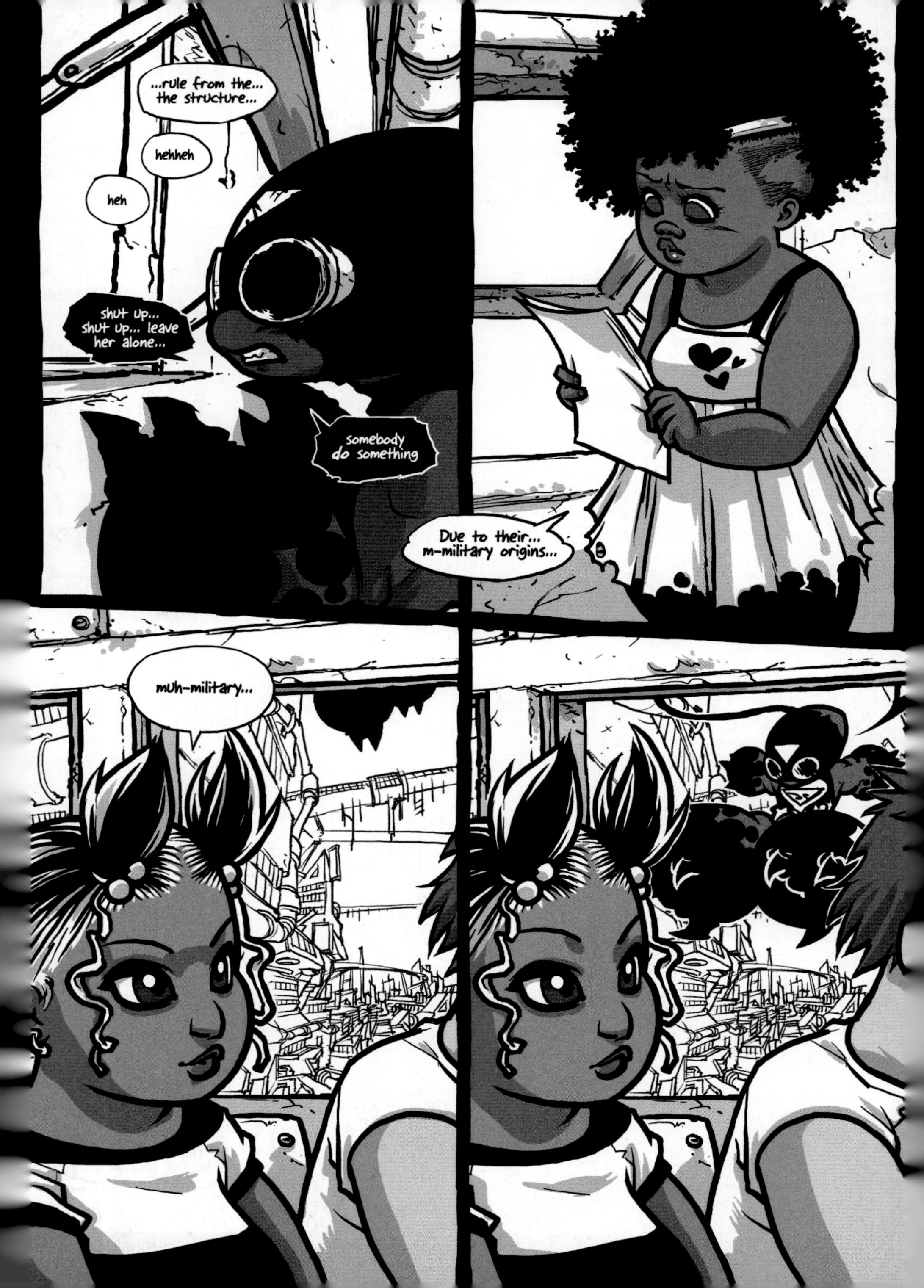
...rule from the...
the structure...
hehheh
heh
shut up...
shut up... leave
her alone...
somebody
do something
Due to their...
m-military origins...
muh-military...

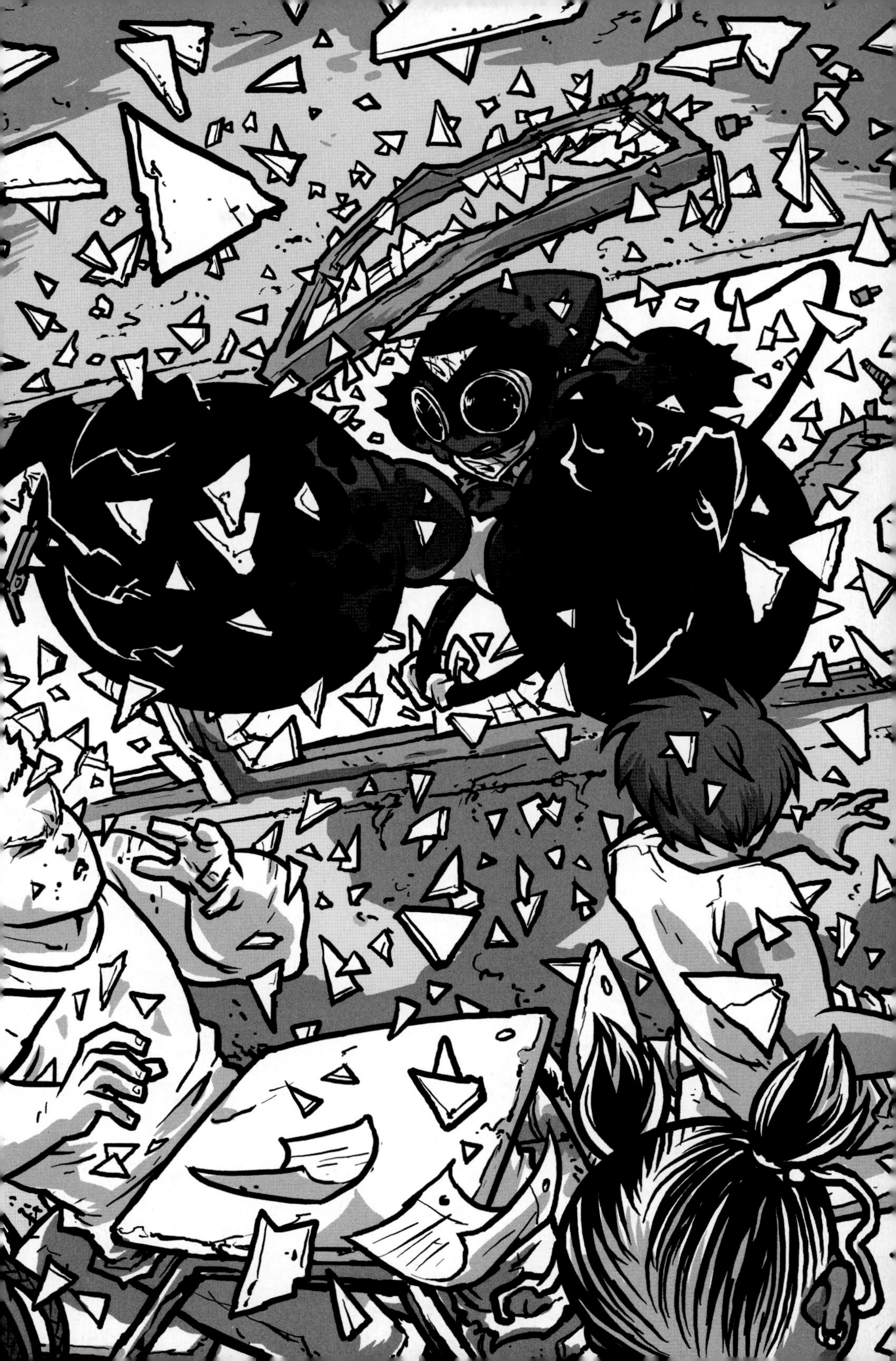

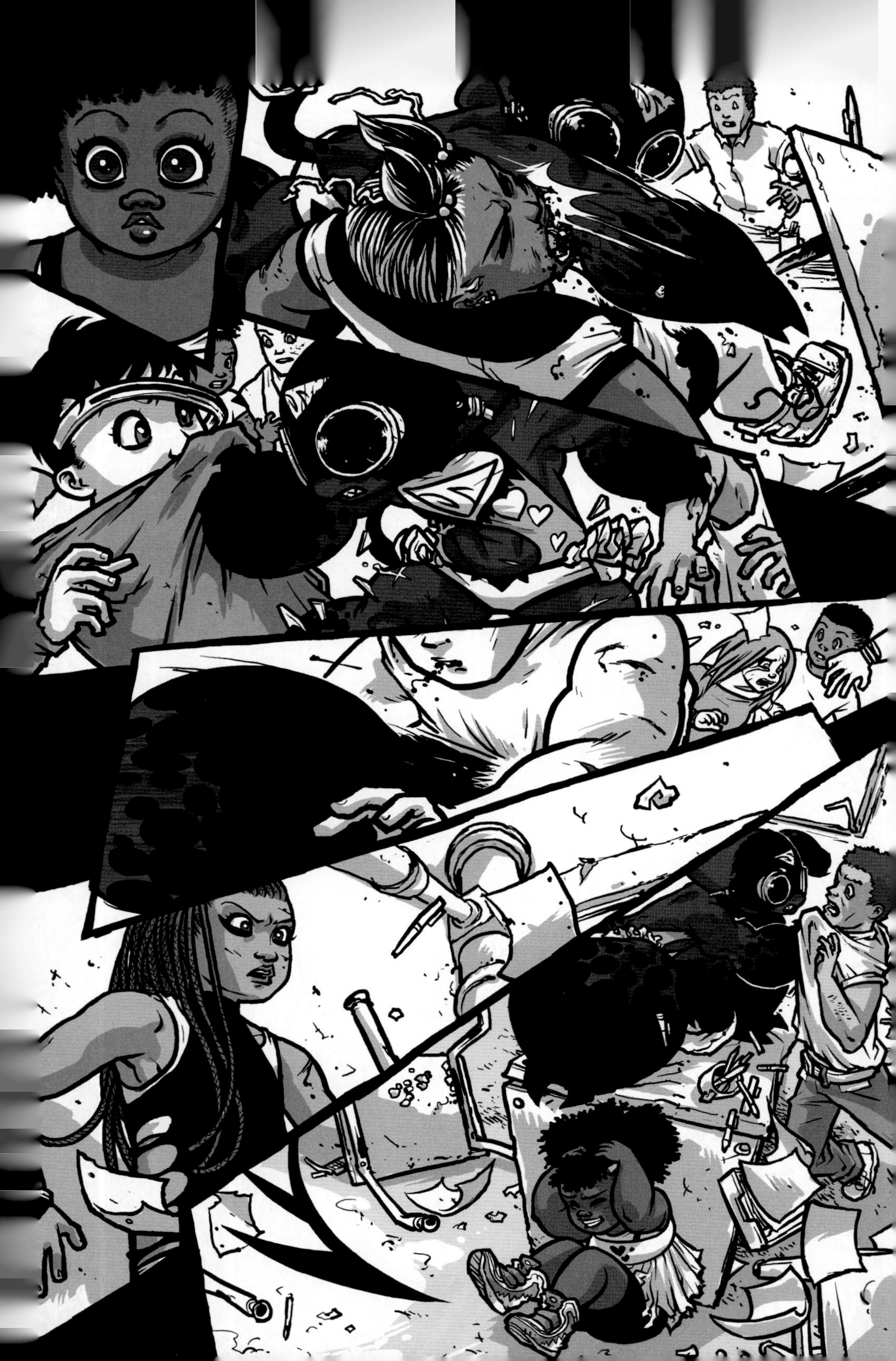

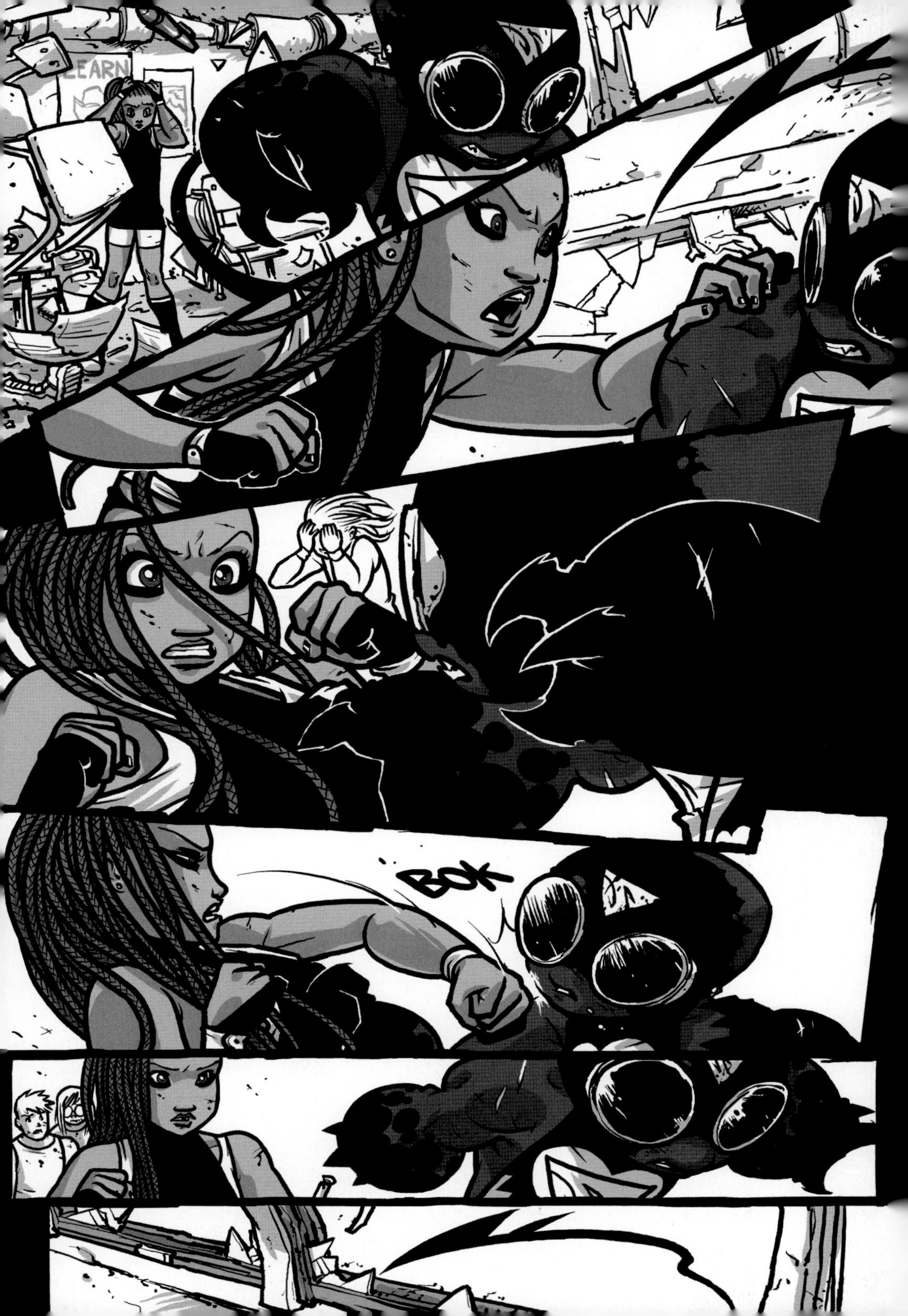
LEARN
BOK

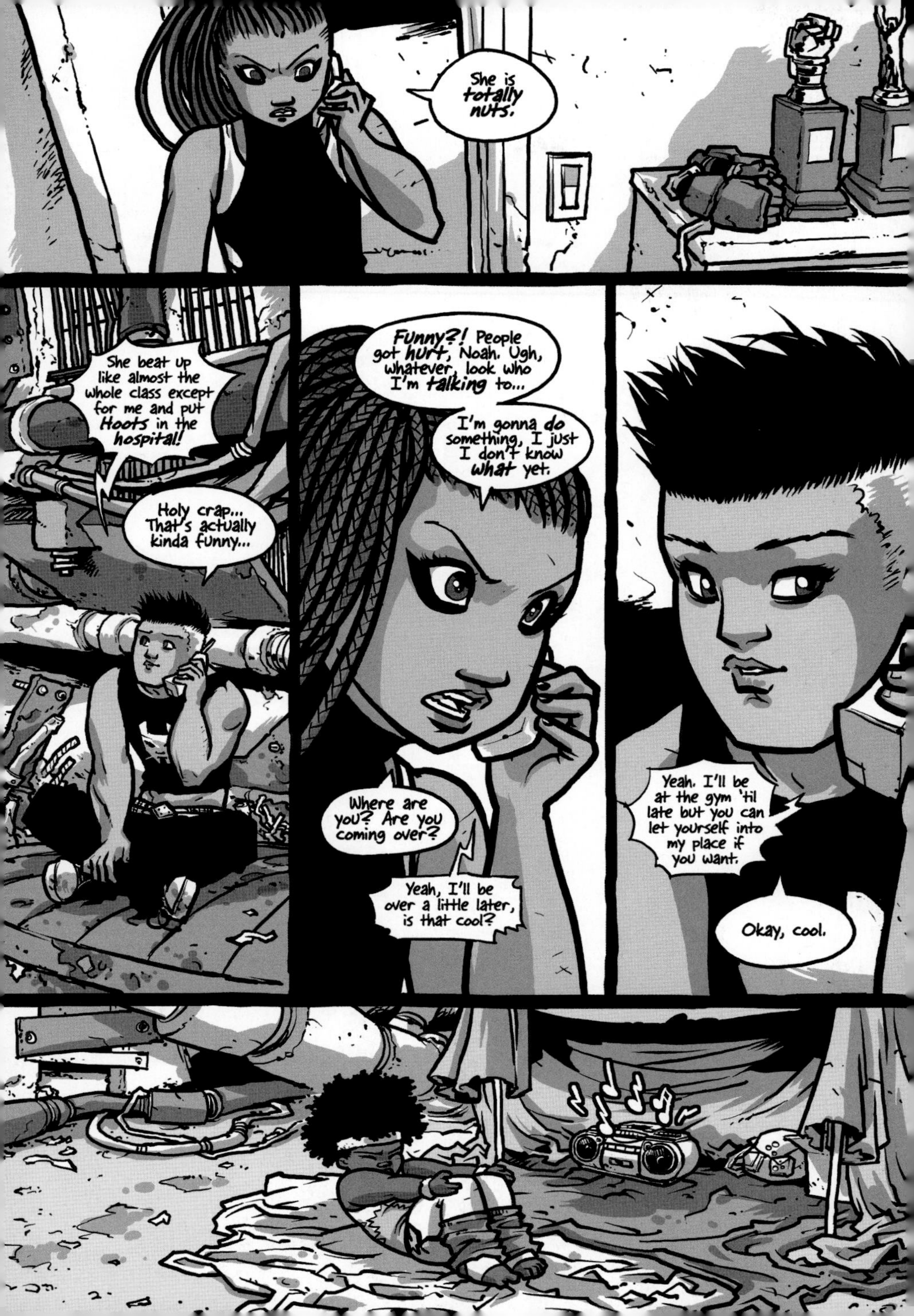
She is totally nuts.
She beat up like almost the whole class except for me and put Hoots in the hospital!
Holy crap... That's actually kinda funny...
Funny?! People got hurt, Noah. Ugh, whatever, look who I'm talking to...
I'm gonna do something, I just I don't know what yet.
Where are you? Are you coming over?
Yeah, I'll be over a little later, is that cool?
Yeah. I'll be at the gym 'til late but you can let yourself into my place if you want.
Okay, cool.

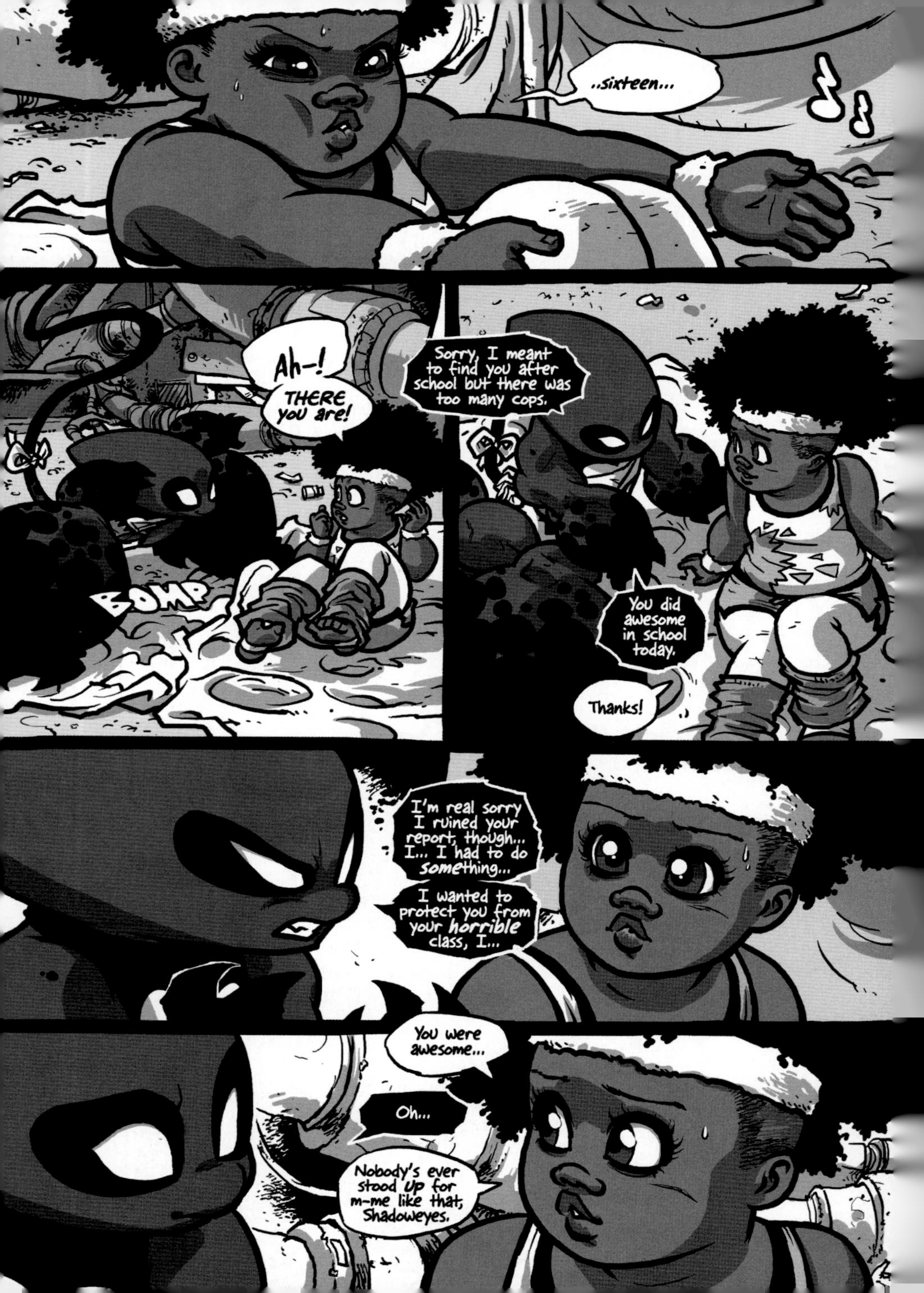
..sixteen...
Ah-!
THERE you are!
BOMP
Sorry, I meant to find you after school but there was too many cops.
You did awesome in school today.
Thanks!
I'm real sorry I ruined your report, though... I... I had to do something...
I wanted to protect you from your horrible class, I...
You were awesome...
Oh...
Nobody's ever stood up for m-me like that, Shadoweyes.

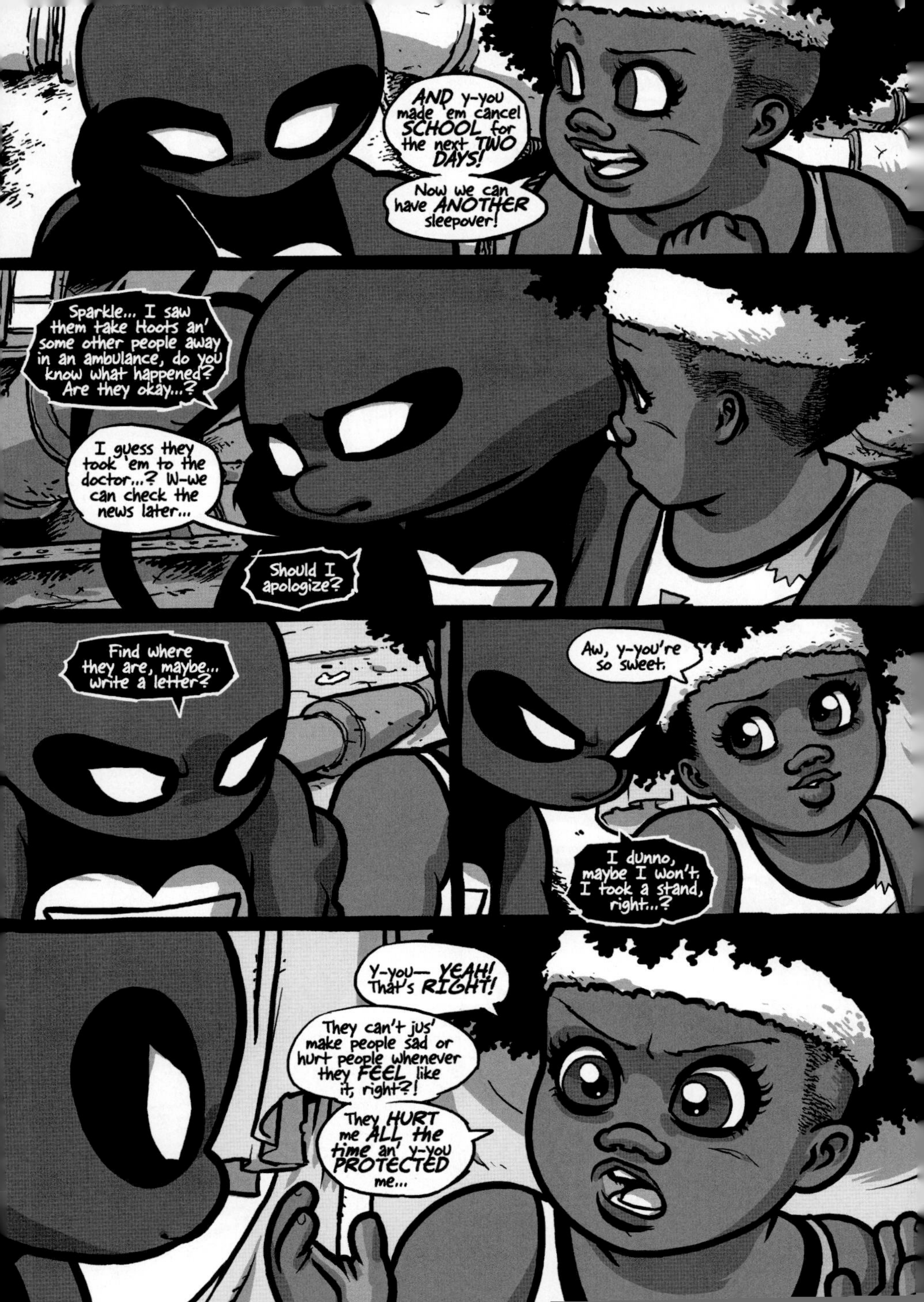
AND y-you made 'em cancel SCHOOL for the next TWO DAYS!
Now we can have ANOTHER sleepover!
Sparkle... I saw them take Hoots an' some other people away in an ambulance, do you know what happened? Are they okay...?
I guess they took 'em to the doctor...? W-we can check the news later...
Should I apologize?
Find where they are, maybe... write a letter?
Aw, y-you're so sweet.
I dunno, maybe I won't. I took a stand, right...?
Y-you— YEAH! That's RIGHT!
They can't jus' make people sad or hurt people whenever they FEEL like it, right?!
They HURT me ALL the time an' y-you PROTECTED me...

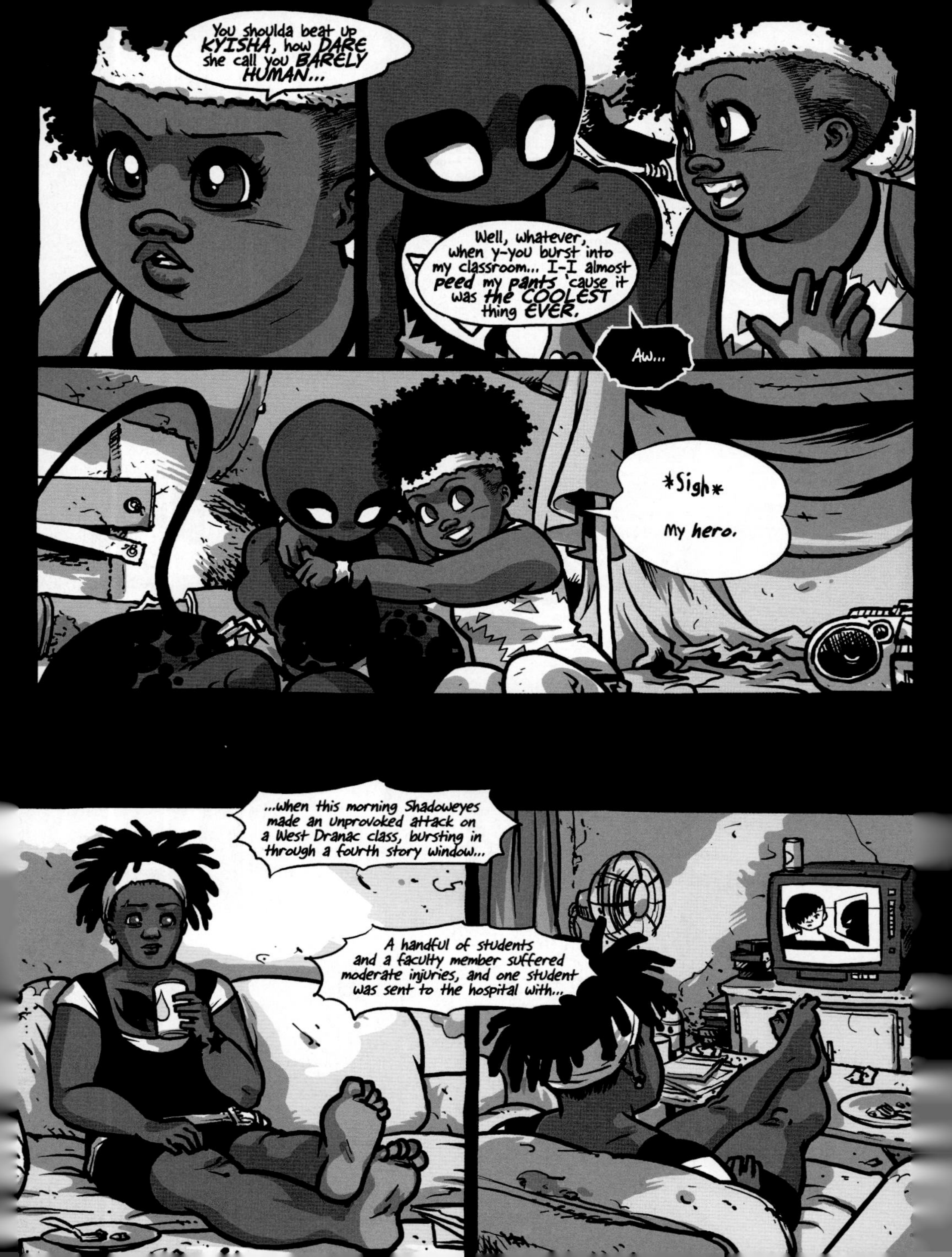
You shoulda beat up KYISHA, how DARE she call you BARELY HUMAN...
Well, whatever, when y-you burst into my classroom... I-I almost peed my pants 'cause it was the COOLEST thing EVER.
Aw...
Sigh My hero.
...when this morning Shadoweyes made an unprovoked attack on a West Dranac class, bursting in through a fourth story window...
A handful of students and a faculty member suffered moderate injuries, and one student was sent to the hospital with...

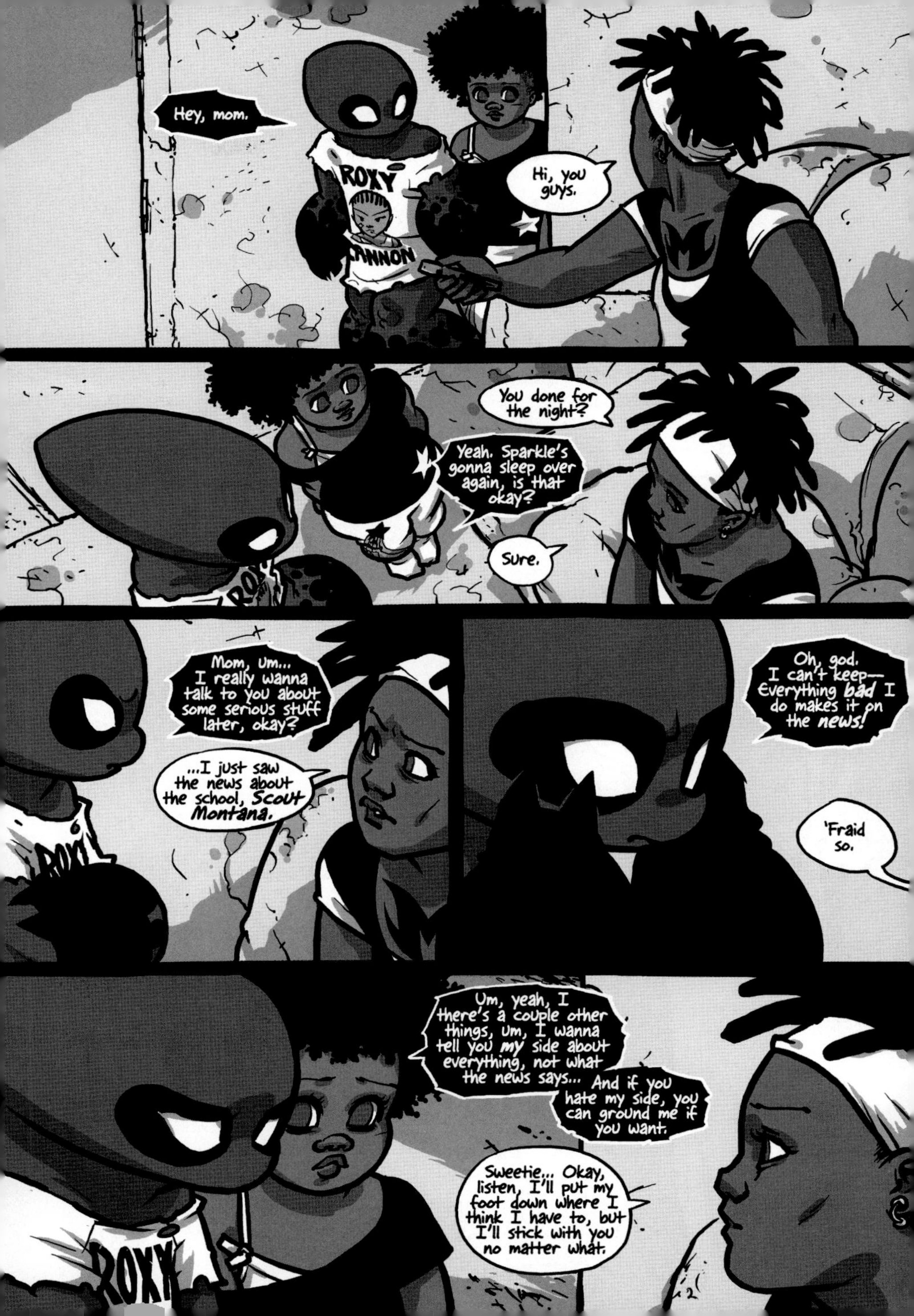
Hey, mom.
Hi, you guys.
You done for the night?
Yeah. Sparkle's gonna sleep over again, is that okay?
Sure.
Mom, um... I really wanna talk to you about some serious stuff later, okay?
...I just saw the news about the school, Scout Montana.
Oh, god. I can't keep— Everything bad I do makes it on the news!
'Fraid so.
Um, yeah, I there's a couple other things, um, I wanna tell you my side about everything, not what the news says...
And if you hate my side, you can ground me if you want.
Sweetie... Okay, listen, I'll put my foot down where I think I have to, but I'll stick with you no matter what.

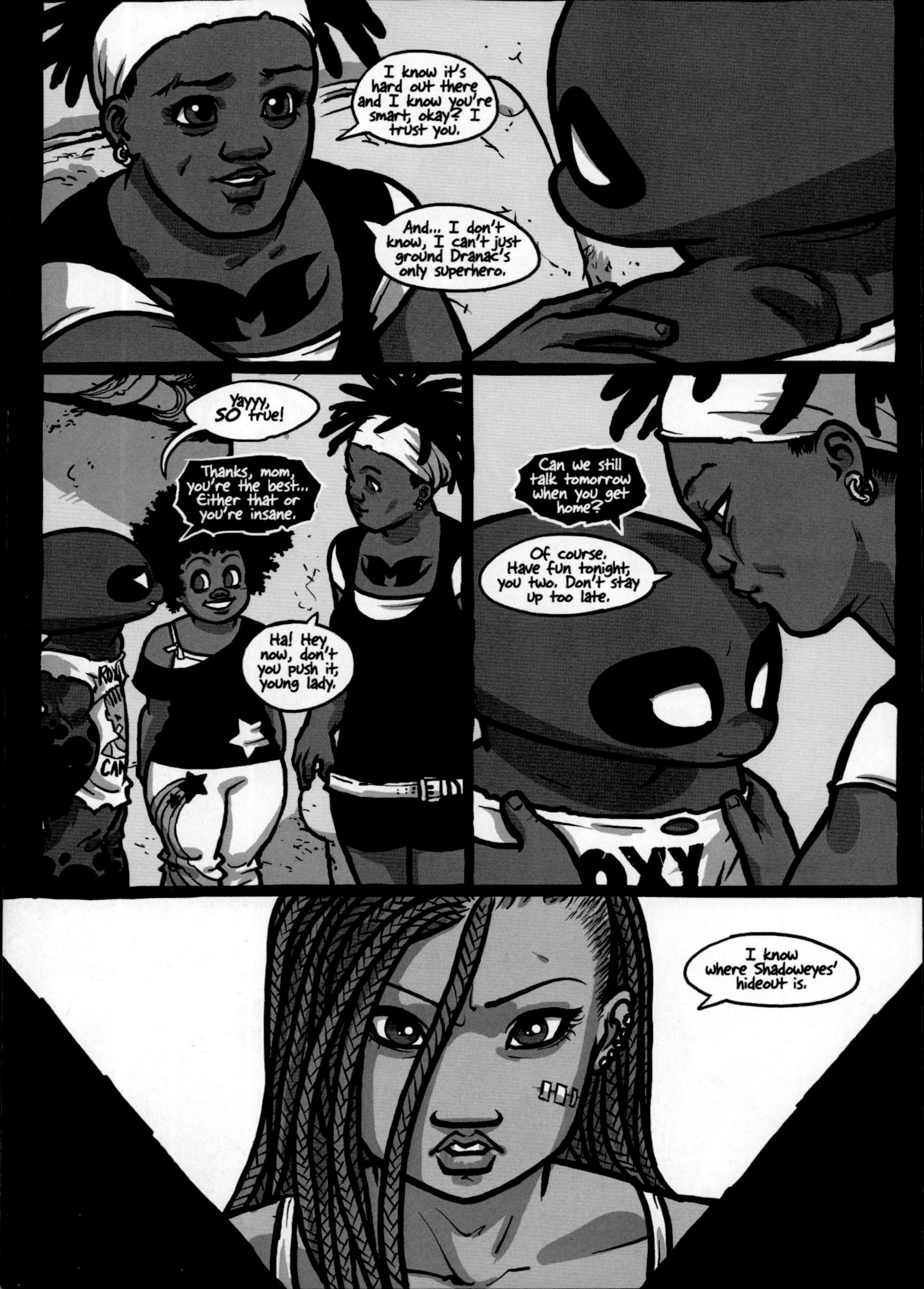
I know it's hard out there and I know you're smart, okay? I trust you.
And... I don't know, I can't just ground Dranac's only superhero.
Yayyy, SO true!
Thanks, mom, you're the best... Either that or you're insane.
Ha! Hey, now, don't you push it, young lady.
Can we still talk tomorrow when you get home?
Of course. Have fun tonight, you two. Don't stay up too late.
I know where Shadoweyes' hideout is.

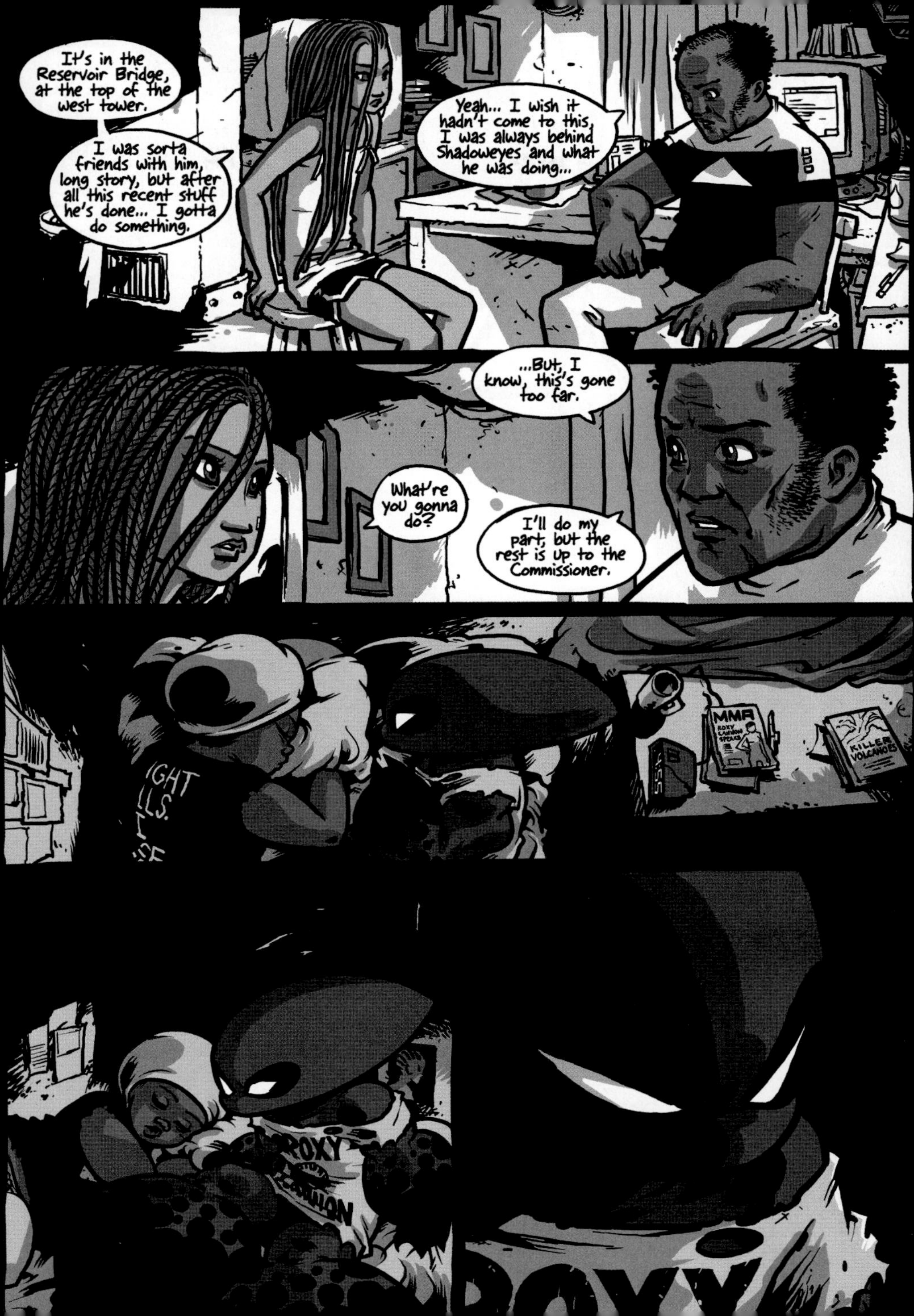
It's in the Reservoir Bridge, at the top of the west tower.
I was sorta friends with him, long story, but after all this recent stuff he's done... I gotta do something.
Yeah... I wish it hadn't come to this, I was always behind Shadoweyes and what he was doing...
...But, I know, this's gone too far.
What're you gonna do?
I'll do my part, but the rest is up to the Commissioner.
MMA
KILLER VOLCANOES
ROXY
CANNON

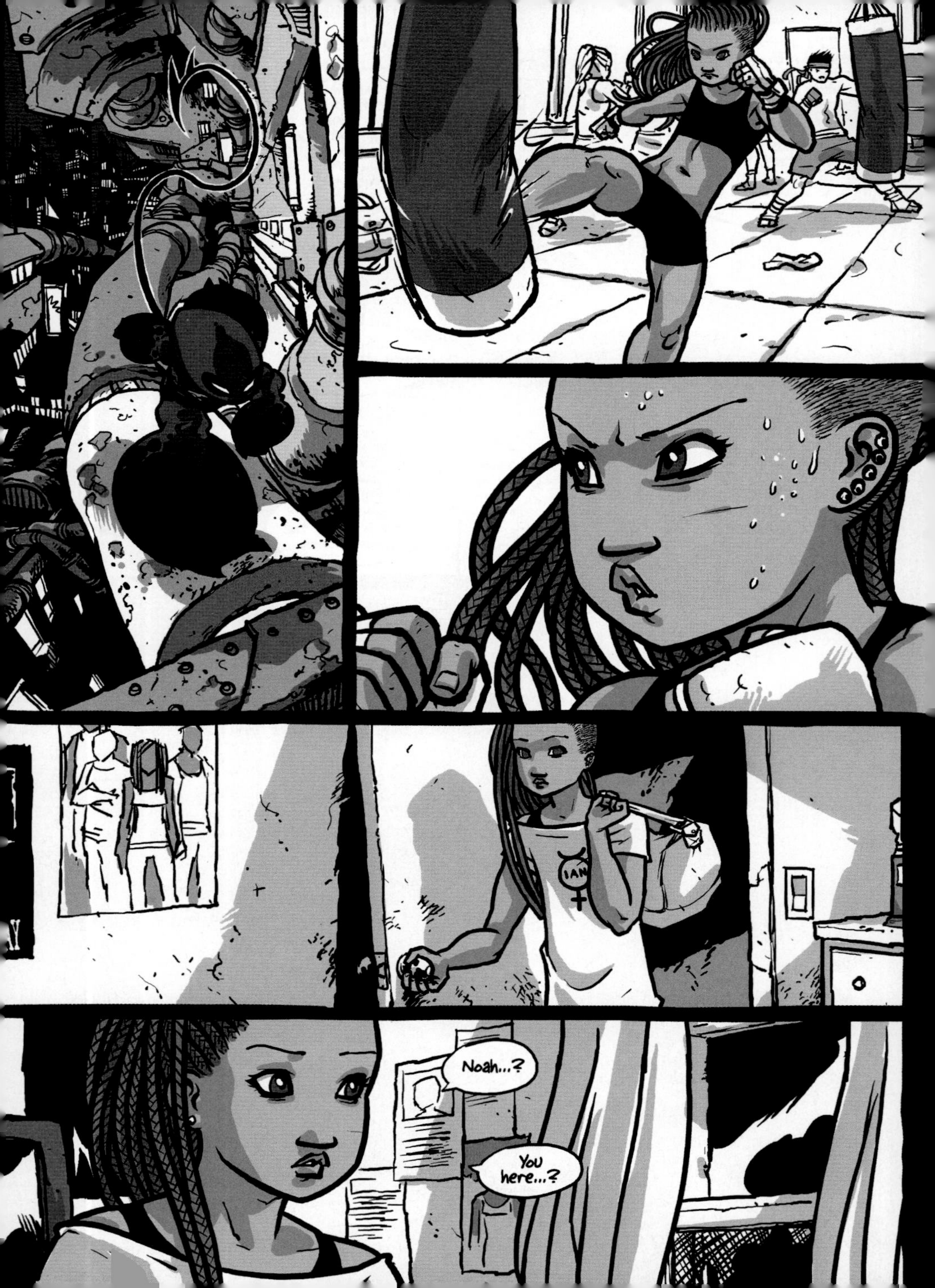

Noah...?
You here...?

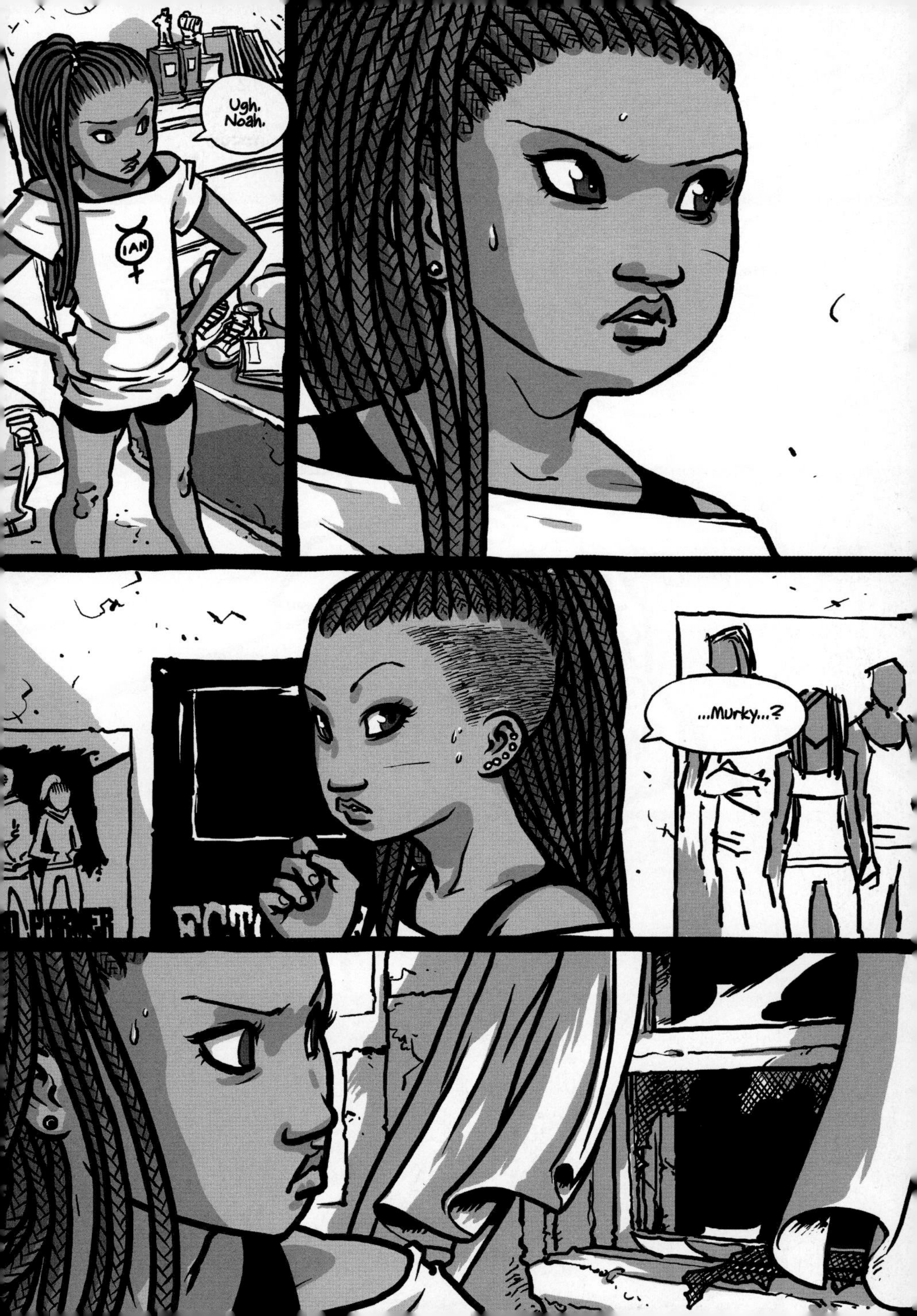
Ugh. Noah.
IAN
...Murky...?

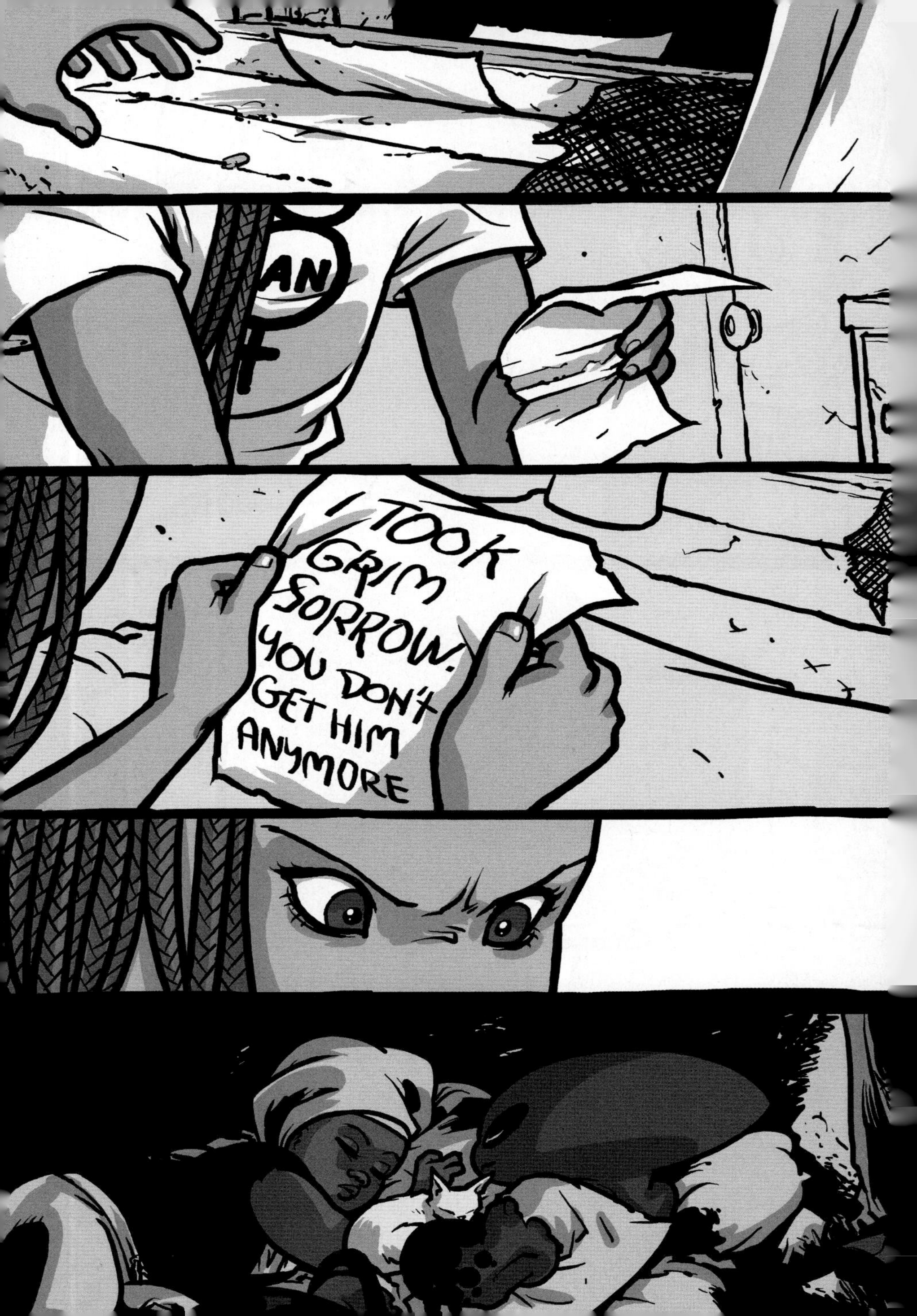
AN
I TOOK GRIM SORROW. YOU DON'T GET HIM ANYMORE

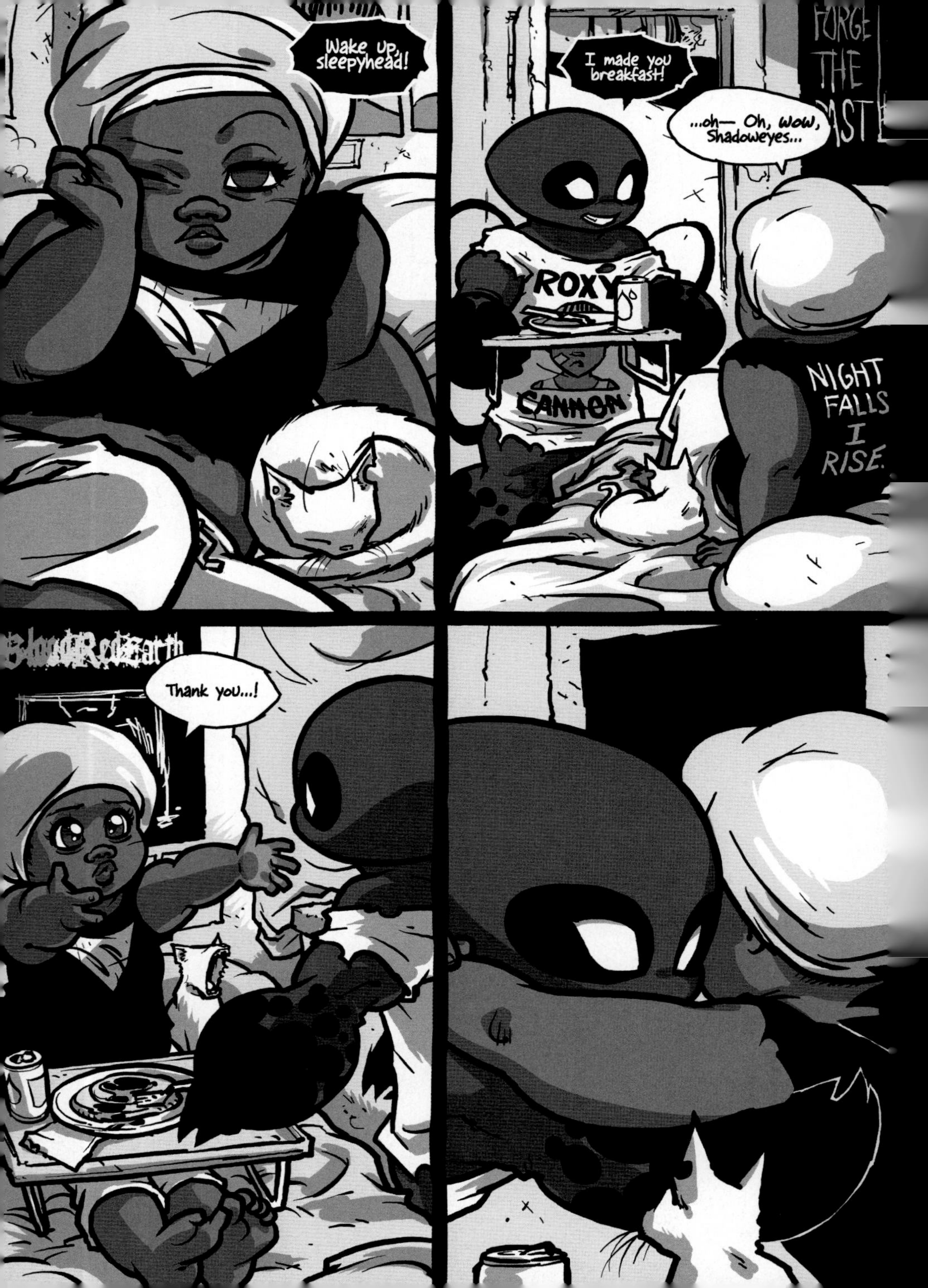
Wake up, sleepyhead!
I made you breakfast!
FORGE THE FASTE
...oh— Oh, wow, Shadoweyes...
ROXY CANNON
NIGHT FALLS I RISE.
Thank you...!

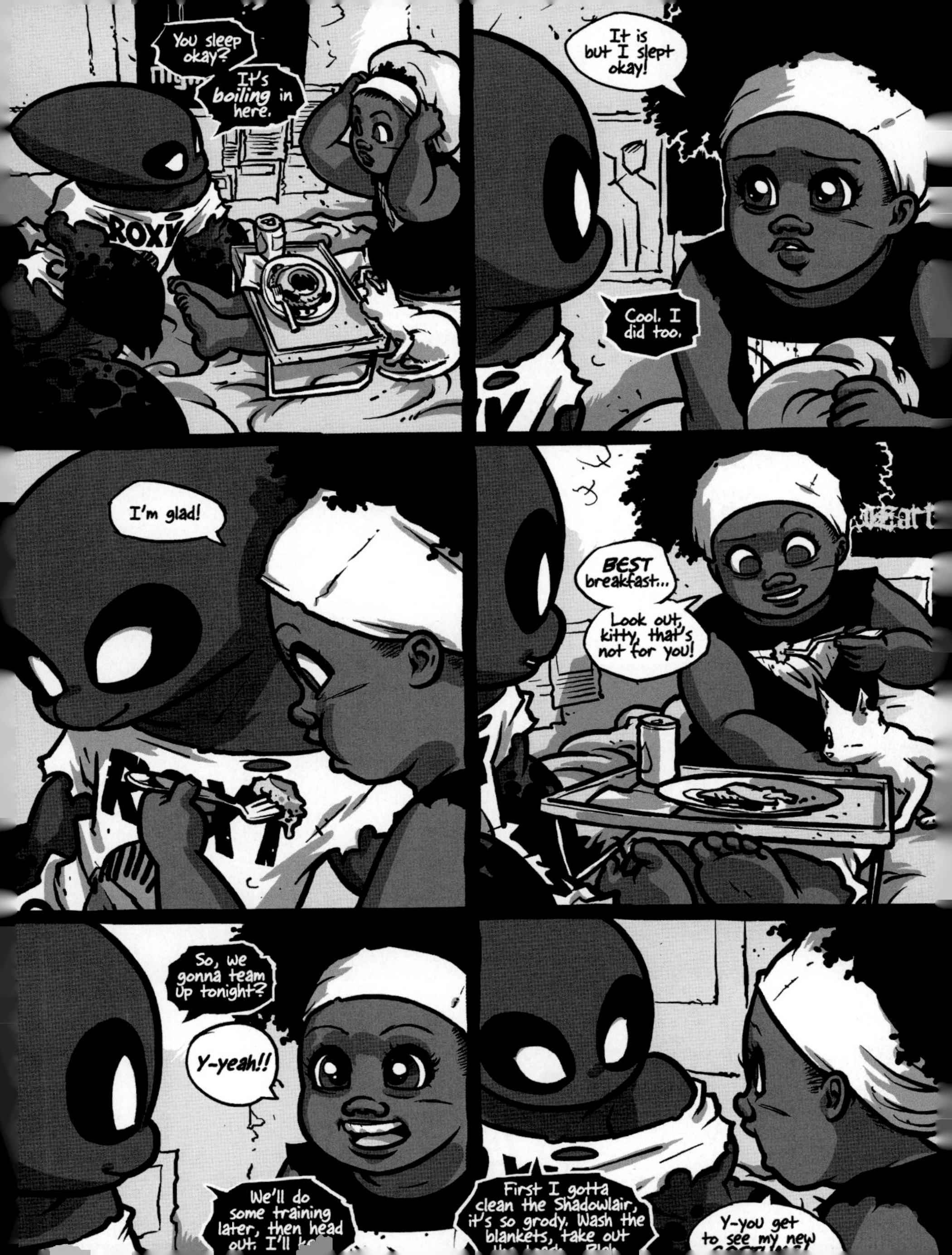
You sleep okay?
It's boiling in here.
It is but I slept okay!
Cool. I did too.
I'm glad!
BEST breakfast...
Look out, kitty, that's not for you!
So, we gonna team up tonight?
Y-yeah!!
We'll do some training later, then head
First I gotta clean the Shadowlair, it's so grody. Wash the blankets, take out
Y-you get to see my new

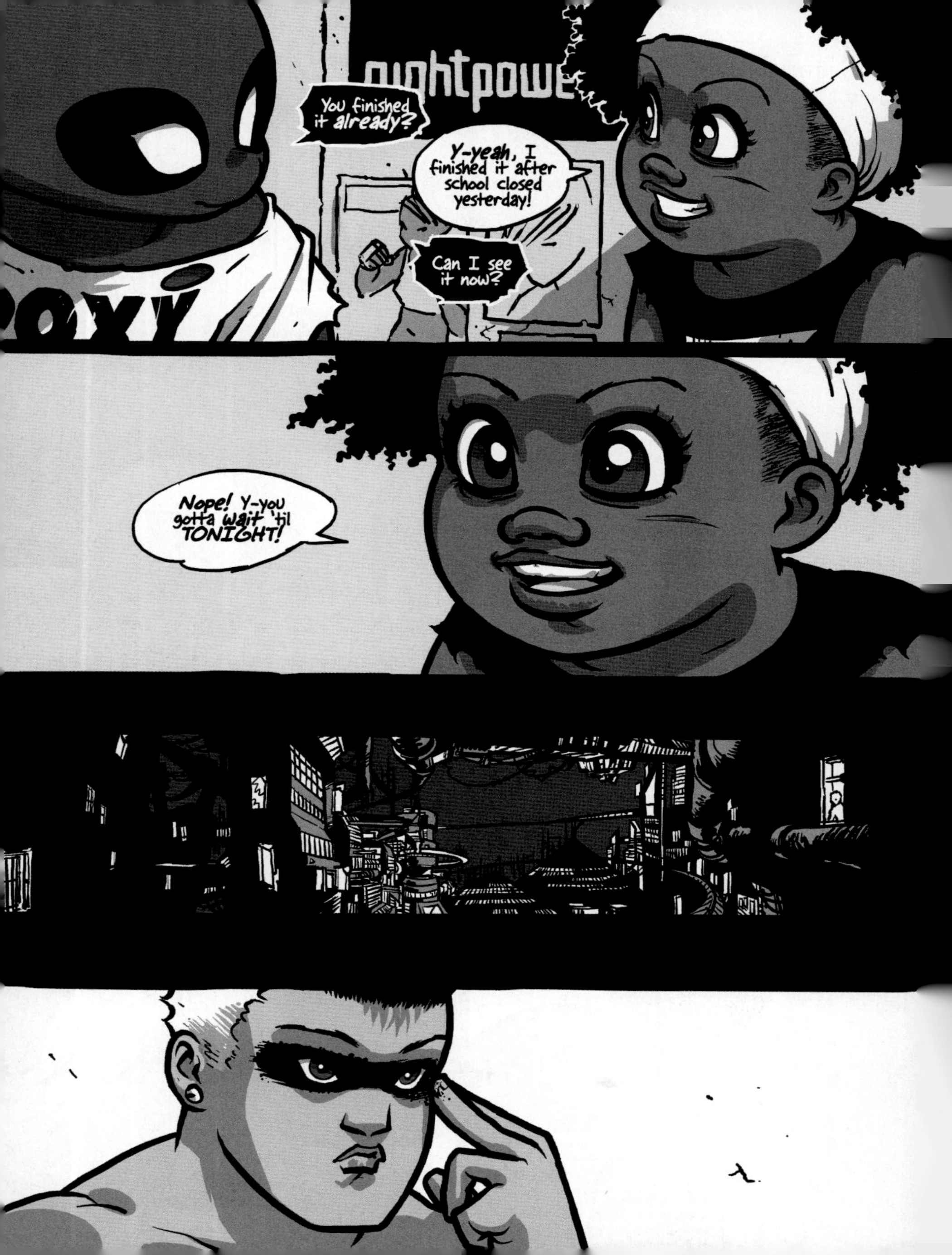
nightpowe
You finished it already?
Y-yeah, I finished it after school closed yesterday!
Can I see it now?
Nope! Y-you gotta wait 'til TONIGHT!

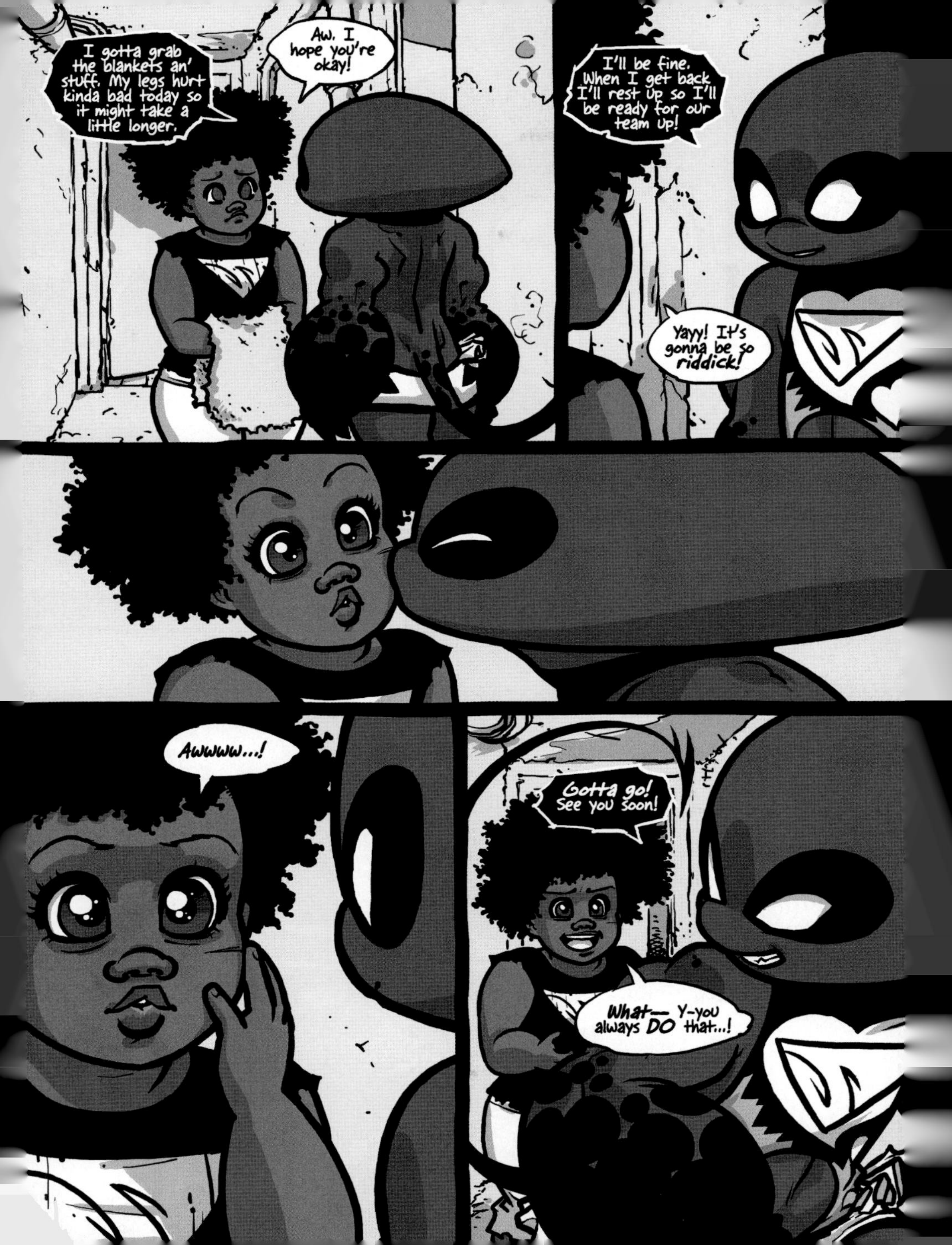
I gotta grab the blankets an' stuff. My legs hurt kinda bad today so it might take a little longer.
Aw. I hope you're okay!
I'll be fine. When I get back I'll rest up so I'll be ready for our team up!
Yayy! It's gonna be so riddick!
Awwww...!
Gotta go! See you soon!
What— Y-you always DO that...!

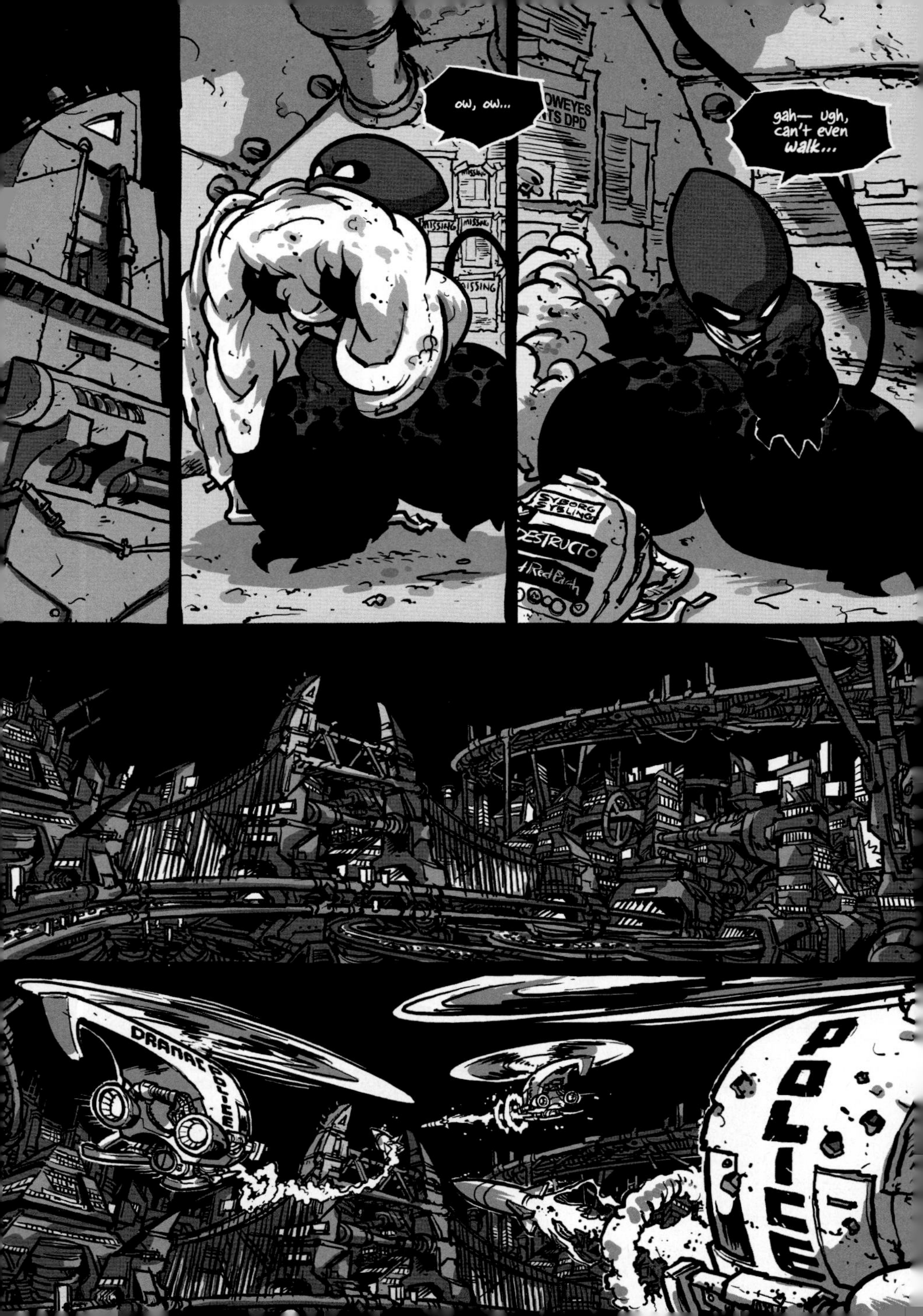
ow, ow...
gah— ugh, can't even walk...
MISSING
SYBORG SYBLING
DESTRUCTO
POLICE
POLICE

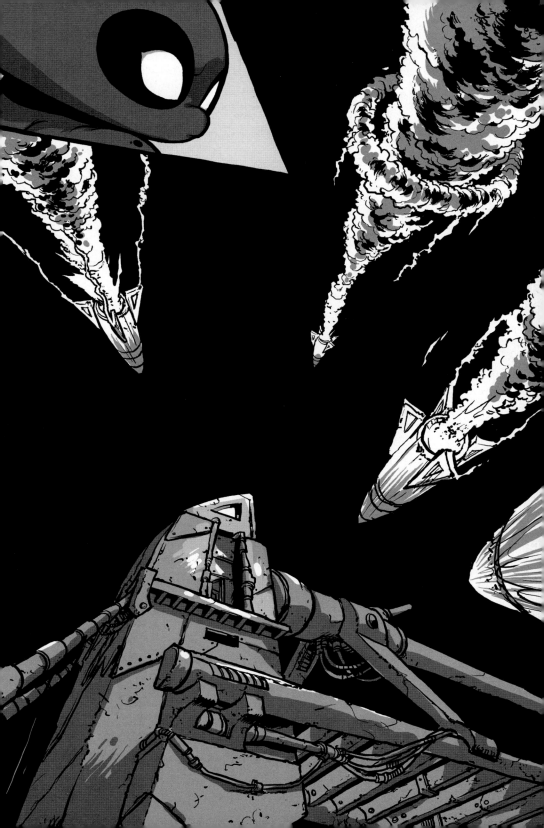

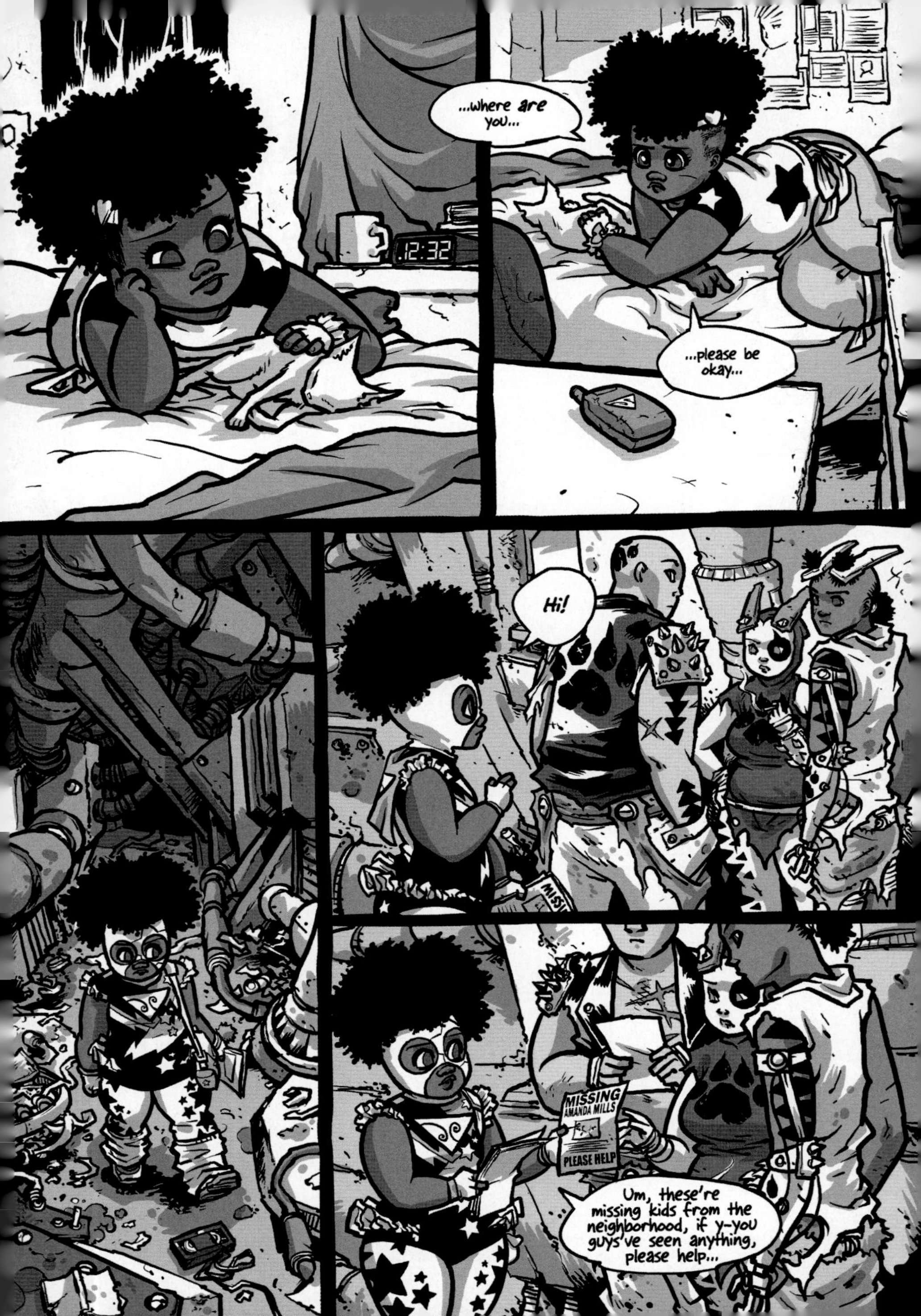
12:32
...where are you...
...please be okay...
Hi!
MISSING
AMANDA MILLS
PLEASE HELP
Um, these're missing kids from the neighborhood, if y-you guys've seen anything, please help...

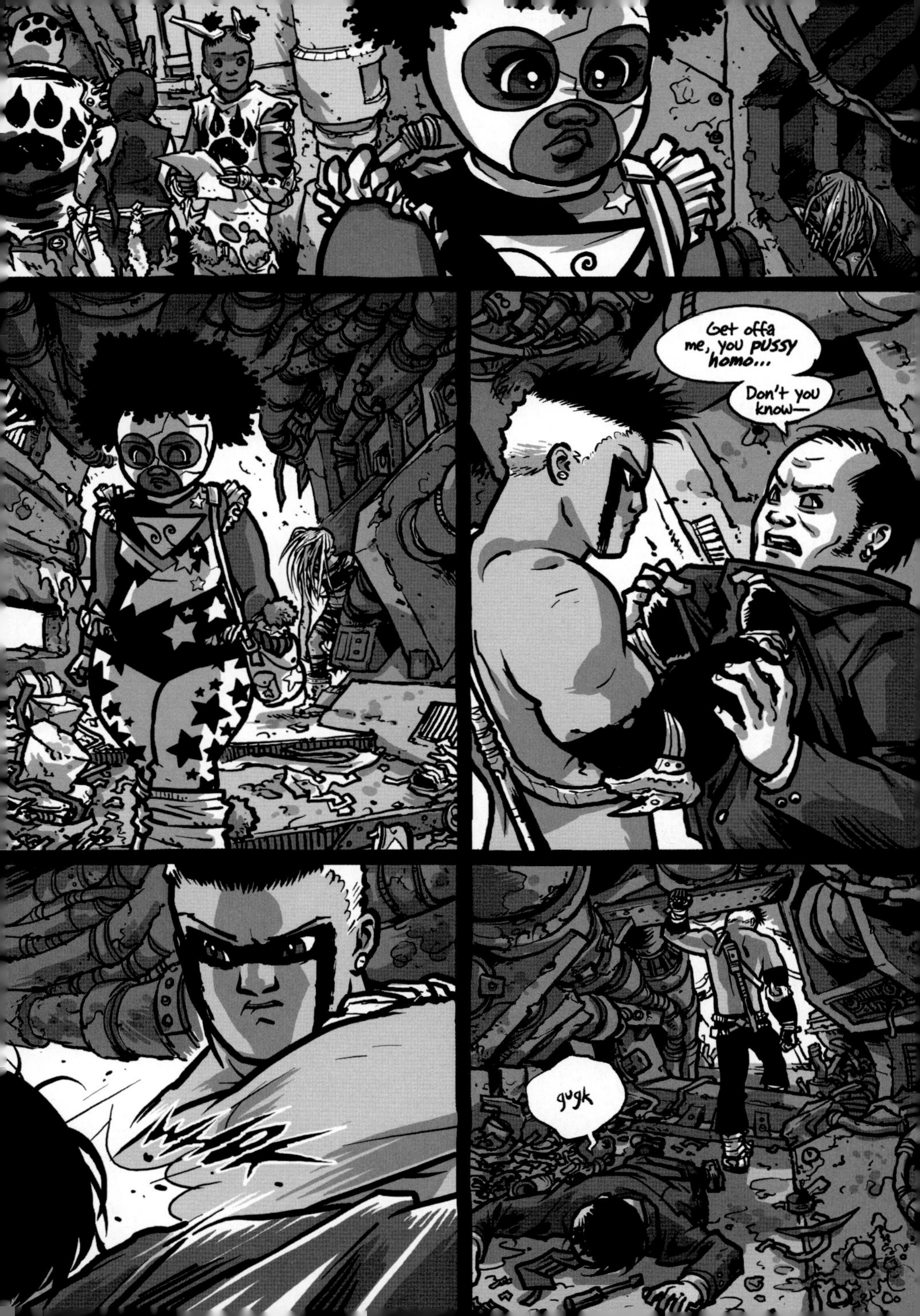

Get offa me, you PUSSY homo...
Don't you know—
gugk

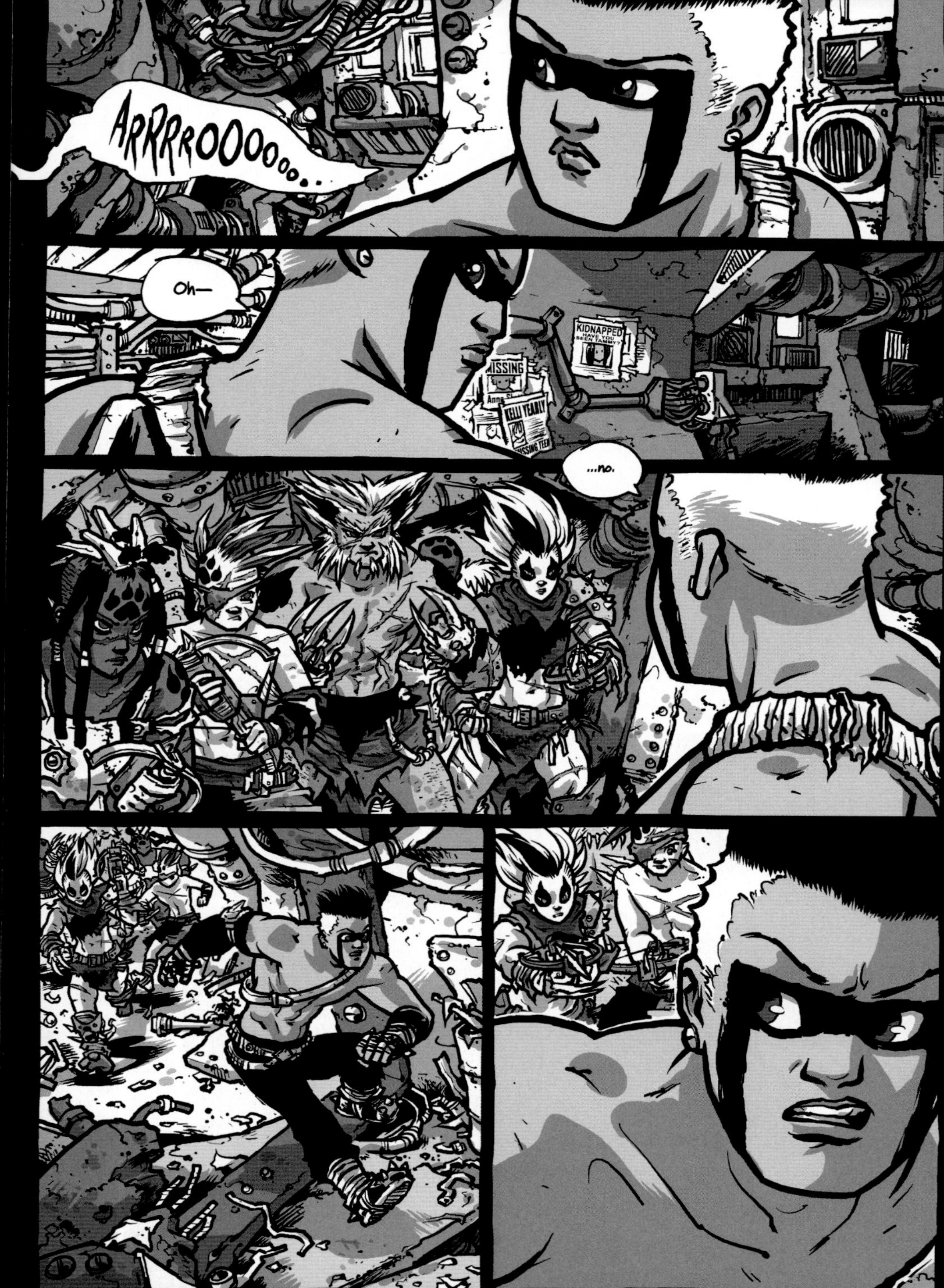
ARRRROOOOoo...
Oh—
KIDNAPPED
HAVE YOU SEEN TAMMY?
MISSING
KELLI YEARLY
MISSING TEEN
...no.

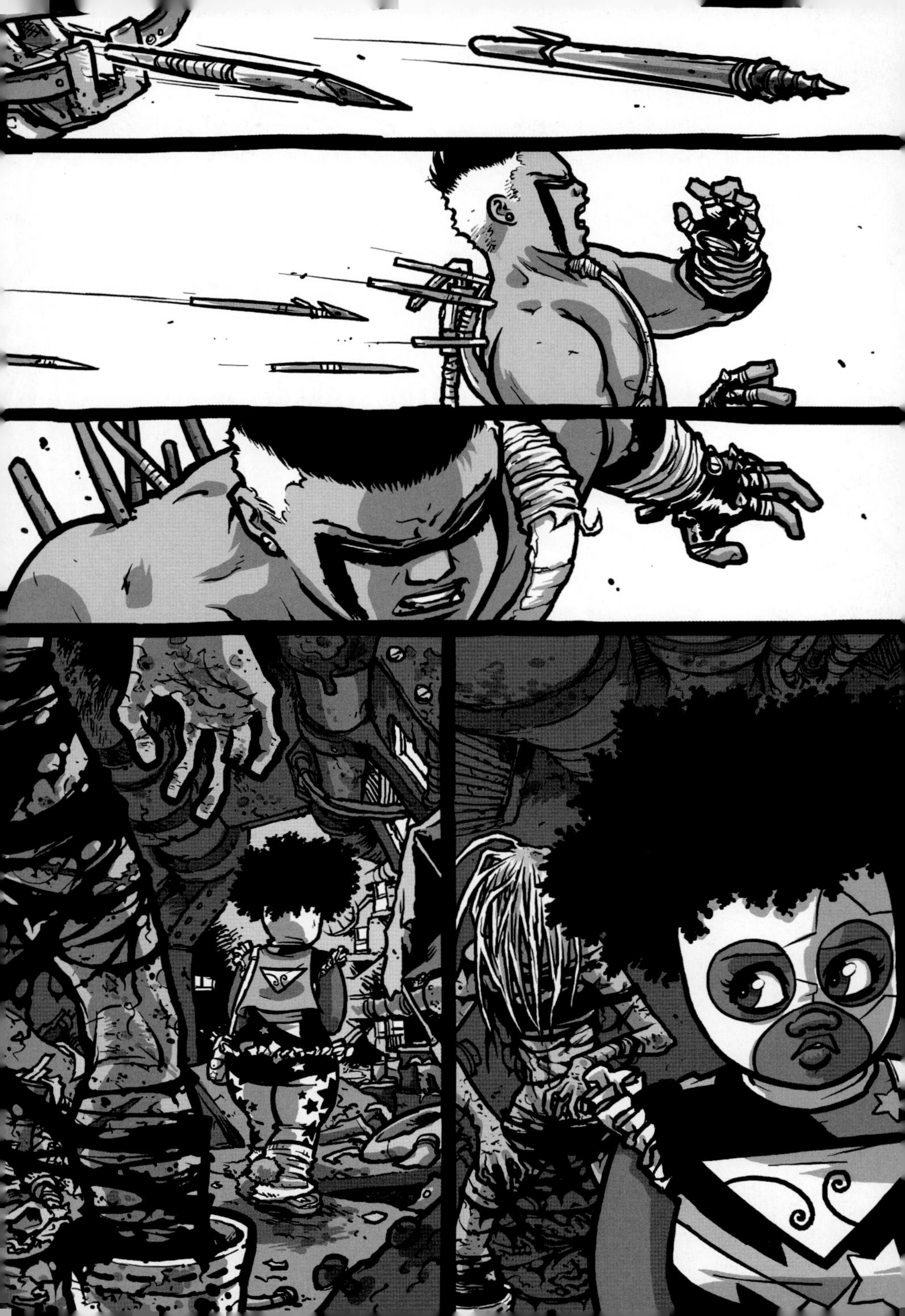

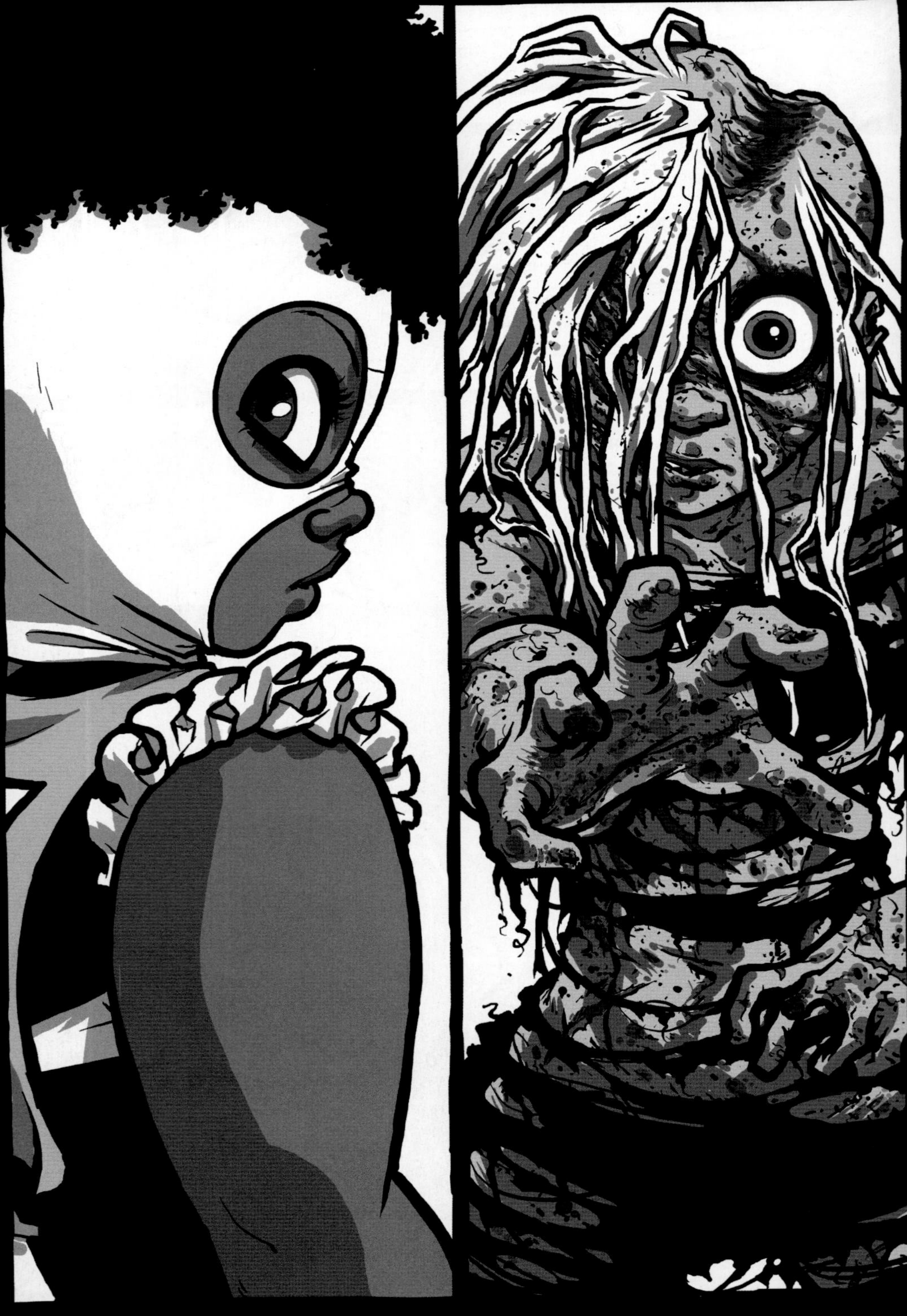

tinued in
MASKED